Inside China's Legal System

CHANDOS
ASIAN STUDIES SERIES
CONTEMPORARY ISSUES AND TRENDS

Series Editor: Professor Chris Rowley,
Centre for Research on Asian Management, Cass Business School,
City University, UK; HEAD Foundation, Singapore
(email: c.rowley@city.ac.uk)

Chandos Publishing is pleased to publish this major Series of books entitled *Asian Studies: Contemporary Issues and Trends*. The Series Editor is Professor Chris Rowley, Director, Centre for Research on Asian Management, City University, UK and Director, Research and Publications, HEAD Foundation, Singapore.

Asia has clearly undergone some major transformations in recent years and books in the Series examine this transformation from a number of perspectives: economic, management, social, political and cultural. We seek authors from a broad range of areas and disciplinary interests: covering, for example, business/management, political science, social science, history, sociology, gender studies, ethnography, economics and international relations, etc.

Importantly, the Series examines both current developments and possible future trends. The Series is aimed at an international market of academics and professionals working in the area. The books have been specially commissioned from leading authors. The objective is to provide the reader with an authoritative view of current thinking.

New authors: we would be delighted to hear from you if you have an idea for a book. We are interested in both shorter, practically orientated publications (45,000+ words) and longer, theoretical monographs (75,000–100,000 words). Our books can be single, joint or multi-author volumes. If you have an idea for a book, please contact the publishers or Professor Chris Rowley, the Series Editor.

Dr Glyn Jones
Chandos Publishing
Email: gjones@chandospublishing.com
www.chandospublishing.com

Professor Chris Rowley
Cass Business School, City University
Email: c.rowley@city.ac.uk
www.cass.city.ac.uk/faculty/c.rowley

Chandos Publishing: Chandos Publishing is an imprint of Woodhead Publishing Limited. The aim of Chandos Publishing is to publish books of the highest possible standard: books that are both intellectually stimulating and innovative.

We are delighted and proud to count our authors from such well-known international organisations as the Asian Institute of Technology, Tsinghua University, Kookmin University, Kobe University, Kyoto Sangyo University, London School of Economics, University of Oxford, Michigan State University, Getty Research Library, University of Texas at Austin, University of South Australia, University of Newcastle, Australia, University of Melbourne, ILO, Max-Planck Institute, Duke University and the leading law firm Clifford Chance.

A key feature of Chandos Publishing's activities is the service it offers its authors and customers. Chandos Publishing recognises that its authors are at the core of its publishing ethos, and authors are treated in a friendly, efficient and timely manner. Chandos Publishing's books are marketed on an international basis, via its range of overseas agents and representatives.

Professor Chris Rowley, BA, MA (Warwick), DPhil (Nuffield College, Oxford) is subject group leader and the inaugural professor of human resource management at Cass Business School, City University, London, UK, and director of research and publications for the HEAD Foundation, Singapore. He is the founding director of the multidisciplinary and internationally networked Centre for Research on Asian Management (www.cass.city.ac. uk/cram/index.html) and editor of the leading journal *Asia Pacific Business Review* (www.tandf.co.uk/journals/titles/13602381.asp). He is well known and highly regarded in the area, with visiting appointments at leading Asian universities and top journal editorial boards in the UK, Asia and the US. He has given a range of talks and lectures to universities, companies and organisations internationally with research and consultancy experience with unions, business and government, and his previous employment includes varied work in both the public and private sectors. Professor Rowley researches in a range of areas, including international and comparative human resource management and Asia Pacific management and business. He has been awarded grants from the British Academy and an ESRC AIM International Study Fellowship, and gained a five-year RCUK Fellowship in Asian business and management. He acts as a reviewer for many funding bodies, as well as for numerous journals and publishers. Professor Rowley publishes extensively, including in leading US and UK journals, with over 370 articles, books, chapters and other contributions.

Bulk orders: some organisations buy a number of copies of our books. If you are interested in doing this, we would be pleased to discuss a discount. Please email wp@woodheadpublishing.com or telephone +44 (0) 1223 499140.

Inside China's Legal System

CHANG WANG
AND
NATHAN H. MADSON

CHANDOS
PUBLISHING

Oxford Cambridge New Delhi

Chandos Publishing
Hexagon House
Avenue 4
Station Lane
Witney
Oxford OX28 4BN
UK
Tel: +44(0) 1993 848726
Email: info@chandospublishing.com
www.chandospublishing.com

Chandos Publishing is an imprint of Woodhead Publishing Limited

Woodhead Publishing Limited
80 High Street
Sawston
Cambridge CB22 3HJ
UK
Tel: +44(0) 1223 499140
Fax: +44(0) 1223 832819
www.woodheadpublishing.com

First published in 2013

ISBN: 978-0-85709-460-5 (print)
ISBN: 978-0-85709-461-2 (online)

© C. Wang and N.H. Madson, 2013

Typeset by Domex e-Data Pvt. Ltd., India
Printed in the UK and USA.

To Rick King
Chang Wang

To my parents
Nathan H. Madson

Contents

List of abbreviations

CECC	Congressional-Executive Commission on China (United States)
CPC	Communist Party of China
DSD	Domestic Security Department
GDP	gross domestic product
ICC	International Criminal Court
ICCPR	International Covenant on Civil and Political Rights
ICJ	International Court of Justice
IMF	International Monetary Fund
KMT	Kuomintang
NPC	National People's Congress
OECD	Organisation for Economic Co-operation and Development
PRC	People's Republic of China
RTL	re-education through labor
SPC	Supreme People's Court
TRIPS	Agreement on Trade-Related Aspects of Intellectual Property Rights
WJP	World Justice Project

Acknowledgments

While sitting down to write a book seems to be a solitary affair, there are many people who are essential to the writing process and who deserve many more thanks than we could ever extend here.

This book would never have been completed without the dedication and hard work of Christopher Luehr and John Fitzgerald. Thank you both for your comments and the countless hours you poured into this book. Your work truly made it more than a collection of thoughts, ideas and theories.

We would also like to thank the Honorable Justice Paul Anderson of the Minnesota Supreme Court and Professor David Weissbrodt, the Regents Professor and Fredrikson & Byron Professor of Law at the University of Minnesota Law School. We cannot thank you enough for taking the time to write thoughtful forewords and serving as references throughout the writing process.

Thank you also to Al Maleson for envisioning this project long before the first words were ever written, and his support and sage advice during the year of writing.

We thank Dr Glyn Jones, George Knott and Ed Gibbons at Chandos Publishing for their vision, diligent work and patience. Thanks so much to our wonderful copyeditor, Cherry Ekins, for her extremely diligent, thoughtful and extensive editing. Her wise suggestions and professional attention to the details make this volume a complete one. Thanks also to Harriet Clayton for putting together a pleasing cover design.

For allowing us to use his translation of Charter '08 we would like to express our gratitude to Professor Perry Link, the Chancellorial Chair for Innovative Teaching Comparative Literature & Foreign Languages at the University of California at Riverside, and the *New York Review of Books*.

Thank you to the students at the University of Minnesota Law School and the William Mitchell College of Law for serving as a sounding board as this book came to fruition.

Finally, we would like to express our heartfelt gratitude to our families, friends and colleagues.

Chang Wang and Nathan H. Madson
August 2013

Foreword 1

Most of us who have the privilege to work within the American constitutional system are very proud of this form of government and willing to talk about it. We frequently become strong advocates for our form of government when visiting with persons from other countries, especially countries with emerging democracies. But we have to be careful not to forget that countries developing their own systems of government, particularly judicial systems, have their own history and culture and thus will develop in several different ways. Most of these countries must, in their own particular way, seek to establish and maintain a system that guarantees the existence of the rule of law. Those of us who serve in government positions in the United States genuinely want to help other countries achieve their goals, but we must be willing to grant those countries sufficient room to do it in a way that works for them.

Those of us from the United States who engage in these efforts should explain why and how our system of government has worked well for us. We should emphasize the fact that there are several important fundamental principles that provide the foundation of our system. These principles include a commitment to the rule of law, a constitution approved by the people, separation of powers, judicial independence and the concept of judicial review of governmental acts that may violate individual rights or a constitutional mandate. But it is a grave mistake for us to overstate our case and claim that our system will work well everywhere. Such an approach can have the same effect as pounding a square wooden peg into a round hole: it does not work well and results in many splinters. We need to explain our form of government but provide enough latitude so our listeners have an opportunity not only to learn about our system but also to evaluate it to see what may work well for their own country. Then we must encourage them to take our best, leave the rest, and employ the best in their own country.

A good starting point for a conversation about our American democracy with representatives from another country is a discussion about the history, culture, government and especially the legal system of their country. This approach may appear to be simple and obvious, but it is often overlooked and even ignored. But its importance to a person's credibility can never be overestimated. Making this initial effort shows respect for your listener. Make an effort to know something about each country and its people. Doing so will lead to a more meaningful sharing of perspectives and ideas about each other's countries. It will also provide a great antidote to mistaken assumptions and diplomatic blunders.

An understanding and appreciation of the importance of our own history when discussing different legal systems should not be underestimated. I readily concede that I have a strong bias in favor of this approach, given that I am a history buff who values a historical perspective. It is difficult to talk to representatives from other countries about their need to establish the rule of law, create an independent judiciary, improve human rights or get more women lawyers and judges without acknowledging our own history. On this latter point, my own experience is informative.

When I was a law student at the University of Minnesota Law School in the late 1960s, we only had one female judge in Minnesota and very few women lawyers. In my class of over 200, there were only four women. When I visit with my female classmates today, they remind me how difficult it was for them to attend law school at that time. It was not unusual for professors to chastise women students on the grounds that they had no business being there, they were there only to get a husband and in the process they were taking the place of a male student who needed to attend law school so he could get a good job as a lawyer and feed his family. In many ways, I was oblivious to the travails of my female colleagues. It took many years to heighten my awareness as to the value that my female peers could bring and have brought to our system of government. While my female colleagues from those days assure me that I always treated them with respect, I am often amazed at how oblivious I was to how different their experience was from mine. We have come a long way in a short period of time, but we cannot forget our past, and we need to share that past with others.

One point I wish to make by using the foregoing example is that, as advocates for our system of government, we must acknowledge that our system is still evolving and much of this evolution is recent. We must understand, appreciate and discuss this recent history. We need to appreciate the fact that a key ingredient in our system is our ability to reinvent ourselves periodically. Then we can explain, in a credible manner, how our system of government has flourished because of the presence of women judges and persons of color. Always make it an objective to explain to others that for the rule of law to flourish, a government must have the ability to incorporate change peacefully so that the government can better reflect the citizens it serves.

I have on two occasions been invited by a branch of the Chinese government to lecture in China on issues such as American federalism, the rule of law and the importance of judicial independence. On my first trip I had a 12-day window for travel and lecturing. I was able to present eight lectures at five of the top ten law schools, a police academy, a training school for judges and an undergraduate university. I also participated in 16 meetings with justices of the supreme courts in Beijing, Shanghai and Hangzhou, law school deans, police academy presidents, police officers and several members of the legal community. It was an extraordinarily interesting and challenging educational and cultural experience, and all the more interesting because I was in China shortly after the major earthquake in Sichuan province.

There were times during my visit when I thought that I might be in over my head. I was worried the Chinese would discover that at heart I was just a farm kid from Minnesota who did not have much to offer. But my fears did not turn out to be justified. I discovered that as a product of our American democracy who has had the privilege to serve in high public office, I had much to share. That said, I must caution everyone not to trust anyone – including me – who pretends to tell you the truth about China. It is very difficult, if not impossible, to know such truth. The most anyone who is a student or keen observer of China can do is to share facts, information and personal insights, observations and perspectives about this country that has recently become an economic powerhouse.

When talking about China, I generally begin my discussions by comparing our two governments. In the United States we have a separation of powers which provides a system of checks and balances. China has central party rule with central authority, and there are very few, if any, checks and balances. In the United States we have an independent judiciary. An independent judiciary does not exist, nor is it presently desired, in China. In the United States we have existed under the concept of the rule *of* law for over two centuries. China puts a premium on the concept of rule *by* law. Many Chinese are very proud of their system of rule *by* law. But do not be mistaken: there is a huge difference between the rule *of* law and rule *by* law.

In the United States we have free speech guaranteed by the First Amendment to our constitution. In China the press and media are essentially the mouth and tongue of the Communist Party. There are severe restrictions on the free communication of ideas: I need go no further than note the compromises on internet accessibility and information that China demands of companies such as Google. In the United States we have the right to access public documents. In China access to information is deemed a privilege, not a right. Easy access to information is critically important to a form of government that is controlled by the people. This free flow of information allows us to hold our public officials accountable and correct our mistakes. Early twentieth-century journalist William Allen White said it well:

> You can have neither wise laws nor free enforcement of wise laws unless there is free expression of the wisdom of the people – and alas, their folly with it. But if there is freedom, folly will die of its own poison, and wisdom will survive.

In the United States we have open access to court records. In China, party government and the courts operate in secrecy. We have, for the most part, an open and transparent system of government. In China everything is run by the party from the top down, and mostly in secret. Any valid organizational chart of the Chinese government will show a direct line that invariably runs from the courts to a political and judicial committee of the Communist Party. This structure means that the courts in China are subordinate to the party – the party controls the courts through its political and judicial committee. Thus the judiciary is not free from the party's political influence. There is a saying in China that the most important cases are decided by politics; medium-sized cases are decided by money and influence; and only the smallest cases are decided under the law, if they get decided at all. This is a system governed under rule *by* law, not the rule *of* law.

Nevertheless, when I was invited to China to talk about our American democratic society, I was given free rein to describe our form of government and make whatever comparisons with China's government that I chose. So the question becomes: why was I given this broad latitude to speak? I believe it can be explained by acknowledging that some real change is occurring in China. I saw some of this change up close when I observed a more open attitude by the government when it dealt with events following the 2008 earthquake in Sichuan province. But the real questions remain: how much change will there be, and how soon?

Based upon my admittedly limited knowledge about China, I would conclude that most of the current reforms in China have their roots in the changes in Chinese culture that occurred between 1980 and 1989 – the decade leading up to Tiananmen Square. The 1989 Tiananmen Square protest is obviously a seminal event in China's modern history, not unlike 11 September 2001 is for the United States. Following Tiananmen Square, there was an increased level of government-sponsored suppression of certain activities in Chinese society – the activities that had been moving China in the direction of being a more open society. This suppression led to a more nationalistic attitude and further restrictions on Chinese society.

But again change appears to be in the wind. In the last few years Chinese leaders seem to be more willing to acknowledge the fact that, if China is going to move forward as a leader in the international economy and play its rightful role as a world power, it must move beyond its post-Tiananmen Square attitudes. The big question is how it will do it and how fast. I believe China's leaders are exploring their alternatives. There is a legitimate internal inquiry going on – it may even be an internal quandary. In the end, I believe that this legitimate interest in making some change is why I have twice been invited to lecture in China. I believe there is a genuine interest in what we Americans may be able to contribute to this process of change, particularly in the area of our perspectives on the law.

My colleague in Minnesota's judiciary, Judge Kevin Burke, is correct when he notes that economic forces are driving change in China. China's leaders know their country is a world economic power and acknowledge that, at least in the economic sphere, China needs some semblance of the rule of law if it is going to thrive. But the leadership in China is justifiably worried about the implications of such change, even if the change is controlled and modest. Students of Chinese history and culture who are aware of the multifaceted nature of the Chinese character know that these concerns are not unfounded. Those in power, if they want to retain it, have reason to be concerned about what may happen once the rule-of-law genie gets out of the bottle. Even modest reforms can, once put in place, lead to dramatic changes that bring with them some unforeseen collateral consequences. If and when the rule-of-law genie does get out of the bottle – even if it is initially limited to the economic sphere – it could easily become uncontrollable for the current leadership in China. The rule of law may spread to other areas of society such as political freedom and human rights, a spread that can threaten the established power structure.

As I noted earlier, there is a real hunger in China for Western ideas, especially American ideas. The Chinese are legitimately interested in any substantive ideas we are willing to share with them. In part, this interest stems from an appreciation of what we have achieved as a society. Nevertheless, the Chinese are concerned about what change may bring. Thus they are proceeding carefully, with deliberation, and in ways that are often difficult for us to understand. It is also apparent that whatever changes they will make, they intend to make them on their own terms.

Most of us in the United States know that during the twenty-first century we face significant competition from China. But I left China believing that the United States and other Western countries have something special that gives us an advantage in this competition – our freedom. Despite all the energy, intellectual engagement and overwhelming manpower that I saw in China, I believe the United States can not only survive but thrive in the face of this economic challenge. The reason is that the current government structure in China still requires most of the people to confine their thinking to specific and often isolated thought silos. Thinking in China still tends to remain under restraint; it is intentionally confined by government policies. The Chinese people do not have the intellectual freedom and exchange that we enjoy. If we in the United States maintain our freedom and traditional ability to think outside the envelope and be innovative, we will do fine. Again, as noted earlier, because of the freedoms we enjoy we have the ability to reinvent ourselves periodically in order to meet changing circumstances. It is an advantage we must work to preserve.

There is another significant advantage that freedom of expression not only allows, but promotes. Here I refer to what Mark Twain once termed a 'discriminating irreverence'. This discriminating irreverence strengthens our society because it is one of the ways we hold our leaders accountable. It most frequently manifests itself through our use of humor.

When visiting the United States in the 1880s, British poet and culture critic Matthew Arnold lamented what he viewed as a pervasive lack of discipline in our society. Arnold especially lamented the lack of awe and respect Americans had for those who were better than others. In pointing out this deficiency he noted that there was one institution of American life that struck him as a particularly bad idea. That was what he called the role of a 'funny man' who, he said, 'is a national misfortune there'. The primary target of Arnold's criticism is a person we now universally regard as a national treasure – journalist, novelist, social critic and skeptic Mark Twain. Twain had an excellent and profound response to Arnold's criticism, and it is an observation that the leaders in China should note and ponder. Twain said, 'A discriminating irreverence is the creator and protector of human liberty.'

This book by Chang Wang and Nathan H. Madson attempts to provide as complete a picture as is presently possible of the Chinese legal system. It is based on their understanding of the posture and position that the Communist Party of China has taken with respect to the rule of law. The authors note the reluctance of China's current leaders to see the rule of law too firmly grounded in the human rights/civil rights area, but yet that same leadership understands its utility in many other areas of Chinese society. During my numerous conversations about the Chinese legal system with Chang Wang and upon reading the authors' manuscript, I have gained great respect for their insights and perceptions as to how the Chinese legal system works. They demonstrate a unique ability to comprehend the complex interrelation of politics and the court, political structure with both rule *by* law and rule *of* law, and the impact of these factors on those who are ruled – governed – under these competing and often incompatible concepts.

As previously indicated, I have over the past few years met with several delegations of judges and lawyers from China. As a result of these meetings I have gained some understanding of how difficult it is to establish the concept of rule of law in China and to develop an understanding of the American concept of rule of law. Without question, China's progress in this area will be one of fits and starts. We need to appreciate that sometimes it may appear as though there are two steps forward and one step back – or even one step forward and two steps back. But if there is to be progress – more steps forward than there are steps back – we need people like the authors and their scholarship to help us gain a better insight into the vast and mysterious Chinese legal system. We need people like them to help us understand China's historical and cultural roots and current context, and to break down barriers of language, complexity and communication that can impede or even prevent those who want to understand China better from accomplishing their goal.

Justice Paul H. Anderson
Minnesota Supreme Court
USA

Foreword 2

The significance of China in the world today can scarcely be overstated, though it may seem a cliché to say so. The magnitude of its engagement with the world has become enormous since the reform period of the late 1970s. Through trade, media, culture and politics, Chinese influence reaches across the globe. It is this influence that makes Chinese law and legal process such vital topics of discussion. Attorneys and scholars engaged in international law and relations, be it trade, business, human rights or other international legal matters, will most likely encounter Chinese legal personnel and institutions.

So why is China's legal system so important? A country's legal system is a major component of its influence on the global stage. And China has a lot of influence. One reason for this is its size and relative power. Consider the following.

- China has the world's largest population, estimated to be 1.34 billion people in 2012.[1]

- China is Asia's largest country[2] and the world's fourth largest by land area,[3] with 14 bordering countries (tying with Russia for the largest number of bordering countries).[4]

- China's economy is the world's second largest,[5] with a GDP of $8.3 trillion (2012).[6]

- China's economy is also one of the world's fastest growing: *The Economist* estimated that the Chinese economy grew by an average of 10.5 percent per year from 2001 to 2010.[7]

- China's international power is notable: it is one of the few nuclear powers[8] and fields the world's largest standing army.[9]

- China is also one of only five permanent members of the UN Security Council, giving it veto power over Security Council resolutions.[10]

China's ubiquity extends into cyberspace. The country now has more than 500 million internet users, which is the largest online population in the world.[11] According to a recent study, Twitter's most active country is China, with 35.5 million users in early 2012.[12] The use of Twitter is apparently taking place in spite of it being blocked by the Chinese government.[13] China's own micro-blog service, Sina Weibo, has attracted over 300 million users.[14]

Beyond its formidable physical, political and economic presence, China's global impact is widespread. It is the world's largest producer and consumer of coal, as well as the second-largest oil user.[15] It should come as no surprise that China's level of CO_2 pollution exceeds that of any other country.[16]

China also sends the world's largest number of students abroad and Chinese are the largest single nationality in the foreign student population of the United States.[17] Outside of OECD countries, China is one of the largest providers of development aid through what are referred to as 'South-South cooperation' efforts.[18]

The size and reach of China raise questions about human rights as well. In this realm too, China is associated with large numbers. Two examples are illustrative. First, China has the world's second-largest prison population (after the United States), with over 1.5 million in custody in 2012.[19] In spite of laws that prohibit the abuse of prisoners, human rights reports indicate that detention conditions in Chinese jails are often extremely harsh, with prisoners being routinely tortured or otherwise mistreated.[20] It is well known that China carries out the largest number of executions in the world, though that number is difficult to calculate as executions are kept secret by the government.[21] It has been estimated that China executes around 4,000 people a year.[22]

Second, China is home to one of the largest newspaper industries in the world, boasting over 1,900 newspapers with growing circulation.[23] The circulation of China's largest newspaper, *Cankao Xiaoxi* (*Reference News*) exceeds that of the *Wall Street Journal*, the most widely read newspaper in the United States.[24] China's media are, however, subject to strict government control and the content is frequently censored. The press freedom watchdog group Reporters without Borders ranked China seventh from last in its 2013 Press Freedom Index, at 173 out of 179 countries reviewed.[25]

In recent years China has become an increasingly active player in the realm of international law. It has signed or acceded to more than 300 treaties,[26] and also currently has membership in more than 100 intergovernmental organizations.[27] In 2010 the International Monetary Fund (IMF) increased China's contribution quota, raising its voting rights along with this,[28] thus giving it a more forceful voice in IMF policy.

China's approach to international arbitration mechanisms has tended to be a cautious one, although the broad trend has been one of increased engagement.[29] Since the reform period of the late 1970s, China has become a party to many economic treaties that involve adjudication clauses, including the World Trade Organization treaty. It does not, however, acknowledge jurisdiction through the International Court of Justice (ICJ) or the International Criminal Court (ICC). In spite of this reluctance, China has engaged with both bodies on some level, for example expressing its concern over the ICC's jurisdiction during the drafting of the Rome Statute, and sending a delegation to the ICJ to express concern over Kosovo's declaration of independence in 2008.

China has also become a significant bilateral aid donor, extending its influence further. In the past decade or so it has become Africa's largest trading partner, exceeding Africa's trade volume with the United States and Europe. Additionally, between 2009 and 2011 the number of loans China issued to developing nations, especially in Africa, exceeded that of the World Bank. While Chinese support has not completely displaced Western development funding, it has come to be viewed as a viable alternative. Chinese development loans and investments usually come with no human rights conditions attached, unlike those of many Western donors (inconsistently applied as those conditions may be).

While the Chinese government tends to view national sovereignty as paramount in a way that differs from many Western countries, it has also exhibited a desire to be a part of international legal mechanisms. For example, while China tends to view human rights criticisms as interference in its internal affairs, it has become a party to many significant human rights treaties, including:

- the International Covenant on Economic, Social and Cultural Rights (2001)
- the Convention on the Elimination of All Forms of Racial Discrimination (1981)
- the Convention on the Elimination of All Forms of Discrimination against Women (1980)
- the Convention against Torture and Other Cruel, Inhuman or Degrading Punishment (1988)

- the Convention on the Rights of the Child (1992)
- the Convention Relating to the Status of Refugees (1982)
- the Convention on the Prevention and Punishment of the Crime of Genocide (1983).

It is also a party to the four Geneva Conventions on the law of armed conflict. While China frequently asserts its sovereignty on matters of human rights, its ratification of and accession to human rights treaties demonstrate a desire to be part of the international community and engage with other countries.

These facts and figures provide some understanding of why China's legal system is so important. While China's presence in world affairs is ubiquitous, its laws and legal system are generally not well understood, especially in the West. To understand China's actions in the realm of international law better, it is instructive to examine how the Chinese legal system functions and evolves over time.

This volume provides the reader with unique insight into the Chinese legal system, including the historical, social and political contexts in which it operates. Its holistic and insider perspective carry with it valuable knowledge unavailable to most Western lawyers and scholars. As China's interaction with international entities increases – whether these entities are other countries, transnational corporations, media outlets or intergovernmental or non-governmental organizations – its legal system will come into play in both civil and criminal matters.

Throughout 2,500 years of Chinese history Confucianism and legalism have battled for control as the dominant school of thought underlying the Chinese legal system. The primary idea behind Confucianism is governance by education, persuasion and moral example. In an ideal Confucian society, morality – rather than the wishes of the people in general – serves as the foundation of law. Confucianism assumes that if people are kept in line by governmental measures or threats of punishment, the people's primary objective will be to stay out of prison. Subjects will behave well not because of any true sense of honor in good behavior or shame in punishment, but simply because of the threat of punishment. The Confucian ideal is to lead by virtue and control. Leaders are expected to lead by example and their subjects will follow. Confucius (551–479 BCE) believed that leaders should craft a code of conduct and keep it secret from ordinary citizens. In the last 20 years there has been a resurgence of Confucianism within mainland China.

Legalists have the same ultimate goal of social order, but seek to use a set of written rules, physical force and a uniform administrative apparatus to impose this order. Every subject is equal before the law, and as such a legal code should be published and understandable by the people in general. They believe the legal code should run the state, not individual rulers. Throughout Chinese history the school of thought shaping the Chinese legal system has flowed between Confucianism and legalism, with primary dominance by the Confucian ideology.

Along with trying to decide the school of thought to follow, the Chinese legal system has struggled with determining how to incorporate Western influence into its legal system. Though China prides itself on developing outside of Western influence, it is undeniable that the West and its influence have played some role in the creation of the People's Republic of China. China distrusts the West in part because of negative historical interactions, such as the Boxer Rebellion and unequal treaties forged between China and Western countries between 1842 and 1949. There has been a general agreement within China that a lot could be learned from the West on how to strengthen itself, but little agreement on how to learn, how much to learn and how fast the learning could be implemented. As China determines how much to take from the Western legal system, a modern Chinese system has begun to develop. Building a legal system is, however, a process that cannot be completed in the span of three decades or even a generation. Hence the Chinese legal system today cannot and should not be compared with that of Western countries such as the United States.

The Chinese legal system is used as a tool to enhance and improve the governance of the Communist Party of China (CPC). It is considered unacceptable for individuals to use the law against the party or hold the party accountable for its actions. There is a separate party system of discipline to deal with members who violate party law, rules and regulations. Party members do not face the 'legal system' or 'criminal justice system'; instead they face the *shuanggui* system run by CPC internal affairs officers. Unlike most countries in the West, the judiciary in China is not independent from the CPC. Accordingly, there can be no judicial reform, nor can judges correct party members' misinterpretation of the law. Rather, the judiciary is meant to support CPC decisions, regardless of what they may be. One Chinese lawyer has said, 'In China, the big cases are about politics, the mid-sized cases are about influence and only the small cases deal with actual law.'[30] Unlike the US legal system, the Chinese court system is inquisitorial, not adversarial. In an inquisitorial system judges play an active role in interrogating witnesses and the parties, rather than remaining neutral referees. According to the 1995 Judge's Law there are three possible routes to becoming a judge: immediately after law school, after graduating from college and working as a judicial clerk for a year or as a former member of the military who is appointed as a judge. Under the Chinese constitution there are four levels of courts, and a loss at one level can be appealed to a higher court.

David Weissbrodt
Regents Professor and Fredrikson & Byron Professor of Law
University of Minnesota Law School

Notes

1. CIA World Factbook (2013) 'China'; available at: *https://www.cia.gov/library/publications/the-world-factbook/geos/ch.html* (accessed: 14 February 2013).
2. Nations Online (undated) 'Countries of the world by area'; available at: *www.nationsonline.org/oneworld/countries_by_area.htm* (accessed: 14 February 2013).
3. Ibid.
4. CIA World Factbook, note 1 above; CIA World Factbook (2013) 'Russia'; available at: *https://www.cia.gov/library/publications/the-world-factbook/geos/rs.html* (accessed: 14 February 2013).
5. World Bank (undated) 'China overview'; available at: *www.worldbank.org/en/country/china/overview* (accessed: 14 February 2013).
6. *Bloomberg News* (2013) 'China eclipses U.S. as biggest trading nation', *Bloomberg News*, 10 February; available at: *www.bloomberg.com/news/2013-02-09/china-passes-u-s-to-become-the-world-s-biggest-trading-nation.html* (accessed: 22 July 2013).
7. *The Economist* (2011) 'The dating game', *The Economist* online, 27 December; available at: *www.economist.com/blogs/dailychart/2010/12/save_date* (accessed: 22 July 2013).
8. Wendy Frieman (2004) *China, Arms Control, and Non-Proliferation (Politics in Asia)*. London: Routledge, p. 10.
9. Barbara A. Weightman (2011) *Dragons and Tigers: A Geography of South, East, and Southeast Asia*, 3rd edn. New York: Wiley, p. 366.
10. David L. Bosco (2009) *Five to Rule Them All: The UN Security Council and the Making of the Modern World*. New York: Oxford University Press, p. 2.
11. Michael Kan (2012) 'China's internet users cross 500 million', *PC World*, 15 January; available at: *www.pcworld.com/article/248229/chinas_internet_users_cross_500_million.html* (accessed: 22 July 2013).

12. GlobalWebIndex (2012) 'Social platform adoption trends 2012', 26 September; available at: *http://thenextweb.com/asia/2012/09/26/surprise-twitters-active-country-china-where-blocked* (accessed: 22 July 2013).

13. Ibid.

14. Ellyne Phneah (2012) 'Sina Weibo hits 300 million users but costs rise', ZDNet, 16 May; available at: *www.zdnet.com/sina-weibo-hits-300-million-users-but-costs-rise-2062304817* (accessed: 22 July 2013).

15. US Energy Information Administration (2012) 'China: country analysis brief'; available at: *www.eia.gov/countries/country-data.cfm?fips=CH* (accessed: 14 February 2013).

16. John Vidal and David Adam (2007) 'China overtakes US as world's biggest CO_2 emitter', *The Guardian*, 19 June; available at: *www.guardian.co.uk/environment/2007/jun/19/china.usnews* (accessed: 22 July 2013).

17. John Wang (2012) 'China sends more students abroad than any other country', *Epoch Times*, 21 September; available at: *www.theepochtimes.com/n2/china-news/china-sends-more-students-abroad-than-any-other-country-295022.html* (accessed: 22 July 2013). The University of Minnesota has the largest Chinese student population of any university in the United States.

18. UN Development Programme (2011) *Towards Human Resilience: Sustaining MDG Progress in an Age of Economic Uncertainty*. New York: UNDP, p. 147.

19. International Centre for Prison Studies (2012) 'World prison brief'; available at: *www.prisonstudies.org/info/worldbrief/wpb_country.php?country=91* (accessed: 14 February 2012).

20. Manfred Nowak (2006) 'Communication on human rights', Special Rapporteur on Torture and Other Cruel, Inhuman or Degrading Treatment or Punishment, Civil and Political Rights, Including the Question of Torture and Detention, UN Doc. E/CN.4/2006/6/Add.6, 10 March.

21. Cleveland Ferguson III (2012) 'International human rights', *International Law*, 46: 389, 401.

22. Keith Bradsher (2012) 'After decades of pressure, China pledges to stop organ transplants after executions', *New York Times*, 24 March, p. A7.

23. Matt Velker (2011) 'Top 10 daily newspapers in China'; available at: *www.china.org.cn/top10/2011-10/31/content_23772241.htm* (accessed: 22 July 2013).

24. Ibid.; Tess Stynes (2012) 'U.S. newspaper circulation slips further', *Wall Street Journal*, 30 October; available at: *http://online.wsj.com/article/SB10001424052970203335504578088643882363414.html* (accessed: 22 July 2013).

25. Reporters without Borders (2013) 'World Press Freedom Index 2013'; available at: *http://en.rsf.org/press-freedom-index-2013,1054.html* (accessed: 14 February 2013).

26. Statement by Duan Jielong, Director-General of Treaty and Law Department, Ministry of Foreign Affairs of China, at Sixth Committee of 61st Session of UN General Assembly, 17 October 2006; available at: *www.china-un.org/eng/chinaandun/legalaffairs/sixthcommittee/t349635.htm* (accessed: 22 July 2013).

27. IndexMundi (2013) 'China'; available at: *www.indexmundi.com/china/international_organization_participation.html* (accessed: 14 February 2013).

28. International Monetary Fund (2010) 'IMF executive board approves major overhaul of quotas and governance', Press Release No. 10/418, 5 November; available at: *www.imf.org/external/np/sec/pr/2010/pr10418.htm* (accessed: 22 July 2013).

29. Julian Ku (2012) 'China and the future of international adjudication', *Maryland Journal of International Law*, 27: 154; Monika C.E. Heymann (2008) 'International law and the settlement of investment disputes relating to China', *Journal of International Economic Law*, 11: 507, 526; Christopher Shen (2004) 'International arbitration and enforcement in China: historical perspectives and current trends', *Currents in International Trade Law Journal*, 14: 69–70.

30. Zhang Jinping, an environmental lawyer in China, quoted in Sui-Lee Wee (2013) 'China cancer village tests law against pollution', Reuters News, 16 January; available at: *www.reuters.com/article/2012/01/16/us-china-pollution-lawsuit-idUSTRE80F0RH20120116* (accessed: 22 July 2013).

About the authors

Chang Wang is an associate professor of law at the College of Comparative Law, China University of Political Science and Law; he is also the chief research and academic officer at Thomson Reuters, the world's leading source of intelligent information for businesses and professionals.

Chang is the second Chinese national ever elected to the prestigious American Law Institute, the vice-chair of the Legal Education and Specialist Certification Committee at the American Bar Association (ABA) and a member of the ABA Human Rights Council. He also serves on the ABA steering groups for Chinese law and immigration and naturalization law. He is a visiting scholar at the American Bar Foundation, a research institute for the empirical study of law. He is adjunct professor of law at the University of Minnesota Law School and William Mitchell College of Law in the United States; visiting professor of law at the University of Bern Faculty of Law and University of Lucerne Faculty of Law in Switzerland; visiting professor at the University of Milan in Italy; and a guest professor of law at Beijing Foreign Studies University in China. He is also a guest lecturer in American law and culture at Beijing Royal School, an elite private high school in China. Since 2007 he has been a member of the Central Civil and Judiciary Committee of the China Association for Promoting Democracy, the fourth-largest political party in China. He is a board member of the *Journal of Transnational Legal Issues*, a law review journal based in Lucerne, Switzerland. In 2013 he was awarded the Erasmus Mundus scholarship by the European Commission.

Chang received a BFA in filmmaking from Beijing Film Academy, an MA in comparative literature and comparative cultural studies from Peking (Beijing) University, an MA in American art history from the University of Illinois at Urbana-Champaign and a juris doctor from the University of Minnesota Law School. He has been admitted into law practice in Minnesota, the District of Columbia and federal courts. He specializes in comparative law, internet law, art law and immigration law.

He has published two books – *The End of the Avant-Garde: Comparative Cultural Studies* and *Legal Research in American Law* – and numerous essays and academic papers, in both English and Chinese, dealing with law, critical theory and art history. Chang Wang also writes a bi-weekly column on the history, law, arts and culture of the United States and Minnesota for *Minnesota Times*, a Chinese-language newspaper based in the Twin Cities.

Nathan H. Madson is an attorney based in St Paul and currently works with FindLaw, a Thomson Reuters business. He graduated from the University of Minnesota Law School in 2011 with a specialization in human rights law, and from the George Washington University with a

BA in international affairs (Asian studies) in 2008. He has worked extensively within the field of human rights, at the Advocates for Human Rights, the Center for Victims of Torture, the US Committee for Refugees and Immigrants, and OutFront Minnesota, among others. In October 2011 he formed his own non-profit organization, Queer Legal Aid Society, with two colleagues.

Nathan has researched and written on Uyghur issues, non-normative methods of legal reform, transitional justice, linguistic human rights, legal anthropology and Chinese law. He has published two articles with the *National Lawyers' Guild Review*. The first provides a detailed accounting of the work the AIDS Coalition to Unleash Power did in the 1980s and 1990s, analyzing the different methods the organization used to change HIV and AIDS policies. The second is a case study of the situation in Russia for lesbian, gay, bisexual and transgender people and the ways in which they can use international human rights norms to advocate for their rights. Nathan is also a member of the *National Lawyers' Guild Review* editorial board.

Introduction:
justice with a Chinese face

This book discusses the development of legal discourse and the ever-increasing influence of Western jurisprudence in contemporary China through comparative law. We discuss at length the formation of 'rule by law' as a grand narrative in its historical context, the controversy around different interpretations of human rights and the burgeoning civil rights movements in the People's Republic of China (PRC).[1]

The book begins with a study of the legal traditions and core assumptions underlying the current role of law in China, followed by a comparative analysis of the respective legal conventions and beliefs in China and the West.

The book examines Western, especially American, influences in specific areas of Chinese law, and the role US jurisprudence has played and could play in the 'modernization' of the Chinese legal system. Attention is paid to cross-cultural misunderstanding and misinterpretation, and the interaction between culture and law.

Readers are given an opportunity to look at China's place in the world, question general assumptions of universal values, observe the dominant legal themes and their development in China, and compare and contrast Western and Chinese legal conventions. The book will help readers better understand the legal system of China, and possibly predict legal actions and outcomes taken by the PRC government. It is designed to provide an introduction to the nature, history and function of law in China; foster comparative legal analysis and critical thinking; and equip future practitioners to address legal situations arising from their work with China.

There are three main parts to the book. The first part, 'Historical views', gives an overview of the development of the legal system in China. Starting with the competing schools of legal thought – Confucianism and legalism – we move from the legal systems of imperial China to the Republic of China and finally the People's Republic of China. Part I ends with a discussion of the growing influence the West has had on China's current legal structure.

Part II, 'The players', examines the individuals, government bodies and bureaucracies that have a prominent role in China's legal system. It is not just laws that compose the legal system of the PRC, but also the courts, procuratorates and judges who explain what the laws mean. Moreover, lawyers, police and secret police all play an important role. Finally, no analysis of the Chinese legal system would be complete without some discussion of the Communist Party of China (CPC).

The final part, 'Case studies', explains civil, criminal and administrative laws through case studies. In addition to describing important selections from these three bodies of law, we look at their implementation. Though China is not a common law system, and thus does not follow case precedent, the case studies still give the reader a broader understanding of the Chinese legal system than he or she would gain by solely reading statutes.

A 'socialist system of laws with Chinese characteristics'

On 8 March 2011 Wu Bangguo, chairman of the Standing Committee of the National People's Congress (NPC), announced 'A socialist system of laws with Chinese characteristics has been established on schedule in China.'[2] He hailed this as a major milestone in the history of the development of the country's socialist democratic legal system. Delivering a report on behalf of the Standing Committee at the parliament's annual session, Wu claimed: 'We now have a complete set of types of laws covering all areas of social relations, with basic and major laws of each type already in place, together with comprehensive corresponding administrative regulations and local statutes', and 'Overall, the system of laws is scientific, harmonious and consistent.'[3]

Wu said that by the end of 2010 China had enacted 236 laws, more than 690 administrative regulations and over 8,600 local statutes. Moreover, the government had completed the work of reviewing current laws, administrative regulations and local statutes. Wu's report culminated in the assertion that within contemporary China 'there are laws to cover every area of economic, political, cultural, social and ecological development'.[4]

When Wu asserts that China has adopted a 'socialist system of laws with Chinese characteristics', what does he mean? Is it a civil law system in which core principles are codified into a referenced system which serves as the primary source of law? Or does he mean a common law system that gives great precedential weight to case law, the law developed by judges through decisions of courts and similar tribunals?

In his report, Wu said:

> the socialist system of laws with Chinese characteristics is based on the situation and realities in China, complies with the requirements for reform, opening up and socialist modernization, and represents the will of the Party and the people. The system is rooted in the Constitution and has several types of laws, including laws related to the Constitution, civil laws and commercial laws, as its backbone.[5]

According to Wu, the system also has 'different levels of legal force, reflected in laws, administrative regulations, and local statutes'.[6]

Though the socialist system claims to reflect the 'situation and realities in China', what is Wu referencing? Obviously, different people and different groups have different views on what constitutes the current situation and realities in the country, but should the situation and realities perceived by the CPC be considered more 'authentic' than other interpretations? There are 80 million members of the Communist Party of China; while they control the political and economic resources in China, they only compose a small fraction of its 1.3 billion citizens. If there is a discrepancy between the CPC and the rest of the population as to the situation and realities in the country, who should prevail?

At the same time that Wu Bangguo declared the establishment of a socialist system of laws with Chinese characteristics, he also rejected political reform, saying that a democratization of China or any real relaxation of the CPC's control could throw the country into turmoil. While advocating for the status quo, he presented the 'five nos': no multiparty election; no diversified guiding principles; no separation of powers; no federal system; and no privatization. 'We have made a solemn declaration that we will not employ a system of multiple parties holding office in rotation; diversify our guiding thought; separate executive, legislative and judicial powers; use a bicameral or federal system; or carry out privatisation,' Wu proclaimed.[7] It was believed this speech was directed at those parties that were calling for a liberal democracy in the wake of the Arab Spring.[8]

Historical reforms in Chinese law

In 1911 the Qing dynasty, the last imperial dynasty in China, was overthrown by the Hsinhai Revolution led by Dr Sun Yat-sen, ending more than 3,000 years of imperial rule and ushering China into modernity. Prior to the fall of imperial China, however, there had been a few attempts at creating a modern, democratic-like legal system.

In 1898, for example, the Hundred Days' Reform sought to modify the existing imperial legal system. Ultimately the movement failed after only 104 days, as the Empress Dowager Cixi led a *coup d'état* against Emperor Guangxu, discontinuing his attempt at modernization.

Some of the changes Emperor Guangxu had sought included using capitalism, as well as manufacturing, to bring China into the Industrial Age; building a modern and strong military; reforming the civil service examination system; streamlining the bureaucracy to eliminate positions with little or no work; ending the absolute monarchy and replacing it with a democratic constitutional monarchy; and modernizing the education system. The reform movement ultimately failed, yet that failure helped push for the eventual fall of the Qing dynasty. The revolutionary forces who would overthrow the government in 1911 saw the resistance to political and legal reforms by the conservative forces as confirmation that the only way to bring about change was by a complete revolution.

In 1902 there was another attempt to change the legal system. Succumbing to foreign pressures to modernize, the Chinese endeavored to reform their legal system by incorporating various bits and pieces of several countries' existing systems. While still maintaining parts of the Grand Qing codex, a Chinese legal reform commission inserted Japanese legal vocabulary and portions of the German civil code into the existing Chinese framework. The commission leading this reform was composed of two ministers of legal revision, and also consulted foreign legal experts. While it made considerable progress in reforming the legal system, the fall of the Qing dynasty ultimately prevented any of those changes from being implemented.[9]

As the legal commission was crafting its proposals, the Empress Dowager Cixi was concerned that any political instability caused by enacting too many reforms too quickly would threaten control by the throne. Thus in 1906 she issued the 'Five No Discussion', or *wu bu yi*, directive, forbidding any changes to five core components of the imperial political system: the Grand Council, akin to an inner circle of advisors; the Eight Banners, the official classification of all Manchurian families who reinforced imperial military and economic power; the Imperial Household Department, which managed the affairs of the imperial family; the Hanlin Academy, a highly selective school that worked closely with the Imperial Court; and eunuchs, who held high-ranking positions within the court.[10] No matter what political reforms Cixi was willing to allow, these five core areas would remain out of reach. This was problematic to the reformers, because these five were precisely the targets of the proposed reform.

There is no evidence whatsoever to suggest that Wu was following Cixi's precedent when he issued his own Five Nos. He was simply clarifying that there were certain core parts of the contemporary Chinese legal system that would not change, as any change in these core values would likely put the CPC's authority in question. Wu and the party were unwilling to part with some aspects of the Chinese legal model, despite the fact that the issues he refused to discuss are the very issues that cause such strife within Chinese society.

Comparing Chinese and American legal systems

Although American law has been developing since the United States declared its independence, the Chinese legal system, in its most recent iteration, only started in 1979, following the end of the Cultural Revolution and after China reopened its doors to the outside world. Though there were laws and a legal system prior to this time, the entire system was almost disassembled during the decade-long Cultural Revolution: the Ministry of Justice was disbanded, law schools were closed and the legal profession was eliminated.

It was not until 1979 that Deng Xiaoping began to revive the Chinese legal community and craft a new and modern legal system. Since that time the system has continued to grow and evolve, along with other relatively modern structures, such as commercialism. Since the end of the Cultural Revolution numerous laws and regulations have been passed, enacted and amended. By August 2011 there were 240 national laws, 706 administrative regulations and 8,600 local regulations in effect.[11] There has also been a sharp increase in the numbers of civil and criminal cases appearing before Chinese courts, incidents of arbitration and mediation, and patent and trademark registrations.[12] All these reflect an increasingly sophisticated and comprehensive legal system in the making.

As a common law country, the United States and its legal system are deeply steeped in precedent, relying heavily on a judge's interpretation of both the codified law and previous judicial decisions. With few exceptions, judicial decisions are important factors in resolving legal matters. In contrast, Chinese law is a 'socialist legal system with Chinese characteristics'. What this means, in effect, is that the Chinese legal system is in place to support socialism and the CPC. The law is used as a tool to reinforce party rule and strengthen its decisions, not to provide a system of checks and balances against government control.

The US legal system incorporates checks and balances, federalism and separation of powers in an attempt to prevent one branch of government holding more power than others. By dividing up the responsibilities of government among the different branches and making no branch accountable to the others, each branch of government can act independently and according to its own interpretation of what is in the best interest of the country. This is true even if each interpretation is in conflict with the other branches. The Chinese system of government, however, is based on single-party rule. The Chinese constitution formally ensures that the CPC is the dominant political party in the country and is in charge of all aspects of the government.

In an effort to maintain complete control, the judiciary is not independent of the CPC. The CPC retains a great deal of power over the legal system and the judiciary. This includes a prohibition of judicial review, meaning judges lack the ability to review governmental actions. Unlike the US judiciary, the Chinese judiciary has been struggling with corruption and professional incompetency; the US judiciary is arguably the least corrupt of the three branches of government, in part because of its independence. American judges do not report to other branches of the government and they are able to review government actions without influence from the other branches. This creates a rule *of* law system in the United States, but a rule *by* law system within China.

American perspectives on Chinese law

As China plays an ever-increasing role within global politics and commerce, the United States has taken a growing interest in monitoring conditions within the country. One of the ways in which the US government does this is through the Congressional-Executive Commission on China (CECC), which comprises 18 members of Congress (nine senators and nine representatives) and five presidentially appointed senior officials. It was first created by Congress in 2000, and tasked with reporting to the president and Congress on human rights and rule of law concerns within China.[13] In 2012 the CECC reported:

> Two countervailing trends exemplified human rights and rule of law developments in China this past year [2012]. On the one hand, the Commission observed the Chinese people… exercising the basic freedoms to which they are entitled and demanding recognition of these rights from their leaders… At the same time, the Commission observed a deepening disconnect between the growing demands of the Chinese people and the Chinese government's ability and desire to meet such demands… Chinese officials appeared more concerned with 'maintaining stability' and preserving the status quo than with addressing the grassroots calls for reform taking place all over China.[14]

With one sentence, the commission captured the US government's understanding of rule of law in China, noting a 'deepening disconnect between the growing demands of the Chinese people and the Chinese government's ability and desire to meet such demands'.

The report continues: 'The Chinese government and Communist Party failed to keep pace with citizens' rising demands. In many areas, officials responded with half-measures that did not fully address citizen concerns and in some cases increased the government's capacity for abuse.'[15] The CECC listed the passing of the amended Criminal Procedure Law, including a new section that permits the secret detention of individuals and the use of torture against dissidents, as an example of the abuse used by the Chinese government.

This is not to say that the CECC's report was entirely negative. The commission noted the progress China has made, citing the government's improvements in environmental administration and the proposed reforms to the Hukou system – a system which currently 'limits the rights of Chinese citizens to freely determine their permanent place of residence'.[16] Nevertheless, 'In other areas, reform and forward movement have simply stalled. On the issue of the International Covenant on Civil and Political Rights (ICCPR), which Chinese officials have expressed an intent to ratify for a number of years, the government's position remained unchanged.'[17] Not only has the government failed to ratify the covenant, but it has not even mentioned a deadline by which it would commit to ratifying it.

One of the main components of the report discusses 12 major human rights issues within China: freedom of expression, workers' rights, criminal justice, freedom of religion, ethnic minority rights, population planning, freedom of residence and movement, status of women, human trafficking, North Korean refugees in China, public health and the environment.[18] Though the report goes into great detail about all 12 facets of human rights, it notes that 'In the name of "social management," the Party and government expanded their reach into society, enhancing surveillance and monitoring of not only democracy and rights advocates but also the citizenry at large.'[19]

The second section documents the development of the rule of law. The CECC focuses mostly on civil society, the institution of democratic governance, the commercial rule of law and access to justice. While there may have been some improvements in the last year, the CECC argues that China must create a 'highly efficient modern government that operates under the rule of law' if it wishes to strengthen its commitment to the rule of law.[20] Ultimately, the report implies that China eschews efficiency within the government and fails to make its decisions according to the rule of law.

The US Department of State's most recent (2011) annual country report on human rights practices reiterates this view, saying the PRC 'is an authoritarian state in which the Chinese Communist Party (CCP) constitutionally is the paramount authority. CCP members hold almost all top government, police, and military positions.'[21] Going further, the Department of State criticized specific human rights practices:

> Deterioration in key aspects of the country's human rights situation continued. Repression and coercion, particularly against organizations and individuals involved in rights advocacy and public interest issues, were routine. Individuals and groups seen as politically sensitive by the authorities continued to face tight restrictions on their freedom to assemble, practice religion, and travel. Efforts to silence political activists and public interest lawyers were stepped up, and, increasingly, authorities resorted to extralegal measures including enforced disappearance, 'soft detention,' and strict house arrest, including house arrest of family members, to prevent the public voicing of independent opinions.[22]

Other abuses included:

> Public interest law firms that took on sensitive cases continued to face harassment, disbarment of legal staff, and closure. The

authorities increased attempts to limit freedom of speech and to control the press, the Internet, and Internet access. The authorities continued severe cultural and religious repression of ethnic minorities in Xinjiang Uighur Autonomous Region (XUAR) and Tibetan areas. Abuses peaked around high-profile events, such as the visit of foreign officials, sensitive anniversaries, and in response to Internet-based calls for 'Jasmine Revolution' protests.[23]

A third report demonstrating US perspectives on the Chinese legal system is one by the US-China Economic and Security Review Commission, a non-partisan group that reports to the legislative branch and monitors what effect bilateral trade between the United States and the PRC has on American national security. The commission also presents an annual report to Congress on its findings.

Investigating 'China's military buildup, proliferation practices, regional economic and security impacts, U.S.-China bilateral programs, economic transfers, energy, U.S. capital markets, WTO compliance, and the implication of restrictions on speech and access to information in China', the commission found that 'China is undergoing a period of intense political transition and economic challenge that will test the ability of the Chinese Communist Party... to maintain its control over the country.'[24] While the commission noted the need for the Chinese government to reform, it also opined that the CPC has been making fewer market reforms and has become increasingly involved in the economy.[25]

Human rights commentary and the Chinese response

One major area of frequently heated dispute between the United States and China is human rights. As noted earlier, the United States sees China as an authoritarian regime that, at times, refuses to accept the universal values of liberty, justice and the pursuit of happiness and denies its citizens the protection of fundamental political rights. On the other hand, China believes it is being prejudiced by stereotype and that the United States has misunderstood its unique system and socialist characteristics.

There are indeed different understandings of 'human rights', yet many believe these rights to be universal and egalitarian: 'The freedoms, immunities, and benefits that, according to modern values (esp. at an international level), all human beings should be able to claim as a matter of right in the society in which they live.'[26] The Universal Declaration of Human Rights lists 30 different rights that are considered to be universal,[27] yet this non-binding declaration has not been adopted by the PRC. Instead, China defines 'human rights' as a combination of 'economic, social, and cultural rights' ('Right to work; Right to basic living standards; Right to social security; Right to health; Right to education; Cultural rights; and Environmental rights'), and 'civil and political rights' ('Rights of the person; Rights of detainees; Right to a fair trial; Freedom of religious belief; Right to be informed; Right to participate; Right to be heard; and Right to oversee').[28] These are a much more narrowly defined set of rights than those recognized by the Universal Declaration of Human Rights.

The World Justice Project (WJP), a US non-profit organization and a project of the American Bar Association, has ranked 97 countries, covering 90 percent of the world's population, on a variety of factors in an effort to determine a country's rule of law index. The index is a measure of a country's commitment to the rule of law, or, as defined by the WJP:

> The government and its officials and agents are accountable under the law… the laws are clear, publicized, stable and fair, and protect fundamental rights, including the security of persons and property… the process by which the laws are enacted, administered, and enforced is accessible, efficient, and fair… [and] justice is delivered by competent, ethical, and independent representatives and neutrals who are of sufficient number, have adequate resources, and reflect the makeup of the communities they serve.[29]

In 2012 the WJP examined eight factors – limited government powers, absence of corruption, order and security, fundamental rights, open government, regulatory enforcement, civil justice and criminal justice – and ranked countries on a global scale, on a regional scale and within similar income groupings to determine whether they comply with the rule of law.

According to the organization, China did quite poorly globally, but even worse within its region. While it was ranked 32 of 97 countries in order and security (its highest ranking on the global scale), it only ranked 9 of 14 countries within the region. The other areas in which China received higher scores, at least within the global ranking, were criminal justice (39) and absence of corruption (40). Regionally, however, those scores were 11 and 8, respectively. When ranked on open government (69), regulatory enforcement (80), civil justice (82), limited government powers (86) and fundamental rights (94), China did not do very well; these scores ranged between 11 and 13 on the regional scale. China's income group rankings were commensurate with its global and regional rankings.

Diving deeper into the rule of law index, the WJP examined individual sub-factors that contributed to China's scores. Understandably, China did well on civil conflict being effectively eliminated, the absence of crime and having an effective criminal investigation system. On the other hand, it did poorly on having non-governmental checks on governmental powers; individual freedoms, such as the freedoms of opinion and expression, of belief and religion, and of assembly and association; and freedom from inappropriate governmental influence in the criminal justice and civil law system. China's scores on the sub-factors on which it ranked the lowest were also the sub-factors in which there was the greatest difference between China's score and the top scores in the world and region.

The political leadership in the CPC changed in November 2012, at its Eighteenth National Congress. Subsequently, the Chinese government and presidency changed in March 2013, when the Twelfth National People's Congress of China was held.

The Eighteenth CPC National Congress elected the Eighteenth CPC Central Committee, and saw the number of Politburo Standing Committee seats reduced from nine to seven. The heads of the propaganda and public security (police) portfolios were downgraded to the level of the Politburo from their previous seats on the Standing Committee of the Politburo.[30] This reflects the party's concerns over the ever-increasing power of the police; at the same time the CPC was making an effort to control the propaganda and police force firmly, ensuring they are in line with the party agenda (discussed more later).

As for the police force, extralegal and illegal practices in recent years have become a major complaint in the aforementioned reports and by Chinese intellectuals. In the area of law, intellectuals saw some success in crafting a 'corps of professional judges and [instituting] a less draconian regime of punishment for criminals. Although these reforms remained largely in place in 2012, they co-existed with the increasingly egregious actions of both civil and armed police in the suppression of rising dissent.'[31] Ultimately, whether these reforms remain depends on the new powers within the CPC.

The call for reform was happening while the government was split on how to deal with dissent. Party General Secretary Hu Jintao and Premier Wen Jiabao emphasized the need for 'social stability' and utilized large showings of police and public security forces to discourage individuals from doing anything of which the government would not approve. At the same time, the now-disgraced party chief of Chongqing municipality, Bo Xilai, worked to convict as many people within organized crime as possible in an effort to send a message to those considering criminal behavior.

This is not to say that the Chinese government's approach to law and order is focused solely on organized crime. The concept of 'social contradictions' speaks to the discord that arises between the 'people' and their 'enemies', although contemporary understandings of 'enemies' include anyone who is:

> suspected of destabilizing society, threatening the territorial integrity of the nation or questioning the ultimate authority of the Communist party. These days, 'social contradictions' is a term often used euphemistically to describe social conflicts between the disaffected masses and the objects of their disaffection: local government officials, developers and, in some cases, company bosses.[32]

In its current attempt to punish the enemies of the people, the government uses 'the overt application of state power via vast police actions' to stop corruption and organized crime.[33]

What both models of law enforcement presuppose, however, is that the interests of the people and those of the CPC are aligned. If this assumption were true, then the government would potentially be making great strides in maintaining a harmonious society. Instead, there has been a growing distance between the masses and the party, which has led to mass protests and social unrest and a strong governmental response.[34] 'After 2007, the "harmonious society" was less about "building" a certain kind of society and more about "protecting" the status quo against those who dared to dissent.'[35] In effect, this has led to a concern that the government can do nothing to stop the abuse of power, because the 'main tension in the country is not between the authorities and a few rogue dissidents, but between China's ultimate interest group – the Party – and a building source of opposition – the people themselves'.[36]

In late January 2013 Human Rights Watch, an international non-profit organization, issued its 2012 country reports. Within the report on China, the authors highlighted the end of the Wen Jiabao and Hu Jintao government:

> That era saw sustained economic growth, urbanization, and China's rise as a global power, but little progress on human rights. The government rolled back protections on the administration of justice, presided over a significant rise in social unrest, including the largest inter-ethnic incidents in decades in Tibet and Xinjiang, and expanded the power of the security apparatus.[37]

In addition, the Human Rights Watch report noted that in its 2012–2015 National Human Rights Action Plan[38] the government continued to argue that the political and legal situations within the country prohibit widespread reform and democratic changes. The new plan put forth the 'principle of practicality', in which the government would recognize only those international human rights obligations that are practical to enforce. Previously, China had acknowledged some universal human rights, but this new approach is based on the understanding that 'national conditions' within China preclude it from 'participatory politics'.[39]

In response to the report by Human Rights Watch, the China *Global Times*, a party-owned newspaper based in Beijing, published an article challenging the findings. Citing Shen Tong, a law professor at Nankai University in Tianjin, the *Global Times* argued that the report was 'one-sided'.[40] The professor claimed the report failed to account for the progress China had made in 2012, including changes within the civil and criminal procedures laws. While Shen did admit that the Chinese government still had room to improve upon its human rights situation, he noted that there is no government with a perfect record.

Indeed, there still is room for improvement. In early 2011 numerous political dissidents, human rights advocates and lawyers were arrested by security forces in fear of an imminent 'Jasmine Revolution' in China. These individuals were arrested without warrant because they were under suspicion of being somehow connected to the anonymous calls for protests. During this crackdown more than 200 people were put under house arrest, 50 human rights advocates were held in extralegal detention and 15 people were criminally sentenced for inciting subversion to state power.[41]

Another common issue facing human rights activists and protesters is disappearances. Disappearances have increased in recent years, now rivaling the number of extralegal detentions since the late 1980s. Often the individuals arrested had no idea of the charges against them and their next-of-kin had no clue as to their whereabouts.

Another form of informal detention that the government uses against both activists and their relatives, presumably under the ancient concept of 'guilty by association', is house arrest. One of the most prominent relatives to be detained by police is Liu Xia, the wife of Nobel Peace laureate Liu Xiaobo, who has been under house arrest since her husband was first awarded the prize.[42] While being held by security forces, be it at home or in a police department, is considered informal detention, the US State Department's country report on human rights practices for China notes that 'The law grants police broad administrative detention powers and the ability to detain individuals for extended periods without formal arrest or criminal charges.'[43] In 2011 the State Department recorded numerous journalists, human rights activists, unregistered religious leaders and former political prisoners, as well as their family members, who were arbitrarily detained or held under house arrest.[44]

As attention is drawn to these extralegal procedures, however, the government has responded by amending the Criminal Procedure Law to legalize them.[45] Instead of working to eliminate such extralegal actions from public security practice, the CPC attempts to normalize the practices, taking them from an extralegal or illegal status to an accepted and legal one.

Questions raised by the Chinese legal system

It is undeniable that there is considerable debate on China's approach to the law, its legal system and its human rights. Questions raised by scholars of China include the following.

- Can China have capitalism without democracy?
- Are there alternative approaches to becoming a prosperous society?
- Can China operate under a substitute for or alternative to the rule of law?
- Are the values of liberty, justice and the pursuit of happiness truly universal?

- Is there a different definition of 'human rights'?
- Is China correct to argue that it is different, and thus cannot be held to the same rules and expectations as other countries?

Ultimately, these questions cannot be answered without looking at the arguments on both sides of the debate.

The British author Martin Jacques believes China will surpass the United States in economic output by 2027 and be the leader of global output by 2050. He eloquently articulates the Chinese government's stance that the 'Western idea of democracy' does not and should not work in China. According to Jacques, modern China is decidedly different from the West, balancing both its traditions and its ancient culture with its drive to move into the future. Jacques opines that China will start to have an influence on many different aspects of life, eventually turning back the tide of Western influence. While the growth of China's economy and political clout may not be in conjunction with democratization, China is still able to influence politics and culture outside its borders.[46]

And this is exactly what the CPC aspires to – the ability to utilize soft power and China's unique cultural identity to gain the respect of the international community. The CPC has worked hard to link itself to the country's Confucian roots, portraying Chinese history as one long, unbroken chain from Confucius to the current party. Along the way, the Chinese culture mixed with communism to form the unique country that it is today.

While this is how the CPC sees itself, there are others who disagree with this interpretation of Chinese history. Gordon Chang, for example, an American attorney who lived in China for years and wrote *The Coming Collapse of China*, said China is nowhere near as powerful as the CPC would have the masses and the international community believe: 'Peer beneath the surface, and there is a weak China, one that is in long-term decline and even on the verge of collapse. The symptoms of decay are to be seen everywhere.'[47] Chang went so far as to predict the fall of the PRC in 2006. Though this collapse did not come to fruition, he continues to maintain that China is on the brink of destruction and the people are one step away from revolution.[48]

It is difficult to deny the economic progress China has made, but Chang notes that the high levels of corruption within the CPC, high rates of unemployment and the large number of people growing disillusioned by the party indicate that progress is at best superficial and more likely illusory. Moreover, Chang believes the general lack of leadership is making it more difficult for the CPC to maintain control of the country, stating the government 'knows how to suppress but it no longer has the power to lead'.[49] Should the party falter in its suppression, the people may be unwilling to remain true to communism.

In an article for *Foreign Policy*, Professor Pei Minxin, a leading expert on governance in China, argues that US policy toward China is based on a faulty assumption – that the CPC will be in power for the foreseeable future.[50] Pei says there are many signs which indicate the fall of the CPC:

> The latest news from Beijing is indicative of Chinese weakness: a persistent slowdown of economic growth, a glut of unsold goods, rising bad bank loans, a bursting real estate bubble, and a vicious power struggle at the top, coupled with unending political scandals.[51]

Pei and Chang both crafted arguments countering China's claim that it was different, and thus could not be compared to the West or held to the same requirements as other members of the international community.[52] While the CPC may claim it is possible to move toward a capitalist society without ever democratizing, to Pei and Chang the 'Red Capitalism' adopted by the PRC is not actually capitalism. Rather, Red Capitalism is merely a combination of political repression and corruption; rule by man and rule by law are not sufficient alternatives to the rule of law.

Perhaps, however, it is Chinese lawyers who are best qualified to talk about their legal system. As one Chinese lawyer told Reuters, 'In China, the big cases are about politics, the mid-sized cases are about influence and only the small cases deal with law.'[53] It should be mentioned that the lawyer who made this comment did so anonymously, which indicates both an honest description of the legal system and one with which the CPC would not agree. In addition, writer Murong Xuecun described the legal system in the following terms:

> countless laws are enacted, and then countless procedures are created, followed by countless enforcement regulations and detailed judicial interpretations, but ultimately it is up to the political leaders to decide who wins and who loses a case. In my country, many cases cannot be pursued in the courts. Even if legal action is taken, courts can refuse to hear a case. Even if the case is heard in court, the judgement [sic] is made well before the hearing starts.[54]

Both the lawyer and the writer are implying that the Chinese legal system is composed of everything but the law. This system is not a 'rule of law' as defined by the United Nations: 'a principle of governance in which all persons, institutions and entities, public and private, including the State itself, are accountable to laws that are publicly promulgated, equally enforced and independently adjudicated, and which are consistent with international human rights norms and standards'.[55] It is a 'rule by law' system – the CPC uses the law to support its rule. Perhaps no one is more articulate on the subject than Wu Bangguo, who in March 2013 delivered the NPC Standing Committee work report for the last time as chairman of the NPC. He said: 'We provided legal and institutional guarantees that the party's line, principles and policies were implemented, and ensured that the party fully played its role as the leadership core in exercising overall leadership and coordinating everyone's efforts.'[56] To anybody who still has any doubt of the 'socialist system of laws with Chinese characteristics', Wu made it abundantly clear that the law is a tool to implement the CPC's line, principles and policies: the party is above the law.

Positive developments

Leading Chinese jurist Professor Jiang Ping has argued that 'China's rule of law is in full retreat',[57] yet there have also been some positive developments in recent years that can be seen as an attempt to improve or adjust the system to a certain degree.

Downgrading of the CPC Central Politics and Law Committee

In 2012 the CPC reorganized the Politburo Standing Committee by excluding the secretary of the Central Politics and Law Committee, the individual responsible for the police and public security forces.[58] The newly appointed Meng Jianzhu was, for the first time, not simultaneously elected to the Standing Committee, which holds nearly all the decision-making power in the country. China researchers in Hong Kong opine that the demotion of the position may be, in part, due to the previous secretary's connection with Bo Xilai and Wang Lijun (the former police chief of Chongqing who fled to the US consulate in an effort to seek political asylum and allegedly gave US officials incriminating evidence on Bo). Throughout the Bo Xilai incident, concerns were raised about Bo's methods of using internal security forces to achieve political ends, embarrassing the Central Politics and Law Committee.

Researchers warn, however, that the government will continue to rely upon domestic security and this restructuring could be seen as the CPC reasserting control over the police and public security apparatuses. This change has taken place at the regional and provincial levels as well.

Possible end of the re-education through labor system

Outside of the Chinese courts exists a system of forced-labor camps designed to 're-educate' minor criminals and other undesirables, such as individuals using drugs or participating in banned religious groups, dissenters and those who 'aggressively' petition.[59] The re-education through labor system has been used since 1957 to jail individuals for up to four years without them ever appearing before a court. There are rumors of change, however; officials within Guangdong province, the deputy director of the China Law Society in Beijing and a report from Xinhua, the state news agency, have all hinted at a reformed labor-camp system. According to Xinhua, 'with the development of society and the legal system [the re-education through labor system] defects have become more and more evident'.[60]

For the labor system to be reformed, however, more needs to be done at the legislative level. Even if the CPC announces changes to or the end of the system, if there are no accompanying comprehensive legal changes to end this form of extralegal detention, use of re-education through labor will continue. Ultimately, however, even an announcement by the CPC that extralegal detention or, more specifically, re-education through labor is inappropriate would be a move in the right direction. As stated in a recent *New York Times* article:

> Nonetheless it would be an important step forward, removing what has remained for decades a crippling obstacle toward realizing a fundamental requirement of any system of the rule of law: that no one accused of a crime can be deprived of liberty without a fair trial before a court. It would be a good start.[61]

Increasing calls for constitutionalism

Finally, there has been a push by intellectuals and members of the CPC for 'Chinese leaders to govern in accordance with the Constitution'.[62] Between December 2012 and January 2013 several pieces in scholarly journals and newspapers requested a greater commitment to constitutionalism within China's ruling elite. One editorial was even published in the *Study Times*, a publication associated with the Central Party School. The article called for the CPC to create a committee which would guarantee that no laws passed by the NPC would violate the constitution.[63]

Following the leadership transition in November 2012, a law professor with Peking University organized a conference in Beijing to discuss how best to force the government to comply with the constitution and, more broadly, how to create reform.[64]

Wu's statements may serve as an answer to these calls for an emphasis on constitutionalism: 'We fully understood the essential difference between China's system of people's congresses and Western capitalist countries' systems of state power, resolutely resisted the influence of all kinds of erroneous thought and theories, and maintained a firm and clear position on major issues of principle.'[65]

The CPC may seek to borrow suitable aspects of other countries' systems, but it will never adopt a Western-style democracy that would undermine the ultimate authority of the party.

This book

In the case of China, the facts, studies and research support two extremes: the imminent collapse of the CPC and the PRC as a whole, or that the PRC will one day take the leading role in the global economy and serve as a pre-eminent world power. There are also empirical evidence and sound analyses that support a variety of other outcomes.

This book, however, offers the reader a look inside the Chinese legal system, from its innermost workings to the larger themes surrounding the rule of law. While we hope to provide as complete a picture of the legal system as possible, the best that any legal scholar or scholar of China can do is present the facts and an interpretation of those facts.

In this book we are not only trying to locate and critically evaluate resources and materials on Chinese legal and political systems, history and current affairs, but also attempting to understand diverse philosophies and cultures within and across Chinese society. Specifically, we explain the philosophical underpinnings of the Chinese legal and political systems, and differing viewpoints on universal values (including justice, liberty, freedom, democracy and human rights) in China and the United States. In addition, we compare competing arguments based on those differences and analyze the evidence used to support those arguments.

We introduce the distinctive paradigms and discursive patterns of law and politics in China, and encourage readers to examine the materials, read and 'listen' to both sides of the debate. We hope readers will compare, analyze, think critically and reach their own conclusions on the Chinese legal system. We try to break through the traditional dichotomy of Chinese learning versus Western learning to interpret legal cases, political events and cultural phenomena from a comparative perspective, exposing the hidden rationales underscoring the historical and ideological narratives. Moreover, this book reveals frequent misunderstandings that occur while attempting to find commonalities between the different cultures.

Furthermore, this comparative perspective offers a vantage point from which we can think critically. As a result, we are less willing to accept presumptions, as we know that any presumption is rebuttable when paradigms shift. And we do hope that this little book helps us to understand China and ourselves a little better.

Notes

1. While many of these concepts could also be discussed within the context of Taiwan, this book focuses exclusively on mainland China, the PRC.
2. China's legislative goal of forming a socialist system of laws with Chinese characteristics by 2010 was set forth at the Fifteenth National Congress of the CPC in 1997.
3. Xinhua (2011) 'Socialist system of laws established in China', Xinhua, 10 March; available at: *www.china.org.cn/china/NPC_CPPCC_2011/2011-03/10/content_22099470.htm* (accessed: 22 July 2013).
4. Ibid.
5. Ibid.
6. Ibid.
7. Government of China (2011) 'Full text: work report of NPC Standing Committee (2011)', 18 March; available at: *http://english.gov.cn/official/2011-03/18/content_1827230_5.htm* (accessed: 19 July 2013).
8. See Shi Jiangtao (2012) 'Beijing slams door on political reform', *South China Morning Post*, 28 March; available at: *www.scmp.com/article/740532/beijing-slams-door-political-reform* (accessed: 22 July 2013).

9. See generally Zhao Xiaogeng (2010) *Legal History of China* (*Zhongguo Fazhi Shi*). Beijing: Renmin University Press.
10. Liu Qingsong (2011) 'From four things not to change to five things not to discuss', *Energy Review*, 2011(5): 124; available at: *www.indaa.com.cn/zz/nypl/201105/201105/P020110510 518418462479.pdf* (accessed: 23 July 2013).
11. Information Office of the State Council (2011) *Socialist Legal System with Chinese Characteristics*, October. Beijing: Information Office of the State Council, Appendix.
12. Ibid.
13. Congressional-Executive Commission on China (2012) '2012 annual report', *www.cecc.gov/publications/annual-reports/2012-annual-report* (accessed: 19 July 2013).
14. Ibid.
15. Ibid., p. 2.
16. Ibid.
17. Ibid., p. 3.
18. Ibid., table of contents.
19. Ibid.
20. Ibid., p. 5.
21. US Department of State, Bureau of Democrary, Human Rights and Labor (2011) 'Country reports on human rights practices for 2011: China'; available at: *www.state.gov/j/drl/rls/hrrpt/humanrightsreport/index.htm?dlid=186268* (accessed: 22 July 2013).
22. Ibid., p. 3.
23. Ibid.
24. Ibid.
25. Ibid., p. 25.
26. *Black's Law Dictionary* (2009) 'Human rights', *Black's Law Dictionary*. St Paul, MN: Thomson West.
27. 'Universal Declaration of Human Rights'; available at: www.un.org/en/documents/udhr/ (accessed: 22 July 2013).
28. People's Republic of China (2012) 'National Human Rights Action Plan of China (2012–2015)'; available at: *http://english.gov.cn/2012-06/11/content_2158183.htm* (accessed: 22 July 2013).
29. World Justice Project (undated) 'What is the rule of law?'; available at: *www.worldjusticeproject.org/what-rule-law* (accessed: 23 July 2013).
30. Willy Lam (2012) 'Finalizing the 18th Party Congress: setting the stage for reform?', *China Brief*, 12(18): 6–7.
31. ANU College of Asia and the Pacific (2012) 'The China Story yearbook 2012', p. 68; available at: *www.thechinastory.org/wp-content/uploads/2012/07/ ChinaStory2012_ch03.pdf* (accessed: 23 July 2013).
32. Ibid., p. 71.
33. Ibid., p. 72.
34. Ibid., p. 74.
35. Ibid.
36. Ibid., p. 86.

37. Human Rights Watch (2013) 'World report 2013'; available at: *www.hrw.org/world-report/2013/country-chapters/china* (accessed: 23 July 2013).
38. People's Republic of China, note 28 above.
39. Human Rights Watch, note 37 above.
40. Xinhua (2012) 'Expert challenges HRW report on China's legal reform', Xinhua, 4 February; available at: *www.globaltimes.cn/content/760044.shtml* (accessed: 23 July 2013).
41. US Department of State, note 21 above.
42. Xin Yu and Wei Ling (2013) 'Activists visit Liu Xia', trans. Wei Ling, Radio Free Asia, 1 January; available at: *www.rfa.org/english/news/china/nobel-01012013110843.html* (accessed: 23 July 2013).
43. US Department of State, note 21 above.
44. Ibid.
45. Ibid.
46. Martin Jacques (2009) *When China Rules the World: The End of the Western World and the Birth of a New Global Order.* New York: Penguin Books.
47. Gordon G. Chang (2001) *The Coming Collapse of China.* New York: Random House, p. 2.
48. See generally ibid.
49. Ibid., p. 2.
50. Pei Minxin (2012) 'Everything you think you know about China is wrong', *Foreign Policy*, 29 August; available at: *www.foreignpolicy.com/articles/2012/08/29/everything_you_think_you_know_about_china_is_wrong* (accessed: 23 July 2013).
51. Ibid.
52. Pei Minxin (2008) *China's Trapped Transition: The Limits of Developmental Autocracy.* Boston, MA: First Harvard University Press.
53. Sui-Lee Wee (2012) 'China cancer village tests law against pollution', Reuters, 16 January; available at: *www.reuters.com/article/2012/01/16/us-china-pollution-lawsuit-idUSTRE80F0RH20120116* (accessed: 23 July 2013).
54. Market Cruncher (2011) 'Murong Xuecun: behind the Chinese façade lies a monster', Market Cruncher, 23 November; available at: *http://marketcruncher.com/2011/11/ 23/murong-xuecun-behind-the-chinese-facade-lies-a-monster/* (accessed: 23 July 2013).
55. UN Rule of Law (undated) 'What is rule of law?'; available at: *www.unrol.org/article.aspx?article_id=3* (accessed: 23 July 2013).
56. Sina (2013) 'Full text: work report of NPC Standing Committee', Xinhua English, 20 March; available at: *http://english.sina.com/china/2013/0320/573404.html* (accessed: 19 July 2013).
57. *China Digital Times* (2010) 'Jiang Ping (江平): "China's rule of law is in full retreat"', *China Digital Times*, 2 March; available at: *http://chinadigitaltimes.net/2010/03/jiang-ping-%E6%B1%9F%E5%B9%B3-chinas-rule-of-law-is-in-full-retreat/* (accessed: 19 July 2013).
58. BBC (2012) 'China leaders reassert control over security portfolio', BBC News, 21 November; available at: *www.bbc.co.uk/news/world-asia-china-20422303* (accessed: 21 November 2012).

59. Stanley Lubman (2013) 'Will re-education through labor end soon?', *China Realtime Report*, 4 February; available at: *http://blogs.wsj.com/chinarealtime/2013/02/04/will-re-education-through-labor-end-soon/* (accessed: 23 July 2013).

60. Ren Ke (2012) 'Commentary: reform of labor re-education system inevitable', Xinhua, 11 October; available at: *http://news.xinhuanet.com/english/indepth/2012-10/11/c_131900685.htm* (accessed: 19 July 2013).

61. Nicholas Bequelin (2013) 'Re-education revisited', *New York Times*, 29 January; available at: *www.nytimes.com/2013/01/30/opinion/global/re-education-revisited.html?_r=1&* (accessed: 23 July 2013).

62. Edward Wong and Jonathan Ansfield (2013) 'Reformers aim to get China to live up to own constitution', *New York Times*, 3 February; available at: *www.nytimes.com/2013/02/04/world/asia/reformers-aim-to-get-china-to-live-up-to-own-constitution.html?pagewanted=all&_r=2&* (accessed: 23 July 2013).

63. Quoted in ibid.

64. Ibid.

65. Sina, note 56 above.

Part I
Historical views

Philosophical underpinnings of the Chinese legal system

Abstract: This chapter covers the two main schools of thought that have shaped the contemporary Chinese legal system: Confucianism and legalism. It seeks to develop the basics of both philosophies by explaining the times and cultures in which each emerged. The chapter also explains the current effort by the People's Republic of China and the Communist Party of China to make certain Confucian symbols more prevalent in an attempt to forge a link between Confucius's time and the present. Finally, some of the dichotomies and paradoxes of the Chinese legal system are introduced.

Key words: Confucius, legalists, Communist Party of China, hidden rules, morality.

For about 2,500 years two opposing schools of thought – Confucianism and legalism – have provided the philosophical underpinnings for China's legal system. Throughout China's history the two schools have vied for supremacy. After examining the history and tenets of Confucianism and legalism, it is clear that China's current system is legalistic, but still retains a Confucian face.

Confucianism

Confucius lived from 551 to 479 BCE, but his teachings and philosophy influence Chinese thought and action to this day.[1] The primary idea behind Confucianism is governance by education, persuasion and moral example.[2] In an ideal Confucian society, morality, rather than the wishes of the populace, serves as the foundation for harmony.[3]

Confucianism also envisions a society based on a hierarchical system in which each individual's role is determined by his or her position in society, as well as by familial and personal relationships.

Within the family unit, all individuals fall within a rigid hierarchy. Those with more subordinate positions in the hierarchy hold a general duty of obedience to the superior members of the family. Though there is considerable emphasis on the duties the lower-ranked family members owe to their higher-ranked relatives (two cardinal virtues of an ideal Confucian household are filial piety and obedience), those in superior positions have a reciprocal duty of caring, support and guidance to the subordinate members.

This idea of obedience and rigid application of hierarchical status also applied on a national scale. The same moral values and codes of conduct that prevailed in a family unit extended to the society and nation as a whole – the nation was, in effect, an extended family. This concept is reflected in the Chinese word 'nation/state' or *guo jia* (国家). The first character means 'nation' and the second means 'family'. As within the family unit, loyalty and obedience to rulers were paramount virtues within society. In the same vein, the rulers are to behave toward those they govern in the same caring way in which fathers were encouraged to behave toward their children.

Within Confucianism there are five constant virtues or *wu chang* (五常). In descending order of importance, the virtues are benevolence or *ren* (仁), righteousness or *yi* (义), propriety or *li* (理), wisdom or *zhi* (智) and fidelity or *xin* (信). These five ethical principles regulated society in ancient China,[4] though translating *xin* presents some difficulty, because the character combines the separate characters for 'people' and 'speech', meaning 'to persist in what one said' or 'one's deeds match one's words'. The meaning is best described as being similar to the English words fidelity, integrity, honesty, trust, faith or promise, but it does not directly correspond with any of these individual words.

The five constant virtues were important in determining who was a 'true gentleman' in ancient Chinese society. Regardless of a person's class or social status, he was expected to exhibit the five virtues and use proper conduct toward others.

This also applied to the way in which rulers were expected to govern. A leader, from local bureaucrat to emperor, was supposed to govern with benevolent concern for the well-being of his subjects. One reason those in charge were expected to live by the five constant virtues is that the Confucian concept of government involves leading by example. The belief was that if individuals in the government are virtuous, their subjects will be virtuous as well.[5]

Another Confucian assumption is that if people are kept in line by governmental measures or threats of punishment, the people's primary goal will be to stay out of prison. Subjects will behave well not because of any true sense of honor in good behavior or shame in bad behavior, but simply because of the threat of punishment. Instead, the Confucian ideal is to lead by virtue and control, or to regulate one's subjects by *li* (propriety). This, in turn, will cultivate a sense of honor and respect among the people.[6]

Part of the Confucian ideology is that people are born good and can improve themselves through learning. When the government focuses on educating its citizens, especially by exemplifying morality, individuals will take note. With enough education and examples of good leadership to follow, citizens will become model citizens.

This assumption led, in part, to the creation of the 'parent official', with the idea that government officials should be held to a higher level of morality than ordinary citizens, and should treat the citizens as their children. They are expected to show a certain degree of benevolence, so that the population can, in turn, regard officials as parent figures. The same parent-child relationship existed between rulers and ministers. The phrase 'ruler, ruler; minister, minister; father, father; son, son' sums up the Confucian idea of living up to one's job title – meaning that rulers should behave like rulers, ministers like ministers and so forth.[7] The underlying principle is that things should accord with their names and individuals must accept their societal roles. By refusing to accept one's role in society, an individual risks destroying the natural harmony.

The Confucian emphasis on a government that can lead by example is best exemplified by the following story:

> At one point, Tsze-kung, a student of Confucius, asked Confucius about government and Confucius replied, 'The requisites of government are that there be sufficiency of food, sufficiency of military equipment, and the confidence of the people in their ruler.'

> Tsze-kung said, 'If it cannot be helped, and one of these must be dispensed with, which of the three should be forgone first?

> 'The military equipment,' said Confucius.

> Tsze-kung again asked, 'If it cannot be helped, and one of the remaining two must be dispensed with, which of them should be forgone?'

The Master answered, 'Part with the food. From ancient times, death has been the lot of all men; but if the people have no faith in their rulers, there is no justification for the state.'[8]

By this, Confucius meant that the social order is threatened whenever people fail to act according to their prescribed roles. The belief was that individuals who followed and respected their assigned roles would also respect the government, its officials and their statuses within Chinese society. Those individuals who disrespect officials could potentially start rebellions, which, according to Confucius, was the gravest of crimes.[9]

Confucius's view of law

Though Confucius is regarded in the West as one of history's great legal minds, a creator of law in the East, and his image is carved on the US Supreme Court building next those of Moses and Solon, Confucius did not like law. Rather, he believed that if a society was virtuous and moral, its citizens would behave. Creating and publishing laws, then punishing people for violating them, would just encourage people to do whatever they could to avoid punishment. According to Confucius, it was better to craft a code and keep it secret from ordinary citizens. Doing so would allow those who enforced the code to use some moral judgment and discretion in applying it.[10]

Confucius was concerned that a code provided little flexibility and failed to recognize the circumstances behind a potentially criminal action. In addition, he thought that if individuals focused solely on escaping punishment, those in the higher social classes would have little reason to remain virtuous:

> If the people's behavior is governed wholly by its response to an 'objective' and invariant code of penal law, the *raison d'être* of the ruling class as an ethical vanguard will be undermined; and the people, after thoroughly familiarizing themselves with the provisions of the law, will simply develop enormous ingenuity and resourcefulness in evading the law.[11]

Confucius's view of history

While there is no vocabulary for 'bad government' in Confucian ideology, Confucius was aware that some leaders were less than scrupulous. In his history *Spring and Autumn Annals* or *Chun Qiu* (春秋), he carefully concealed certain portions of the truth so as to present the kingdom of Lu in a better light.[12] It was Confucius's idea that if history was truthful, the people would lose faith in the government. Therefore misrepresenting, ignoring and hiding the truth in history writing and editing are allowed, even necessary. Overall, the work was relatively deceptive, in order to preserve the reputation of the government better.

Critical thinking on Confucius

Within Confucianism, the presumption is that human beings are fundamentally good. Confucianism believes people will internalize acceptable norms and only take proper actions. This will not only lead to a harmonious social order, but will also improve an individual's inner character and the overall quality of society.

Because Confucius assumed that men would do what was expected of them in an effort to create a harmonious society, his idea of governance lacked a system of checks and balances. Under the assumption that a ruler would rule with benevolence and treat his or her subjects as a parent would treat a child, Confucius failed to offer safeguards against a ruler who was tyrannical. Without such safeguards in place, Confucian society could become a 'rule by man' system, as opposed to one that is governed by the rule of law. Confucianism's emphasis on unquestioning obedience to authority makes it particularly difficult if a ruler is less than benevolent.

This call for blind obedience sparked discussion well past the lifetime of Confucius. In his 1918 book *Madman's Diary*, Lu Xun (1881–1936), one of the fathers of modern Chinese literature, attacked Confucianism as an oppressive and hypocritical morality that thinly conceals and encourages exploitation, injustice, inequality, passivity and conformity. He also argued that it has had a negative effect on the Chinese people.[13]

Lu claimed that he had read two authoritative books on Confucianism, *Four Books* and *Five Classics*, and had begun to see the words 'Eat people' between the lines of text. Lu used this reference to cannibalism to highlight his perception of hypocrisy within Confucianism.[14] Noting that unquestioning acceptance of authority stifled personal liberty, innovation and critical thinking, Lu accused the Chinese government of exploiting the public's obedience by corruptly taking from the people they were supposed to protect.

By 1919 Lu Xun's critiques of Confucian ideals had taken hold, and many Chinese intellectuals believed these traditional values were responsible for the country's decline and moral bankruptcy. It was between 1915 and 1923 that the New Cultural Movement was also taking place. Lu wrote that Confucius's China praised age, men and the collective society at the expense of young people, women, individualism and general creativity. Moreover, Confucian China's devotion to tradition prevented innovation and was making it impossible for China to join the modern world. In Lu's opinion, China needed to abandon Confucian ideals and modernize.[15]

Mao Zedong was another strong opponent of Confucianism. After 1949 the Communist Party of China (CPC) no longer regarded Confucius as a saint, and in the early 1970s Chairman Mao and the CPC started an anti-Confucius campaign.[16] From 1973 to the end of the Cultural Revolution in 1976 Mao sought to reinterpret history through a Maoist and communist lens. Coincidentally, he chose to rewrite history in much the same way Confucius had done centuries before. Mao also encouraged the public to contrast the failings of Confucius and Confucianism with the benefits of Maoism and communism. He did this by linking himself and his image to that of the first emperor of China, Qin Shihuang, who had also opposed Confucianism and favored legalism.

The resurgence of Confucianism in China

In all, Confucius was largely unpopular from 1949 to 1979. Within the past 30 years, however, there has been a resurgence of Confucianism within mainland China: 'It fits in with a general tendency by the current regime to emphasize continuity with the past.'[17] The current CPC officials have found that Confucius's concept of a harmonious society has gone far to create a stable social situation in contemporary China.

Not only has the current administration revived Confucius and many of his ideals for a harmonious society, but it has also gone so far as to establish Confucius Institutes in numerous countries around the world to increase its soft power overseas. Though China is officially socialist and Mao is the human representation of its ideology, the government consciously chose to use Confucius's name and image to promote its language and culture internationally. Rather than focusing on the divergent social theories of communism and Confucianism, the current leadership is using Confucianism to communicate that, as it was in the days of Confucius, China is a great country. Because the CPC has brought the country back to prominence, it wishes to promote a sense of national pride, even if that means venerating the once-discredited Confucius.[18]

Though Confucianism and Chinese communism seem to be at odds, there are certain common themes: both schools of thought place considerable emphasis on harmony and stability. Confucius's ideal of a harmonious society and the current regime's desire for stability are quite similar.

As communist rule continues in China, a movement to respect the past has developed. The CPC has been reimagining history as an unbroken and unified path from ancient China and Confucius to present-day China and Mao. In essence, the government is seeking to gloss over its past disputes with Confucianism and portray China as a continuous civilization. Thus the CPC has been working in recent years to present Confucius as a symbol of the glamour and beauty of the past, rather than as a symbol of decadent imperial traditions.

During the Cultural Revolution the CPC brought Maoism to the sanctity of a religion, but after the death of Mao, the trial of the Gang of Four (including Mao's wife) and the revelation of the horrors of the Cultural Revolution, Maoism as a belief system began to fade. This left many people with a desire for something new, something to believe in and to fulfill their spiritual needs. This spiritual void left many in the CPC uneasy, believing that religion could undermine the party's authority; thus, perhaps in an effort both to address the spiritual needs of the people and to maintain their own authority, the CPC has attempted to reconcile Confucianism with communism.

While some see the current regime's use of Confucianism as an attempt to rework an old idea to serve a new goal, others believe the regime is still attempting to claim moral superiority despite the fact that it is morally bankrupt. The CPC's attempt to assert superiority and merge it with a Confucian morality is best evidenced by its incorporation of Confucianism into the Beijing Olympics. The government had 3,000 Confucian disciples on display and used the Confucian quotes 'When a friend comes from afar, is that not delightful?', and 'All men are brothers.'[19] By relying on Confucian imagery while simultaneously extolling Chinese virtues of hospitality, the government hoped to convey to the global community its link to Confucius.

Mencius 孟子

Mencius was a pupil of Confucius's grandson Zisi, and has been revered as a sage and one of the most important Confucian intellectuals. While this interpretation of Confucius's teachings is considered to represent orthodox Confucianism, Mencius did not agree with Confucius on many aspects of the ideal Confucian society. In contrast to Confucius's high regard for the ruling elite, Mencius focused on the importance of everyday citizens. In another sharp departure, Mencius said that rulers can be overthrown if they are tyrannical, corrupt or brutal. For example, when asked about the overthrow of notoriously ruthless King Zhou of the Shang dynasty, Mencius replied, 'I have merely heard of killing a villain Zhou, but I have not heard of murdering the ruler.'[20]

Each emperor and dynasty believed they ruled with a 'mandate of heaven' or *tianming* (天命): heaven offered a mandate to each new dynasty, yet this right to govern was not permanent. If an emperor failed to carry out his role correctly, for example if he failed to rule justly, heaven could transfer the mandate to another ruler. Rulers were required to behave toward those below them as a parent would treat a child; failing to do so would strip the ruler of his or her right to be treated with deference. Mencius said that though a ruler does deserve considerable respect, he or she must also answer to the people and society: 'The people are to be valued most, the altars of the grain and the land [traditional symbols of state vitality] next, the ruler least. Hence winning the favor of the common people you become Emperor....'[21] Mencius's vision of an ideal leader is best described as a benevolent dictator, someone who places greater importance on morality than on pragmatism.

Legalism

Legalism is the teaching of Chinese utilitarian political philosophers during the Warring States period (475–221 BCE) and after who emerged to counter Confucianism. These philosophers advocated that law should be publicly promulgated principles and standards of conduct backed by powerful state coercion. In essence, they were the first organized group of people who promoted what many in the West would recognize as the rule of law.

Though legalists had the same ultimate goal as Confucius – maintaining social order and the authority of the ruler – their proposed method of achieving that goal was very different. Whereas Confucius had advocated a society based on morality, education and modeling what was proper, 'the legalists sought to use a set of written rules, physical force, and a uniform administrative apparatus to impose order on society'.[22]

Han Fei Zi was one of the most important legalistic thinkers. His theories of rule focused on three qualities: law or *fa* (法), tactics or *shu* (术) and legitimacy or *shi* (势).[23] Unlike Confucius, Han believed that every subject was equal before the law, which required the legal code to be published and understandable. Not only should everyone have knowledge of the laws, but individuals should be rewarded for following the law – and punished for breaking it. Han was also a proponent of rule of law, and believed that even a weak ruler could enforce the legal code with some strength. Accordingly, it was ultimately the legal code that ran the state, not the individual ruler.

The second requirement for a functional government was a certain degree of secret methods or tactics, applied to ensure that no one else would take over control. A ruler needed to keep his predilections and motivations secret, in order to convince the public that the only way to stay on the right side of the law was to follow it. If individuals knew that certain behaviors were appreciated by the ruler, people might try to garner favor to avoid punishment.

Though a ruler may carry certain power and respect, according to the legalists it was the position that truly held the power, not the individual filling it. If a ruler wanted to succeed, he needed to respond to the people. Being rigid and insisting on demonstrating power would undermine the ruler's legitimacy.[24]

Because legalists recognized that people could be corrupt or tyrannical, they were not willing to rely on merely setting a moral example to encourage good behavior. Rather, they needed a system of punishment for lawbreakers.[25] Whereas Western societies typically offer four basic justifications for punishment – retribution, deterrence, rehabilitation and incapacitation – legalism only offered one: deterrence.

Han argued for extremely harsh punishment in order to deter criminal behavior adequately. According to Han, a proper punishment was execution or torture. Legalists sought to use punishment as a tool of fear that prevented the population from acting against the criminal code or rulers. Unlike Confucians, legalists maintained that punishments need not fit the crime; instead, the ruler should impose harsh punishment even for the slightest wrongdoings.[26] This concept of disproportionality in the Chinese criminal justice tradition is exemplified by the numerous types of torturous corporal punishments prevalent in imperial China.[27]

To force citizens to behave as the government wished, even if the government's wishes went against the citizens' interests or will, legalists sought to use universally applied laws. The theory was that because no one, regardless of status, could escape prosecution, everyone would follow the law.

This theory corresponded with the legalists' general belief about humanity. Unlike Confucius, they thought that everyone was born self-interested and evil, so there needed to be a system to impose order. Without intervention, people would behave selfishly, causing widespread social unrest.

With their goal of instilling fear in individuals, legalists disagreed with the Confucian idea that a ruler should be respected for his moral and virtuous behavior. Instead, said the legalists, rulers needed to be feared for their punishments and respected for the way in which they rewarded law-abiding citizens. Rewards, however, were not to be generously distributed. As Shang Yang said, 'In a well-ordered nation, punishment is endemic, reward scarce.'[28]

Legalism did not last long in China. After the Qin dynasty collapsed (see below), legalism was soon abandoned and its teachings discredited. This does not mean, however, that legalism was forgotten in China.[29] Many of its traditions persisted within individual households and groups of households. The idea of guilt by association, for example, emerged from the legalist tradition.

Qin and the first emperor

Qin Shi Huang (秦始皇) was king of the Chinese state of Qin from 246 to 221 BCE, and unified China. His empire consisted of approximately one-third of the territory of modern China, and he served as the first emperor until his death in 210 BCE.[30] Though the previous Warring States era had been particularly violent, it had also been a time of free thought. In an effort to unify both China and political thought, however, Qin followed the advice of his chancellor, Li Si, and undertook to burn all history books. Not only did this give Qin the ability to control what was taught, but it served as a sharp break from the traditional Chinese reverence for books and learning. He also banned all ideologies other than legalism.

The emperor was concerned that members of the intellectual community were publicly praising him, but using scholarly works to breed dissent among the people. Qin sought to write his own history books, believing that the existing histories and books on legal thought would undercut his legitimacy.

Li Si crafted extremely harsh penalties for those who did not comply with this new policy of book burning. If anyone refused to burn his or her books within 30 days of the order, he or she would be sent to build the Great Wall. If an official knew of someone who had not burned his or her books, the official would be equally as guilty. Even those who used ancient texts to comment on the Qin emperor or his government would be executed, as would their families.

In conjunction with the burning of the books or *fenshu* (焚书), Qin also cracked down on the intelligentsia by burying scholars alive, known as *kengru* (坑儒).[31] It was said that when two alchemists lied to the emperor about how to live longer, he chose to bury 460 scholars alive in the capital. Though advised not to take such a violent and extreme measure after the country had already been unified, Qin could not be persuaded otherwise. The concern was that those who still followed Confucianism would become upset and possibly raise unrest. Only 15 years later, in 206 BCE, the Qin dynasty was overthrown and replaced by the Han dynasty.

This was the first noted burning of books or burying of scholars in China. Because books were treated as extremely valuable items and scholars had long been respected and revered, the emperor's actions had a significant impact. It was not until 1957 that similar actions would be taken again. During the Anti-Rightist Movement and the Cultural Revolution in the mid-twentieth century, the CPC started to persecute intellectuals: approximately 550,000 intellectuals were found guilty of being rightists, and an untold number of books were destroyed.[32]

Hidden rules and law in imperial China

With Confucianism officially readopted by the Han dynasty, and continuing through the final Qing dynasty, it is clear that Confucian thought helped to determine how China was run. One Confucian ideal, that the legal code should not be made readily available to the masses, was quickly adopted, so much so that China has been said to be run by 'hidden rules' rather than by law.

In 1999 Chinese historian and editor Wu Si created the phrase 'hidden rules' or *qian guize* (潜规则) to explain the prevalence of unspoken practices in ancient Chinese society.[33] For example, it was commonly known that an official was to give something of value to a superior on several different occasions during the year. Though it was not an official part of the legal code, and was actually considered illegal, nearly everyone complied with this practice. Failing to do so often led to punishment or disfavor.

Another hidden rule was that the government had the right to harm its citizens. Contrary to the Confucian responsibility to protect the people, the government could undertake action that would cause harm to its subjects. Yet another rule was that it was often important to bribe government officials. As some officials had purchased their positions, they saw bribes as a return on their investment. This prevailing attitude created a systematic, inherited and top-down form of corruption.

Many officials used hidden rules to secure the favor of superiors. Within the past decade these rules have become accepted as necessary to 'lubricate the channels'. The use of such unofficial acts dates back to the Ming and Qing dynasties. The emperors recognized that they could do little about these accepted practices, because removing hidden rules would have required them to execute all their corrupt officials. Because the elimination of most of the country's officials would likely have led to the collapse of their states, emperors were more likely to let hidden rules undermine the established legal system.

For many within the imperial bureaucracy, hidden rules let them get more out of their official statuses than would otherwise be allowed. Even those in lowly positions were able to increase their wealth by abusing their power. Often this exploitation came at the expense of the emperor and the public. As unwritten rules became more rampant, it was important for those in the lower echelons to capitalize on the hidden laws to survive; relying on the actual legal system would have been fruitless when almost no one respected the established laws.[34]

Though there was widespread use of hidden rules within imperial China, the emperor was still the ultimate authority. He was known as the *tianzi* (天子), indicating that his legitimacy was derived from a celestial source (*tian* – 天). As the figurative patriarch of the country, the emperor embodied legislative, judicial and executive power, giving rise to a system of rule by man rather than the rule of law. He served as the final arbiter of people's lives, and was considered to be entirely above the law. Any attempt to limit the emperor's power was seen as treasonous.

The imperial concept of the individual was subsumed within that of the group. Individuals were recognized and acknowledged to have legitimate interests, but they were not considered to be independent of their roles within a group. This meant that individuals in Confucian society could not force courts to respect their personal interests. Without an ability to protect individual interests in opposition to those of the group, China had no place for individual or human rights. Rather, the intent of the law was to create a harmonious social order, and one of the worst crimes was to disrupt the social hierarchy or commit a crime against someone of a higher status.

An individual's status or societal function influenced how he or she was to be dealt with or punished under the law. Inequality before the law also played out in family law, as only the husband, not the wife, could initiate a divorce.

Law versus morality

Because Confucius held such little regard for the legal system, he preferred to rule through morality rather than by law. He presumed that any ruler's actions were moral and benevolent, creating the related presumption that it was the citizen's duty to accept the emperor's actions without question.

This sense that morality was superior to the rule of law created two problems. The first was that those in power were presumed to be good people and unable to make mistakes. This presumption was so strong that anyone who dared to criticize the government was considered a traitor. Much as those who criticize the CPC today may be prosecuted for inciting subversion of state power, it was presumed treason to criticize officials in imperial China. The second problem was that this system created a two-faced sense of morality. While it was of the utmost importance to respect the social hierarchy, there was an insistence on extreme morality.

Lu Xun described an instance of extreme morality in one of the famous '24 paragons of filial piety':[35]

> Kuo Chu has three sons. His mother reduces her food in order to give some to her grandsons. He then discusses with his wife: 'I feel very sad, our mother always spares her food for our sons. She herself does not actually get enough food. You can give birth to more sons. Could you give birth to our mother? Hence, better is it

to bury our sons and let our mother have sufficient food.' His wife agrees with him. Three feet deep they have dug in the ground, but instead of burying their sons, they find some large pieces of gold on which it is written: 'God of wealth gives this gold to the filial Kuo and his wife!'

Another such example of extreme morality was the concept of the chaste widow. In imperial China a widow was expected to remain faithful to her husband and his family after his death. Instead of being able to remarry and get on with her life, she was expected to move in with her husband's family and care for her in-laws until she or they died. When a chaste widow died, the village would commemorate her moral dedication by building a shrine to her. Rather than allowing the woman to move on and find happiness after the death of her husband, she was expected voluntarily to take up a life of servitude for an eventual posthumous shrine.

Just as the emperor simultaneously embodied the legislative, judicial and executive branches of government, there was no separation of powers at the lower levels of government. At all levels, individual officials had multiple powers – with the same officials often acting as administrators, judges and police.

The lack of separation of powers also meant a lack of judicial independence. Because the individual presiding over a trial was often the same person who had apprehended the suspected criminal and also the same person who had initially outlawed the suspect's actions, it was difficult for individuals to receive a fair trial.

Even if a court or administrative official was impartial, magistrates often had little background in the law. Their lack of experience, combined with the relative secrecy of legal norms and policies, encouraged arbitrary court rulings. Moreover, court officials were not required to explain the legal reasoning behind their decisions, further permitting magistrates to come to whatever conclusions they wanted, not necessarily those mandated by the law.

Civil law in imperial China was not nearly as complex as it is today. Though the Tang dynasty did create its own code, it was not meant to resolve private, civil matters. Instead, the legal system was reserved for criminal codes that sought to instill fear and caution into individuals. These Tang dynasty codes could potentially cover virtually any human activity, because administrators could alter a law to make an action criminal. Even if judges did not criminalize a behavior, the code was used to make analogies to existing statutes.

In addition to the lack of civil law, there was a general lack of commercial law. Merchants did not constitute their own class and disputes that arose between them, or between merchants and consumers, were resolved extrajudiciously. One of the first methods of resolving conflict was mediation. Some merchants formed merchant or craft guilds that could act as quasi-judicial bodies. Elders also often served as arbitrators or mediators for commercial conflicts.

Penal codes

Governments in imperial China were known for cruel and unusual punishments, often disproportionate to the crimes committed. Punishment, however, was not something that individual officials determined. A considerable set of rules instructed officials on what actions deserved punishment and what punishment was required. There was also a very detailed list of actions that were considered harmful to the government, which had their own punishments.

Unlike in Western countries, where law regulates human behaviors, in ancient China almost all human behaviors recognized by law were linked to a punishment, reinforcing the concept that the law in imperial China was criminal in nature. Punishment decisions were based on what would inflict an appropriate degree of pain for the crime committed (but the understanding of an 'appropriate' degree would be considered disproportionate to the crime today).[36] In addition, many officials used torture to get information from both suspects and witnesses.

The infamous story of 'Please Step into the Vat'[37] is perhaps the best example of the nature of the criminal punishments in ancient China.

During the reign of Wu Zeitan, a Tang dynasty empress, two officials, Zhou Xing and Lai Junchen, were tasked with extracting confessions from suspects and prosecuting those who were allegedly trying to overthrow Wu. Zhou and Lai's targets ranged from commoners to civil and military officials, and the two judges would create a case against individuals and get the information they needed by torturing them with inhumane corporal punishment.

Empress Wu then received a letter that said Zhou had been plotting with others to overthrow her. She directed Lai to look into the matter and handle Zhou as he would any other suspect – with little compassion. Though Lai was an experienced judge, he was concerned that Zhou would not be affected by his normal tactics and would not easily confess. Knowing that if he failed in finding Zhou guilty he would face the wrath of the empress, he finally came to a solution.

Lai invited Zhou to a grand feast at which both drank heavily. After they were both quite intoxicated, Lai pretended to sigh and remarked to Zhou that sometimes he was not able to get people to confess. He asked Zhou if he had any suggestions, and Zhou told him to get a large vat that was extremely hot and surrounded by fire. When the prisoner stepped into the vat, he would surely make a confession, said Zhou.

Hearing this, Lai ordered a vat to be brought before them, and lit a charcoal fire as Zhou had said. Turning to Zhou, he told him about the letter and the accusation of plotting a rebellion. Lai then invited Zhou to step into the vat, at which point Zhou fell to his knees and admitted his guilt.

Though this happened in the Tang dynasty, there is a modern equivalent. In the late 2000s the police chief of Chongqing, Wen Qiang, was accused of taking more than RMB12 million (US$1.76 million) in bribes. He was prosecuted and executed by his successor, Wang Lijun, but Wen warned Wang that the same thing would happen to him. With laws on the books but no real enforcement, the officials in charge had essentially unconstrained power. As Wen predicted, Wang later found himself in trouble as well (see Chapter 4).

No lawyers or legal profession

By Western definitions, China did not really have a stable legal system or legal profession until 1979. Until that point there had been no uniform rules governing the country, and officials had depended on Confucian morality to rule. Though some believe Confucian ideals offered an alternative to the traditional Western legal system, and the collection of various penal rules served as an early form of codification, there had actually never been a stable system that allowed for the rule of law.[38] Rather, there had been abuse of power, corruption and hidden rules.

As famed sinologist John King Fairbanks put it:

> The concept of law is one of the glories of Western civilization, but in China Legalism, although it profoundly influenced the Chinese attitude toward all law, has been a despised term for more than two thousand years. This is because the legalist concept of law fell far short of the Roman. Whereas Western law has been conceived of as a human embodiment of some higher order of God or nature, the law of the legalists represented only the ruler's fiat. China developed little or no civil law to protect the citizen; law remained

largely administrative and penal, something the people attempted to avoid as much as possible.[39]

Though many ordinary citizens in China attempted to avoid the legal system, they were often unaware of what was illegal. Since the Tang dynasty there has been a legal code, but it was often unpublished and only available for magistrates who tried cases. These officials had no legal training and were merely appointed to make legal decisions based on a code to which the public did not have access. This often meant that court decisions were arbitrary and, because judges were not required to explain the rationale behind their decisions, there was little opportunity to appeal a decision.

The Chinese legal system has only recently allowed for true criminal defense, since legal education and lawyers were relatively unknown in ancient China. The legal system was purely in the hands of the emperor and his officials, who were responsible for all alterations, additions to and promulgations of the law, and this monopoly continued into the twentieth century.

Notes

1. See generally Jonathan Clements (2008) *Confucius: A Biography*. Stroud: Sutton Publishing.
2. Ibid.
3. See generally Confucius ([c. 551–479 BCE] 2003) *Confucius: Analects – With Selections from Traditional Commentaries*, trans. E. Slingerland. Indianapolis, IN: Hackett Publishing.
4. Dagobert Runes (1983) *Dictionary of Philosophy*. New York: Philosophical Library, p. 338.
5. Epiphanius Wilson (1900) *The Wisdom of Confucius*. New York: Colonial Press, p. 153.
6. Ibid., p. 152.
7. See generally ibid.
8. Confucius ([c.551–479 BCE] 1938) *The Analects of Confucius*, trans. and annotated by Arthur Waley. London: George Allen & Unwin; available at: *www.humanistictexts.org/confucius.htm* (accessed: 4 August 2013).
9. Wilson, note 5 above, p. 153.
10. Benjamin I. Schwarz (1985) *The World of Thought in Ancient China*. Cambridge, MA: President and Fellows of Harvard College, p. 326.
11. Ibid., p. 327.
12. Confucius (c. 551–479 BCE) *Spring and Autumn Annals*; English translation available at: *www.chinaknowledge.de/Literature/Classics/chunqiuzuozhuan.html* (accessed: 4 August 2013).

13. Lu Xun (1918) *Madman's Diary*; English translation available at: *www.marxists.org/archive/lu-xun/1918/04/x01.htm* (accessed: 4 August 2013).
14. Jeremy Tambling (2007) *Madmen and Other Survivors: Reading Lu Xun's Fiction*. Hong Kong: Hong Kong University Press.
15. Jeffrey N. Wasserstrom (2010) *China in the 21st Century; What Everyone Needs to Know*. New York: Oxford University Press, p. 9.
16. See generally Jonathan Spence (1990) *The Search for Modern China*. New York: W.W. Norton.
17. Wasserstrom, note 15 above, p. 11.
18. Ibid., p. 12.
19. Confucius, note 8 above.
20. Mencius (c. 300 BCE) *Mencius*; English translation available at: *www.acmuller.net/con-dao/mencius.html* (accessed: 4 August 2013).
21. Ibid.
22. Klaus Mühlhahn (2009) *Criminal Justice in China: A History*. Cambridge, MA: Harvard University Press, p. 19.
23. Burton Watson (1964) *Han Fei Tzu: Basic Writings*. New York: Columbia University Press.
24. Mühlhahn, note 22 above, p. 20.
25. Patrick D. McAnany (2010) 'Justification for punishment (Punishment)', Online Grolier Multimedia Encyclopedia, August; available at: *http://auth.grolier.com/* (accessed: 16 September 2010).
26. Mühlhahn, note 22 above, p. 20.
27. Ibid.
28. Shang Yang (1928) 'The Book of Lord Shang'; English translation available at: *http://ctext.org/shang-jun-shu* (accessed: 4 August 2013).
29. Justin Wintle (2006) *The Timeline History of China*. New York: Sterling Publishing, p. 59.
30. Ibid.
31. Ibid.
32. Ibid.
33. Wu Si (2009) 潜规则: 中国历史中的真实游戏 (*Hidden Rules: The Real Game in Chinese History*). Shanghai: Fudan University Press.
34. Zhu Yuan (2009) 'Tacit rules undermine nation's rule of law', *China Daily*, 1 July, p. 8; available at: *www.chinadaily.com.cn/opinion/2009-07/01/content_8342355.htm* (accessed: 3 March 2013).
35. Lu Xun (1926) 'The 24 paragons of filial piety', *Mang Yuang Biweekly*, 10 May; English translation available at: *www.ruf.rice.edu/~asia/24ParagonsFilialPiety.html* (accessed: 4 August 2013).
36. Mühlhahn, note 22 above, pp. 14–15.
37. Chinese explanation available at: *http://baike.baidu.com/view/54359.htm* (accessed: 4 August 2013).
38. Junfan Zhang (1997) 中国法律的传统与近代转型 (*The Change of Legal Traditions in Modern China*). Beijing: Law Press, p. 234.
39. John King Fairbank (1960) *East Asia: The Great Tradition*. Boston, MA: Houghton Mifflin, p. 84.

China and the Western influence

Abstract: This chapter covers the more than 200-year history of China's interactions with the West. From Chinese feelings of victimhood derived from the '100 years of humiliation' to the enclave system following the Treaty of Nanjing and the balance between Chinese nationalism and Western learning, the chapter tries to ground China's current relationship with the West by exploring various historical interactions. The *ti-yong* dichotomy is also introduced, describing a way of incorporating Western learning while still staying true to China's uniqueness. Additionally, the history of the Republic of China and the People's Republic of China is discussed.

Key words: *ti-yong* dichotomy, concession, Sino-Western relations, Republic of China, People's Republic of China.

Although China is much more open today than it was even 20 years ago, it is still adapting to being a member of the global community. Since the West and Japan first took an interest in China, there have been periods of openness as well as periods of latent (or open) hostility to outsiders. These feelings about foreigners have created a complex and evolving attitude toward the global community today.

'100 years of humiliation'

'100 years of humiliation' refers to the period of foreign intervention and imperialism by Western powers and Japan in China between 1839 and 1949.[1] This narrative has been frequently invoked by the Communist Party of China (CPC) as a reminder of Western imperialism, and serves as a rebuttal to foreign criticism of China's human rights abuses.

The preamble of the Constitution of the People's Republic of China (PRC) serves as the official version of modern Chinese history being taught in schools in China:

> After 1840, feudal China was gradually turned into a semi-colonial and semi-feudal country. The Chinese people waged many successive heroic struggles for national independence and liberation and for democracy and freedom.
>
> Great and earthshaking historical changes have taken place in China in the 20th century.
>
> The Revolution of 1911, led by Dr. Sun Yat-sen, abolished the feudal monarchy and gave birth to the Republic of China. But the historic mission of the Chinese people to overthrow imperialism and feudalism remained unaccomplished.
>
> After waging protracted and arduous struggles, armed and otherwise, along a zigzag course, the Chinese people of all nationalities led by the Communist Party of China with Chairman Mao Zedong as its leader ultimately, in 1949, overthrew the rule of imperialism, feudalism and bureaucrat-capitalism, won a great victory in the New-Democratic Revolution and founded the People's Republic of China. Since then the Chinese people have taken control of state power and become masters of the country.[2]

Though China's history predates its contact with the West and the country prides itself on developing outside Western influence, it is undeniable that the West and its influence played some role in the creation of a modern China. China's interactions with the West, however, have created a strong feeling of victimhood dating back to the First Opium War (1839–1842). During the First and Second Opium Wars, China lost to European armies, and since this time outsiders have been called 'foreign devils'[3] and been targets of Chinese nationalists.

Another cause of China's feelings of victimhood was the Boxer Rebellion (1897–1901).[4] When the Boxers rose up against the foreign missions and governments which had taken hold of certain segments of China, they were beaten back. The Boxers were a Chinese peasant-led group that drew inspiration from martial arts and spirituality, both of which were used to combat the foreign influence in China.

The Boxers worked with imperial Qing forces to try to free China of Westerners, who they believed had tarnished the country. In addition to their frustration with Christian missionaries, the Boxers were upset over the burning of the Old Summer Palace in Beijing, Yuanmingyuan (圆明园), by British and French soldiers during the Second Opium War (1856–1860). Yuanmingyuan had been a grand palace and the royal garden of the Qing emperor, but very little of the magnificent treasures, wealth and art was left after it was looted and burned to the ground.

After its loss in both Opium Wars the Qing emperor could no longer reasonably believe that China was the center of the world. Between 1894 and 1895 China and Japan fought the First Sino-Japanese War over control of northeastern China (Manchuria) and the Korean peninsula. Losing in this war as well, the Chinese learned that they were not even the center of Asia. It was these realizations that spurred an attempt to modernize China by self-strengthening.

Unequal treaties between 1842 and 1949 and extraterritoriality

The Boxer Rebellion also developed in response to a series of unequal treaties between China and Western nations, the first of which was the Treaty of Nanjing. The treaty, signed in 1842, ended the First Opium War between Britain and China. Though the treaty saw a definite end to hostilities, it also required the Chinese to cede Hong Kong to the British indefinitely.[5]

The Treaty of Nanjing was one of many unequal treaties that China signed, some of which gave special privileges to foreigners, who were often treated better than the native Chinese. Foreigners created enclaves, or 'concessions', within key Chinese cities in which they were subject to the laws of their own countries rather than Chinese law. This concept of extraterritoriality went so far as to require that foreign nationals be tried by special courts established within their enclaves or by their nations' consular staff.

One of the biggest concessions was the Shanghai settlement. As part of the Treaty of Nanjing, two concessions were carved out of the city of Shanghai: the International Settlement and the French Concession. These extraterritorial zones exhibited many of the characteristics that other foreign enclaves had developed across China, such as Chinese citizens and nationals from non-treaty partners being subject to Chinese law. Though required to follow Chinese law, Chinese officials were unable to try anyone on their own; rather, a Chinese judge was paired with a foreign assessor. Any of the nationals of a treaty power were subject to their respective country's laws, however, and tried in their own consular courts.

The British established the British Supreme Court for China and Japan (1865) and the Americans created the US Court for China (1906) to administer British and American law, respectively, within the International Settlement.[6] The British Supreme Court was responsible for British nationals throughout China, Japan and Korea, and mirrored many of its other extraterritorial courts around the world. The court remained functioning (although only as the Supreme Court for China) until 1943, when the United Kingdom relinquished its extraterritorial rights within China.

The US Court for China was considered another US district court whose appeals were heard before the Ninth Circuit Court of Appeals in San Francisco. Up until its establishment, American nationals used the US consular courts for legal purposes. The US Court for China, which had one judge, applied federal law in China, but it faced difficulties when it came to state criminal and civil matters. When these cases arose, the court applied Alaskan law (then a territory) and the law of Washington, DC, both of which were considered 'American' law. Though the court applied federal law, as it was not located in the United States, constitutional protections did not apply.

The United States and United Kingdom renounced their extra-territoriality in 1943, but it was not until 1999 that the final Western power left China. The last two European territories in China, Hong Kong and Macau, were transferred to the PRC government in 1997 and 1999, respectively. Hong Kong and Macau were not concessions, however, but rather colonies of Britain and Portugal. After their transfer back to China, both regions became special administrative regions and, under the 'one China, two systems' approach, retain many of the same laws and freedoms they had during their colonial administration.

Hong Kong and Macau were both acquired by European powers through unequal treaties, as well. Though the treaties that China agreed to during the late nineteenth and early twentieth centuries are recognized as being unfair to the Chinese, the phrase 'unequal treaties' did not appear until the twentieth century. Although the Chinese government entered into these agreements, they were rarely negotiated and were often imposed on China after military defeats. In effect, these treaties subrogated China to being a semi-colonial or less-than-sovereign state. In addition to the concessions and colonies, the Chinese were forced to pay reparations and open their ports to foreign traders.

Since 1620 there had been a constant flow of Westerners into China, mostly British, who attempted to change the country.[7] Though this effort to modernize the Middle Kingdom continued until 1960, it ultimately failed. Everyone, no matter what their cause, be it medicine, Christianity or some other source of reformation, made very little headway. They failed in part because China has long blazed its own path and done things the Chinese way. One-man attempts to change the nation were ultimately useless.[8]

Not everyone has seen Western colonialism as something negative, however. In a controversial interview with Hong Kong's *Liberation Monthly* (now called *Open Magazine*), the writer Liu Xiaobo said that bringing China to modernity would take 300 years of colonialism:

> In 100 years of colonialism, Hong Kong has changed to what we see today. With China being so big, of course it would require 300 years as a colony for it to be able to transform into how Hong Kong is today. I have my doubts as to whether 300 years would be enough.[9]

Mao, on the other hand, would not have agreed with Liu. He identified himself as a nationalist and someone who fought against foreign influences, but some have argued that he was in league with the Soviets or could have been a foreign agent subverting state power, which by definition would be treason.[10] Mao's influence and his distrust of the West are still felt, however. His effect on China was deep, and 'the Mao era continues to reside within the inner being of China in a somewhat unconscious way. It manifests itself in nationalistic and chauvinistic responses, sensitivity to slights and slurs, a constant awareness of China's comparative standing and a lingering uncertainty about its own strengths and whether it is still a victim or not.'[11] The problem, of course, is that China no longer is a victim. This perception of victimhood, however, has made it extremely difficult for the country to feel as if it is part of the international community.

Nationalism

Though Chinese sentiments toward the West started to improve in the lead-up to the 2008 Beijing Olympics, this did not last long. Throughout the Olympics, the Chinese government utilized the Confucian saying, 'When a friend comes from afar, is that not delightful?' By using this phrase, the CPC created the illusion that athletes, coaches and fans were all coming to China to see the Chinese, restoring some of the importance they felt they had lost. This illusion collapsed, however, when the Norwegian Nobel Committee selected author Liu Xiaobo for the Nobel Peace Prize in 2010.

This incident made the CPC realize that the international community did not see the Chinese government in a favorable light. This devastating experience forced the CPC to retreat and close itself off again. It cracked down on dissidents and took an iron-fisted approach to those it believed were trying to overthrow the government. Questioning the government or even expressing displeasure with a governmental policy was seen as being a tool of Western imperialism, reigniting China's long-standing feeling of victimhood.

Another example of this 'victim' status was the controversy surrounding air pollution in Beijing in 2012. Chinese officials have long said that the country is not to be judged according to international norms or treaties, in part because China's development is uniquely Chinese. When American and other foreign diplomats started posting hourly updates on Chinese air and light pollution that contradicted official Chinese sources, Chinese officials became incensed.

Curiously, however, Chinese politicians pointed to international treaties and norms in requesting that foreigners respect local Chinese law. For example, one official said, 'China's air quality monitoring and information release involve the public interest and are up to the government. Foreign consulates in China taking it on themselves to monitor air quality and release the information online... goes against the spirit of the Vienna convention.'[12] The Vienna Convention requires that diplomats respect and follow the laws of the country in which they are stationed.

Surprisingly, however, the Chinese government soon reconsidered its position and dropped its accusations that the US embassy was violating international law. The government also started to publish more accurate reports of air pollution in some of the major cities, an uncommon move by the CPC.[13]

Another example of this ultrasensitivity is the way political dissidents are treated. The authorities often call political activists who criticize the party dictatorship or specific policies 'foreign agents'. When writer Yu Jie was arrested and beaten by Beijing police in October 2010, he was informed that one of his crimes was befriending the Nobel laureate Liu Xiaobo. Police accused him of working with Liu as 'tools of imperialism used to subvert China'.[14] Similarly, Beijing police officer Dong Yansheng yelled at human rights lawyer Pu Zhiqiang: 'you are a f**king traitor and running dog for the western countries. You received foreign media interviews, just like Liu Xiaobo, you are a damn f**king traitor to your motherland!'[15]

These accusations are largely unsupported and, to an outsider, appear to be ridiculous. The larger historical narrative of '100 years of humiliation', however, sheds some light on why the government is so suspicious of outside influences and views foreign involvement as one of the most heinous of crimes. For years the Chinese have felt besieged and subjugated by outsiders after having been, conceivably, one of the largest powers in Asia. Now, as the CPC and China find a place within the international community, they also find themselves criticized for a variety of reasons, which reminds them of their years as a semi-colonial state.

The Foreign Affairs Movement and the *ti-yong* dichotomy

Following China's defeat in the First Sino-Japanese War, it became readily apparent to Chinese officials that there was a great need for reform. Though there was general agreement that China could learn a lot from the West on how to strengthen itself, there was very little agreement on how to learn, how much to learn and how fast the learning could be implemented. The concern was that China should not lose its uniqueness and traditional values as it tried to craft widespread reforms and fundamental changes throughout the country.

Initially, the imperial court looked to Japan and its reforms during the 1867 Meiji Restoration. The Qing dynasty's reform, however, did not achieve the same success. From the Japanese Meiji Restoration came a highly centralized bureaucratic government and a constitution that allowed for an elected parliamentary body. In addition to governmental reforms, the Japanese people gained communication and transportation systems that facilitated continuing modernization. The industrial sector started to grow rapidly, and relied on new technology rather than the semi-ancient technology that was prevalent before Japan's leap forward.[16] This industrial success also contributed to the tremendous strength of the Japanese navy and army. Finally, the people rid themselves of the previous feudal system and restrictions that confined individuals to the class into which they were born. Part of this relative social fluidity came from widespread education reforms.

Unfortunately, very little of this was achieved in China. Similar to the Meiji Restoration, the Chinese Foreign Affairs Movement was an attempt to extract Western knowledge to bolster Chinese power. The principle of the movement was articulated by Zhang Zhidong, who in 1898 published *Exhortation to Study*.[17] In it, he insisted on a method of relatively conservative reform, summarized in the phrase 'Chinese learning for fundamental principles, or *ti*, and Western learning for practical application, or *yong*'. This dichotomy of *ti* (体) and *yong* (用) eventually ruled how China was to interact with the West. China wanted to ensure that Chinese learning remained the essence or *ti*, while Western learning was only to be used for practical development or *yong*. After seeing Japan's great successes, China sought to bring in technical experts, engineers and manufacturers to acquire the knowledge to recreate and adapt Western weapons and machines. Many in China believed that the West's power came from its deadly and effective arms and warships. Thus imperial officials hired experts to build the ships, munitions and other weapons they believed would give China the capacity to become a great military power.

With the single phrase 'Chinese learning for fundamental principles and Western learning for practical application' or '*zhongxue wei ti, xixue wei yong*' (中学为体,西学为用), Zhang Zhidong captured the need for both inner (Chinese) and outer (Western) learning. According to Jonathan Spence:

> this was a culturally reassuring position in a time of ambiguous, often painful, change. It affirmed that there was indeed a fundamental structure of Chinese moral and philosophical values that gave continuity and meaning to the civilization. Holding on to that belief, China could then afford to adopt quickly and dramatically all sorts of Western practices, and to hire Western advisers.[18]

The *ti-yong* dichotomy, or the balance between inner/Chinese and outer/Western learnings, allowed the Chinese government to restrict its reforms to what it saw as secondary or supportive functionalities. Adopting or importing Western techniques for technology and the military did not require a reformation of the government, Confucian ideals or the moral foundation that ruled China. Rather, the Western learning could further traditional Chinese social goals, making them almost symbiotic in nature. This complex process of inner versus outer learning also transformed China from a state of being to a state of learning in the late nineteenth century.

Though *ti* and *yong* have long been present in China, their definitions have changed over time. Until 1912 internal learning meant following Confucian ideals, but between 1912 and 1979 there were major changes to what was considered Chinese 'essence'. At first, *ti* somewhat mirrored the Confucian thought that was present in imperial China; after 1949 and the establishment of the PRC, however, *ti* exclusively meant Maoism. Yet since the end of the Cultural Revolution there has been some debate as to exactly what *ti* means: communist ideology or nationalism?

Similarly, the meaning of *yong* has also changed over time. Initially, in the 1860s, it meant acquiring Western military technology, but by the 1880s it had expanded to include commercial and industrial growth. In the late 1890s *yong* meant adapting a constitutional monarchy with a parliamentary system of government. Though it quickly turned its back on them, in 1919 during the May Fourth Movement China introduced 'Mr Democracy' and 'Mr Science' from the West.[19] Throughout the span of Mao's control of the government, China prided itself on disavowing learning from the West and tried to move forward solely by internal Chinese learning. Starting in the 1970s, however, the government came up with the 'four modernizations' it would take from the West: agriculture, industry, national defense, and science and technology. The political activist Wei Jingsheng also declared the need for a 'fifth modernization' – democracy – though this was not accepted by the CPC.[20]

The failed '100 days reform' in 1898 and late Qing reforms

Before the establishment of the Republic of China, Emperor Guangxu of the late Qing dynasty attempted to reform China. The Empress Dowager Cixi let the reform movement run for only 100 days before she stopped it and executed six of its leaders; another two senior leaders went into exile.[21] One of the proposed reforms was to make the traditional civil service exam system more modern and eliminate those positions that required little or no work but still provided a salary (known as sinecures). There was also a push to abandon the education system, which was based mainly on studying Confucian texts, and to incorporate subjects like mathematics and science into the curriculum. The reformers believed they could utilize commerce, manufacturing and capitalism to industrialize the nation quickly.

In addition to these social and economic changes, the reformers sought to change the basic structure of the Chinese government and economy. One of the first things they tried was to build up the military, both in size and in strength. They also wanted to change the government to a constitutional monarchy from an absolute monarchy: there would still be an emperor, but the government would be largely a democracy. By supporting a capitalist approach, the reformers believed that the economy could be greatly strengthened. Though the emperor had given the reform movement the task of transforming China, the more powerful empress dowager gave the movement very little time to accomplish any of its goals before ending it and executing its leaders.

From 1902 to 1912, the last decade of the late Qing dynasty (1644–1912), there was an unprecedented effort to modernize Chinese law to accommodate social changes, under pressure from foreign powers. Drawing upon Japanese legal vocabulary and usage, Chinese jurists and officials translated and incorporated considerable amounts of the German civil code into the Grand Qing Codex.[22] The government established a legal reform commission, appointed two ministers of 'legal revision' (one of whom was Wu Tingfang, the ambassador to the United States) and hired foreign legal experts as consultants.[23] Unfortunately, the Qing dynasty collapsed before any transformative legal reforms were ready for implementation.

Republic of China

On 1 October 1911 the forces of the Chinese Revolutionary Alliance or Tongmenghui (同盟会) initiated what would become the Xinhai Revolution and the end of the Qing dynasty. The revolution started with the Wuchang uprising in October and ended with the last emperor, Puyi, abdicating on 12 February 1912, although fighting among warlords continued for the next 16 years. One of the leaders of the revolution, Dr Sun Yat-sen, believed that the newly formed Republic of China would develop in three phases: unification by military rule, political tutelage and constitutional democracy.[24]

A decade after the establishment of the Republic of China, Chiang Kai-shek and the Kuomintang (KMT) began to fight against the widespread feudal system in China and sought to tackle the nation's warlords in an attempt to unite the country. In 1927 Chiang finally beat back the warlords and established a capital in Nanjing.

The Republic of China enjoyed a short-lived period of enlightened legal process, which featured a judicial system independent from other branches of government. The era was also characterized by openness throughout Chinese society to foreign influences and Western perspectives on legal thought. In 1915 the American lawyer and missionary Charles W. Rankin established the Comparative Law School of China in Shanghai.[25] Patterned after the American model of legal education, the school devoted considerable effort to teaching Anglo-American law.[26]

During the same period, China once again used the German civil code as a prototype for legislative reform. Six sets of codes (the constitution, the civil code, the code of civil procedure, the criminal code, the code of criminal procedure, and the administrative and administrative procedure laws) were promulgated as the foundation of a brand-new legal system. By the early 1930s the government had also formalized the procedures through which to publish and preserve court judgments. Many of the cases issued during this period began to have precedential value, especially those involving succession of land, bigamy and concubinage.[27]

In 1912 the Provisional Constitution of the Republic of China was first promulgated, and it remained in effect until 1928. The KMT crafted a Western-style government with a Western-influenced legal system, and the constitution created both a president and a parliament. The powers of the president were relatively weak in comparison to the legislature, however. Unlike under imperial rule, the court system was independent of other branches of the government.

The basis of this government would be a strong parliamentary system, as found in the West. Unlike Western democracies, however, Sun wanted to expand the traditional three-branch government to include the examination and control branches or *yuan* (院).

Though the party adopted a series of legal and penal codes, they were rarely enforced beyond Nanjing. Because the KMT used Western models, it did away with social or collective punishments, preferring individual sanctions. This clashed with the traditional Chinese method of law and punishment, and the codes derived from the German legal system did not make much of an impact at the local level. The KMT had thought this type of 'equal before the law' approach would stabilize the country, but it was ultimately abandoned with the threats posed by the CPC and the Japanese.[28]

It was the Second Sino-Japanese War and Second World War that eventually ended the Republic of China. Starting in July 1937, the republic fought the Japanese incursion into Chinese territory. Though the Chinese, with the help of the Allies, eventually beat back the

Japanese, communist forces under the command of Mao Zedong drove Chiang and the KMT to Taiwan. The CPC established the People's Republic of China on the mainland while the expelled Nationalist government continued in Taiwan as the Republic of China. This interruption of the Republic of China also saw the end of its progress in legal reform. The PRC no longer recognized the legitimacy of the Republic of China after 1949: it abolished the Nationalist legal system, including the judiciary, rescinded the entire existing body of law and began to construct its own 'socialist' legal system by drawing heavily on the Soviet experience.

'The People's Republic'

The PRC's history can be divided into two periods: the Mao era (1949–1978) and the Deng Xiaoping and post-Deng years (1979 to the present). In terms of the legal system, these two periods share common features but are distinguished by different doctrinal ideologies. Under Mao's leadership, the government took a hostile view toward formalized legal systems. Mao and his party 'saw the law as creating constraints upon their power'.[29] In addition:

> The legal system itself was deliberately targeted for attack as being counterrevolutionary, and indeed, the very idea of 'law' was rejected. Legal institutions such as courts and procuratorates were shut down or paralyzed, law schools were closed, and members of the legal community were forced to shift professions or were sent down to farms to learn from peasants.[30]

Jerome Cohen has also noted that following the defeat of the KMT and the establishment of the PRC, there was a distinct lack of a legal system:

> It took the PRC thirty years to begin to seriously fill the legislative vacuum, and that enormous task has not yet been completed. Until 1979 it had been difficult to speak more than tentatively of a PRC legal system. To be sure, there was in the mid-1950s, after endless campaigns against landlords, rich peasants, urban businessmen and counterrevolutionaries, an effort to import the Soviet legal model that had developed from Leninist origins. But the 'anti-rightist' movement

of 1957–9, which was a reaction to the condemnations against the Communist Party voiced during the immediately preceding 'Let a Hundred Flowers Bloom' period, wrote finis to that second Chinese experiment with a Western import. For over two decades, until the Cultural Revolution ended and Deng Xiaoping and his comrades announced the new policy of 'opening and reform', the PRC lacked most of the identifiable features of a formal legal system.[31]

After 1979 Deng Xiaoping and his party instituted an 'open door' policy which took a utilitarian approach to the reconstruction of social order and the legal system. The law came to be viewed as a useful instrument to support the country's economic growth. Over the past three decades China has made significant progress in developing a legal system that in many ways is consistent with international norms. Prolific legislative activities and increased emphasis on the implementation and enforcement of law are positive steps toward a stable legal environment.[32]

China is clearly in a period of transition: 'Building a legal system is a process that cannot be completed in the span of three decades or even in a generation… [therefore] such a fledging system cannot realistically be compared with that of the United States', argues Daniel C.K. Chow.[33] China's legal 'system' differs from that of the United States not only in maturity and sophistication, but also in fundamental values. The 'system' being developed in China does not follow the principle of 'rule of law' – following a clear and consistent set of laws – but rather 'rule by law' – using the law as an instrument to control the masses. Throughout the modernization of China's system, Western influences should not be underestimated, as the development of a contemporary Chinese legal system, 'like [that of] many other developing nations around the world, has been a process of westernization'.[34] The same is true for the development of the legal profession, legal education and legal information systems in China.

There has also been a paradigm shift during the past 30 years: 'Concepts such as the rule of law and individual rights are derived from western political traditions and have no equivalents in Chinese history.'[35] But the Chinese have long accepted Zhang's plausible argument of 'Chinese learning for fundamental principles and Western learning for practical application', which appears to serve as the rationale behind the control over information and knowledge. Ironically, the standard to evaluate China's success in developing a modern legal system is whether it can function effectively in the international community by speaking the kind of legal language that is universally accepted.

Anti-Rightist Movement, Great Leap Forward and Great Famine

Starting in 1957, Mao and the CPC were concerned about growing dissent among intellectuals, leading to the Anti-Rightist Movement. Those who criticized the party, its officials or its policies were termed 'rightists' (because the CPC saw and continues to see itself as a leftist revolutionary party, meaning that anyone who is against the party is a rightist or counterrevolutionary), publicly humiliated and punished. In essence, the Anti-Rightist Movement was an effort to purge intellectuals who were independent thinkers. The practice of labeling someone a rightist was a form of political revenge, and continues to the present day. The ideological campaign has been an important party tool to remove those who vocalize their dissent.

Following the Anti-Rightist Movement, Mao attempted to modernize China through the Great Leap Forward. He laid out an unrealistic policy that he believed would make China a serious world power and bring the country into the modern age. Unfortunately, misguided policies encouraged false reporting of the abilities of the nation's farmers, leading to the Great Famine (1959–1961). Known as the 'three-year natural disaster', no one was ever held responsible for the 30 million deaths from starvation during this man-made famine.[36]

Cultural Revolution

Another stumbling block for the Chinese legal system was the ten-year period between 1966 and 1976, known as the Cultural Revolution. Throughout the Cultural Revolution there was nearly constant turmoil and approximately 400,000 people died.[37] In addition, there were nearly 1 million victims and over 100 million participants in the chaotic Red Terror.[38]

The Cultural Revolution was not so much an enforcement of communist and revolutionary ideals as it was a state-sponsored cycle of violence, riots and persecution. The Red Guard, many of whom were teenagers and young adults, fervently sought to root out enemies of the state and protect Chairman Mao. This eventually led to the abolishment of the legal and educational systems and the collapse of the economy. Beyond the human victims of the Cultural Revolution, the Red Guard also destroyed many historical sites, antiquities and anything else that represented or celebrated traditional Chinese culture.[39]

Throughout the Cultural Revolution there was detailed record-keeping on individuals who were deemed to be threats to the state. Despite the records, many intellectuals who died at this time were merely labeled as having been tortured to death. Curiously, many of the records do not mention a crime, nor list who did the torturing. After the Cultural Revolution ended, some members of the Red Guard climbed the ranks of the CPC and are currently in power.[40]

Throughout the Mao era of the PRC, the legal system was used as a tool to control the population, remove 'counterrevolutionaries' and promote socialism. The legal system and the law were utilized by the CPC to give it legitimacy and achieve party goals. The criminal justice system relied very little on justice and focused more on creating class struggle.

In the earliest days of the PRC the legal system closely resembled the Soviet form of legal bureaucracy, but in 1954 a new constitution was adopted. The new constitution reified the Soviet-style bureaucracy while simultaneously bequeathing considerable power to the Standing Committee of the National People's Congress.

Though the CPC had complete control over the law and the legal system, the party still was concerned that the law was curbing its power and rivaling it for control of the country. Thus, in 1957, the legal system was slowly dismantled until, during the Cultural Revolution, it was ultimately abolished.

One of the last major legal milestones in the Mao era of the PRC was the creation of the 1975 constitution. In an effort to ease concerns over loss of power, the Maoists lifted many of the constitutional restraints that the 1954 constitution had created, thus 'legalizing' many illegal acts by the Red Guards and Maoists during the Cultural Revolution. The new constitution shored up the power of the CPC and did away with many of the protections that had been in the previous constitution, such as eliminating the procuratorate and vesting the police with many of its former judicial powers. Many trials were conducted by revolutionary committees or mobs. The constitution removed the provision on equality before the law, making it easier to utilize the law as a weapon against political enemies. Moreover, it allowed for arbitrary arrest and detainment, and eliminated an individual's ability to pick up and move.

The Cultural Revolution claimed the lives of several million people and inflicted cruel and inhuman treatments on hundreds of millions of others. The number of victims, especially the death toll of the mass killings perpetrated by the Red Guards, police, military and mobs, is still regarded as a 'state secret' by the authorities. They do maintain statistics for so-called 'abnormal deaths' across China, however. Professor Song

Yongyi has reviewed different studies of the 'abnormal death' phenomenon: the death toll during the Cultural Revolution estimated in these studies averages approximately 2.95 million.[41]

The widespread mass killings during the Cultural Revolution consisted of five types:

- mass terror encouraged by the government – victims were humiliated and then killed by mobs or forced to commit suicide in streets or other public places
- direct killing of unarmed civilians by armed forces
- pogroms against traditional 'class enemies' by government-led perpetrators, such as local security officers, militias and masses
- killings as part of political witch-hunts (a large number of suspects of alleged conspiratorial groups were tortured to death during investigations)
- summary execution of captives – disarmed prisoners from factional armed conflicts.[42]

Very few of these mass killings have been investigated, and very few of those responsible have ever been prosecuted.

In July 2012 a man in his 80s from Zhejiang province was arrested for a killing in 1967. He was tried at a district court, convicted and sentenced to three-and-a-half years in jail. This unprecedented trial sparked debates over seemingly selective justice, because the party leadership which stirred up the social and political upheaval and ordered the mass killings has never been held accountable.[43]

The trial of the Gang of Four

When Mao died and the Cultural Revolution ended, the CPC needed to find scapegoats for the tremendous death and destruction that happened during the ten-year event. Because Mao was still revered as a national hero, the Gang of Four were put on trial in 1981 for taking control of the state and party leadership. In addition, they were tried for the political persecution of 750,000 people during the Cultural Revolution and the deaths of 34,375.

The Gang of Four consisted of Jiang Qing, the former wife of Mao Zedong, Yao Wenyuan, Zhang Chunqiao and Wang Hongwen, all of whom were top party members during the Cultural Revolution. Of the four, Jiang defended herself, saying she was merely following Mao's orders at all times. She also stood accused of targeting artists and hiring 40 people to dress as Red Guards and persecute specific writers and performers in Shanghai, where she had previously worked as an actress.

Though the crimes of the Cultural Revolution were perpetrated by numerous individuals, only a small number of people, among them the Gang of Four and a former general, Lin Biao, were found to be the counterrevolutionary forces that were responsible for the atrocities. Lin was killed in 1971 in a plane crash over Mongolia, shortly after what appeared to be a coup against Mao.

In the end, Jiang and Zhang were both sentenced to death, but their sentences were later commuted to life imprisonment. Wang was sentenced to life in prison and Yao to 20 years.

The case of Yu Luoke

At no point in history has China been an open society in which disagreement with the government was allowed. Any and all dissent was seen by the government as outright disloyalty, in part because of the long history of Confucian values in China. Confucius was a proponent of a rigidly enforced hierarchy, in which those in charge were to be followed without question. Failing to conform to the hierarchy would cause social unrest (see Chapter 1).

Though China has long distrusted dissent, especially during the Cultural Revolution, a culture of deceit developed. The system of deceit and deception presented a protection for people who disagreed with the ways in which the government operated behind a veneer of compliance.

A number of people have had the courage to stand alone. One man, Yu Luoke, was imprisoned between 1968 and 1970 before ultimately being executed on 5 March 1970.

Yu had been a constant critic of the Cultural Revolution and what he called 'political manipulation' in China. Though he was not able to go to university because of his parents' status as capitalists, he garnered notoriety as a writer and essayist. Yu quickly became famous, especially after his essays on equality were published. He also wrote that the Chinese people had a right to revolution. Though these essays were in the public domain and denounced by Chinese officials, it was one particular article entitled 'On family background' that truly sparked outrage.

'On family background' criticized the theory that people's political beliefs were the product of their blood relationships – that is, the children of revolutionaries were also revolutionaries and the children of 'the six black classes' (landlords, rich peasants, counterrevolutionaries, bad elements, rightists and capitalists) could never be more than reactionaries.

Yu was arrested and charged with 'counterrevolutionary' crime. After two years in prison, he was publicly executed in Beijing in 1970, aged 27.

The case of Zhang Zhixin

Another intellectual, Zhang Zhixin, was also sent to prison and then executed as a counterrevolutionary. Her conviction was based on uttering a criticism of Jiang Qing, or Madame Mao, the woman who would ultimately be tried as one of the Gang of Four for crimes committed in the Cultural Revolution:

> I have doubts about Jiang Qing (Madame Mao). What's wrong with making critical remarks about her? Why shouldn't Jiang Qing's problems be revealed? We should even expose the Central Cultural Revolution Group... Why should we go along with the notion that even if you do not understand, you must obey? If this is allowed to continue, the situation will get out of control. This is all an effort to fortify Chairman Mao's reputation and that of Lin Biao. I personally have no trust in Lin Biao.[44]

Zhang was arrested and imprisoned for six years before being executed on 4 April 1975.

Tiananmen

In the spring and summer of 1989 a new movement for democracy started to brew in Beijing, ultimately leading to the Tiananmen incident of 4 June. The leaders of this movement were primarily students and young people who protested corruption and the secretive way in which law and politics were handled in China.

Throughout the spring, discontent with the CPC spread until martial law was declared in Beijing on 19 May. The intellectuals who were gathering in Tiananmen Square in the middle of the city issued a 'Six-point statement on the current situation':

> Therefore, we appeal for the disagreements encountered in the top leadership's secretive decision-making process to be openly judged and decided upon by the people of the entire country; that a special session of the National People's Congress be convened to intervene under the supreme power granted by the constitution; that an ad hoc delegation of the Chinese Communist Party meet to examine the recent work of the Politburo...[45]

On 24 May, 57 of the 120 members of the Standing Committee of the National People's Congress chose to convene a special session regarding the implementation of martial law, but the committee did not meet because of the impending crackdown. A regular session of the Standing Committee was to be held on 20 June, yet it was also cancelled. The Standing Committee never had a chance to review the constitutionality of the martial law.

There have been a variety of interpretations of the 1989 Tiananmen incident. While some see the crackdown as a human rights violation of international proportions, the CPC has been insistent that it is a matter of state sovereignty and an internal affair, arguing that foreign governments have no right to interfere, or even to criticize. Others argued that the crackdown was necessary for the country: without it, China would not have enjoyed its stable political environment and remarkable economic growth for the past two decades. Some are hesitant to talk about what happened in 1989, saying that bringing it up prevents people from moving on.

Zhao Ziyang was the CPC general secretary at the time of the incident. Throughout the standoff and the student demonstrations he insisted that the incident be resolved peacefully, knowing that it would also be the end of his career. Ultimately, however, his wishes were disregarded and the army moved in to quash the student movement. Zhao was stripped of his position and placed under house arrest for 16 years until his death in 2005.

In 2009 his secret memoir was published in both Chinese and English. In it he noted, after long and difficult deliberation, that Chinese and other socialist attempts to incorporate democracy into the government had been ineffective. Zhao admits the Chinese system is not one in which the people are in charge, but rather they are ruled by a few individuals or even a single person. In a surprising revelation, Zhao also said that he believed the Western parliamentary democratic system has demonstrated the most vitality, and is the best possible type of government available.[46]

Notes

1. Alison Adcock Kaufman (2010) 'The "century of humiliation," then and now: Chinese perceptions of the international order', *Pacific Focus*, 25(1): 1–33.
2. National People's Congress (1984) 'Constitution of the People's Republic of China', Preamble. Beijing: NPC.
3. See generally Robert Bickers (2012) *The Scramble for China: Foreign Devils in the Qing Empire, 1832–1914*. New York: Penguin Global.
4. Jonathan Spence (1990) *The Search for Modern China*. New York: W.W. Norton, p. 140.
5. Susanna Hoe and Derek Roebuck (2010) *The Taking of Hong Kong: Charles and Clara Elliot in China Waters*. Hong Kong: Hong Kong University Press.
6. Wellington Koo (1912) *The Status of Aliens in China*. New York: Columbia University.
7. See generally Jonathan Spence (1980) *To Change China: Foreign Advisers in China*. London: Penguin Books.
8. Ibid.
9. Liu Xiaobo (1988) 'Liu Xiaobo, the "dark horse" of literature', *Open Magazine*, 27 November.
10. See generally Jung Chang and Jon Holiday (2005) *Mao, the Unknown Story*. London: Jonathan Cape.
11. Five Books Interview (2012) 'Orville Schell on China and the US', 5 January; available at: *http://fivebooks.com/interviews/orville-schell-on-china-and-us* (accessed: 5 August 2013).
12. Tania Branigan and Reuters (2012) 'China warns foreign embassies publishing smog readings is illegal', *The Guardian*, 5 June; available at: *www.guardian.co.uk/world/2012/jun/05/china-embassies-smog-readings-illegal* (accessed: 5 August 2013).
13. Jaime A. FlorCruz (2012) 'Beijing's New Year surprise: PM 2.5 readings', CNN, 27 January; available at: *www.cnn.com/2012/01/27/world/asia/florcruz-china-pollution* (accessed: 5 August 2013).
14. Yu Jie (2012) 'Exposing CPC tyranny and running to the free world: my statement on leaving China', trans. Human Rights in China; available at: *www.hrichina.org/content/5778* (accessed: 5 August 2013).
15. Pu Zhiqiang (2010) 'Pu Zhiqiang takes on his police interrogator, and tweets it', 29 October, trans. *China Digital Times*; available at: *http://chinadigitaltimes.net/2010/10/pu-zhiqiang-takes-on-his-police-interrogator-and-tweets-it/* (accessed: 5 August 2013). Censored language in the original.

16. See generally William Beasley (1972) *The Meiji Restoration*. Stanford, CA: Stanford University Press.
17. Zhang Zhidong (1898) *Exhortation to Study*, private publication, 5 May. An English translation by Samuel I. Woodbridge was published by Fleming H. Revell Company in 1900, with the title *China's Only Hope: An Appeal*; available at: *http://archive.org/details/chinasonlyhopeap00zhan* (accessed: 5 August 2013).
18. Spence, note 4 above, p. 225.
19. Ibid.
20. Wei Jingsheng (1999) 'The fifth modernization', English translation in Orville Schell and David Shambaugh (eds) *The China Reader: The Reform Era*. New York: Random House, p. 165.
21. Spence, note 4 above, pp. 224–30.
22. See Demei Zhang (2003) 探索与抉择——晚清法律移植研究 (*Exploration and Choice: The Transplantation of Laws in Late Qing Dynasty*). Beijing: Qinghua University Press.
23. Ibid., pp. 25, 100.
24. Spence, note 4 above, pp. 275–300.
25. Alison Conner (2003) 'The Comparative Law School of China', in C. Stephen Hsu (ed.) *Understanding China's Legal System, Essays in Honor of Jerome Cohen*. New York: New York University Press, p. 211.
26. Ibid., p. 210.
27. Priscilla M.F. Laung (2005) *Selected Edition of China Law Reports: 1991–2004*. Beijing: People's Court Press/Renmin University Press, p. 21.
28. Spence, note 4 above, pp. 361–403.
29. Daniel C.K. Chow (2009) *The Legal System of the People's Republic of China in a Nutshell*, 2nd edn. St Paul, MN: Thomson West, p. 56.
30. Ibid., p. 59.
31. Jerome Cohen (undated) 'The PRC legal system at sixty'; available at: *www.usasialaw.org/?p=58* (accessed: 2 February 2013).
32. James M. Zimmerman (2005) *China Law Deskbook: A Legal Guide for Foreign-Invested Enterprises*, 2nd edn. Chicago, IL: American Bar Association, p. 70.
33. Chow, note 29 above, pp. 61–2.
34. Ibid., p. 64.
35. Ibid., p. 64, fn. 42.
36. Frank Dikötter (2011) *Mao's Great Famine: The History of China's Most Devastating Catastrophe, 1958–1962*. New York: Walker & Company.
37. Roderick MacFarquhar and Michael Schoenhals (2008) *Mao's Last Revolution*. Boston, MA: Belknap Press.
38. 'Red Terror' here refers to mass campaigns of the Red Guards (a mass paramilitary social movement of young people who were mobilized by Mao Zedong in 1966) in China from August 1966 to September 1967, marking the start of the Cultural Revolution (1966–1976). See ibid., p. 102: 'Although the human toll of some subsequent phases of the movement was greater, it was the in-your-face nature of the "red terror" of August–September 196[7] that stuck in popular memory.'
39. MacFarquhar and Schoenhals, ibid.

40. Qian Liqun (2012) 'Concerns of Red Guards in politics', *DW News*, 19 February; available at: *http://opinion.dwnews.com/news/2012-02-19/5860 4631-all.html* (accessed: 5 August 2013).

41. Song Yongyi (2011) 'Chronological index: chronology of mass killings during the Chinese Cultural Revolution (1966–1976)', Online Encyclopedia of Mass Violence, 25 August; available at: *www.massviolence.org/ Chronology-of-Mass-Killings-during-the-Chinese-Cultural?cs=print* (accessed: 5 August 2013).

42. Ibid.

43. AFP (2013) 'Jail for rare China Cultural Revolution murder case', Agence France Presse, 3 April; available at: *www.france24.com/en/20130403-jail- rare-china-cultural-revolution-murder-case* (accessed: 30 April 2013).

44. Zheng Yi (1997) *Scarlet Memorial: Tales of Cannibalism in Modern China.* Boulder, CO: Westview Press.

45. Liang Zhang (1989) 'The Tiananmen papers', *World Affairs*, 152(3): 146.

46. Zhao Ziyang (2009) *Prisoner of the State: The Secret Journal of Chinese Premier Zhao Ziyang*, trans. Bao Pu. New York: Simon & Schuster.

Part II
The players

The judiciary

Abstract: The creation and evolution of the non-independent judiciary are discussed. The place of the judiciary within the grand scheme of the Communist Party of China is covered, as well as the relation between the head of the courts and the procuratorates and other important branches of government. The chapter also examines the structure of the courts, their roles and responsibilities, and the challenges facing them.

Key words: Supreme People's Court, Supreme People's Procuratorate, Communist Party of China, judiciary.

The party and the judiciary

He Weifang, one of the most influential 'public intellectuals', a title normally reserved for progressive, liberal, pro-democracy professors, lawyers, writers and artists, once told Australian journalist Richard McGregor: 'As an organization, the Party sits outside, and above the law. It should have a legal identity, in other words, a person to sue, but it is not even registered as an organization. The Party exists outside the legal system altogether.'[1] What He meant was that the Communist Party of China, unlike for example the US government, cannot be held accountable for its actions within the court system. The CPC remains wholly separate from the courts and their decisions.

As noted in the Introduction of this book, in March 2011, in his annual report on the work of the Standing Committee of China's National People's Congress (NPC), its leader Wu Bangguo announced that China had established 'a socialist legal system with Chinese characteristics'.[2] Jerome Cohen, an expert on Chinese law, noted that Wu's assessment was problematic, arguing that this phrase does not adequately describe the current situation. Instead, 'a Chinese Communist political-legal system' would be more accurate.[3] For Cohen, the inextricable connection between the CPC and the courts, even though the party could not be sued within the courts, precluded China from having a true legal system. This raises the questions of whether the CPC controls the law and, if so, is this a problem?

The answers depends on how you define 'rule of law'. Randall Peerenboom, a legal scholar of China, believes that 'one of the virtues of a thin conception of rule of law is that it is compatible with various forms of government, including in theory single party socialism'.[4] Therefore, 'a leadership role for the Party is potentially consistent with a Statist Socialist and Neoauthoritarian rule of law'.[5]

There are, however, several understandings of what 'rule of law' means, including a formalist or 'thin' and a substantive or 'thick' definition. Formalist definitions do not make a judgment about the 'justness' of law itself, but define specific procedural attributes that a legal framework must have to comply with the rule of law.[6] Substantive conceptions go beyond this to include certain rights that are said to be based on, or derived from, the rule of law.[7]

Peerenboom's argument is questionable because 'thin' definitions of the rule of law only mean that the law is not absolutely supreme, but there is no presumption of the 'justness' of the law itself or of procedural justice. In China's situation, where the CPC controls the entire legal system and operates above the law, this is fundamentally at odds with a substantive concept of the 'rule of law', which requires equality before the law and due process.

Black's Law Dictionary defines the 'rule of law' as 'the doctrine that every person is subject to the ordinary law within the jurisdiction',[8] for example, all persons within the United States are subject to the same law. No one has particular rights and protections that others do not have, and the system of laws that apply to an individual does not differ based on status or membership to a particular group.

None of these three definitions accurately fits in the PRC's situation – there is a separate CPC disciplinary system to deal with party members who violate party rules, laws and regulations. These members do not face the 'legal system' or 'criminal justice system'; instead they face the *shuanggui* (双规) system run by the CPC's internal affairs officers. The *shuanggui* system is covered more fully in Chapter 7.

Moreover, in China the Supreme People's Court (SPC), the highest court in the land, is not independent. The SPC president is a member of the CPC Central Politics and Law Committee, and reports to the chair of the committee.[9] And, in the international law context, 'the "Rule of

Law" is generally understood to refer to a principle of governance in which all persons, institutions, and entities, including the State itself, are accountable to laws consistent with international human rights norms and standards'.[10] As mentioned above, the CPC itself is not accountable to the law or international human rights norms and standards, meaning China does not conform to a Western-style rule of law system.

The mindset behind the party-controlled legal system hearkens back to the *ti-yong* philosophy discussed in Chapter 2. In this situation the CPC is the *ti* or essence, while the law, and specifically rule of law, is the *yong* or function. The party believes the law is merely a tool to enhance or improve its governance, therefore it is absolutely unacceptable for individuals to use the law against the party or hold the party accountable for its actions. Under this party-controlled structure, logically the entire judiciary should be a functional organ of the party.

The CPC Central Politics and Law Committee or *Zhongguo gongchandang zhongyang zhengfa weiyuanhui* (中国共产党中央政法委员会) is the organization responsible for all legal enforcement authorities, including the courts, prosecutors and police force. As with many political organs in the country, there are provincial, municipal, county and autonomous region equivalents to the national committee. A Politburo Standing Committee member leads the body.

During the Cultural Revolution the committee's predecessor was purged by the government and the smaller equivalent was led by the then head of secret police. It was after the Tiananmen Square incident in 1989 that the CPC became convinced of the need to control the legal system fully again, so the committee was re-established.[11]

As of today, the composition of the Central Politics and Law Committee is as shown below:[12]

- Chair: Meng Jianzhu, a member of the CPC Politburo
- Vice-chair: Guo Shengkun, police chief of China (minister of public security)
- Member 1: Zhou Qiang, president of the SPC (chief justice)
- Member 2: president of the Supreme People's Procuratorate (chief procurator)
- Member 3: Zhou Benshun, general secretary of the committee
- Member 4: Geng Huichang, minister of national security
- Member 5: Wu Aiying, minister of justice
- Member 6: Li Dongsheng, vice-minister of public security

- Member 7: Du Jincai, a general from the military, vice-chair of the General Political Department of the CPC Military Committee
- Member 8: Wang Jianping, general of armed police
- Member 9: Chen Xunqiu, vice-chair of Committee for Comprehensive Management of Social Security; associate general secretary of the committee.

This committee reports to the Standing Committee of the Politburo of the CPC Central Committee, the highest authority of the CPC:[13] the members of the Central Politics and Law Committee report to its chair, who reports to the Standing Committee of the Politburo.[14] Thus the chief justice and the chief prosecutor of China both report to the chair of the Central Politics and Law Committee, a committee inside the CPC and supervised by the Standing Committee. And they have equal status to the minister of national security, minister of justice and minister of public security. The judiciary is not independent at all – it is just like any other department within the government. In addition, the chair of the Central Politics and Law Committee is a former minister of public security (police chief); he now supervises the chief justice and chief prosecutor of China.

From this structure we see clear and solid reporting lines: both the courts and the prosecutors directly report to a member of the Politburo, and are ranked lower than the police chief. In fact, they have dotted reporting lines to the police chief because he is also the vice-chair of the committee.

Non-independent judiciary

Unlike most countries in the West, the idea of an independent judiciary is not appealing to the CPC. With no separation of powers there is no independent judicial branch. The NPC, the Chinese national legislature, selects the chief justice of the Supreme People's Court, other justices and senior SPC judges.

While it may seem that the NPC and its Standing Committee are in control of the SPC, the SPC actually reports to the Central Politics and Law Committee of the CPC Standing Committee. In China, law is understood to be a function of and a support to the rule of the party, meaning that a judiciary which challenges the government or the party is contradictory to the goal of the judiciary:

According to orthodox theory as officially proclaimed in mainland China, law is ultimately an instrument of the people's democratic dictatorship and thus of communist party leadership in the construction of socialism; law is party policy elevated into the will of the state through the legislative process. Judges' fidelity to the law should, if this concept of law is correct, never override their loyalty to the principle of party leadership.[15]

What this means is that there can be no judicial review, nor can judges correct the party's misinterpretation of the law. Rather, the judiciary is meant to support party decisions, regardless of what they may be.

When the communist government first crafted a constitution in 1954, it modeled it after the Soviet Union and Article 78 attempted to create a court that would 'administer justice independently and [be] subject only to the law'.[16] For the next three years the courts were relatively autonomous when it came to ordinary decision-making, but the party provided guidance for overarching judicial policies.[17] After the Anti-Rightist Movement of 1957, however, the CPC took back control of the judiciary and its decisions. A party committee or secretary would determine how a case was to be examined, approved and adjudicated.[18]

Then, during the Cultural Revolution, the concept of merging police, procuratorate and court or *Gong Jian Fa* (公检法) emerged.[19] The police-procuratorate-court were three tools to enforce the CPC's rule and eliminate the people it believed to be anti-revolutionary.[20] In effect, it replaced the courts and prioritized public security (police) and the procuratorate over the courts.

It was not until 1978 that the third plenary session of the Eleventh CPC Central Committee sought to strengthen the judicial system. In 1978 the PRC entered a period of reform and opening or *gaige kaifang* (改革开放), during which the CPC wanted to 'make China a modern, powerful socialist country before the end of this century'.[21] As part of this reformation the NPC promulgated its first criminal law and law of criminal procedure in 1979, and also created the Organic Law of the People's Courts. These legal reforms were meant to set up standardized systems of arrests, investigations and adjudication of criminal trials.

When reading the Organic Law of the People's Courts, it may seem like the judiciary gained its independence: 'The people's courts shall exercise judicial power *independently*, in accordance with the provisions of law, and shall not be subject to interference by any administrative organ, public organization or individual.'[22] The CPC is not, however, classified as an administrative organ or a public organization, meaning it still can and does exert influence over the courts. In addition, Article 3 says that the courts must:

> safeguard the system of dictatorship of the proletariat, maintain the socialist legal system and public order, protect socialist property owned by the entire people, collective property owned by working people and the legitimate private property of citizens, the citizens' right of the person and their democratic and other rights, and ensure the smooth progress of the socialist revolution and socialist construction in the country. The people's courts, in all their activities, educate citizens in loyalty to their socialist motherland and voluntary observance of the Constitution and laws.

Though Article 4 gives the veneer of independence, Article 3 very clearly defines the purpose and role of the court – support the party and its rule.

This idea that the courts were meant to support the CPC was reiterated by Luo Gan in 2007. Luo, then chair of the Central Politics and Law Committee, announced that while the Chinese courts needed to be on par with other countries' judicial systems, they still needed to support the party: 'There is no question about where legal departments should stand,' he said. 'The correct political stand is where Party stands.'[23] For Luo, using the law to hold the party accountable is unacceptable. Legal departments, i.e. police, procuratorate, court or *Gong Jian Fa*, are of the party, by the party and for the party.

Again, in 2011, the NPC's chairman, Wu Bangguo, said that China could suffer instability and domestic upheaval if it started to adopt Western reforms.[24] Democratic reforms would undermine the CPC's control, and Wu promulgated the five 'nos': 'no multi-party election; no diversified guiding principles, no separation of powers, no federal system, and no privatization'.[25] For Wu, the courts in China are the courts of the party, not the court of law or court of equity, thus no judicial review of the party's executive or legislative power is permitted.

As Murong Xuecun, a former lawyer and a Chinese novelist, put it:

> In my country, the legal system works like this: countless laws are enacted, and then countless procedures are created, followed by countless enforcement regulations and detailed judicial interpretations, but ultimately it is up to the political leaders to decide who wins and who loses a case. In my country, many cases cannot be pursued in the courts. Even if legal action is taken, courts can refuse to hear a case. Even if the case is heard in court, the judgment is made well before the hearing starts.[26]

Structure

It was really in 1979 that the NPC allowed the court to serve as a judicial body. Up to that time, the courts were viewed with suspicion and the CPC mainly delegated their power to other governmental bodies. Between November 1980 and January 1981, however, the courts played a prominent role in the trial of the Gang of Four and other members of the 'Lin-Jiang cliques'.[27] Not only were former major government players on trial, but the Chinese government hoped to show that they were being treated just like any other citizens of the PRC. Though the government hoped these trials would demonstrate to a global audience that China had a functioning and impartial legal system, many people watching might have thought the showcase trials were more political than they were legal.

Shortly before the trial of the Gang of Four, the Ministry of Justice was re-established in 1979, after having been decommissioned for 20 years. The ministry was meant to support and administer the newly formed legal system. It relied on local bureaus and judicial departments to find funding for the courts, manage and train the new cadres of judicial employees, and ensure that legal research was done properly. The ministry also served as a liaison between Chinese and foreign judicial bodies.

At the very top of the court system is the Supreme People's Court, which can review the decisions of all lower courts and has jurisdiction over all regular and special courts. The SPC is in Beijing and reports to the Standing Committee of the NPC, which also elects the president of the SPC. Both because the chief justice is elected by the Standing Committee and because the SPC reports directly to it, this sends a clear message that the legislative and judicial branches are not equals. It also reinforces the role of the court to uphold the CPC-socialist system.

It is not just courts that have an influence on the adjudication of Chinese trials, however. The Organic Law of the People's Courts mandates that any major case must be reviewed for errors in finding of facts or application of law by an adjudication committee. Adjudication committees are found at every level of the courts and are often composed of the chief (president) and associate judges (vice-presidents) of the court, who are appointed by the respective standing committee of the people's congress. Adjudication committees also review conflicts and determine when a chief judge must withdraw from a case. When an adjudication committee has ruled on a case, frequently before the trial, the court must follow that decision.

China's four-tiered court system was established by two legal documents: the Organic Law of the People's Courts (1980) and the Constitution of the People's Republic of China of 1982. At the bottom are the local people's courts. There are three levels of people's courts, and the fourth tier is the Supreme People's Court in Beijing. Outside the main court system are the specialty courts.

The local people's courts serve as courts of first instance, meaning they hear and try civil and criminal cases. They are divided into primary, intermediate and higher people's courts. The basic courts are in individual towns, municipalities and autonomous communities. Intermediate courts deal with issues at the prefecture level; autonomous prefectures and municipalities also have intermediate courts. Finally, the higher people's courts are at the provincial and autonomous regional levels. Special municipalities also fall within their purview.

Above the local people's courts is the SPC, located in the capital. Not only does it act as the appellate court for and administrator of the local people's courts, but it also serves that role for the special people's courts. With the exception of Hong Kong and Macau, which have British- and Portuguese-based legal systems, respectively, the Supreme People's Court is the final appellate court in the nation. Hong Kong and Macau have distinct and separate court systems.

Finally, there are several courts of special jurisdiction that hear 'cases of counter-revolutionary activity, plundering, bribery, sabotage, or indifference to duty that result in severe damage to military facilities, work place, or government property or threaten the safety of soldiers or workers'.[28] These include the Railway Transport Court of China, the Maritime Court of China, the Military Court of China and a court that deals with forestry. Though these courts focus on specific issues, their decisions can be appealed to the SPC as well.

Military courts make up the largest group of special courts and try all treason and espionage cases. Although they are independent of civilian courts and directly subordinate to the Ministry of National Defense, their decisions are reviewed by the SPC. These military courts were first established in 1954 to protect the special interests of all commanders, political commissars and soldiers, but they ceased to function during the Cultural Revolution (1966–1976). Military courts and procuratorates were reinstituted in October 1978, and open military trials resumed in December of that year.

In addition to the court system, there are levels of prosecuting offices that correspond to each level of the court. At the very top is the Supreme People's Procuratorate (covered in the next chapter).

Supreme People's Court

The Supreme People's Court of China was established on 1 October 1949, the same day that the PRC was established. The chief justice was Shen Junru, a late Qing dynasty legal scholar. Chief justices can serve no more than two successive five-year terms, and by 2012 there had been 12 different chief justices of the SPC. Under the chief is one first-level justice and 11 second-level justices – two of whom are female – all of whom serve as leaders of the court. In addition, the SPC includes more than 200 judges who meet in smaller tribunals to decide cases.

No judicial review

Black's Law Dictionary defines 'judicial review' as:

> the doctrine under which legislative and executive actions are subject to review (and possible invalidation) by the judiciary... Judicial review is an example of the separation of powers in a modern governmental system (where the judiciary is one of three branches of government). This principle is interpreted differently in different jurisdictions, which also have differing views on the different hierarchy of governmental norms. As a result, the procedure and scope of judicial review differs from country to country and state to state.[29]

Because the judiciary at every level ranks lower than the legislative branch at the same level, the SPC and lower courts do not have the power of judicial review. Allowing the courts to determine the constitutionality of legislation would not only be impossible because of the lack of separation between the two branches, but would also defeat what the CPC believes the purpose of the judiciary to be: to support the rule of the party.

Hierarchical administrative organ

The whole court system functions as an administrative agency with a clearly defined hierarchy. According to the Judge's Law of the People's Republic of China, there are 12 levels of judges, which form a hierarchy paralleling that of the CPC. It also mirrors the government's civil service program, in which there are 15 levels of cadres or civil servants.

Inside the SPC are four civil tribunals, two criminal tribunals, one administrative tribunal and 19 departments and offices. The SPC organ also includes the People's Court Press (legal publishing), the People's Court News (legal news), National Judges College (judicial training) and National Judges Association/National Female Judges Association.

Under the SPC there are 31 provincial higher people's courts, 360 intermediate people's courts and more than 3,000 district people's courts. Every court reports to the court directly above it; every court directly supervises the courts below. Every court has a CPC committee as a managing authority. Each level of court is also essentially responsible to local political power (CPC committee and executive organ) at the same level, a responsibility reinforced by local control over court finances.

Double jurisdictions

The whole court system in China is based on the principle of 'two-trials-to-conclude-a-case':[30] one trial at first instance, and one trial on appeal. During either trial, issues of both fact and law are argued and adjudicated. The SPC, like provincial higher and intermediate people's courts, is both a trial court and an appellate court. It exercises appellate jurisdiction over all the lower courts, as well as original jurisdiction in important cases at the national level. In the latter case, the SPC could rehear its own case in order to conclude it.[31]

Judicial interpretation in place of case law

China is a civil law jurisdiction (Hong Kong, in contrast, is a common law jurisdiction), thus Chinese judges do not make law by adjudicating cases and controversies. The SPC does have an important legislative function, however, which it exercises by promulgating judicial interpretations and documents providing general rules for courts to follow in adjudicating cases.

The SPC, acting on its own or sometimes jointly with the Supreme People's Procuratorate, may issue a short or long reply, in question-and-answer format, to specific questions of law submitted by lower courts. The SPC may also issue long and systematic documents to interpret or elaborate on legislative provisions, and to supplement or even fill in the gaps in existing legislation. These latter documents are basically legislative in nature.

Courts do not regulate and supervise attorneys

The SPC and lower courts in China do not regulate and supervise lawyers. According to the Law of the People's Republic of China on Lawyers, provincial-level bureaus of justice examine and approve attorney license applications, and the national-level Ministry of Justice issues national unified attorney licenses. The Ministry of Justice and its lower branches regulate and supervise attorneys; the SPC and its lower courts do not have the authority to supervise any attorneys other than their own judges and clerks.

Are *fayuan* courts?

The Chinese word for 'court' is *fayuan* (法院), but courts in China do not operate and do not have the same base goals as courts in the West. As defined by the *Oxford Companion to Law*, a court is 'a form of tribunal, often a governmental institution, with the authority to adjudicate legal disputes between parties and carry out the administration of justice in civil, criminal, and administrative matters in accordance with the rule of law'.[32] By this definition, a court needs to operate under the rule of law – a concept that is outside of government control. Moreover, rule of law does not inherently support any particular kind of government, but rather a government that respect its citizens' rights.

However, Article 3 of the Organic Law of the People's Courts of the People's Republic of China says that the courts must 'safeguard the system of dictatorship of the proletariat, maintain the socialist legal system and public order', making it quite clear that the purpose of the courts is to support the party's rule.

When litigation or criminal prosecution arise that could potentially disrupt the CPC's control over China, it would appear that the court must find a way to adjudicate a case that will protect the system. Unlike a judicial system that offers ordinary citizens a channel to address their grievances and solve disputes and controversies, this system mainly concerns protecting the CPC's leadership.

One particular question that needs to be raised is whether the Chinese *fayuan* really are courts. This is not only a translation issue, but has broader significance in understanding China's legal system. Professor Donald Clarke has contemplated and admitted this is a 'quite difficult' question.[33] To an American, the Chinese *fayuan* might initially appear court-like in nature or, to be more accurate, like the US court system, but going deeper there are many dissimilarities. While the Chinese courts are not practicing under the rule of law and are used as a tool to uphold the CPC, does that make them something other than courts? Must a court mirror the American system to be classified as a court? Are there basic functions or requirements a court must abide by to be a court? If one takes such a hard-and-fast approach, the Chinese *fayuan* might not be considered courts.

Many would argue, however, that China must have courts somewhere and the *fayuan* are the most court-like institutions.[34] There is an assumption that every society must have some kind of court to enable it to function, so Chinese *fayuan* must be considered courts. But there is also debate as to whether the idea that a society must have courts is fact or merely a presumption.[35]

'Judges'

Unlike the American legal system, the Chinese courts, as created by the 1980 Organic Law of the People's Courts and the 1982 constitution, are inquisitorial, not adversarial. This means the judges and assessors will play an active role in interrogating witnesses and parties, rather than remaining neutral referees. A majority of trials are decided by one to three judges and three to five assessors. Assessors are appointed or elected members of the community who are at least 23 years old and have full political rights. If elected, they are elected by local individuals or a people's congress; if appointed, they are appointed by the court itself.[36]

Judges are also elected or appointed by a people's congress at the corresponding level to the court; they can serve a maximum of two five-year terms. Under the Organic Law and the State Constitution, there are four levels of courts and a loss at one level can be appealed to a higher court. Though the law uses the term 'elected', judges are ultimately chosen by the legislative body at the instruction of the CPC at the corresponding level, reifying and strengthening the subordination of the judiciaries to the party.

It was not until 1995 that China first promulgated the Judge's Law. By 2011 the number of judges had grown to about 190,000 and there were 130,000 other members of the court system. As defined by Article 2 of the Judge's Law, judges are:

judicial persons who exercise the judicial authority of the State according to law, and they include the presidents, vice-presidents, members of judicial committees, chief judges and associate chief judges of divisions, judges and assistant judges of the Supreme People's Court, local People's Courts at various levels and special People's Courts such as military courts.

The Judge's Law also dictates how one can become a judge. There are only three possible routes: immediately after law school; after graduating from college and working as a judicial clerk for a year; or as a former member of the military appointed as a judge. Head judges, or presidents of the courts, are appointed by the corresponding people's congress. Though it would appear that judges are then to report to the congress that appointed them, they actually serve the CPC Politics and Law Committee at that level.

Prior to the promulgation of the Judge's Law, many of the judges were inexperienced, not only with their roles in the judiciary but with the law in general. Approximately 57,000 former members of the military were discharged in 1981 by the CPC Central Military Committee and sent to work as 'judges'. Many of these men and women had very little experience with courtrooms and even fewer had formally studied law.[37] It was also noted by Professor He Weifang, a legal scholar at Peking University Law School, that many of these veterans did not consider the judiciary to be a separate profession; rather, they viewed being a judge as they would any other political appointment – one to be filled by CPC members.[38] To these 'judges', being a member of the party is the career, being a 'judge' is probably more like an assignment.

Professor He wrote an article about teaching a class at a judicial training center. When he asked the students whether members of the military can be appointed as doctors since they could be appointed as judges, the class failed to understand his point.[39]

Some of He's most vocal objectors were veterans who had been appointed judges. Though his article repeated many of the ideals put forth in the Judge's Law, which had been published three years earlier, a former lieutenant-colonel who had joined the judiciary issued a response in the official publication of the military.[40] The colonel argued veteran judges are still respected, and an intermediate-level judge has implied that veterans are just as qualified, if not more so, to serve as judges because of their considerable life experience.[41]

Prior to 1995 there were no requirements to becoming a judge; anyone could theoretically be appointed to the position. Though the Organic Law of the People's Courts was first passed in 1980, it was not until the 1995 promulgation of the Judge's Law that there were some restrictions placed on who was allowed to be a judge.

Article 9 of the 1995 Judge's Law lays out the qualifications to becoming a judge, including:

> to be of the nationality of the People's Republic of China; to have reached the age of 23; to endorse the Constitution of the People's Republic of China; to have fine political and professional quality and to be good in conduct; to be in good health; and to have worked for at least two years in the case of graduates from law specialties of colleges or universities or from non-law specialties of colleges or universities but possessing the professional knowledge of law; or to have worked for at least one year in the case of Bachelors of Law; those who have Master's Degree of Law or Doctor's Degree of Law may be not subject to the abovementioned requirements for the number of years set for work.

Though these are considered to be necessary to become a judge, the law also says that anyone who does not meet the educational and experiential requirements can 'receive training so as to meet the qualifications as provided by this Law within a prescribed time limit. The specific measures shall be laid down by the Supreme People's Court.'[42] What would be considered to be the most important requirements in many countries – a knowledge of the law and sufficient experience to hear and decide civil and criminal cases – are the qualifications that can be worked around in China. This could be an effort to promote incapable but loyal judges to the bench – judges who would follow the direction set forth by the legislative branch.

Starting in 2001, the Judge's Law was revised to require anyone serving as a judge in a provincial high court or the SPC to have a postgraduate degree:

> to have worked in law for at least two years in the case of a graduate from a four-year course in the law specialty of an institution of higher education or a graduate from a four-year course in a non-law specialty of such an institution who possesses the professional knowledge of law, and to have worked in law for at least three years in the case of the said graduate to be appointed

judge of a Higher People's Court or the Supreme People's Court; to have worked in law for at least one year in the case of a person holding a Master of Law degree or Doctor of Law degree; or a person holding a master's degree or doctor's degree of non-law specialty who possesses the professional knowledge of law, and to have worked in law for at least two years in the case of the said person to be appointed judge of a Higher People's Court or the Supreme People's Court.[43]

Much like with the previous set of laws, there was an exception made for this requirement as well: 'Where it is really difficult to apply the provisions... regarding the academic qualifications, such qualifications for judges may, upon examination and approval by the Supreme People's Court... be relegated to include graduates from a two-or-three-year course in the law specialty of an institution of higher education.'[44] In essence, this exception allowed a graduate of the Chinese equivalent of an associate's degree program to serve on the highest courts in the nation.

In addition to definitions of who can serve as a judge, there is a list of people who are ineligible for judicial service. According to Article 10, anyone who has been criminally punished or has been fired from public employment is ineligible to serve as a judge.

The Chinese acceptance of judges with little or no legal background is best demonstrated by a former president of the SPC:

> The career of China's chief justice, the President of the Supreme People's Court, Wang Shengjun, nominally the most senior judicial officer in the country, embodies the values of this legal system admirably. Wang has never studied law, and ascended to the post in 2008 through a career in provincial policing in central Anhui Province and then the state security bureaucracy in Beijing. Apart from a degree in history, interrupted by the Cultural Revolution (1966–1976), Wang's only other education has been at the Central Party School in Beijing.[45]

However, 'in the Party's view Wang's political credentials made him perfectly qualified for the senior legal job'.[46]

In March 2013 Zhou Qiang was elected SPC president, i.e. chief justice, at the fifth plenary meeting of the first session of the Twelfth National People's Congress in Beijing. This is good news for the legal profession because Zhou was legally educated and holds two degrees in law.[47]

Judicial examination

In 2011 the method of selecting judges was radically reformed. For the first time, judges were chosen using a national judicial examination. The Judge's Law was updated to reflect that change, stating that 'persons to be appointed judges for the first time shall be selected, through strict examination and appraisal, from among those who have passed the uniform national judicial examination and who are the best qualified for the post, in conformity with the standards of having both ability and political integrity'.[48]

Much like the national lawyer's qualification exam, first administered in 1986 by the Ministry of Justice, a judge's qualification exam administered by the SPC began in 1995. In 2002 a unified exam was administered. This test incorporated the qualifying exams for lawyers, judges and prosecutors. In the first year, however, the pass rate was extremely low; only 6.68 percent of individuals who took the exam passed. Many believe the pass rate was driven down by would-be judges, in part because they were taking the same exam as lawyers.[49]

Judicial corruption

As is to be expected, the Judge's Law includes language that prohibits judicial corruption. Article 7 lists obligations put upon judges, including to be independent of personal bias when hearing facts and law by the opposing sides, to uphold the laws and constitution of the PRC, safeguard a litigant's rights and operate under a series of professional ethics. Unlike Western judiciaries, Chinese judges must also work to protect the state's interests, ensure state secrets are not leaked and remember that the masses have the ultimate legal supervision over the judiciary.

Article 32 of the 2011 law lists unacceptable and prohibited behaviors of Chinese judges. Judges are not allowed:

> to spread statements damaging the prestige of the State; to join illegal organizations; to take part in such activities as assembly, procession and demonstration against the State; and to participate in strikes; to embezzle money or accept bribes; to bend law for personal gain; to extort confessions by torture; to conceal or falsify evidence; to divulge State secrets or secrets of judicial work; to

abuse functions and powers; and to infringe upon the lawful rights and interests of natural persons, legal persons or other organizations; to neglect his or her duty so as to wrongly judge a case or to cause heavy losses to the party concerned; to delay the handling of a case so that work is adversely affected; to take advantage of the functions and powers to seek gain for himself or herself or other people; to engage in profit-making activities; to meet the party concerned or his or her agent without authorization and attend dinners or accept presents given by the party concerned or his or her agent; or to commit other acts in violation of law or discipline.

Oddly enough, the bans on using one's position to increase personal wealth, gain or accept banquets and presents are all prohibitions against normative 'hidden rules' behavior. Under a typical 'hidden rules' system, the expectation is that an individual buys his way into the judiciary and can then get some kind of return for his investment through bribes. Many of the things that judges are forbidden from doing constitute some of the largest problems within the judicial system. Though they have been legislated against, judges are often tempted to and do engage in corrupt practices. As described in the US Department of State country report on human rights practices for China:

> The law provides criminal penalties for official corruption; however, the government did not implement the law effectively, and officials frequently engaged in corrupt practices with impunity. Many cases of corruption involved areas that were heavily regulated by the government and therefore susceptible to fraud, bribery, and kickbacks, such as land usage rights, real estate, and infrastructure development.[50]

There are some limited measures trying to control judicial corruption, and two provincial people's courts have taken a stand against it. The Higher People's Court of Chongqing Municipality banned the family members of judges from taking bribes or money from lawyers; and the Higher People's Court of Fujian Province prohibited judges and parties to a case from meeting in private.[51]

Despite these moves to eliminate it, there are numerous stories of judges and court officials being publicly accused of corruption. The Wuhan Intermediate Court saw 44 lawyers and 13 judges being questioned about abusing power and taking bribes in March 2004.[52]

Two months later the chief judge of the Hunan Provincial High Court was arrested on bribery charges with ten other members of the court. He was ultimately sentenced to death, with a two-year suspension of the sentence.[53] In 2005 and 2006 judges at the Fuyang and Shenzhen intermediate courts were arrested for bribery. The Fuyang judges were also charged with using prostitutes and gambling.[54] The Shenzhen judges had first been investigated by the CPC under the *shuanggui* system before being arrested and prosecuted by police.[55]

It was Huang Songyou who truly illustrated Chinese judicial corruption, however. Huang was the SPC vice-president and one of the senior associate justices, but was questioned under the *shuanggui* system in October 2008. The CPC disciplinary officers were investigating reports of corruption. Ultimately, Huang was stripped of his title. In 2010 he was also criminally convicted of corruption and given a life sentence. In total, it was believed that Huang had collected RMB3.9 million or $570,000 in bribes. It was also thought that his history of embezzlement traced back to when he was a judge in Guangdong.[56]

Procuratorates

Drawing from the Soviet Union model, the public procuratorate was a governmental department that prosecutes criminal offenses. Established prior to the Cultural Revolution, the procuratorates were abolished by the CPC Central Committee in 1969; between 1969 and 1979 all prosecutions were handled by the police and public security forces.[57] In 1979 the Organic Law of the People's Procuratorates was promulgated and re-established the procuratorates. This law was subsequently amended in 1983, and the Public Procurators Law was also passed in 1995.

The Organic Law of the People's Procuratorates shares many similarities with the Organic Law of the People's Courts. Article 1 states that 'The people's procuratorates of the People's Republic of China are state organs for legal supervision.' Article 4 elaborates on their purpose:

> The people's procuratorates shall, through exercising their procuratorial authority, suppress all treasonous activities, all activities to dismember the state and other counterrevolutionary activities, and strike at counterrevolutionaries and other criminals, so as to

safeguard the unification of the country, the system of proletarian dictatorship and the socialist legal system; to maintain public order and order in production, education, scientific research and other work and in the life of the people; to protect the socialist property owned by the whole people and by the collectives of the working masses, and the private property lawfully owned by citizens; to protect the citizens' rights of the person and their democratic and other rights; and to ensure the smooth progress of the socialist modernization... The people's procuratorates, through procuratorial activities, educate the citizens to be loyal to their socialist motherland, to consciously observe the Constitution and the laws and to actively fight against illegal activities.

Article 12 cautions: 'The arrest of any citizen, unless decided on by a people's court, must be subject to the approval of a people's procuratorate.'

Again, the role of the procuratorates is clear: to ensure that the party remains in control and the socialist system survives. This lends support to the prosecution and conviction of people labeled enemies of the state or traitors, or anyone whose actions are of national concern.

Similarly, there are many commonalities between this law and the Judge's Law:

Public Procurators are the procuratorial personnel who exercise the procuratorial authority of the State according to law, including chief procurators, deputy chief procurators (the Procurator-General, Deputy Procurators-General of the Supreme People's Procuratorate), members of procuratorial committees, procurators and assistant procurators of the Supreme People's Procuratorate, local People's Procuratorates at various levels and special People's Procuratorates such as military Procuratorates... The functions and duties of Public Procurators are as follows: to supervise the enforcement of laws according to law; to make public prosecution on behalf of the State; to investigate criminal cases directly accepted by the People's Procuratorates as provided by law; and other functions and duties as provided by law.[58]

Though the procuratorates and procurators are completely separate from and governed by different laws than the courts and judges, they are influenced by many of the same things. For one, there have been many stories of corruption with procuratorates. Many procurators do not have legal or sufficient educational backgrounds to prosecute cases properly.[59]

This is not, of course, true across all the procuratorates. The current president of the Supreme People's Procuratorate, Cao Jianming, is not only a graduate from a top Shanghai law school but was also a law professor and dean of a law school before being appointed to the Supreme People's Court. In 1999 Cao became SPC vice-president, and in 2008 he was appointed to his present post.

Though Cao has considerable legal experience, he is also heavily influenced by the CPC. As Supreme People's Procuratorate president he is part of the CPC Central Politics and Law Committee, but his role in the committee is lower than that of the police chief, meaning that prosecutors answer to the police and public security. This ranking is replicated at city, county and provincial levels. While Article 5(3) of the Organic Law of the People's Procuratorate says that the role of the procuratorates is to determine what police actions are legal, they actually report to the police. At some of the lowest levels they do review some police work, but they are unable to correct anything that appears to be illegal. The courts rank above the procuratorates but also below the police.

Access to court information

In 1979 Deng Xiaoping instituted the 'open door' policy, which took a utilitarian approach to the reconstruction of social order and the legal system. The law came to be viewed as a useful instrument to support the country's economic growth. Over the past three decades China has made significant progress in developing a legal system that in many ways is consistent with international norms. Prolific legislative activities and increased emphasis on the implementation and enforcement of law are positive steps toward a stable legal environment.[60]

Legal publishing in China is a state-controlled enterprise and has historically been restricted.[61] Before 1979, legal bibliographic systems and legal research methods were primitive. Standardized and advanced techniques for organizing legal information, such as codification, indexing, cataloging and superseding, were not implemented by legal publishers until the early 1990s.[62] The failure to develop an effective method of organizing information and disseminating legal knowledge can be explained by the long-standing and well-established tradition that access to information and knowledge in China is a privilege, not a right.[63]

Beyond the traditional disregard for equal access to information, the lack of technical infrastructure was also responsible for the underdevelopment of a modern legal information system. China had 'neither a central government clearinghouse like the United States Government Printing Office for disseminating government information nor a depository library system to have libraries house the government publications and provide public access to them'.[64] Government documents, even those with legal implications, could be classified as 'state secrets', only available to the officials who executed them. This again is a unique characteristic that echoes imperial practices. In 2007 the State Council promulgated the PRC Regulations for the Disclosure of Government Information.[65] No doubt the regulations, along with 'electronic government projects' (a set of websites established by central and local governments to transfer some government functions online), contributed to the development of a legal information system in China.

The 1990s witnessed an unparalleled economic growth in China driven by vast foreign investment, privatization of commercial and industrial entities, and technological advances. Sir Francis Bacon's dictum 'knowledge is power'[66] became a motivating force and mantra across the country. Demands for more information and more knowledge increased throughout all segments of society. Consequently, the collection, management and distribution of knowledge came to be viewed as having both social and economic benefits. Legal information in particular was seen as a body of information potentially of high market value.

In 1995 Peking University, the country's oldest and most prestigious university, launched Chinalawinfo, the first online Chinese legal information database. This effort was followed by other technological ventures:

> Facilitated with modern technology and aiming to catch up with sophisticated online services, such as Westlaw and LexisNexis, law publishers, online products entrepreneurs, law schools, law firms, and even law enforcement departments, are committing themselves to create comprehensive databases and electronic legal services.[67]

In 1999, with strong government support, Tsinghua University launched China National Knowledge Infrastructure, the largest digital value-added information library in China and a nationwide knowledge-sharing platform.

Notes

1. Richard McGregor (2010) *The Party: The Secret World of China's Communist Rulers*. New York: HarperCollins, p. 22.
2. Wu Bangguo (2011) '2011 report on the Standing Committee of China's National People's Congress', National People's Congress of China, Beijing.
3. Jerome Cohen (2011) 'Law unto itself', *South China Morning Post*, 30 March; available at: *www.usasialaw.org/wp-content/uploads/2011/03/2011.3.30-SCMP-Cohen-Law-unto-itself.pdf* (accessed: 6 August 2013); see also Jerome Cohen (2011) 'A socialist legal system with Chinese characteristics', 30 March; available at: *www.usasialaw.org/?p=5279* (accessed: 2 February 2013).
4. Randall Peerenboom (2002) *China's Long March toward Rule of Law*. Cambridge: Cambridge University Press, p. 212.
5. Ibid.
6. Paul P. Craig (1997) 'Formal and substantive conceptions of the rule of law: an analytical framework', *Public Law*, 21: 467.
7. Ibid.
8. *Black's Law Dictionary* (2009) 'Rule of law', *Black's Law Dictionary*, 9th edn. St Paul, MN: Thomson West, p. 1448.
9. Communist Party of China (undated) 'Central Politics and Law Committee'; available at: *http://cpc.people.com.cn/GB/64114/64135/* (accessed: 6 August 2013).
10. Hassan B. Jallow (2009) 'Justice and the rule of law: a global perspective', *International Lawyers*, 43(1): 77.
11. Albert H.Y. Chen (2004) *An Introduction to the Legal System of the People's Republic of China*, 3rd edn. Hong Kong: LexisNexis Butterworths, p. 151.
12. Chinapeace (2013) 'New leadership of the Central Politics and Law Committee announced'; available at: *www.chinapeace.org.cn/* (accessed: 6 August 2013).
13. Chinese Communist Party News (undated) 'A brief introduction of the Central Politics and Law Committee of the CPC'; available at: *http://cpc.people.com.cn/GB/64114/64135/5994757.html* (accessed: 12 August 2013).
14. Sohu News (2013) 'Analyzing the combination of the Central Politics and Law Committee'; available at: *http://news.sohu.com/s2013/dianji-1120/* (accessed: 12 August 2013).
15. Chen, note 11 above, p. 151.
16. Ibid., p. 152.
17. Ibid.
18. Ibid.
19. Baidu Baike (2013) 'Gong Jian Fa'; available at: *http://baike.baidu.com/view/333187.htm* (accessed: 6 August 2013).
20. Ibid.
21. Third Plenum of the 11th CPC Central Committee (1978) 'Communiqué of the third plenary session of the 11th Central Committee of the Communist Party of China', adopted 22 December; available at *www.bjreview.com.cn/90th/2011-04/26/content_357494_3.htm* (accessed: 12 August 2013).

22. Organic Law of the People's Courts, Article 4, emphasis added.
23. Quoted in McGregor, note 1 above, p. 25.
24. Quoted in Shi Jiangtao (2011) 'Beijing slams door on political reform', *South China Morning Post*, 11 March.
25. Quoted in ibid.
26. Quoted in Market Cruncher (2011) 'Murong Xuecun: behind the Chinese façade lies a monster', Market Cruncher, 23 November; available at: *http://marketcruncher.com/2011/11/23/murong-xuecun-behind-the-chinese-facade-lies-a-monster/* (accessed: 6 August 2013).
27. Leo Goodstadt (1982) 'The trial of the Lin-Jiang cliques: China's return to the rule of law', *Hong Kong Law Journal*, 31: 12.
28. Government of China (2005) 'Judicial system of the People's Republic of China', 29 August; available at: *http://english.gov.cn/2005-08/29/content_27294.htm.* (accessed: 6 August 2013).
29. *Black's Law Dictionary* (2009) 'Judicial review', *Black's Law Dictionary*, 9th edn. St Paul, MN: Thomson West, p. 924.
30. Government of China, note 28 above.
31. Organic Law of the People's Courts, Article 31.
32. David Walker (1980) *The Oxford Companion to Law*. Oxford: Oxford University Press, p. 301.
33. Donald Clarke (2011) 'Are Chinese fayuan (法院) courts?'; available at: *http://lawprofessors.typepad.com/china_law_prof_blog/2011/06/are-chinese-fayuan-%E6%B3%95% E9%99%A2-courts.html* (accessed: 6 August 2013).
34. Ibid.
35. Ibid.
36. Organic Law of the People's Courts, Article 37.
37. McGregor, note 1 above, p. 114.
38. He Weifang (贺卫方) (1998) 'Veterans became judges (复转军人进法院)', *Southern Weekend Newspaper* (南方周末), 2 January.
39. Ibid.
40. Cao Ruilin (曹瑞林) (1998) 'Why ex-servicemen cannot come to the court (复转军人缘何不能进法院)', *China National Defense News* (中国国防报), 2 October.
41. Ibid.
42. Judge's Law of the People's Republic of China (1995), Article 9.
43. Judge's Law of the People's Republic of China (2001), Article 9.
44. Ibid.
45. McGregor, note 1 above, p. 24.
46. Ibid.
47. Xinhua News (2013) 'Profile: China's chief justice, procurator: carrying public hopes for justice', Xinhua News, 17 March; available at: *http://news.xinhuanet.com/english/china/2013-03/17/c_132240866.htm* (accessed: 6 August 2013).
48. Judge's Law of the People's Republic of China (2011), Article 12.
49. *Southern Weekend Newspaper* (南方周末) (2002) 'Low passing rate; many judges failed the judicial exam (通过率偏低, 众多法官被司法考试绊倒)', *Southern Weekend Newspaper*, 12 July; available at: *www.china.com.cn/chinese/law/172458.htm* (accessed: 6 August 2013).

50. US Department of State, Bureau of Democracy, Human Rights and Labor (2011) 'Country reports on human rights practices for 2011: China'; available at: *www.state.gov/j/drl/rls/hrrpt/humanrightsreport/index.htm?dlid=186268* (accessed: 6 August 2013).

51. Ibid.

52. China Youth News (2006) 'Wuhan Intermediate Court corruption continues; the reason of failed supervision questioned', 13 October; available at: *http://news.xinhuanet.com/legal/2006-10/13/content_5197141.htm* (accessed: 12 August 2013).

53. A. Cheng and Wei Juan (2006) 'The fall of Wu Zhenming, former president of Hunan High Court', *Wutian Gold News*, 15 November; available at: *http://review.jcrb.com/200708/ca631535.htm* (accessed: 12 August 2013).

54. *People's Daily* (2005) 'Eating, drinking, prostitution, and gambling: perspective on the group corruption of Fuyang Intermediary Court', *People's Daily*, 30 April; available at: *http://politics.people.com.cn/GB/1026/3362116.html* (accessed: 12 August 2013).

55. Xinhua News Agency (2006) 'It is all bankrupt's fault', 6 November; available at: *http://news.sina.com.cn/c/2006-11-06/111211438273.shtml* (accessed: 12 August 2013).

56. BBC (2010) 'China jails senior judge for life over corruption', BBC News, 19 January; available at: *http://news.bbc.co.uk/2/hi/asia-pacific/8467064.stm* (accessed: 6 August 2013).

57. Chen, note 11 above, p. 160.

58. Organic Law of the People's Procuratorates, Article 2.

59. Chen, note 11 above, p. 163.

60. James M. Zimmerman (2005) *China Law Deskbook: A Legal Guide for Foreign-Invested Enterprises*, 2nd edn. Chicago, IL: American Bar Association, p. 70.

61. Even in the early 1990s, the State Council promulgated Administration Provisions on Legal Compilation Editing and Publishing (29 July 1990), followed by Notice of the Press and Publication Administration on the Implementation of the State Council's Administrative Provisions on Legal Compilation Editing and Publishing (22 December 1991). These are efforts to regulate legal publishing business.

62. Joan Liu and Wei Luo (2003) 'A complete research guide to the laws of the People's Republic of China (PRC)', 15 January; available at: *www.llrx.com/features/prc.htm* (accessed: 6 August 2013).

63. Imperial China did not fully respect individual rights. Confucianism values order: 'The people may be made to follow a path of action, but they may not be made to understand it.' (Confucius, 551–479 BCE.)

64. Liu and Luo, note 62 above, fn. 36.

65. State Council (2007) '中华人民共和国政府信息公开条 (PRC Regulations for the Disclosure of Government Information)', promulgated 5 April, effective 1 May, State Council, Beijing.

66. Francis Bacon (1597) 'Meditations Sacrae', reported in John Bartlett (1980) *Familiar Quotations*, 15th edn. New York: Little, Brown, p. 179.

67. Liu and Luo, note 62 above, fn. 36.

The police

Abstract: The next big player in the Chinese legal system, the police, is covered in this chapter. The different components of public security are defined, the role of the police is elaborated upon and the laws governing police officers are explained. The concept of maintaining stability, the focal point of police activity, is discussed, as well as the work of the Domestic Security Department. Finally, some representative cases show how police operate and some of the concerns regarding public security.

Key words: public security, police, Domestic Security Department, internet police, Wen Qiang, Wang Lijun.

Definitions

Within the Chinese government, the role of public security cannot be overstated. Headed by the Ministry of Public Security, the public security forces include police and special police units, as well as the public security bureaus. The ministry is a cabinet-level government agency in charge of law enforcement. The police chief, the head of the Ministry of Public Security, is a member of the Central Politics and Law Committee, CPC Central Committee. Meng Jianzhu, the committee's chair, was the former police chief, thus a former police chief supervises the current chief justice (the president of the Supreme People's Court) and chief procurator (president of the Supreme People's Procuratorate), as well as the current police chief. Though the chief justice and chief procurator are officially independent, they report to the Central Politics and Law Committee.

The Ministry of Public Security is parallel to the Ministry of State Security, which is the principal national security agency. The Ministry of State Security focuses primarily on foreign intelligence, but also involves itself in some domestic security matters. The Ministry of Public Security, however, is dedicated exclusively to internal and domestic security issues.

The Ministry of Public Security also supervises public security bureaus at provincial, municipal and county levels. Provincial public security bureaus, in turn, administer county- or district-level public security sub-bureaus and branch bureaus, which perform a role similar to larger police stations. The lowest-level outposts are police posts, which perform a role similar to small, local police stations. The ministry does not, however, directly supervise the People's Armed Police, a paramilitary or gendarmerie force primarily responsible for civilian policing and fire rescue duties in the PRC. The special police units are like American SWAT units of the Chinese People's Armed Police at the provincial and municipal levels. There is at least one unit in each Chinese province to offer services when requested by the local police or other law enforcement agencies. It is when the government is trying to suppress and contain mass protests, however, that local police and special police units work the closest.

Overview

Role of the police and security apparatus

The primary domestic security force is the police within the Ministry of Public Security. As mentioned, the Ministry of State Security has some domestic security responsibilities, but is primarily concerned with external threats. Other contributors to domestic security include civilian municipal security forces or 'urban management' officials. These officials are often employed by local police jurisdictions to help enforce local regulations.

The US State Department 2011 country report on human rights practices in China says there is little judicial oversight of police forces, nor has police power been moderated by other government departments.[1] This lack of checks and balances may have led to the considerable corruption of police, including brutality and participating in extrajudicial detention and extortion. Though there was acknowledgment of police corruption in 2009 by domestic news sources and the Supreme People's Procuratorate, these extrajudicial actions have not stopped. News outlets also reported convictions of public security officials who had been tried for the death of suspects and prisoners in 2009. While members of the government have spoken about police misconduct, the procuratorate ranks below the police, meaning that even a condemnation by the chief procuratorate would not necessarily stop police corruption.[2]

Police

The majority of the 2 million police officers in China are not adequately trained or compensated.[3] Many work in stations that are only responsible for about 10,000 people, and generally wait for people to come to them with problems rather than actively trying to prevent crime. Despite this relaxed approach, many people are wary of the police. Though city dwellers are generally more comfortable with the police than rural villagers, the urban populations still have a degree of distrust. This may be, in part, because officers have spent more time reinforcing tight government control of the citizenry than solving the crimes that people bring to them. As such, the family and friends of crime victims are often angry and upset with law enforcement's inability to pursue justice.

The CPC, in preparation for the 60-year anniversary of communist rule, involved all 2 million police officers around the country in an effort to ease discontent before the October 2009 anniversary.[4] Starting in December 2008, the officers were given the additional task of going out to listen to ordinary citizens' complaints. As can be imagined, many of the things that are most important to people are those that most directly impact them, such as their safety and security.

This does not mean, of course, that the police force is being reformed. There have still been reports of excess, such as the death of a traffic officer from Shenzhen in December 2009.[5] In its coverage of the story, the *China Daily* reported that the officer had died at a banquet he had been forced to attend. While at the banquet he had drunk heavily, passed out on a couch and then suffocated. The officer, Chen Lusheng, was named a martyr, despite the circumstances surrounding his death, because it was determined that he had died in the line of duty.[6] It is believed, however, that this was so his family could be compensated for his death.

Police investigations

Regardless of what police are investigating, many police stations lack the technology and equipment that are found in nearly all Western stations. Police are unable to utilize many of the scientific- and forensic-based investigative techniques widely used in other parts of the world. Many local patrols do not have cameras, cars or computers, much less any of the more nuanced equipment that is necessary for something like DNA analysis. Some officers even still use finger cuffs because they do not have handcuffs.

Moreover, one extremely common method of investigation is actually illegal. Under both Chinese and, arguably, international law, it is illegal to torture a confession out of someone. Chinese law makes any confession obtained through torture inadmissible in court, but the police allegedly frequently torture suspects or witnesses. Officers have also been known to arrest people who are expected to give testimony that either the police or other government officials would rather not have come out. In an effort to combat these widespread practices and in light of a prominent case of forced confession, the government announced that it would be recording interrogations.[7] The incident spurring this reform was a man being released after serving 11 years for the murder of his wife – only after the wife turned out to be alive was the man released. The man's arresting officer killed himself after it was revealed that he had tortured the suspect for a confession.[8]

Governing law

One of the laws governing the police is the People's Police Law of the People's Republic of China. Article 26 lays out the basic requirements to becoming an officer, including 'to be a citizen who has reached the age of 18; to endorse the Constitution of the People's Republic of China; to have fine political and professional quality and good conduct; to be in good health; to have an educational background of senior middle school or above; [and] to become a people's policeman out of his or her own volition'. If an applicant has 'been subjected to criminal punishment for commission of a crime or been discharged from public employment', however, he or she will not be admitted to the force.[9] Though it may seem this clause is to ensure criminals are not recruited to the police, it also means that anyone convicted of political crimes or dismissed from state employment for questioning the CPC is prohibited from joining the force.

According to Article 2, the police are required to 'safeguard State security, maintain public order, protect citizens' personal safety and freedom and their legal property, protect public property, and prevent, stop and punish illegal and criminal activities'. In addition to being the public security forces on the street and in police stations, the police work in 'State security organs, prisons and organs in charge of re-education through labor, as well as judicial policemen working in the People's Courts and the People's Procuratorates'.[10] The concept of re-education through labor is addressed later in the chapter.

The police who work in the main public security organs are tasked with a variety of duties:

> to prevent, stop and investigate illegal and criminal activities; to maintain public order and stop acts that endanger public order; to ensure traffic safety, maintain traffic order and deal with traffic accidents; to organize and carry out fire prevention and control and supervise routine fire protection; to control firearms and ammunition, and keep under surveillance knives, inflammables, explosives, deadly poisons, radioactive materials and other dangerous articles; to administer special trades and professions as provided by laws and regulations; to serve as bodyguards for persons specially designated by the State and protect important places and installations; to keep under control assemblies, processions and demonstrations; to administer affairs of household registration, citizens' nationality, and entry into and exit from the territory, and handle matters concerning aliens' residence and travel within the territory of China; to maintain public order along the border (frontier) areas; to execute criminal punishment with respect to criminals sentenced to public surveillance, criminal detention, or deprived of political rights and criminals serving sentences outside prison, and to exercise supervision over and inspection of criminals who are granted suspension of execution or parole; to supervise and administer the work of protecting the computer information system; to guide and supervise the work of security in State organs, public organizations, enterprises, institutions, and major construction projects; and guide mass organizations such as public security committees in their work of maintaining public order and preventing crime; and other duties as stipulated by laws and regulations.[11]

Moreover, Article 6 requires that police officers do all this in accordance with Chinese law.

Article 9 dictates how officers can interrogate suspects. The law says that interrogations may be done in an effort to maintain public order and as long as the officer has an appropriate certificate. After the interrogation is complete 'the person may be taken to a public security organ for further interrogation upon approval of this public security organ'.[12] For the public security organ to approve prolonged interrogation, the individual to be interrogated must 'be accused of a criminal offense; be suspected of committing an offense on the scene; be suspected of committing an offense and be of unknown identity; [or carry] articles that [were] probably obtained illegally'.[13]

Individuals can be held for a maximum of 24 hours, starting from the minute they enter the public security organ. In special cases, however, interrogation 'may be extended to 48 hours upon approval by the public security organ at or above the county level'[14] if the police determine that they wish to continue to hold the individual for further interrogation or other 'compulsory measures'.[15] If they do not, or if the public security organ cannot make its decision within the allotted time, the individual must be released. In addition, the suspect's family or the organization for which he or she works must be notified if extended interrogation is approved; if it is not, the individual must be released immediately.

Additionally, according to this law, Chinese police cannot hold anyone without informing a family member or employer of the individual's detention.[16] Regardless, arbitrary detention is not uncommon. The law grants police broad administrative detention powers and the ability to detain individuals for extended periods without formal arrest or criminal charges.

Police detention beyond 37 days requires prosecutorial approval of a formal arrest. After arrest, police are authorized to detain a suspect for up to an additional seven months while the case is investigated.[17]

> After the completion of a police investigation, an additional 45 days of detention are allowed for the procuratorate to determine whether to file criminal charges. If charges are filed, authorities can detain a suspect for an additional 45 days before beginning judicial proceedings. In practice police sometimes detain persons beyond the period allowed by law. Pretrial detention periods of a year or longer were common. The law stipulates that detainees be allowed to meet with defense counsel before criminal charges are filed. Police often violated this right.[18]

There are specific things that police officers cannot do, without exception. They may not 'spread statements that damage the prestige of the State... join illegal organizations... take part in such activities as assembly, procession and demonstration... [or] take part in strikes'.[19] While Article 22 lists a set of prohibited activities, it does not adequately define what constitutes an infraction. It is also forbidden to engage in a variety of illegal activities or do police work outside the letter of the law. In addition to spreading statements that damage the prestige of the state, there is no clear definition of what 'other acts in violation of law and discipline' means. Moreover, there is no specification of what the punishment would be if an officer did violate this article.

Re-education through labor

Though China's judicial system is designed to punish criminals, there is also a system of administrative detention that is managed by the police. The re-education through labor (RTL) system can be used to lock up people accused of minor crimes for one to three years. Typical crimes that may be dealt with through RTL instead of the criminal justice system include 'petty theft, prostitution, and trafficking illegal drugs, as well as religious or political dissidents'.[20] Non-judicial panels, known as 'labor re-education panels', may remand persons to RTL camps or other administrative detention for up to three years without trial. If the panel chooses, it can add a further year of detention.[21]

With no checks and balances in place, there is no way to challenge questionable detentions. The detentions themselves have been the subject of many reports, some indicating that many of the people assigned to work camps are forced into political education.[22] The political education aspects of the camps are often accompanied by torture, and occasionally death by torture.[23]

The RTL system, 'in place since the 1950s, was originally used to suppress those whom government deemed counterrevolutionaries. More recently, re-education through labor has proven an effective tool for local authorities to silence opponents.'[24]

In 1998 China signed the International Covenant on Civil and Political Rights (ICCPR), but it has yet to ratify the civil rights treaty. Under Article 9(4) of the ICCPR, the RTL system is a violation of international human rights: 'Anyone who is deprived of his liberty by arrest or detention shall be entitled to take proceedings before a court, in order that that court may decide without delay on the lawfulness of his detention and order his release if the detention is not lawful.' Since China has not yet ratified the convention, it cannot be held responsible under international law. But if the prohibition on extrajudicial detentions is part of customary international law, it does not matter that China has not ratified the ICCPR: if a legal norm has reached the level of customary international law, any country, regardless of if it has signed a treaty, can be held responsible for a violation. We will not go into whether extrajudicial detention has reached such a legally binding status.

Moreover, the Chinese Ministry of Justice, and specifically Wang Gongyi, the vice-director of the Institute of Justice Research, has confirmed that RTL violates the Chinese constitution and the Criminal Procedure Law.[25] Interestingly, however, Wang has also said that the extrajudicial detentions violate the ICCPR, which implies that Wang believes China should be held to the convention's standards.[26]

Tang Hui's case

Tang Hui is the mother of an 11-year-old girl who was raped. The young girl had gone missing for three months in 2006 before she was found at a local spa, where she had been forced into prostitution and was beaten and raped multiple times. In 2008 two suspects in the case were sentenced to death, two more were sentenced to life in prison and a final two were charged with rape and given less-than-life sentences. Tang was extremely upset with the verdict and tried to appeal for harsher sentences, but it took her until June 2012 to have the suspects resentenced to two death penalties, four life sentences and a 15-year sentence for a seventh defendant.

To get the longer sentences, Tang blocked traffic in front of the court building and camped out in the hallways of the courthouse. The public security forces detained her and held that she had disrupted the social order, sentencing her to 18 months of RTL.

Bloggers on the Chinese social hub and microblog Weibo expressed their outrage that a mother who had crusaded for justice for her young daughter had been sentenced to hard labor. The *People's Daily*, a government-run newspaper, reported the investigation and also posted to Weibo saying that 'a country's greatness cannot be solely supported by GDP and Olympic gold medals, but should encompass people's rights and dignity, social fairness and justice'.[27] This progressive take on Tang's detention came as a shock to many, including the netizens, who said that the paper is 'serving the people' at last. In August 2012 Tang was released from a labor camp in Yongzhou, only one week after receiving her 18-month sentence.[28]

There have been indications that the CPC is considering 'reforming' or even abolishing RTL. Meng Jianzhu, chair of the CPC Central Politics and Law Committee, told the NPC Standing Committee in January 2013 that 'the CPC Central Committee has deliberated' the reform and 'the system of re-education through labor is expected to come to a stop this year once the Standing Committee of the National People's Congress (NPC) approves the proposal'.[29] This news was immediately well received by many. Sophie Richardson, China director of Human Rights Watch, commented: 'This decision, if it truly puts an end to Re-Education Through Labor, would be an indisputable step towards establishing rule of law in China. Courageous activists and ordinary citizens have long fought to end this system of arbitrary detention.'[30]

Nevertheless, there are doubts. Professor Jerome Cohen analyzed the true meaning of Meng's statement:

> What did Meng mean? There are many possibilities. Did he simply mean that, in the exercise of its discretion, the police would at least temporarily suspend sending a couple of hundred thousand defenceless people to labour camps each year? Did he also mean that, in the coming months, the more than 300 existing re-education through labour sites would be emptied of their current occupants?

> Or did he mean even less – that the government would only change the name of this notorious punishment but keep it in substance? Ever since its formal establishment in 1957, the police have lobbied tenaciously to retain this instrument of control, which subjects individuals to long-term detention in the name of social 'harmony' without bothering to seek their indictment by prosecutors and trial, conviction, sentencing and appellate review by courts.[31]

Maintaining stability or *weiwen*

High cost of increased spending on police in China

Maintaining stability, or *weiwen* (维稳), is a policy that was first introduced in the 1990s, but it became a priority to the CPC in the preparation for the Beijing Olympics. Initially there was little structure to *weiwen* and very few critiques from either inside or outside the country as the government spent more money on police and increased domestic security. Over the last few years, however, the amount of money spent on maintaining stability has grown tremendously.

In March 2011 the budget for domestic security was more than that spent on the military for the first time ever.[32] At the time, it was estimated that the amount of money set aside for *weiwen* would be RMB624.4 billion ($95 billion); the People's Liberation Army was only to spend RMB601.1 billion ($91.5 billion).[33] Just two years earlier the domestic security budget was RMB514 billion, slightly under the RMB532 billion spent by the military.[34]

In an interview with Reuters, Nicholas Bequelin, a researcher for China Human Rights Watch, said 'there's a vicious circle that more security leads to more security',[35] while a political scientist with Tongji University in Shanghai, Xie Yue, suggested that the 'system is very sensitive to any instability or contention'.[36] In an interview with *The Guardian*, Xie said the increase in spending indicates that it has been difficult to maintain control within China's borders.[37]

A Shanghai paper reported in May 2010 that domestic security spending rose at a faster rate than that for welfare, hospitals and schools.[38] In addition, domestic security often comprised a larger portion of the budget. The increased spending has led some local government officials to force members of local grassroots communities to put millions of yuan into a fund each year.[39] When there is some kind of social unrest or a protest, money is drawn from these funds to help cover domestic security expenses.

A professor from the Chinese Academy of Administration, a university that trains government officials, wrote, 'many local government departments don't put themselves in the shoes of people in hardship and try to solve the fundamental problems at their root'; instead, they are concerned with 'how to increase and maintain security camera systems, how to increase uniformed police and plain clothes security staff'.[40] This is, in part, because many officials' promotions are based on a points system, in which the number of protests is a factor.

As more money is spent on domestic security, funds are increasingly diverted from other sectors, including budgets used to maintain the country's economy. Of course, with funding disappearing, more people will likely grow restless, increasing the need for domestic security officials to maintain stability. This is creating a cycle in which increased spending on *weiwen* will lead to an increased need for *weiwen*. As one observer has noted, 'the current model of stability has reached the point where it cannot continue'.[41] It has also been said that 'China swaddles all its big meetings, events and sensitive dates with police and guards to scare off trouble-makers, extinguish protests and project power.'[42] Ultimately, the government is terrified of anything that threatens its power over the people.

The expenses associated with the deep-seeded 'stability' that the CPC is trying to portray may soon lead to social unrest. According to a political scientist at the Chinese Academy of Social Sciences, Yu Jianrong, 'What may happen in China in the future is that there are more outbreaks of local turmoil.'[43]

The system of maintaining stability falls under the mandate of the Central Politics and Law Committee of the CPC's Central Committee. It was determined that this committee was the appropriate place for *weiwen* because it mostly involved security issues and the Central Politics and Law Committee is charged with oversight of the internal security system, law enforcement agencies and judiciary. Since the ramp-up to the 2008 Olympics, maintaining stability has become a large part of the committee's work.

In a general sense, maintaining stability has given police wide authority to achieve their goals – in effect, police can use any tool at their disposal in this effort. Those involved with maintaining stability are only responsible to the CPC, and there is no or little supervision of the tools and approaches they use in attaining their goals. Ironically, these forces have little or no incentive actually to achieve stability, because they themselves will be rendered useless should real stability be established. The jobs, funding, power and influence of the forces maintaining stability all depend on a constant instable state. This sounds counterintuitive at first, but it is logical: police and other domestic security officers are being incentivized to prod and stir social unrest so they can then move in to create the veneer of stability and contentment. This is one of the reasons why police have little interest in resolving crimes or dealing with petitioners' requests for justice. It also is why police have used excessive force with citizens – it drives people into social conflicts or petitioning for police accountability.

The current incentive program for domestic security officers under *weiwen* is similar to one used during the Taiping Rebellion,[44] when the emperor gathered forces to quash unrest among the masses. By paying them in proportion to how many rebels they killed, the emperor created an incentive for his forces to kill innocent civilians without bothering to check if they were actual rebels. Much more recently, this paradox has been replicated with Chen Guangcheng, a human rights attorney. When he was sentenced to house arrest, the government paid local people to guard Chen.[45] The economic benefit of doing this led to hundreds of people coming to stand guard outside his home.

What the *weiwen* system fails to address, however, is where the need for internal security has come from. The official line has left the program up for interpretation by saying that the money is being spent to maintain stability, without defining what stability and instability are or what methods are allowable under *weiwen*. This indicates that the government is using the system as a catch-all for dealing with people it perceives to be dissidents or troublemakers.

'*Guobao*' and 'drinking tea'

The Domestic Security Department (DSD) or *guonei anquan baowei zhidui* (国内安全保卫支队) is often better known by its homonym, 'national treasure' or *guobao* (国保). The department, a part of the police force within the Ministry of Public Security, is very similar to a secret police force. Its reach is felt throughout the police and domestic security system, despite maintaining strict secrecy, though its main responsibility is to watch human rights advocates, political and religious dissidents, petitioners and other groups deemed to be subversive by the Chinese government, whether in the economic, cultural or educational sphere.

The DSD's primary goal is to ensure that the CPC's control is not compromised, the 'regime of the People's Democratic Dictatorship' is maintained and the socialist system of modernization can continue without hindrance. These mandates clearly make anyone who questions the government or could potentially, in the government's eyes, disrupt communist rule a focus of the DSD. The Chinese information site Baidu Baike has listed three groups of people as the primary targets of DSD officers' interrogations:

> People who have social influence – they do not need to be social celebrities, but within China, they have broad social networks or become spokespeople of a group with common experience[, p]eople who have their own distinct views in the economic, cultural and political domain, they possess different views from the authorities or 'main melody' and insist on expressing their views[, p]ossibly related to rights protection – protecting economic rights, such as apartment owners of urban residential blocks or peasants who lost their land; protecting political rights, such as journalists, writers who insist on freedom of the press or freedom of expression, or house church members who maintain their beliefs, or Tibetan Buddhists who support the Dalai Lama.[46]

The DSD is composed of its office and several information-gathering branches that work on a variety of 'subversive' or otherwise questionable groups of people.

To Chinese netizens and others familiar with the political landscape, 'drinking tea' or *hecha* (喝茶) is one of the most common ways in which Domestic Security personnel conduct their work. The *guobao* uses the pretext of inviting someone to drink tea as a way to conduct an informal interrogation. The phrase still has the connotation of being 'summoned and interrogated by the state security police'.[47] An invitation to drink tea follows a relatively standard procedure. The person to be interrogated is approached by two or more members of the *guobao* at either his or her home or work. Sometimes the individual is called up or even stopped in the street, but the actual 'tea' is generally held in police stations. On occasion the interrogation happens in an out-of-the-way and empty office or classroom, or even sometimes in someone's home. These interrogations last up to several hours.[48]

Who are being hecha-ed and for what reasons?

As listed above, a wide variety of people may become of interest to the Domestic Security personnel. DSD officers actively investigate and interrogate those people they believe could cause problems for the country, whether it is for their online messages, going to a memorial for a woman who self-immolated in protest of a governmental demolition project, writing about Tibet, Xinjiang, the Tiananmen Square incident or democracy and freedom, associating oneself with the Jasmine Revolution or signing Charter '08, the charter that led to Liu Xiaobo's arrest and 11-year jail sentence. Other cases which have led to state security police interrogations were for expressing support for the Norwegian Nobel Committee's decision to award the Nobel Peace Prize to Liu Xiaobo, attending or planning to attend events hosted by Ai Weiwei before his arrest and secret detention, and signing online petitions for such causes as the detention of a Uyghur scholar or improving prison management.[49] Sometimes the *guobao* will ask people to *hecha* not because of their own activities but because of the actions of someone close to them. In one instance, a young man was interrogated in his workplace about his roommate's work with a non-governmental organization.[50] The officers also asked the man to spy on his roommate.

In the book *Close Encounters with the Chinese PSB*, the editors Xu Youyu and Hua Ze sought to document why people were asked to drink tea with the *guobao*. Nearly all those interrogated were writers, artists, journalists, activists or lawyers, and many were questioned about activities similar to those listed above, which may be why one of the editors made the bold claim that China has already become a 'police state'.[51]

Internet police

Integral to keeping the restricted access to the internet in place, commonly referred to as the Great Firewall, are the internet police. With over 50,000 people working in this force in bureaus in 500 different cities, the officers scout around the web to find people who have committed internet crimes. The material that is considered illegal under Chinese restrictions is reactionary, harmful or pornographic. Because the job does not have an aspect of danger or publicity to it, many internet police are plain-clothes officers who appear like any other science and technology professionals. These officers, however, rely on the same investigation skills that are necessary to solve crimes.

The internet police are mainly responsible for what could be the largest number of cyber-dissidents jailed in the world. Because many of these individuals were found guilty of internet crimes, such as signing online petitions, communicating with foreign groups that are deemed hostile to Chinese authority, challenging regulations or demanding overall improvements for the Chinese people, the internet police have played a large role in their arrests and convictions.

These actions help to create a controlled set of information available to Chinese citizens. Despite the widespread restrictions, there is no general internet censorship law; rather, all regulations come from the propaganda department of the CPC, but are enforced by provincial branches of the state-run internet service providers.

Detention, torture and extrajudicial killings

Chinese police have relatively little oversight, giving them tremendous power to do whatever they want, whether as part of an investigation or outside official business. This unchecked power has, unfortunately, led to numerous reports of human rights abuses.[52] Human rights scholars, as well as American researchers with the US Department of State, have compiled a considerable number of serious violations.

For example, Chinese police are known to hold people secretly and participate in disappearances. This practice is prohibited by both Chinese law and international human rights law. While these actions are currently illegal, some government officials have made proposals to make disappearances and arbitrary detention legal under Chinese law and for the law to apply retroactively.

Two of the most famous cases of disappearances involved human and civil rights activists. The lawyer Gao Zhisheng, who had previously represented Christians and members of the Falun Gong, was finally freed from secret detention on 16 December 2011 more than two years after he was forcibly disappeared in August 2009.[53] Though released from secret detention, he was sent to prison for three years after he allegedly violated the conditions of his parole as part of his five-year suspended sentence. Gao's disappearance had garnered considerable worldwide attention and was the focus of many human rights organizations' campaigns and internet-based petitions.

The second infamous disappearance of a human rights advocate is that of Hada, an ethnic Mongolian activist from Inner Mongolia. He, his wife and his son were arrested and continue to be held in secret detention without ever appearing in front of a judge or even being formally charged with a crime.[54] Hada had previously been imprisoned for 15 years for founding the Southern Mongolia Democracy Alliance, and was freed in 2010. This organization asked for a referendum on Inner Mongolia, and Hada was convicted of espionage and separatism.

In addition, some ten people who were involved in the 4 June 1989 Tiananmen Square demonstrations are still in prison.[55] This figure was provided by the Duihua Foundation, a human rights organization, but some people believe the number of former student activists imprisoned is actually much higher.

Beyond the disappearances, there have been a number of arbitrary arrests and detentions linked to public security forces.[56] Though police have the ability to hold people administratively without ever arresting them, a proposed change to the criminal procedure laws would give police the power to detain people extralegally if they are suspected of crimes involving terrorism, state secrets or extraordinary corruption.

In 1988 China ratified the UN Convention against Torture and Other Cruel, Inhuman or Degrading Treatment or Punishment, making torture and many other forms of punishment illegal in China. This meant China had to adopt legislation enshrining this ban on torture and degrading punishment. As it currently stands, Chinese law prevents police and prison guards from physically abusing, torturing, beating or encouraging or forcing others to beat, or insulting the dignity of prisoners and detainees.[57] A 2010 law also prevents evidence or confessions gained through torture from being admitted into evidence in court. Despite these protections in place, many prisoners and detainees have reported extensive physical and psychological abuse,[58] including being beaten and hit, denied sleep, given electric shocks and forced to sit staring at the wall for hours.

Though any individual or group could conceivably be tortured, generally religious and political dissidents are more likely to be abused by public security forces.[59] One lawyer, Jiang Tianyong, was taken into police custody on 19 February 2011 and released in April.[60] He was never formally arrested or charged with a crime, but for two months he was tortured. He was forced to sit without moving for up to 15 hours at a time. Throughout his detention he was repeatedly interrogated, and was severely beaten during his first two days of detention.

In February 2012 the UN Committee against Torture, the investigative body attached to the convention, issued its concerns about the use of torture in China. It noted that members of the Chinese police forces were consistently using torture to get information and confessions from people, in violation of both Chinese and international laws. The committee also found that while the Chinese government was trying to address the problem through the criminal justice system, much of the torture that was happening was during administrative detentions or in the RTL system.

Another major site of torture within China is *ankang* (安康) or psychiatric hospitals. These are 22 high-security mental health facilities that held more than 40,000 people from 1998 until May 2010,[61] when an official with the Ministry of Public Security, the government agency that runs the hospitals, announced that it was only appropriate for individuals who had demonstrated some kind of criminal behavior to be admitted to them.[62] Of course, because political crimes are considered criminal behavior under Chinese law, political and religious dissidents, members of the Falun Gong and the Chinese Democracy Party, and those who frequently petition the government may still be admitted to *ankang* centers.

These mental health facilities were officially designed to house the criminally insane, but the ministry has involuntarily detained dissidents alongside individuals with serious mental health issues. There have been reports that individuals at *ankang* facilities have been subjected to forced psychiatric treatment, electric-shock therapy and involuntary medication.[63] The rules surrounding how an individual is committed to an *ankang* facility are shrouded in secrecy and there does not appear to be a way for detainees to question or protest a designation of mental illness.

One example of an individual being detained in a psychiatric hospital is that of petitioner Hu Dongsheng. Hu was detained, physically abused and forcibly returned to Hefei, Anhui province, where he was quickly committed to an *ankang* facility.[64] Hu had been at the Beijing office of the Ministry of Public Security on 29 April 2011, petitioning people's complaints of a forced demolition, when he was detained. Nor was this the first time Hu had been sent to a psychiatric hospital for excessive petitioning.

In addition to detention and torture, there have been reports of extrajudicial killings of police detainees. Government officials in Wukan, Guangdong province, asked villagers to designate representatives to settle a local dispute.[65] The villagers were protesting the government's sale of village land, and the representatives tried to negotiate with officials. Ultimately the negotiations failed, and police arrested the representatives on 11 December 2011. On 13 December government officials announced that one representative had died in custody, allegedly of a heart attack, but his relatives say he had been tortured and beaten to death. This was, of course, denied by the local procuratorate.[66]

Arbitrary, extrajudicial and unlawful killings are some of the most severe of human rights abuses, and a lack of documented custodial deaths calls into question China's desire or ability to rein in excessive police force. In addition, the lack of documentation means that the number of people who died in custody is unknown and could potentially be much larger than the number of officially documented custodial deaths.

Yang Jia case

Yang Jia was an unemployed young man whose life was changed while in police custody. Though many believe he crossed a line when he killed six police officers on 1 July 2008, some in China consider him to be a 'hero'.[67]

Yang's first encounter with police was in early 2007 in Shanxi province. The 28-year-old was stopped by local police as he was waiting in a train station. The officers took the young man to a police station for an interrogation, during which they repeatedly hit Yang, knocking out his front tooth. After he was eventually released, Yang turned to petitioning, both for his medical expenses and for a legal issue that involved his mother. He repeatedly petitioned for himself and for her, so much so that she was detained for two weeks in March 2007 because police said the petitioning had become unlawful.

An already frustrated Yang was again detained by police in October 2007.[68] He was visiting Shanghai, and police from the Zhabei district police station brought him in for questioning, alleging he had stolen a bicycle. Yang defiantly told police that he had rented the bicycle (which was true) and was unaware that it had been stolen. During his interrogation he was severely beaten and heavily bruised on his back and arms. He also testified during his trial that officers had insulted him during his interrogation.

Upon his release, he tried to file complaints and petition for redress again.[69] Yang wanted officers to admit that they were wrong, and also petitioned for compensation. When police finally responded to his petitions several months after the incident, they determined that he had been reasonably treated and officers had a 'legal basis' for their actions. Many believe that it was the repeated physical abuse and harassment by police and the humiliation of their justifications that led Yang to his actions on 1 July.

On that day, Yang returned to Shanghai and the Zhabei police station with a homemade explosive, a hammer and a long knife.[70] When he first walked into the police station he detonated and threw the explosive, distracting the guards, then cut the throats of four police officers before going to the upper floors. There he killed two more officers and injured five others. He was stopped when police contained him and trained their guns on him. He allegedly told police, 'Just shoot me, I've had enough.'[71]

Yang's trial was postponed because of the 2008 Summer Olympics.[72] Eventually, on 27 August 2008, he was tried and convicted in one hour during a closed-door trial at Shanghai No. 2 Intermediate People's Court. Four days after his trial, Xinhua confirmed that Yang was convicted of premeditated murder and had been sentenced to death. His sentence was upheld by an appellate court, and it was determined that Yang was of sound mind on 20 October 2008. Yang's case was eventually brought to the Supreme People's Court, where his sentence was reviewed and confirmed. He was executed on 26 November 2008.

Wen Qiang case

Unlike Yang Jia, Wen Qiang was a police commissioner who was tried and executed for participating in organized crime.[73] In Chongqing much of the city's organized crime worked in tandem with police officers, there was corruption between city CPC leaders and the gangs, and there were gang members and members of organized crime in public offices and positions of power. An article in *The Telegraph* noted that police stations 'were actually the centre of the prostitution, gambling and drugs rackets'.[74] To uphold the façade that the police were not working with, for and under organized crime lords, some gangsters would occasionally be arrested and sent to prison, but it was reported that the imprisoned gang members suffered no hardships. Organized crime in the city was so entrenched that innocent bystanders would be killed and dismembered and the police would do nothing.

In the midst of all of this was Wen, the former police commissioner. In 2009 the criminals' grip on the city began to loosen as the Chongqing gang trials started. Led by the police chief, Wang Lijun, and the CPC chief of Chongqing municipality, Bo Xilai, the trials lasted for two years. By their end in 2011, 4,781 people had been arrested. Wen was one of those, along with 19 people suspected of being crime bosses, hundreds of gang members, corrupt CPC officials, police officers and six district police chiefs.[75]

Wen and his wife were put on trial in 2010. Wen was tried for corruption and rape, while his wife, Zhou Xiaoya, was charged with taking bribes.[76] Wen was eventually found guilty of raping a university student, not accounting for all of his assets and offering police protection to the Chongqing triads in exchange for RMB16 million ($2.3 million). His wife was also found guilty of accepting bribes, and there was little doubt that both would be convicted. Wen was sentenced to death, while his wife was sentenced to eight years in prison.

Wang Lijun case

Wang Lijun, a former vice-mayor and head of the Public Security Bureau of Chongqing, has also faced trouble with the law, despite being one of the people instrumental in bringing down Wen Qiang and others in the Chongqing gang trials.

Wang's troubles began in February 2012, when he was quickly demoted from his position as vice-mayor of Chongqing after he fled to the US consulate in Chengdu to tell American officials of the death of British businessman Neil Heywood.[77] In telling staff at the consulate of Heywood's murder and its cover-up, and implicating Gu Kailai, wife of his boss Chongqing CPC secretary Bo Xilai, in the death, Wang sought help from the Americans. Whether he was seeking to defect or trying to escape his boss, Wang spent 24 hours in the consulate, starting on 6 February.

When Wang left the consulate, he was escorted by members of the Ministry of State Security to Beijing. Officially, his actions at the consulate were termed a 'serious political incident' by the government.[78]

As Wang not only reported that Gu had killed Heywood, but that Bo had played a role in covering up the murder, Bo's career was immediately in jeopardy.[79] In addition, the until-then positive regime that Bo had put in place, termed the 'Chongqing model' and the 'red culture movement', was at risk of being attacked. Bo had grown famous for instituting the 'Praise Red Communism, Crack Down on Black Crime' or *chang hong, da hei* (唱红打黑) campaign.

The Wang Lijun case reveals several interesting contradictions. For years, Wang had been seen as publicly anti-American and a strong proponent of traditional Maoism.[80] When he felt threatened, however, Wang attempted to abandon communism, the CPC and China by looking for protection at the US consulate.

In addition, Wang served as a police chief in a major city and held numerous titles and guest law professorships, but he was largely uneducated.[81] He had completed middle school, but had no further formal education. His unfamiliarity with the law was demonstrated in thinking that the United States allowed for diplomatic asylum. It appears that Wang thought he could seek asylum from Bo by fleeing to the consulate in Chengdu, but diplomatic asylum is not the same thing as territorial asylum, in which an oppressed individual flees his or her home country and arrives in the United States seeking asylum or refuge. Rather, diplomatic asylum is the granting of refuge to an individual who shows up at a consulate or embassy. This kind of asylum generally causes more tensions and problems with the host country than a diplomat or his or her country is willing to endure, and thus such asylum is rarely recognized.

Wang's closed-door trial for treason began on 13 August 2012.[82] In addition to Wang, four other senior police officials, Guo Weiguo, Li Yang, Wang Pengfei and Wang Zhi, were put on trial for covering up Heywood's murder. On 10 August 2012 the story of how the officers tried to hide Gu and Bo's connections to murder emerged. The officers had hidden evidence, altered interviews and interrogations and, ultimately, had agreed that Heywood had died from too much alcohol.

Chengdu Intermediate People's Court found Wang guilty of defection, accepting bribes of at least RMB3 million, abuse of power and bending the law to selfish ends by covering up Heywood's murder by Bo's wife Gu Kailai. The court sentenced Wang to two years' imprisonment for abuse of power, two years for defection, nine years for bribe-taking and seven for bending the law for selfish ends. In total his sentence is 15 years, but he may serve far less if given parole.[83]

Notes

1. US Department of State, Bureau of Democracy, Human Rights and Labor (2011) 'Country reports on human rights practices for 2011: China (includes Tibet, Hong Kong, and Macau)'; available at: *www.state.gov/j/drl/rls/hrrpt/ humanrightsreport/index.htm?dlid=186268* (accessed: 14 September 2013).
2. Ibid.
3. Jeffrey Hays (2012) 'Police in China', factsanddetails.com, April; available at: *http://factsanddetails.com/china.php?itemid=301&catid=8&subcatid=50* (accessed: 14 September 2013).
4. Ibid.
5. Ibid.
6. Chi-Chi Zhang (2009) 'China labeled a martyr after drinking death', *Boston Globe*, 15 December.
7. Hays, note 3 above.
8. Ibid.
9. People's Police Law of the People's Republic of China, Article 24.
10. Ibid., Article 2.
11. Ibid., Article 6.
12. Ibid., Article 9.
13. Ibid.
14. Ibid.
15. Ibid.
16. Ibid.
17. US Department of State, Bureau of Democracy, Human Rights and Labor (2012) 'Country reports on human rights practices for 2012: China'; available at: *www.state.gov/j/drl/rls/hrrpt/humanrightsreport/index.htm?yea r=2012&dlid=204193* (accessed: 14 September 2013).
18. Ibid.
19. People's Police Law of the People's Republic of China, Article 22.
20. Ministry of Public Security (2005) 'Tentative procedures for labor re-education (劳动教养试行办法)', Article 10; available at: *www.mps.gov.cn/n16/n1996 048/n2283084/2286585.html* (accessed: 14 September 2013).
21. State Council of the PRC (2005) 'Additional regulations for labor re-education (国务院关于劳动教养的补充规定)', III; available at: *www.mps. gov.cn/n16/n1996048/n2283084/2286577.html* (accessed: 14 September 2013).
22. Laogai Research Foundation (2013) 'Original documents on display at the Laogai Museum confirming human rights abuses committed by the Chinese

Communist Party'; available at: *www.laogai.org/blog/original-documents-laogai-museum-confirming-abuses* (accessed: 13 August 2013).

23. Ibid.

24. Brian Spegele (2013) 'China labor camps under fire from state think tank', China Real Time Report, *Wall Street Journal*, 7 August; available at: *http://blogs.wsj.com/chinarealtime/2013/08/07/china-labor-camps-under-fire-from-state-think-tank/* (accessed: 13 August 2013).

25. Wu Jiao (2007) 'New law to abolish laojiao system', *China Daily*, 1 March; available at: *www.chinadaily.com.cn/china/2007-03/01/content_816358.htm* (accessed: 14 September 2013).

26. Ibid.

27. *Wall Street Journal* (2012) 'Mother's labor-camp sentence sparks fury', *Wall Street Journal*, 6 August; available at: *http://blogs.wsj.com/chinarealtime/2012/08/06/mother%E2%80%99s-labor-camp-sentence-sparks-fury/* (accessed: 14 September 2013).

28. *China Daily* (2012) 'Mother of young rape victim heads home', *China Daily*, 11 August; available at: *www.chinadaily.com.cn/china/2012-08/11/content_15665833.htm* (accessed: 14 September 2013).

29. Bai Tiantian and Yan Shuang (2013) 'Re-education to be reformed', *Global Times*, 8 January; available at: *www.globaltimes.cn/content/754403.shtml* (accessed: 14 September 2013).

30. Human Rights Watch (2013) 'China: fully abolish re-education through labor', 8 January; available at: *www.hrw.org/node/112283* (accessed: 14 September 2013).

31. Jerome Cohen (2013) 'Is this really the end of re-education through labour?', *South China Morning Post*, 16 January; available at: *www.scmp.com/comment/insight-opinion/article/1128734/really-end-re-education-through-labour* (accessed: 14 September 2013).

32. Chris Buckley (2011) 'Update 2 – China internal security spending jumps past army budget', Reuters, 5 March; available at: *www.reuters.com/article/2011/03/05/china-unrest-idUSTOE72400920110305* (accessed: 17 September 2013).

33. Ibid.

34. Chris Buckley (2010) 'Analysis: China price for stability raises alarm', Reuters, 14 October; available at: *www.reuters.com/article/2010/10/14/uschina-politics-stability-idUSTRE69D12T20101014* (accessed: 14 September 2013).

35. Ibid.

36. Tania Branigan (2011) 'Wen Jiabao makes pledge to China's poor at National People's Congress', *The Guardian*, 5 March; available at: *www.guardian.co.uk/world/2011/mar/05/wen-jiabao-pledges-china-poor* (accessed: 14 September 2013).

37. Ibid.

38. Buckley, note 34 above.

39. Ibid.

40. Ibid.

41. Ibid.

42. Ibid.

43. Ibid.
44. See generally Yung Wing (1909) *My Life in China and America*. New York: Henry Holt & Co., Chapter 6.
45. Keith B. Richburg (2012) 'In Chen's frightened village, surveillance increases, thugs keep outsiders at bay', *Washington Post*, 11 May; available at *http://articles.washingtonpost.com/2012-05-11/world/35458843_1_dongshigu-chen-guangcheng-village* (accessed: 23 August 2013).
46. Baidu Baike is a Wikipedia-style online dictionary/information portal. Its 'The Domestic Security Department' entry was published anonymously in 2010 at: *http://baike.baidu.com/view/2535288.htm* (accessed: 20 December 2011), but this page has been deleted. A copy of the page with English translation is provided by China Digital Times (2010) 'Internal document of the Domestic Security Department of the Public Security Bureau (Part I)', 26 January; available at: *http://chinadigitaltimes.net/2010/01/internal-document-of-the-domestic-security-department-of-the-public-security-bureau-part-i/* (accessed: 17 September 2013).
47. Ibid.
48. See generally Xu Youyu and Hua Ze (eds) (2012) *Close Encounters with the Chinese PSB* (遭遇警察). Hong Kong: Open Press.
49. Quoted in Yaxue Cao (2012) 'Drinking tea with the state security police – who is being questioned', Seeing Red in China, 1 March; available at: *http://seeingredinchina.com/2012/03/01/drinking-tea-with-the-state-security-police-who-is-being-questioned/* (accessed: 25 August 2013).
50. Ibid.
51. Ibid.
52. US Department of State, note 1 above.
53. Ibid.
54. Ibid.
55. Ibid.
56. Ibid.
57. Ibid.
58. Ibid.
59. Ibid.
60. Ibid.
61. Ibid.
62. Ibid.
63. Ibid.
64. Ibid.
65. Ibid.
66. Ibid.
67. Eva Pils (undated) 'Yang Jia and China's unpopular criminal justice system', Human Rights in China; available at: *www.hrichina.org/crf/article/3702* (accessed: 25 August 2013).
68. Ibid.
69. Ibid.
70. Ibid.
71. Ibid.
72. Ibid.

73. BBC (2009) 'Police held in China gang probe', BBC News, 21 August; available at: *http://news.bbc.co.uk/2/hi/asia-pacific/8213357.stm* (accessed: 25 August 2013).

74. Malcolm Moore (2009) 'China corruption trial exposes capital of graft', *Daily Telegraph*, 17 October; available at: *www.telegraph.co.uk/news/worldnews/asia/china/6357024/China-corruption-trial-exposes-capital-of-graft.html* (accessed: 17 September 2013).

75. Eric Baculinao (2010) 'Will China's corruption crackdown spread?', NBC News, 2 February; available at: *http://worldblog.nbcnews.com/_news/2010/02/02/4376280-will-chinas-corruption-crackdown-spread?lite* (accessed: 25 August 2013).

76. Ibid.

77. Sharon Lafraniere, John F. Burns and Jonathan Ansfield (2012) 'Death of a Briton is thrust to center of China scandal', *New York Times*, 10 April; available at: *www.nytimes.com/2012/04/11/world/asia/detained-party-official-facing-ouster-from-politburo.html?pagewanted=all&_r=0* (accessed: 25 August 2013).

78. Lin Feng and Wen Hua (2012) 'Punishment of Bo Xilai foretells a greater political storm', *Epoch Times*, 11 April; available at: *www.theepochtimes.com/n2/china-news/punishment-of-bo-xilai-foretells-a-greater-political-storm-218661-all.html* (accessed: 25 August 2013).

79. Ibid.

80. Willy Lam (2012) 'Hu draws blood in Wang Lijun scandal', Asia Times Online, 6 March; available at: *www.atimes.com/atimes/China/NC06Ad02.html* (accessed: 25 August 2013).

81. China Vitae (undated) 'Wang Lijun: biography'; available at: *www.chinavitae.com/biography/Wang_Lijun/bio* (accessed: 25 August 2013).

82. Malcolm Moore (2012) 'Neil Heywood scandal: Wang Lijun "has been secretly put on trial"', *Daily Telegraph*, 13 August; available at: *www.telegraph.co.uk/news/worldnews/asia/china/9472663/Neil-Heywood-scandal-Wang-Lijun-has-been-secretly-put-on-trial.html* (accessed: 17 September 2013).

83. Tania Branigan (2012) 'China jails Bo Xilai's fomer police chief Wang Lijun for 15 years', *The Guardian*, 24 September; available at: *www.guardian.co.uk/world/2012/sep/24/china-police-chief-wanglijun-jailed* (accessed: 17 September 2013).

The lawyers

Abstract: This chapter looks at lawyers and their role within the legal system. It starts with the history of the legal profession and its evolution within the People's Republic of China, including the birth of the current profession following the promulgation of relatively recent laws. There is also a discussion of legal education and regulation of the legal profession. The chapter ends with profiles of several well-known lawyers.

Key words: lawyers, legal profession, legal education, Zhang Sizhi, Jiang Ping, Pu Zhiqiang.

Lawyers as a 'bad element'

On 31 July 2012 an edition of the *People's Daily* reported on the need for internal reforms, but also cautioned the United States not to stir up trouble through grassroots groups.[1] Netizens point to one paragraph in particular:

> with 'Internet freedom' as its slogan, [the Americans] will attack 'top down' governance in order to push forward the traditional model of liberal democracy; through the use of... [various] social groups as the core forces, they will push for a 'bottom-up' approach to Chinese governance from the grassroots to lay a foundation for changing China...[2]

Human and civil rights lawyers, those involved in underground religion (family churches and Catholics who are loyal to the Vatican rather than attending Chinese-government-sponsored churches), dissidents, internet heroes (public intellectuals who frequently use the internet as a forum to criticize the government) and disadvantaged groups (migrant workers, unemployed city residents, senior citizens) were labeled as the most unstable segments and easily manipulated by foreign forces.

Netizens quickly dubbed these groups as the new five black categories or *heiwulei* (黑五类), the term for the five groups singled out by Mao for suppression in the 1950s and 1960s.[3] Under Mao, the five black categories were landlords, rich farmers, anti-revolutionists, bad elements and right-wingers. During the Cultural Revolution, Mao insisted that these groups constituted bourgeois elements that were infiltrating the government and society at large, in an attempt to revert China back to capitalism.

The *People's Daily* article deeming lawyers to be one of the five black categories is premised on the belief that the United States is 'penetrating China's lowest classes'.[4] Moreover, it presumes that the United States and the West are trying to influence these five groups in an effort to strengthen their influence in Chinese society. In essence, the article demonstrates the strong hostility toward lawyers, especially those who represent other members of the *heiwulei*; as such, lawyers are seen as rebels and troublemakers.[5]

History of the legal profession in China

Historically there were no lawyers in China, but 'litigation masters' or *songshi* (讼师) and 'knife-pen men' or *daobi xiansheng* (刀笔先生). Though not lawyers, they were still considered part of the legal profession, and were thus the subject of resentment and hostility. These early professionals were able to advise litigants on a case and draft pleadings, but there was no right to represent their clients formally.[6] In fact, it was not until the start of the twentieth century that China reformed its legal system and allowed lawyers to appear in court. Prior to that, there were no formal legal education or legal training programs, and lawyers were not allowed into traditional courts.[7]

The reason why lawyers have long been disrespected is because the Chinese have generally viewed law as a tool of the state, an instrument to rule and punish.[8] The law was not meant to serve as the means for one person to assert a claim against another, nor was it to challenge the government or assert individual rights. Individual rights were not recognized in imperial China.

It was after foreign nations started influencing China, specifically after the First Opium War in 1842, that lawyers began to appear in China. Western lawyers started working within the European concessions and consular courts before finally finding themselves in Chinese courts as well. These attorneys represented both foreigners and Chinese citizens within the courts, yet some Chinese people started to petition the emperor to develop a means of producing Chinese lawyers. One minister for legal reform during the late Qing dynasty, Shen Jiaben, was concerned that foreign lawyers would not honestly aid a Chinese client if it meant hurting the lawyer's fellow countryman. Shen believed that a system of Chinese lawyers would be an effective way to give Chinese citizens a fair hand in trials against Westerners.

It took the 1911 revolution and the overthrow of the imperial system for the legal profession to begin. Lawyers were first recognized by a series of regulations in 1912, the first year of the Republic of China. These early regulations, modeled on Japanese statutes, detailed a lawyer's function and what training and qualifications were required of him. Most importantly, however, the regulations specifically authorized lawyers to appear in Chinese courts.[9]

These laws laid down the basic rules for lawyers. They had to be above the age of 20, graduates of universities of politics and law, and to have passed the lawyer's examination. Initially women were not allowed to become lawyers or practice law; a lawyer also had to be a member of a lawyers' association. The provisional regulations laid down a lawyer's functions in court: they could appear in ordinary and special courts, either appointed by a client or by court order, which marked the first time that lawyers were specifically authorized to appear in Chinese courts. Then in 1917, when the regulations were revised, lawyers were permitted to draft contracts and wills for clients and enter into contracts and other legal documents on a client's behalf.[10]

Between 1927 and 1944 the Republic of China government allowed women to become lawyers.[11] The minimum age was also raised to 21 and the rights of lawyers' associations were expanded to include making proposals to the minister of justice on legal reform. Finally, special procedures for handling the punishment of lawyers were established. These laws constituted the basis of the lawyering system during the Republic of China period and are the origin of the lawyering system in Taiwan.[12]

Lawyers in the PRC

Following the revolution that put the Chinese Communist Party in power, there were three distinct stages of development within the legal profession.

1950 to 1957

The legal system of the Republic of China was abolished following the start of the People's Republic in 1949.[13] The provisional constitution not only abandoned the laws and regulations governing lawyers, but also stripped the country of the entire Kuomintang legal system. Those individuals who had been lawyers in the Republic of China were largely condemned as members of the exploiting class and 'only a few lawyers were upright and fair-minded and dared to speak for the people'.[14] The majority were disbanded under the Circular Concerning the Abolition of Underground Lawyers and Litigation Tricksters (1950), which was issued by an early Ministry of Justice. The circular stopped lawyers' work and disbanded their organizations. With this clean start, the CPC promulgated a new legal system and profession. The General Principles of People's Courts (1950), the Organic Law of the People's Courts (1954) and the Constitution (1954) all contained rules and regulations for lawyers.[15]

Starting in 1954, a handful of large cities, including Beijing and Shanghai, created clinics in which people could receive legal advice, marking some of the first legal work being done in the PRC.[16] The Report Concerning Establishing Our Country's Lawyers' Work was a series of recommendations submitted by the Ministry of Justice in January 1956 that requested a lawyer system regulated by national legislation. These recommendations led to the Provisional Regulations on Lawyers in 1957, and by June of that year there were 817 legal advice offices created across China,[17] and 19 lawyers' associations responsible for 2,500 full-time lawyers and 300 adjunct lawyers scattered across 33 cities.[18]

Though the legal profession had started, lawyers were restricted in what they could do. There were no private law firms. Rather, attorneys were considered to be public servants and provided criminal defense and advised and represented individuals in civil lawsuits. Lawyers were also able to create legal documents for individuals.[19]

1957 to 1977

The legal profession was still relatively young in 1957, but it also was at a turning point. As a precursor to the Cultural Revolution, the Anti-Rightist Movement was a time in which the number of law schools and lawyers started to fall. The decline was due in part to public sentiment toward attorneys during the period. Lawyers were considered to be rightists, and many were exiled to the countryside for their suspected capitalist leanings. Finally, in 1959, the Ministry of Justice and lawyers' organizations were dismantled.

1978 to the present

The foundational documents for the current legal system in China include the 1978 Constitution, the 1979 Organic Law of the People's Courts, the Criminal Law and the Criminal Procedure Law. These created a system of advocacy and a right of defense for criminal suspects.[20] But by 1979 there were still very few lawyers – only 19 registered in Beijing, and just a few hundred in the rest of China.[21]

The defunct Ministry of Justice was also revived in 1979, and tasked with regulating and administering the legal profession. In August 1980 the Standing Committee of the National People's Congress issued the Provisional Regulations of the People's Republic of China on Lawyers, which listed the qualifications, organization, rights and responsibilities of lawyers.[22] Interestingly, the provisions listed lawyers as 'legal workers of the State', making them part of the governmental bureaucracy.[23] The provisions also created 'legal advisory offices' that served as the business organizations where lawyers worked.[24]

These regulations set forth what lawyers were and were not able to do. A lawyer's role was defined as providing assistance to citizens, businesses and the government.[25] They were permitted to act as representatives in civil lawsuits or alternative dispute resolution, legal advisors and criminal defense lawyers; they were also permitted to provide non-litigation support, such as advice and opinions and completing transactional work. The regulations updated the qualifications to become a lawyer: unlike in most countries, lawyers needed to show their dedication to China before receiving permission to practice law.[26] Attorneys needed to 'cherish the PRC, support the socialist system, have the right to vote and stand for election and, moreover, had to be examined and approved by the Bureau of Justice Office affiliated to the provincial government'.[27]

These regulations have allowed the legal profession to grow rapidly. Between 1979 and 1984 there were an estimated 11,000 lawyers in the country, and today there are approximately 200,000.[28] Until 1988 the only place in which lawyers could practice were the state-owned law firms, but in 1988 a cooperative law firm was started in Baoding.[29] As more private law firms appeared on the scene, the Ministry of Justice promulgated the Trial Scheme for Cooperative Law Firms in May 1988.[30] This regulation allowed for private, cooperative law firms, and the Proposals on Deepening Lawyers' Reform of 1993 legalized partnership law firms.[31]

The scope of legal practice has also expanded considerably. Initially, lawyers were quite limited in what they were allowed to do, but regulations have been loosened and lawyers are now practicing in matters of contracts, property, intellectual property and family law, among others. The legal field now encompasses acting as an agent *ad litem* in trademark cases, contract negotiation and patents and copyrights. Within the larger cities, many lawyers work in highly profitable fields of the law.

The diversity of legal practice is probably due to the fact that the amount of legislation has been growing, making it more difficult for individual lawyers to have in-depth knowledge of all fields of the law. When there were relatively few laws and only a few sources of legislation and regulations, lawyers were usually able to develop a sufficient proficiency across all the branches of law, enough to have a general practice.

In a fitting return to China, a number of North American, European and Asian lawyers have moved there. Unlike during imperial China, however, these attorneys are unable to represent clients directly or sign legal documents.[32] Rather, foreign-trained attorneys are only allowed to serve in an advisory capacity. To be able to sign a legal document, they must work with licensed Chinese lawyers.

In 1992 foreign law firms were first allowed into the PRC, and there are now more than 200 within China.[33] The Regulations on the Management of Foreign Law Firms' Representative Offices and the Implementing Rules for the Regulations on the Management of Representative Offices of Foreign Law Firms, passed into law in December 2001 and July 2002 respectively, are the two primary sets of laws governing foreign lawyers. In addition, foreign attorneys are monitored by the Ministry of Justice.

Legal education

The first law school in China, the Legal Political School, was founded in 1907, and by 1909 there were over 40 schools spread across the country.[34] Most of their graduates went into governmental or judicial positions rather than establishing themselves in professional practice.

Higher education in China today

China's higher education is slowly transforming from a unified, centralized, closed and static system into one characterized by more diversification, decentralization, openness and dynamism, stimulating the involvement of local governments and non-state sectors. Most higher education institutions are public bodies, and the higher education branch of government mandates that Chinese institutions of higher education report to a supervising government agency, whether central or provincial. School administrators are also appointed by supervising government agencies, and administrators, faculty and staff are state employees. There are a few private institutions, strictly supervised by local education authorities to ensure they conform to the basic standards of quality.

The number of schools has been rapidly expanding since the 1990s, but the select few 'key schools' are the only institutions of higher education that receive a considerable amount of funding from the government. The other schools continue to be underfunded, putting a strain on teaching resources for current students. The explosion of schools has also led to an increase in the number of college graduates, driving higher unemployment for graduates.

Legal education overview

In mainland China there are two fields of study within the law: broadly defined 'law' (or 'political science and law') and narrowly defined 'legal studies'. The more expansive 'law' includes legal studies, Marxist theory, sociology, political science and public security studies (law enforcement). The narrower 'legal studies' only covers jurisprudence, legal history and domestic, international and other laws.

There are also varieties within Chinese legal education. Beyond traditional undergraduate and graduate legal studies, there are also 'middle professional' and an in-service training certificate through the National Judges College and National Procurators Colleges.[35] Ultimately, however, the purpose of university departments of legal studies is to prepare students for careers in government, teaching and research. This differs from the emphasis of political and law schools, which is to train practitioners to serve in procuratorates, public security organs, courts, law firms and the organs of judicial administration.[36]

A brief history of legal education

The history of legal education in the PRC runs parallel to that of other legal institutions. In 1952 there were only four law schools and four law departments, but a system of legal education was gradually developed from the Soviet model. Soviet legal experts brought educational materials and aided Chinese scholars in teaching. During the Cultural Revolution (1966–1976) all college and university admissions were suspended. For ten years the system of higher education in China was demolished, but in 1977 and 1978 eight law schools reopened.[37] During the next four years 30 universities were approved by the Ministry of Education to establish new legal studies departments.[38]

Since the first law schools opened in 1952 there has been tremendous growth in the number of legal departments across the county. By 2001, 292 law schools and law departments at undergraduate and graduate levels were in operation.[39] This number almost doubled within four years: there were 559 law schools and law departments in 2005; and by 2010 there were more than 600.[40] There are approximately 300,000 undergraduate and graduate law students in China, and the number is growing by 15 percent per year.[41]

The Ministry of Education oversees the universities and colleges that produce lawyers. Within the ministry, the Higher Education Bureau is in charge of accrediting the individual programs, textbooks, curricula, how schools evaluate a student's work and how they allocate their funding. The Guidance Commission of Legal Education (also a subsidiary of the Ministry of Education) supervises and gives advice on legal education.[42] There are a few colleges and universities that do not report to the national Ministry of Education; these institutions are supervised by the Municipal Commissions of Education. Finally, the Ministry of Justice and its subsidiaries grant licenses to practice law, observe attorneys and administer the national judicial examination.

Law schools

Law schools are accredited by the Ministry of Education or provincial-level bureaus of education when a university submits an application on behalf of its law school or legal studies department. Because there is no standard body that accredits all the universities, there are discrepancies in accreditation processes. This has led to a focus on bureaucratic procedures and less of an emphasis on the quality of teaching and education. Outside a few long-standing law schools, most legal education programs are small in scale.

A law program is accredited as long as the college or university has been accredited by an educational authority. This semi-automatic recognition is problematic, because it gives too much discretion and authority over the law program's approval to the college or university administration, which is not an expert in legal education.

Law programs have 16 compulsory subjects: legal theory, Chinese legal history, constitutional law, administrative law and law of administrative litigation, criminal law, criminal procedure, civil procedure, civil law, commercial law, economic law, intellectual property, private international law, international law, international economic law, labor and social security. Traditionally, law programs have placed a greater emphasis on lectures than on discussion, and focused more on doctrines than on case studies and more on presentation of a systematic body of knowledge than on the development of analytical skills. Some programs have departed from these teaching methods, however, recognizing that the traditional mode of legal education does not adequately meet the needs of legal practice. In an attempt to address the needs of practicing lawyers better, more attention is being paid in the leading law schools to case studies, practical lawyering skills, drafting and clinical education.

There remain several major issues within Chinese legal education – a lack of general liberal arts education and practical skills training, for one. In addition, there is a focus on political training, but little time is spent on professional responsibility – only a handful of law schools have professional responsibility courses. Some of these concerns surrounding Chinese legal education can likely be traced to the ambivalent objective of the law and lawyering within the PRC.

Western influence on Chinese legal education

In 1915 the Comparative Law School of China was established in Shanghai by the American lawyer and missionary Charles W. Rankin.[43] It was patterned after the US model of legal education, focusing on Anglo-American law. Since this early American influence, there has been a progressive opening of Chinese legal education:

> Over the past several decades, a salvo of development agencies, donors, NGOs, educational programs, law schools, and academics, many from the U.S., have sought to reform the Chinese legal system

and, particularly, legal education. At the same time, education ministries of the People's Republic of China (PRC), increasingly mindful of the status of Chinese education in a global market, have adapted aspects of the U.S. legal education model in China.[44]

The interest in comparative legal studies is not one way, however. There are currently over 40 law schools offering classes on Chinese law within the United States, and many of the premier Chinese universities have started to offer legal coursework for visiting foreign students.[45] This, in conjunction with several formalized semester or summer study-abroad programs between American and Chinese law schools, can often be approved by the American Bar Association and used toward US graduation requirements.[46] Many of these programs provide an overview of Chinese law, with an emphasis on commercial transactions, or incorporate comparative law components in the coursework.

Law schools that have borrowed from their foreign counterparts have sought to adjust the Chinese legal education system to reach the goal of standardizing the curriculum. For example, within recent years 49 law schools have established a Juris Master program,[47] which only accepts graduates of non-legal majors and takes two years to complete.[48] Its aim is to shift the former focus of 'pure' scholarship within graduate education to a more practical orientation. Westernized programs are also utilizing case method studies in conjunction with the more traditional emphasis on legal theories. Finally, schools are starting to offer clinical programs similar to American law schools; currently more than a dozen Chinese law schools offer such clinics.[49]

Purpose of legal education

It goes without saying that the purpose of legal education in China has retained a distinctive Chinese quality. In comparison to the United States, in which future lawyers are taught to be zealous advocates on behalf of their clients, Chinese law students are primarily trained to be civil servants, researchers, judges or professionals. Unlike American students, Chinese law students are often preparing themselves for a career in politics, whether as a politician or as a member of the CPC; the law and legal system are meant to reinforce the CPC's control.

This difference in purpose is reflected in the skills that Chinese and American law students learn while in school. Chinese students focus on memorizing rules and finding legal theories. As a civil law jurisdiction, Chinese legal theorists are held in more respect than judges:

because in China the law-practice process is from legal theories to statutes and then to the administration of justice. So legal theories are the source, statutes are the bases of judges' decisions, and the administration of justice is simply the mechanical application of legal principles to articles of law. This decides the deductive nature in China's legal-education method.[50]

In contrast, American students develop skills in case analysis and 'issue spotting', or describing the ways in which legal rules are contradictory or create a gap in which there are no laws to regulate a situation. American students are taught to determine a case's holdings and learn how to apply the holdings both broadly and narrowly, creating arguments that support their clients and discredit their opponents.

Regulating lawyers

The Law of the People's Republic of China on Lawyers was promulgated in October 2007 and remains the most prominent source of law on lawyers and lawyering in China. It starts off by defining a lawyer as 'a professional who has acquired a lawyer's practice certificate pursuant to law, and is authorized or designated to provide the parties with legal services'.[51] The law requires that lawyers 'protect the lawful rights and interests of parties, ensure the correct implementation of law, and safeguard fairness and justice of the society', mirroring commandments across many legal systems.[52]

There are also important requirements in regards to professional responsibility. In addition to following the laws and constitution, 'a lawyer must base himself on facts and take law as the criterion. In legal practice, a lawyer shall subject himself to supervision of the State, society and the parties concerned. The legal practice of lawyers according to law shall be protected by law.'[53] It is important to note, however, that the CPC is considered neither an individual, an organization nor a unit under Chinese law, meaning that the party is not obliged to protect a lawyer's rights.

The qualifications necessary to become a lawyer are relatively straightforward. Anyone 'who intends to apply for the legal practice of a lawyer shall meet the following conditions: upholding the Constitution of the People's Republic of China; having passed the unified national judicial examination; having completed a full year's internship at a law firm; and being a person of good character and conduct'.[54] The requirements to uphold the constitution and be a person of good character and conduct may leave room for interpretation, however. Being openly against the CPC or the socialist regime would prevent an individual from becoming a lawyer. In addition, there is no definition of what constitutes good character and conduct.

Interestingly, however, it appears that someone will not be granted a license to practice law unless he or she has been offered a position by a law firm. Part of the application submitted for a lawyer's practice certificate includes 'documents produced by a law firm showing that it agrees to recruit the applicant'.[55] It would seem that a graduate who has not yet been hired by a firm would be unable to practice law. This also means that a recent graduate or group of recent graduates would be unable to form their own law firm. The law defines a law firm as:

> an organization in which lawyers practice law. For the establishment of a law firm, the following conditions shall be met: It has its own name, domicile and articles of association; It is manned with lawyers who conform to the provisions of this Law; The person who intends to establish the firm *shall be a lawyer who has a good deal of experience in the profession* and, in the recent three years, who has not been suspended from legal practice by way of punishment; Its assets are in conformity with the amount specified by the judicial administration department under the state Council.[56]

If an attorney wants to form a partnership law firm, he or she would need at least:

> three or more partners, and the persons who intends to establish such a firm shall be a lawyer with at least three years of experience in the profession. A partnership law firm may be established in the form of general partnership or in the form of specialized general partnership. The partners of such a law firm shall, in accordance with law, bear liability for the debts of the law firm in conformity with the form of partnership.[57]

In addition to defining what a lawyer is, his or her professional responsibilities and where he or she may work, the law dictates what business is appropriate for a lawyer. Article 28 lists a very discrete set of actions that lawyers can perform, many of which are similar to duties of lawyers in the United States.[58]

While performing his or her work, a lawyer cannot be held personally responsible for his or her legal opinions, unless it is determined 'the views he [or she] presents... endanger State security, maliciously slander another person, or seriously disrupt the court order'.[59] The law does not state, however, who would make such a determination nor what the punishment is for such an offense.

Much like within the United States, Chinese lawyers have certain requirements surrounding secrecy and protection of clients' personal information. Article 38 requires anyone who comes to learn state or commercial secrets not to talk about them. The only exception is for lawyers to inform police if they have come to learn of a threat to public security.[60]

There is also a long list of behaviors that are prohibited for lawyers, though it is unclear what would happen to a lawyer who was found to have committed any of the following:

> privately accepting authorization, collecting fees, or accepting money, things of value or other benefits offered by a client; seeking the disputed rights and interests of a party by taking advantage of his provision of legal services; accepting money, things of value or other benefits offered by the other party and infringing the rights and interests of the client through ill-intentioned collusion with the other party or a third party; in violation of regulations, meeting with a judge, prosecutor, arbitrator or another staff member concerned; giving bribes to a judge, prosecutor, arbitrator or another staff member concerned, introducing bribes to them, instigating or inducing a party to resort to bribery, or, by other illegitimate means, attempting to influence their handling of a case in accordance with law; intentionally providing false evidence or intimidating or luring another person into providing false evidence, for the purpose of preventing the other party from obtaining evidence lawfully; instigating or inciting a party into settling disputes by disrupting public order, endangering public security or by other illegal means; or disrupting the order of a court or an arbitration tribunal, or interfering with the normal conduct of litigation or arbitration.[61]

Suspension and disbarment

Two of the most common punishments for a lawyer who violates part of the Law of the People's Republic of China on Lawyers are suspension and disbarment. As described in Article 49, a lawyer can be suspended for six months to a year if he or she has violated the law. In addition, he or she can be fined up to RMB50,000, have his or her lawyer's certificate revoked and face criminal charges, if applicable.[62] The list of violations is very similar to those prohibited by Article 40.[63]

The most serious violation, however, is when 'a lawyer receives criminal punishment for an intentional crime'.[64] If this happens, 'his lawyer's practice certificate shall be revoked by the judicial administration department'.[65]

Loyalty oath

Though it is not stated in the Law of the People's Republic of China on Lawyers, the Ministry of Justice has enacted its own requirement that lawyers proclaim their loyalty to the CPC by taking an oath.[66] Anyone applying for a first-time lawyer's practice certificate or lawyers who need to reinstate their licenses must take a loyalty oath. This new regulation has sparked some controversy, and many human rights lawyers in China who defend individuals accused of criticizing the government have expressed confusion about how to represent their clients while staying true to their oath.[67]

Lawyers must give the following oath to receive a license to practice law:

> I volunteer to become a practicing lawyer of the People's Republic of China and promise to faithfully perform the sacred duties of a socialist-with-Chinese-characteristics legal worker; to be faithful to the motherland and the people; to uphold the leadership of the Chinese Communist Party and the socialist system; to safeguard the dignity of the constitution and the law; to practice on behalf of the people; to be diligent, professional, honest, and corruption-free; to protect the legitimate rights and interests of clients, the correct implementation of the law, and social fairness and justice; and diligently strive for the cause of socialism with Chinese characteristics![68]

While much of the oath is merely a recitation of the requirements laid out in the professional responsibility section of the Law on Lawyers, it also uses 'socialist' or 'socialism' three times. It is quite clear that the oath serves as a reminder of the purpose of the law – to support the party's control. It specifically defines a lawyer's role as to 'uphold the leadership of the Chinese Communist Party and the socialist system'. It is understandable, then, how difficult it must be for human rights lawyers to attempt to hold the party or the state responsible for some kind of violation when they must also ensure that their defense is not a direct accusation against the party and the state.

The ministry has stated that one of the reasons for the oath is to 'effectively improve the ideological and political quality, professional ethics and skills of lawyers'.[69] It also believes the oath will help lawyers to develop many of the core values of being a legal worker.

The oath must be administered within three months of a new attorney acquiring his or her license, though it remains unclear whether attorneys renewing their licenses will be forced to take the oath.[70] This is also the first oath that the Ministry of Justice has required of all lawyers; at times lawyers need to take oaths for smaller lawyers' groups and associations, but this oath appears to apply for any and all new lawyers.[71]

Again, it is worth noting that a lawyer is defined as a 'legal worker'. This hearkens to the 1980 Provisional Regulations on the Work of Lawyers, in which lawyers were classified as a type of government official – meaning they were under government and party control. This provisional law was replaced in 1996 by the Law on Lawyers, which defined lawyers as individual 'practitioners who obtained lawyers' practising certificates in accordance with the law and provide legal services to society'.[72]

New rules for the punishment of lawyers

When it comes to punishing lawyers, the Ministry of Justice promulgated the March 2004 Measures for Punishment in Illegal Actions of Lawyers and Law Firms. These list over 20 violations that can result in a variety of punishments, including garnishment of wages, suspension of practice and disbarment.[73] Some of the actions that have been ruled illegal encompass competitive practices, conflicts of interest and the lawyers' and law firms' connections to the judicial branch. What is most frightening to many lawyers is a proposal that would give judges the ability to disbar a lawyer for up to a year for causing a disruption during a hearing.[74]

Given that the law is meant to support the CPC, it is understandable that the government has regulations in place to control its lawyers. Many lawyers are concerned that the regulations will prevent them from representing their clients, and may also punish lawyers who publicize sensitive trials: 'It fits into a pattern of trying to use the law and regulations like this to tame lawyers. Court order can potentially become whatever [judges] say it is.'[75] This means that any lawyer who attempts to blog information about his or her case publicly without the permission of the judge could face punishment.

The specific section of concern may only apply to real-time reporting, but because of the flexibility with which laws can be interpreted and the power judges have to issue orders, it is possible that it can be more broadly interpreted. Some lawyers believe they can be punished simply because a judge does not like them, but the vice-president of the Supreme People's Court has said that the public is apt to believe lawyers who accuse judges and the courts of wrongdoing.

In practice, this law has prevented lawyers and family members of defendants from speaking out because they are not sure of their rights under the law. Families of defendants were often unaware of their rights or under intense pressure to remain silent.

'They came for lawyers'

The concerns that lawyers report, from their ability to practice to their safety, have been documented by international human rights organizations, for example Amnesty International. At least as early as 2009, lawyers alleged that members of the Chinese government, especially the police force, were harassing, disbarring or suspending, torturing and detaining attorneys.[76] The lawyers at most risk are those who have taken on issues of human rights, civil rights or other sensitive topics. The more lawyers try to assert everyone's rights and equality before the law, the more the government has attempted to control and limit attorneys.[77]

Fearing a potential 'Jasmine Revolution' as a chain reaction in response to the 'Arab Spring' in 2011, the Chinese government cracked down on lawyers covering traditionally sensitive issues, including religion, property rights and freedom of expression: 'Human rights lawyers are being targeted as they try to use the law to protect citizens against the excesses of the state.'[78] One way the government has curtailed or discouraged the undertaking of human rights cases is by requiring lawyers and law firms to go through an annual assessment. Those attorneys who have worked on controversial cases or topics often fail, and temporarily or permanently lose their licenses.[79]

The law that prohibits a lawyer from commenting on a case (see above) also includes restrictions on which types of clients can be represented and broadens the crime of inciting subversion during legal defense.[80] This has the largest impact on ethnic minority groups, such as Uyghurs and Tibetans, religious groups like the Falun Gong and those who have fought government action. It leaves a considerable number of people without access to legal counsel or competent legal representation. As one human rights activist has argued, 'If lawyers fear taking on "sensitive cases", especially those involving official misconduct, then the Chinese people cannot rely on the law for redress, and officials have carte blanche to act with impunity.'[81]

As lawyers have become more involved with human and civil rights, the government has marked them for punishment, censure and violence.[82] The fear is that lawyers will use the law to push for democratic reforms and challenge government officials. The threats appear to be working, as very few of China's approximately 204,000 lawyers are willing to take on sensitive cases.[83]

Professor Jerome Cohen posits that the cause of the social unrest which led to fears of a Jasmine Revolution has come from the government's 'own success in rapidly transforming China's economy, opening its society, and raising the Chinese people's awareness of their rights'.[84] Starting with the reforms crafted by Deng Xiaoping in 1978, there has been increasing evidence of disparities, social unrest and conflict, including income gaps, abuse by members of the state security forces and the relocation of 20 million people from rural areas to the cities. At the same time, the CPC has created a legal system with rules, regulations and procedure.[85] Starting after the Cultural Revolution, increasing amounts of legislation and constitutional amendments have created individual rights for Chinese citizens and an ease of access to the legal system that had not been present before.

Chinese citizens are also turning to lawyers because other methods of resolving disputes are either not effective or cause more problems than they are worth.[86] The long-standing extralegal petition process has seen few results and many petitioners find themselves extrajudicially detained for disrupting society. Professor Cohen points out that this creates a contradiction within the party:

They crave the reinforced status that comes from the legitimacy that a rule of law confers on governments at home and abroad. But they also want to avoid the embarrassment and loss of dictatorial control that might occur if lawyers were permitted to challenge their power, even if only before courts that remain under the party's thumb.[87]

Cohen says the government's response has been to use both legal and extralegal methods of scaring lawyers away from taking any case or supporting any cause that does not solidify party control.

Lawyers, law professors and troublemakers: Zhang Sizhi, Jiang Ping, Pu Zhiqiang

Zhang Sizhi: 'a lawyer never wins'

Zhang Sizhi was born in 1927, and was an early member of the CPC. He was one of the expeditionary forces in India in 1943 and took control of the Beiping regional court in 1949. By 1956 he had been ordered to Beijing to establish a legal advisory office, but he was sentenced to 20 years of re-education after being labeled a rightist in 1957. He gained notoriety by defending the Gang of Four following the Cultural Revolution, and continues to serve as a defense attorney today.

Since defending Mao's wife, Jiang Qing, one of the Four, he has participated in a number of rights-based cases, though he says, 'I never win the politically sensitive cases I take.'[88] Despite his lack of success in the courtroom, some consider him to be 'the conscience of the society'. Zhang has also been an outspoken advocate for legal reform and the need for an independent legal system. He notes the seeming contradiction of individuals with little to no legal training or experience assuming powerful roles within the judiciary. As Zhang points out, 'in the current environment, it has become almost a rule of the game'.[89]

Jiang Ping

Jiang Ping is an extremely well-respected lawyer from Ningbo, Zhejiang province. He enrolled at Yenching University in 1948, but went to the Soviet Union in 1951 to study at Moscow State University. Upon graduating, he became a professor at Beijing College of Political Science and Law, now China University of Political Science and Law. Eventually he became president of China University of Political Science and Law, but left his job in 1990 because he had sided with the student demonstrators during the Tiananmen Square incident of 1989. Currently he is a professor at China University of Political Science and Law, an arbitrator and advisor with the Beijing Arbitration Commission and works with the China International Economic and Trade Arbitration Commission.

Jiang was active in much of the legislation that was promulgated in the 1990s. He was involved with the General Principles of Civil Law (the civil code), Property Law, Trust Law, Administrative Litigation Law and many of the other laws that now form the backbone of the Chinese legal system. He also served as the vice chair of the Law Committee of the National People's Congress.

Jiang Ping admitted:

> Strictly speaking, in the 30 years of reform what I did was call for private rights. I chose civil law and private rights because those areas were weak in China, or rather in a China with such strong public powers, private rights were always in a weak position. Private rights include the rights of private enterprise, of private property, and perhaps even broader personal rights.[90]

Jiang has also worked hard to create a system of rule of law in China, though he does believe that 'the rule of law is in retreat. Or perhaps, building the rule of law, judicial reform, and political reform are all moving backwards.'[91] He opines, however, that there is an increased interest in rule of law within China. More citizens understand their rights and lawyers are striving both to make money and to protect individuals' human rights.[92]

Pu Zhiqiang

A younger-generation civil rights lawyer, Pu Zhiqiang is known for his work in human rights. Pu focuses on freedom of the press, product safety and defamation, but he has also done considerable work on behalf of writers and journalists. The sensitive cases he has taken on, however, have led to him being monitored, arrested and questioned.

Pu first gained notoriety as a student in the 1989 democracy movement. Despite it being an overt political action, he returns to Tiananmen Square each year to commemorate the demonstrations that took place. In his legal practice, he defended the writers Wu Chuntao and Chen Guidi in 2004 against charges of libel for their book *A Survey of Chinese Peasants*. One reporter noted that Pu's defense made it seem 'as if... the Communist Party itself... [was] the one on trial'.[93] Pu also won a case in which the judiciary recognized the right of a magazine and journalists to publish material as long as the stories are not derived from hearsay.[94]

One of the most recent incidents in which Pu was involved was a disagreement with the deputy director of Fengtai Section of the Beijing Public Security Bureau Domestic Security Department.[95] After Pu's friend, Liu Xiaobo, was announced as the Nobel Peace Prize laureate, Pu was detained,[96] taken to Fanjiacun police station and pressured not to do any interviews about the Nobel Prize. The deputy director told Pu that Liu's award was the work of anti-Chinese forces, and his support of Liu and giving interviews to members of the media associated him with those anti-Chinese sentiments.[97] Pu responded:

Awarding Liu Xiaobo is the mainstream civilization's [the world's] acknowledgment of his peaceful, non-violent efforts. Such good news cannot be hidden or suppressed, and I am excited and send Xiaobo and his wife my best greetings. The Chinese Communist Party needs to learn how to face the fact that the Nobel Peace Prize Award winner is sitting in a dark jail in China. Hu Jintao and Wen Jiabao don't know what to do about this, so it's time to lift the media censorship, pave a way for the whole society to reach a consensus, and move forward. You are acting blindly and this will just further tarnish the image of your party bosses.[98]

This response led the director to accuse Liu of denouncing the party and put Pu under his control or *guanzhi* (管制). The concept of control, however, is a criminal punishment that can only be applied by a court after a guilty verdict.[99] Pu argued that because he was neither breaking the law nor had been found guilty of any crime, the director had no right to put him under his control.

During his interrogation, Pu was asked about his participation in drafting Charter '08. Pu denied having anything to do with drafting the document, reiterating that he only signed it.

Li Zhuang case

To understand the sometimes competing ideologies within China's legal system – professionalism and populism – it is important to look at the trial of Li Zhuang, a Beijing-based lawyer who went to Chongqing to help those accused of being members of Chongqing's organized crime gangs between 2009 and 2011.[100] Li was ultimately accused of, tried for and convicted of pushing a client to give false testimony.[101] He was sentenced to 30 months in prison.

Prior to the case that made him famous, this lawyer had been creating a name for himself as someone who would stand up to the procuratorates.[102] In 2007 he represented a client in Shahe, Hebei province, and read through considerable documentation before he finally found evidence that his client had made a false admission while he was tortured. Following his defense in the courtroom, Li was taken into custody for five hours. He then unsuccessfully sued the police department.

While Li appealed his conviction for pushing his client into false testimony, he quickly gave in. Later, he spoke with the judge and insisted that the trial in which the alleged false testimony was given was based on 'clear facts and sound evidence'.[103] In a second appeal Li's sentence was reduced to 18 months, but Li claimed that judicial officials had violated some kind of agreement, alluding to his guilty plea having been encouraged by certain government departments.

Though it appears Li would have fought, he believed cooperation with authorities would be better for him.[104] In reality, however, his case demonstrates the power judicial officials hold and what may happen when they believe punishment is in order.

It was Li's second trial, however, that truly split legal observers into two camps. One year after his initial trial on fabricating evidence, he was tried again on the same charges in an alleged earlier incident in Shanghai.[105] In both trials, many lawyers and observers believe that Li was innocent, and Li himself argued that he had been framed. His trials appeared to many to be an improper use of the courts for political gain.[106]

This claim has been further substantiated by the fact that court procedure was not followed in either case. Li's lawyers were unable to cross-examine his accusers, and Li himself was unable to confront his accusers.[107] The fear among the legal community is that something similar could happen again, and a second conviction would make it clear that jail time could follow the defense of a sensitive client. Ultimately, however, the second charge was dropped.

Notes

1. China Digital Times (2012) 'Netizen voices: blasting the *People's Daily*', China Digital Times, 3 August; available at: *http://chinadigitaltimes.net/2012/08/141150/* (accessed: 11 August 2013).
2. Ibid.
3. Ibid.
4. Ibid.
5. Ibid.
6. Albert H.Y. Chen (2004) *An Introduction to the Legal System of the People's Republic of China*, 3rd edn. Hong Kong: LexisNexis Butterworths, p. 164.
7. *Oxford International Encyclopedia of Legal History*, Vol. 4. New York: Oxford University Press, p. 45.
8. Li Yuwen (2000) 'Lawyers in China: a "flourishing" profession in a rapidly changing society?', French Centre for Research on Contemporary China, January; available at: *www.cefc.com.hk/pccpa.php?aid=1605* (accessed: 11 August 2013).
9. *Oxford International Encyclopedia of Legal History*, note 7 above, p. 45.
10. Li, note 8 above.
11. Ibid.
12. Chen, note 6 above, p. 165.
13. Li, note 8 above.
14. Ibid.
15. Ibid.
16. Ibid.
17. Ibid.
18. Ibid.
19. Ibid.
20. Ibid.
21. Hilderbrandt International (2005) 'China: opportunities in the legal services market', research report, Hilderbrandt International, Washington, DC, December, p. 7.
22. Li, note 8 above.
23. Ibid.
24. Ibid.
25. Ibid.
26. Ibid.
27. Ibid.
28. Ibid.
29. Ibid.
30. Ibid.
31. Ibid.
32. American Bar Association (2012) 'Restrictions continue in China for U.S. lawyers', American Bar Association, October; available at: *www.americanbar.org/publications/governmental_affairs_periodicals/washingtonletter/2012/october/lawyersinchina.html* (accessed: 11 August 2013)

33. China Briefing (2012) 'Foreign law firms in China – 2012 listings', China Briefing, 7 February; available at: *www.china-briefing.com/news/2012/02/07/foreign-law-firms-in-china-2012-listings.html* (accessed: 25 August 2013).
34. Carl F. Minzner (2012) 'The rise and fall of Chinese legal education', *Fordham International Law Journal*, 36(2): 340.
35. Ibid., p. 373.
36. China University of Political Science and Law (undated) 'Brief introduction to China University of Political Science and Law'; available at: *www.cupl.edu.cn/html/en/col1105/column_1105_1.html* (accessed: 25 August 2013).
37. Minzner, note 34 above, p. 377.
38. Ibid.
39. Han Dayuan (2010) 'Chinese legal education: now, challenge, and prospects'; available at: *www.iias.sinica.edu.tw/upload/conferences/20100611/1-1/1-1-2.pdf* (accessed: 25 August 2013).
40. Ibid.
41. Ibid.
42. Ibid.
43. Alison W. Conner (2003) 'The Comparative Law School in China', in Stephen Hsu (ed.) *Understanding China's Legal System*. New York: New York University Press, p. 211.
44. Matthew S. Eric (2009) 'Legal education reform in China through U.S.-inspired transplants', *Journal of Legal Education*, 59(1): 60.
45. Wei Luo (2011) 'Chinese law courses offered by North American law schools'; available at: *http://law.wustl.edu/chinalaw/clcourse.html* (accessed: 25 August 2013).
46. Ibid.
47. Baidu Baike (2013) 'Juris Master'; available at: *http://baike.baidu.com/view/146616.htm* (accessed: 25 August 2013).
48. Ibid.
49. Han, note 39 above.
50. Ibid.
51. Law of the People's Republic of China on Lawyers (2007), Article 2.
52. Ibid.
53. Ibid., Article 3.
54. Ibid., Article 5.
55. Ibid., Article 6.
56. Ibid., Article 14, emphasis added.
57. Ibid., Article 15.
58. Ibid., Article 28.
59. Ibid., Article 37.
60. Ibid., Article 38.
61. Ibid., Article 40.
62. Ibid., Article 49.
63. Ibid.
64. Ibid.
65. Ibid.
66. Voice of America (2012) 'China orders communist loyalty oaths for lawyers', VOA News, 21 March; available at: *http://blogs.voanews.com/*

breaking-news/2012/03/21/china-orders-communist-loyalty-oaths-for-lawyers/ (accessed: 11 August 2013).

67. Ibid.
68. Ministry of Justice (2012) 'Ministry of Justice issues decision establishing a system of notification for swearing in lawyers', 21 March; available at: *www.moj.gov.cn/index/content/2012-03/21/content_3445267.htm* (accessed: 11 August 2013).
69. Voice of America, note 66 above.
70. Ibid.
71. Ibid.
72. Law of the People's Republic of China on Lawyers, Article 2.
73. Measures for Punishment in Illegal Actions of Lawyers and Law Firms (2004).
74. Tania Branigan (2012) 'China: lawyers fear new regulation against "disrupting" hearings', *The Guardian*, 29 August; available at: *www.theguardian.com/world/2012/aug/29/china-lawyers-regulation-disrupting-hearings* (accessed: 25 August 2013).
75. Ibid.
76. Amnesty International (2011) 'China: dark times for lawyers as repression intensifies', Amnesty International, 30 June; available at: *www.amnesty.org/en/news-and-updates/china-dark-times-lawyers-repression-intensifies-2011-06-30* (accessed: 11 August 2013).
77. Ibid.
78. Ibid.
79. Ibid.
80. Ibid.
81. Ibid.
82. Amnesty International (2011) 'Against the law: crackdown on China's human rights lawyers deepens', Amnesty International, 30 June; available at: *www.amnesty.org/en/library/info/ASA17/018/2011/en* (accessed: 11 August 2013).
83. Ibid.
84. Jerome A. Cohen (2011) 'First, they came for the lawyers', *Foreign Policy*, 12 July; available at: *www.foreignpolicy.com/articles/2011/07/12/first_they_came_for_the_lawyers* (accessed: 11 August 2013).
85. Ibid.
86. Ibid.
87. Ibid.
88. Zhang Sizhi (2001) *My Defense Statements and Dreams*. Shanghai: Xuelin Press, p. 1.
89. Jonathan Watts (2006) 'Mao casts long shadow over China', *The Guardian*, 15 May; available at: *www.guardian.co.uk/world/2006/may/16/china.jonathanwatts* (accessed: 11 August 2013).
90. Jiang Ping (2010) 'China's rule of law is in full retreat', 2 March; available at: *http://lawprofessors.typepad.com/china_law_prof_blog/2010/03/jiang-ping-chinas-rule-of-law-is-in-full-retreat.html* (accessed: 11 August 2013).
91. Ibid.

92. Excerpt from Jiang Ping's 28 December 2009 speech at All China Lawyers Association annual meeting. The speech was later published in *Chinese Lawyers Digest* (律师文摘); available at: *http://news.mylegist. com/1604/2010-02-21/21028.html* (accessed: 1 June 2011).

93. Philip P. Pan (2004) 'In China, turning the law into the people's protector', *Washington Post*, 28 December, p. A01.

94. *Southern Weekly* (2012) 'Tough attorney Pu Zhiqiang', *Southern Weekly*, No. 38; available at: *www.nbweekly.com/news/people/201209/31342. aspx* (accessed: 25 August 2013).

95. Ibid.

96. China Digital Times (2010) 'Pu Zhiqiang takes on his police interrogator, and tweets it', China Digital Times, 29 October; available at: *http://china digitaltimes.net/2010/10/pu-zhiqiang-takes-on-his-police-interrogator-and-tweets-it/* (accessed: 11 August 2013).

97. Ibid.

98. Ibid.

99. Ibid.

100. Caixin Online (2010) 'Who is Li Zhuang?'; available at: *http://topics. english.caixin.com/2010/lizhuang/* (accessed: 11 August 2013).

101. Ibid.

102. Ibid.

103. Ibid.

104. *Wall Street Journal* (2011) 'China drops charges against lawyer', *Wall Street Journal*, 23 April; available at: *http://online.wsj.com/article/ SB100014240 5274870390700457627859352831616.html* (accessed: 11 August 2013).

105. Ibid.

106. Ian Johnson (2011) 'Trial in China tests limits of legal system reform', *New York Times*, 19 April; available at: *www.nytimes.com/2011/04/20/ world/asia/20china.html?_r=0* (accessed: 11 August 2013).

107. Ibid.

Part III
Case studies

6

Civil laws and cases

Abstract: This chapter delves into civil law within the People's Republic of China. In addition to the general principles of Chinese law, contract law, property law, tort law, intellectual property and commercial law are covered. Key aspects of civil procedure are introduced and explained. The chapter concludes with representative cases selected by the Supreme People's Court as decisions that create quasi-case law.

Key words: civil law, civil procedure, contract law, property law, tort law, intellectual property, commercial law.

While many countries in the West have long had a civil law tradition, it was not until the Qing dynasty started looking at foreign legal systems in an effort to reform its own that civil law began to develop in China. It was the Communist Party of China's major economic and legal reforms of 1979, however, that truly were the start of a civil law system in the People's Republic of China.

General principles of civil law

The General Principles of the Civil Law of the People's Republic of China went into effect in 1987 and form the main source of civil law in the country.[1] It is a set of principles that draws heavily from the German civil code and works to provide a uniform framework for interpreting the PRC's civil laws. The General Principles contain not only civil law but also civil rights and obligations and liabilities under civil law. Though the Chinese government has tried to consolidate the civil laws into a comprehensive code, this has never been done successfully or without controversy.

The General Principles define a natural person or citizen in the second chapter, which also explains who has the 'capacity for civil rights and capacity for civil conduct'. As defined in Article 9, 'A citizen shall have the capacity for civil rights from birth to death and shall enjoy civil rights and assume civil obligations in accordance with the law', and Article 11, 'A citizen aged 18 or over shall be an adult. He shall have full capacity for civil conduct, may independently engage in civil activities and shall be called a person with full capacity for civil conduct.' As in the West, partnerships and businesses are defined in the section on citizenship. The following chapter defines the entities that are treated similarly to individual persons. These 'legal persons' include enterprises, official organs, institutions and social organizations, and economic associations.

Chapter 5 names the four civil rights available to natural and legal persons: property, creditors, intellectual property and personal rights. The sixth chapter lays out the consequences for breach of contract and infringement of rights. It also explains the various ways in which someone in breach can be held liable. The following chapters explain various other provisions related to civil law, including how the law applies with regard to foreigners.

As with most laws in the PRC, the civil law has a very specific purpose that is elucidated in Article 1 of the General Principles:

> This Law is formulated in accordance with the Constitution and the actual situation in our country, drawing upon our practical experience in civil activities, for the purpose of protecting the lawful civil rights and interests of citizens and legal persons and correctly adjusting civil relations, so as to meet the needs of the developing socialist modernization.

The law also states that everyone involved in a civil dispute will be treated equally.[2]

Though Article 9 says that all citizens have civil rights (and obligations) from birth to death, Article 18 explains that only at the age of 18 will a citizen have the full spectrum of civil rights; 18 is also defined as the age of majority, but if an individual's 'main source of income is his own labour', he or she may gain access to his or her full capacity for civil rights before the age of majority.[3]

As defined by Article 36, 'A legal person shall be an organization that has capacity for civil rights and capacity for civil conduct and independently enjoys civil rights and assumes civil obligations in accordance with the law.' It will only have its capacity for civil activity for the duration of the organization. In addition, Article 37 lays out some specific requirements for a legal person, including that it has sufficient money and property; that it was created legally; that it is named, organized and has its own premises or location; and that it can be held civilly liable. If an organization is unable to meet these criteria, it will not be recognized as a legal person. These organizations can include enterprises (both Chinese and Chinese-foreign joint ventures), but they must be properly registered with an administrative agency.

Though Chapter 5 of the General Principles contains some substantive law, many categories of civil law were later expanded into their own separate codified laws (discussed in greater detail later in this chapter). Some of the articles in Chapter 5 are basic definitions, such as Article 71's definition of 'property ownership' as 'the owner's rights to lawfully possess, utilize, profit from and dispose of his property'.

Curiously, the law does not define creditors and debtors in financial terms; instead, it refers to a debtor as a legal person that has obligations under a special relationship (a debt) to the individual who holds the rights to the debt (the creditor).[4] In addition, a 'creditor shall have the right to demand that the debtor fulfill his obligations as specified by the contract or according to legal provisions'.[5] Contracts are defined as 'an agreement whereby the parties establish, change or terminate their civil relationship. Lawfully established contracts shall be protected by law.'[6]

Following the rights to life and health, Article 99 expounds upon a citizen's right to a name. This right (as well as the prohibition against interfering with it) not only applies to natural persons, but also to legal persons, individual partnerships, enterprises and individual businesses. The chapter on personal rights protects against the use of a citizen's 'portrait' without his or her consent,[7] which ties into the right of reputation: 'The personality of citizens shall be protected by law, and the use of insults, libel or other means to damage the reputation of citizens or legal persons shall be prohibited.'[8]

Chapter 5's final provisions include protection of honorary titles and marriages of choice. Article 105 explicitly states that 'Women shall enjoy equal civil rights with men', but the preceding article lists vulnerable groups whose rights are protected by law: mothers, the 'handicapped', 'old people', children and families.

Immediately following the chapter on personal rights are the laws regarding civil liability. Article 106 provides a general overview, stating that there is civil liability for breach of contract and violation of property rights, and that strict liability is applicable when indicated by the law.

The chapter also lays the groundwork for torts and tort liabilities. Article 134 states:

> The main methods of bearing civil liability shall be: cessation of infringements; removal of obstacles; elimination of dangers; return of property; restoration of original condition; repair, reworking or replacement; compensation for losses; payment of breach of contract damages; elimination of ill effects and rehabilitation of reputation; and extension of apology.

Of course, the General Principles also allow a court to 'serve admonitions, order the offender to sign a pledge of repentance, and confiscate the property used in carrying out illegal activities and the illegal income obtained therefrom. It may also impose fines or detentions as stipulated by law.'[9]

Selected civil laws

Contract law

The Contract Law of the People's Republic of China took effect on 1 October 1999, and remains the primary law governing contracts within China. This most recent iteration has drawn together many pieces of Chinese contract law that had previously been parts of other substantive laws, which has allowed for increased uniformity.[10] Moreover, 'The principles of the freedom of contract, of good faith, and of the fostering of transactions have informed and guided the formulation of the Contract Law and are embodied in many of its major provisions.'[11] The Contract Law has evolved based on the Chinese government's experience with previous contract laws, but it also reflects influences from foreign contract regimes. The law has both general and specific provisions, in addition to rules regarding the formation, fulfillment and breach of contracts. The specific provisions document the numerous varieties of contracts allowable.

As with most Chinese laws, Article 1 lays out the purpose of the law, namely to protect 'the legitimate rights and interests of the parties to contracts, [maintain] the socio-economic order and promote the socialist modernization'.[12] Article 2 defines a contract as:

an agreement on the establishment, alteration or termination of a civil right-obligation relationship between natural persons, legal persons or other organizations as subjects with equal status. Agreements on establishing such personal relationships as marriage, adoption and guardianship shall be governed by the provisions of other laws.

Property law

The Property Law of the People's Republic of China went into effect on 1 October 2007, and covers all aspects of property law within the PRC's civil law system. In a deviation from the purer socialism of years past, the current law supports the protection of private property:

> With the great expansion of personal wealth in China in the past two decades, there was a general sentiment both within the Party and the populace that a new law was necessary to recognize and protect the wealth generated by China's growing private sector. The 2004 amendments to the Constitution, with their greater emphasis on the protection of such rights, [are] a reflection of these same sentiments.[13]

In addition, the drafting of the Property Law differed considerably from the traditional legislative process. Instead of being written behind closed doors, the public submitted approximately 14,000 suggestions that were considered over a decade-long period before the law was finally published and put into effect.[14]

As with other Chinese laws, Article 1 clearly states the law's purpose: to support the 'socialist market economy'.[15] It explains that its purpose is also to 'defin[e] the attribution of things, giv[e] play to the usefulness of things and protect the property right of obligees'.[16] Article 2 then defines 'things' as both personal and real property, and a 'property right' as 'the exclusive right enjoyed by the obligee to directly dominate a given thing according to law, which consists of the right of ownership, the usufruct and the security interest on property'.

Though the Property Law creates private, collective and state ownership, it does not allow for private ownership of real property. Thus the new law does not change the system in which the state owns all the land. Under the current system of land tenure, an individual can own a land-use right, which relies upon the concept of usufruct, or the right of enjoyment from a piece of property that is held in common ownership.[17] Though the Property Law does not grant citizens individual rights over real property, Article 9 does require that any individual who attempts to create, destroy or transfer real property rights must register the change in rights. Article 40 also defines three types of property rights: security, ownership and use.

Article 42 allows for the state to take land, homes and other pieces of real property from those possessing a right of enjoyment. When land is taken, the state will make payments for the cost of the land and the cost of relocating the tenants and other pieces of immovable property for which the law requires compensation. The law ensures that individuals' 'lawful rights and interests shall be protected'.

As part of its control over the land, the CPC carefully restricts what and how much land can be changed from agricultural use to construction projects.[18] The state also makes clear what land it owns and what land belongs to 'the collectives'.[19] Article 47 says, 'Land in the cities belongs to the State. Land in the rural and suburban areas which belongs to the State as is provided for by law is owned by the State.' According to Article 58, however:

> the land, forests, mountains, grasslands, wasteland and tidal flats belong to the collective, as is provided for by law; the buildings, production equipment, water conservancy facilities of farmland that are owned by the collective; the educational, scientific, cultural, public health and sports facilities that are owned by the collective; and other immovables and movables owned by the collective.

In addition, Article 59 explains what power a collective has over its land and property:

> The following matters shall be subject to decision by the members of a given collective in accordance with the statutory procedure: plans for contracting of land, and subcontracting of land to other units or to individuals other than those belonging to the collective; adjustments to be made to the contracted land by the individual persons among themselves who have the right to land contractual management; methods for the use and distribution of such fees as compensations paid for land; such matters as change in ownership of the enterprises invested by the collective; and other matters as provided for by law.

Collectives may include towns, townships, economic organizations and villagers' committees or teams.[20] Any collective is bound by law and administrative regulations in its use, possession, benefit and disposal of land. Article 63 also prohibits the 'illegal possession, looting, private sharing, and destruction of such [collective] property by any units or individuals'. If a collective has made a decision that infringes upon individual members' rights and interests, however, the aggrieved members may apply to a people's court for satisfaction.

Though the Property Law severely restricts the transformation of agricultural land to construction, there have been reports of an increasing number of illegal or controversial decisions to sell property rights to developers.[21] These decisions have led to 'mass incidents', the Chinese euphemism for riots, protests and demonstrations. The *People's Daily* reported approximately 90,000 mass incidents each year from 2007 to 2009, and in 2010 there were around 180,000 such incidents.[22] Some estimate that 65 percent of all mass incidents are directly related to land disputes. Nor have land grabs been isolated incidents; international news agencies have reported over 66 million farmers who have lost some or all of their land in the past ten years.[23]

In regard to personal property, Article 64 of the Property Law explains that individual property rights exist: 'All individual persons shall be entitled to enjoy ownership of such immovables and movables as their lawful incomes, houses, articles for daily use, tools of production, and raw and semi-finished materials.'

Tort liability law

The first comprehensive tort law in China is the Tort Liability Law of the People's Republic, which took effect on 1 July 2010. Within its purview are the more traditional tort topics, including personal injury and medical malpractice, but it also covers actions less commonly found in Western tort law, such as environmental damages and liabilities for individuals who raise animals. Nearly all the tort liabilities are recorded in the Tort Liability Law, in addition to the concepts of mitigating factors and product liability.

The law mandates that a tortfeasor take specific action to stop or remedy any tortious actions, including removing any danger present to an individual, restoring property to individuals who hold an interest in the property and apologizing.[24] The law recognizes both actual damages and emotional distress, providing compensation for both.[25] And, as in the West, the Tort Law provides for joint and several liability (multiple tortfeasors)[26] and contributory fault (tortfeasor and victim are both partially to blame for damages).[27]

Though the law recognizes or provides compensation for numerous types of tortious behavior, it does not always define the incidents which create liability:

> The Tort Law lacks definitions of key terms used or alluded to throughout the Tort Law such as negligence, gross negligence, intentional acts, fraud, misrepresentation, reasonable care, trespass to land, trespass to chattel (property), assault, battery, consent, informed consent, privilege, capacity and lack thereof, and causation. However, the lack of specificity is common in most PRC laws... Liability is based upon an infringement of a person's civil rights, but it is unclear as to the level of culpability – namely, negligence, gross negligence or intentional acts.[28]

Unlike the other civil laws in the Chinese legal system, Article 1 does not mention upholding or protecting the socialist government as one of its purposes. It does, however, seek to 'prevent and sanction tortious acts, and promot[e] social harmony and stability'.[29] Interestingly, Article 2 provides one of the few definitions within the Tort Law:

> Tort liability shall be assumed according to this Law for any infringement of civil rights. For the purpose of this Law, 'civil rights and interests' refer to personal and property rights, including, inter alia, the right to life, right to health, right of name, right of reputation, right of honor, portraiture right, right to privacy, autonomy in marriage, guardianship, ownership, usufruct, security interest in property, copyright, patent, right to exclusive use of trademarks, right of discovery, equity interest and right of inheritance.

Understanding that tort liability comes from an infringement of civil rights, Article 3 explains that it is the person whose rights have been infringed who has the ability to seek tort liability against the tortfeasor. Correspondingly, an individual who has infringed upon someone's rights will be named the tortfeasor. According to Article 6, it appears that the tortfeasor must prove he or she did not commit a tortious act when defending against a claim of tort liability. Furthermore, Article 7 establishes the concept of strict liability, in which a person will be held liable for a tort, regardless of fault, when legal provisions so require.

Without providing an exhaustive list, 'Tort liability is mainly assumed through: cessation of the infringement; removal of obstacle; elimination of danger; restitution of property; restoration to the original state; compensation for loss; formal apology; and elimination of adverse impact and the restoration of reputation.'[30] Article 16 expands upon tort liability in ordering that damages can include medical and rehabilitation care, lost wages, disability payments and funeral and death expenses.

Similar to the American product liability system, a consumer who is injured by a defective product can file a lawsuit against either the manufacturer or the seller.[31] While the manufacturer can be held responsible for products with a defective design, the seller can be held liable if the product is damaged in its care.[32] Though the Tort Liability Law specifies who can be held responsible for product liability, the manufacturer or seller may need to seek compensation from the other party if the infringee filed a lawsuit against the incorrect party.[33]

If a Chinese citizen is harmed by a doctor, nurse or other medical professional, he or she may use Article 54 of the Tort Law to seek compensation for medical damage. In addition, when a medical professional fails in his or her duty to diagnose or apply treatment consistent with the prevailing medical standards, he or she can be held liable for the damage caused.[34] The medical damage liability chapter explains further that:

> Medical personnel shall explain to the patients in the course of diagnosis and treatment their conditions and the medical measures. If surgery, special examination or special treatment is required, medical personnel shall explain to their patients, inter alia, the medical risks and alternative treatment in a timely manner and obtain their written consents. If it is inadvisable to explain the same to the patients, medical persons shall do so with the immediate relatives of the patients and obtain their written consents. If a medical person fails to fulfill his or her obligations… and causes damage to his or her patient, the medical institution shall be liable for compensation.[35]

While Article 55 does mandate that medical professionals receive written consent before treating a patient, Article 56 allows for the lead medical professional to make judgment calls on treatment when consent is unable to be obtained.

The last major section of the Tort Law is the chapter on liability for environmental pollution. As is to be expected, Article 65 provides for tort liability when environmental pollution causes damage. Interestingly, the burden of proof lies with the alleged polluter, for proving both that he or she did not pollute and that there was no causal relationship between the polluter's actions and the damage.[36] As with other chapters in the Tort Law, environmental pollution allows for joint and several liability.[37]

It is clear that the Tort Law was partly influenced by foreign legal regimes, because the very concept of 'tort' did not exist in the Chinese system before the 1980s. It seeks to blend civil and common laws while incorporating a unique 'Chineseness'. One foreign influence was a group of legal scholars from the West – Dr Chuanxi Stephen Hsu, the first Chinese national elected to the American Law Institute, led a translation project to make the Restatement of Torts available in Chinese.[38] Not only did he make US tort laws accessible, but he also commented on several drafts of the Tort Liability Law before it was ultimately published.

Some observers find the promulgated Tort Law both ambitious and incomplete:

> it leaves many important questions unanswered. For example, it is unclear if the Torts [sic] Law should govern administrative torts, state agency torts, or government personnel torts committed in connection with the exercise of official duty. Additionally, the broad coverage of the Torts Law, in terms of rights and interests, creates many ambiguities that require more legislative interpretations or judicial explanations, especially when determining damages and calculating damage awards.[39]

There is also some confusion as to whether the Tort Law or the 1986 Civil Code has control if there is a conflict. Even if conflicts between the two laws were adequately resolved, there is some doubt that the Tort Law is enforceable, especially where the law may affect China's economic interests.

Intellectual property rights

To protect intellectual property rights, the PRC has both promulgated domestic laws and ratified international conventions.[40] The comprehensive system of intellectual property laws was first crafted in 1979, but it has grown through the passage of legislation, administrative regulations and three national laws: the Patent Law, the Trademark Law and the Copyright Law. Moreover, the opinions, circulars and notices issued by the Supreme People's Court have all combined to protect domestic and foreign intellectual property rights in China.

The Patent Law of the People's Republic of China was promulgated in 1984, but it was in 1985 that China ratified the Paris Convention for the Protection of Industrial Property and the Patent Cooperation Treaty (1970). Patents were further strengthened with China's assent to the World Trade Organization in 2001, as its membership required it to sign up to the Agreement on Trade-Related Aspects of Intellectual Property Rights (TRIPS).

Trademarks were first legislated in 1982 in the Trademark Law of the People's Republic of China, later amended in 1993 and 2001. Copyrights are regulated by the Copyright Law of the People's Republic of China and the Implementing Rules for the Copyright Law of the People's Republic of China. The law went into effect in 1990 and the implementing rules in 1991; the rules were amended in 2002.

Commercial law

There is a specific branch of law within China called 'economic' or commercial law which is distinguishable from civil law, though the exact boundaries are not always clear:

> There is a considerable body of literature proposing different theories about the distinction between civil law and economic law in the PRC, although the debate is probably of more academic than practical significance. While civil law has always been a recognized branch of the law for the purpose of legal scholarship in the PRC, the term 'economic law' only became widely used after the beginning of economic reform in 1979.[41]

Civil law consists of many of the topics already covered, including contracts, torts, property and family laws, while economic law regulates economic contracts, companies and partnerships, bankruptcy, anti-monopoly, security transactions, maritime and foreign investment laws.

The development of economic and commercial law started in the early 1980s as China was moving away from a planned economy governed by the CPC's administrative regulations and toward a partial market economy governed, to some degree, by principles of modern capitalism. While there has been increasing reliance on legal and regulatory measures to manage and develop the market economy, it remains quite different from the previous planned economy, which was regulated by administrative measures. The legislation and regulatory measures provide consistency and predictability in economic activities and respect for the integrity of contracts and property rights. There are overlaps between civil law and economic law, but it is more accurate to say the distinction is artificial. Whether artificial or not, Daniel C.K. Chow elucidates:

> economic law... regulat[es] vertical economic relations or economic management relations between higher level and lower levels of the planned sector of the economy as well as some horizontal relations that are closely related to vertical economic relations such as contracts entered into in furtherance of state plans. In addition, some internal structure of economic organizations as well as organizations related to foreign economic activities, such as sino-foreign joint ventures, also fall within the category of economic law.[42]

One of these 'economic' laws is the Company Law of the People's Republic of China, which went into effect in 1994. Since its first promulgation the law has been amended three times, and the newest version took effect in 2006. The three revisions have completely transformed it, leaving very little of the old law in place – an estimated 10 percent of the original law remains. The Company Law regulates limited liability companies and joint stock companies.

The Company Law has a markedly different purpose than the civil laws previously discussed:

> This Law is enacted in order to standardize the organization and behavior of companies, to protect the legitimate rights and interests of companies, shareholders and creditors, to maintain the socio-economic order and to promote the development of the socialist market economy.[43]

Article 3 names companies as legal persons with independent property and property rights. As with other legal persons, companies are responsible for their debts. The amount of liability assumed by shareholders, however, will be limited 'to the extent of the capital contributions subscribed respectively by them; and the shareholders of a company limited by shares shall assume liability towards the company to the extent of the shares subscribed respectively by them'.

For a limited liability company to incorporate, there must be a specific number of shareholders and a specific amount of capital contributions.[44] The shareholders must also have worked together to craft the articles of association. Finally, the company must be named and have 'its own domicile', and its structure must meet the statutory requirements.[45] The shareholders themselves form the shareholders' assembly, which is the 'organ of power of the company'.[46]

In contrast to a limited liability company, a company limited by shares must meet a unique set of requirements:

> The number of promoters conforms to the statutory number; [t]he share capital subscribed for and raised by promoters reaches the statutory minimum amount of capital; [t]he issue of shares and the preparations made for incorporation conform to the provisions of law; [t]he company's articles of association are formulated by the promoters, and such articles of association of a company incorporated by means of share offer are adopted at the inaugural meeting; [t]he company has its name, and its organizational structure conforms to the requirements for a company limited by shares; and [t]he company has its [own] domicile.[47]

One of the requirements of a company limited by shares is that it must have a board of directors.[48] As stipulated in Article 109, the board is composed of five to 19 individuals and can contain:

> representatives from among the staff and workers of the company. Such representatives on a board of directors shall be democratically elected by the staff and workers of the company through the conference of the representatives of the staff and workers, the general meeting of the staff and workers, or through other forms.

This type of company's capital will have shares of equal value that can be transferred between individuals.[49]

Finally, the Company Law allows for two kinds of mergers and acquisitions:

> When a company has another company amalgamated with it, it is merger by amalgamation, and the amalgamated company shall be dissolved. When two or more companies merge to establish a new company, it is merger for new establishment, and all parties being merged shall be dissolved.[50]

The above articles are only applied to Chinese-owned companies, yet the legal system also allows for direct foreign investment. Foreigners may establish branches of a wholly foreign-owned company, establish an equity joint venture or create a contractual joint venture. Each of the three forms of foreign investment comes with its own unique rules and regulations.[51]

As with specific subsections of civil law, there is evidence that the new Company Law may be difficult to implement and slow to create change. While some aspects of the law may cause immediate changes, such as those 'that can be applied automatically by local government officials and that do not require the participation of legal professionals or the courts', many others will require a concerted effort to reshape the Chinese economy.[52] According to Dan Harris, three of the new provisions may be more easily implemented: the reduction in the amount of registered capital, the provision allowing single shareholder limited liability companies, and the provisions that allow for a simplified management structure for limited liability companies with a limited number of shareholders.[53]

But these instantaneous changes are few. Harris points out that numerous factors will likely prevent the widespread reform the CPC thought it was enacting:

> Given the weak judiciary system and a bureaucracy unaccustomed to handling complex corporate law questions, the New [sic] Company Law likely will have little impact on closely held limited liability companies in China. Absent public or institutional demand for such sweeping legislation, the only way the legislation may have any impact is through a combination of massive, government-imposed education and vigorous government enforcement. Since neither of these may happen in China, the New Company law [sic] likely may fail to have the significant impact the drafters hoped for.[54]

Civil procedure

Though the first Civil Procedure Law of the People's Republic of China was adopted in 1982, it has subsequently been revised and the current version took effect in 2013. The law is based on the PRC constitution and 'the experience and actual conditions of our country in the trial of civil cases'.[55] Similar to its foreign counterparts, the Civil Procedure Law's purpose is to regulate civil trials and protect citizens' rights:

The Civil Procedure Law of the People's Republic of China aims to protect the exercise of the litigation rights of the parties and ensure the ascertaining of facts by the people's courts, distinguish right from wrong, apply the law correctly, try civil cases promptly, affirm civil rights and obligations, impose sanctions for civil wrongs, protect the lawful rights and interests of the parties, educate citizens to voluntarily abide by the law, maintain the social and economic order, and guarantee the smooth progress of the socialist construction.[56]

Though Article 5 does state that citizens and foreign nationals are granted the same rights and responsibilities under the Civil Procedure Law, the courts will restrict the rights of foreigners whose countries impose any restrictions on Chinese citizens. With the exception of this caveat, anyone filing civil litigation within the PRC will be subject to the Civil Procedures Law.[57]

Interestingly, Article 6 gives the impression that the courts are independent in civil matters: 'The people's courts shall exercise judicial powers with respect to civil cases. The people's courts shall try civil cases independently in accordance with the law, and shall be subject to no interference by any administrative organ, public organization or individual.' It is important to remember, however, that the CPC is not considered an administrative organ nor a public organization, meaning it may still affect how judges within the people's courts decide civil matters. Otherwise, Articles 7 and 8 guarantee that judges must decide cases purely on the facts and the law, and that all individuals have the same rights when appearing in the people's courts.

The process of civil litigation is very specific: 'In trying civil cases, the people's courts shall, according to the provisions of the law, follow the systems of panel hearing, withdrawal, public trial and the court of second instance being that of last instance.'[58] In addition, a people's court will first try to conduct voluntary conciliation, but if conciliation is not possible the court will render a judgment.[59]

Jurisdiction

In general, primary people's courts will be courts of first instance for civil lawsuits, but there are specific subject matters that primary courts never hear. Instead, intermediate courts serve as the court of first instance for 'major cases involving [a] foreign element; cases that have major impact on the area under their jurisdiction; and cases as determined by the Supreme People's Court to be under the jurisdiction of the intermediate people's courts'.[60] The second type of case, those with 'major impact on the area under their jurisdiction', is not well defined, leaving considerable room for interpretation. Moreover, the high people's courts will serve as courts of first instance over 'cases that have major impact on the area under their jurisdiction'.[61] Finally, the SPC has virtually limitless jurisdiction as a court of first instance, as it can hear 'cases that have major impact on the whole country; and cases that the Supreme People's Court deems it should try'.[62]

The Civil Procedure Law dictates which people's court within the primary-, intermediate- or high-court hierarchy has jurisdiction over a case. Generally, a lawsuit must be brought in the territory in which the defendant has his or her domicile. When the habitual residence is not the same as the domicile, the people's court of the defendant's habitual residence has jurisdiction. When the defendant is a legal but not a natural person, the suit must be brought in the court of the defendant's domicile. And when the case involves multiple defendants of multiple domiciles or habitual residences, the plaintiff may bring the lawsuit in any of the courts that have jurisdiction.[63]

There are some exceptions, however, to the territorial jurisdiction rules listed in Article 21. When the lawsuit concerns a contract dispute, the plaintiff may file the suit in the people's court 'where the contract is performed'.[64] Lawsuits concerning various aspects of the creation or maintenance of a company will be filed in the jurisdiction in which the company is located.[65] Finally, Article 28 allows plaintiffs who are suing on a tort to bring a lawsuit in either the place of the defendant's domicile or the place of the tort.

Trials

A unique aspect of Chinese civil trials is that lawsuits are typically tried by a collegial panel. A collegial panel is always an odd number of judges and judicial assessors, or judges alone.[66] Though they are different, judicial assessors have almost the same rights and responsibilities as judges, but with lower ranks. Courts of both first and second instance will use collegial panels, as well as any court that is rehearing a case.[67] In the case of a retrial, a new collegial panel will be formed.[68] In situations where a civil lawsuit is being decided by summary procedure a single judge will decide the case.[69]

According to Article 48 of the Civil Procedure Law, organizations and legal persons, in addition to citizens, may be parties to a civil lawsuit. The parties will be represented by either legal representatives (legal persons) or their principal heads (organizations). Parties have specific rights during a civil case, including:

> the right to appoint agents, apply for withdrawals, collect and provide evidence, proffer arguments, request conciliation, file an appeal and apply for execution [of a judicial order]. Parties to an action may have access to materials pertaining to the case and make copies thereof and other legal documents pertaining to the case.[70]

In addition, parties can appoint up to two people to act as an agent *ad litem*.[71] These agents may be lawyers, legal service providers, close relatives, staff members or other community members from the organization to which the party belongs.

While anyone can bring a lawsuit, he or she must have a 'direct interest' in the case at hand for a court to accept the suit.[72] In addition, the plaintiff must have a definite defendant and specific allegations giving rise to a civil lawsuit that is recognized and can be heard by a people's court. To initiate the suit, the plaintiff must submit a written statement of complaint to the people's court in which he or she is filing.[73] Because not everyone will be able to make a written complaint, the court will accept oral complaints, which it will then transcribe and notify to the defendant.[74]

Article 121 requires that the statement of complaint must clearly list basic information about both the plaintiff and the defendant (including, surprisingly, the plaintiff's ethnic status), the claims and facts that compose the lawsuit, contact information for witnesses and the evidence to be presented. The court then must accept or reject the case, sending a copy of the statement of complaint to the defendant within five days of accepting it.[75] Within the first 15 days of receiving the statement of complaint the defendant must file a statement of defense, to include much of the same biographical and contact information for the defendant and his or her legal representative.[76] Unlike, for example, the US court system, a defendant's failure to file a statement of defense does not have an effect on the trial itself.[77]

Should the defendant object to the jurisdiction of the people's court, he or she must make an objection within the 15-day period to file the statement of defense.[78] If the defendant fails to do so, his or her objection will be considered waived and it shall be assumed that the defendant accepts the jurisdiction of the people's court. Upon receiving an objection based on jurisdiction, the court will review the objection and either reassign the case to the proper court or reject the objection entirely.

After the plaintiff receives the statement of defense from the court, a public trial will be held.[79] There are some exceptions to the requirement for a public trial, such as when one party requests a private trial for divorce or trade secrets, or if it is determined that state secrets or personal privacy may be compromised.

The court investigation itself is divided into five distinct parts:

> statements by the parties; informing the witnesses of their rights and obligations, giving testimony by the witnesses and reading of the written statements of witnesses that are absent; presentation of documentary evidence, material evidence, audio-visual material and electronic data; reading of expert opinions; and reading of records of inspection.[80]

Court debate, however, will follow its own unique order: 'oral statements by the plaintiff and his agents ad litem; defence by the defendant and his agents ad litem; oral statement or defence by the third party and his agents ad litem; and debate between the two sides'.[81] Following court debate, the collegial panel will hear the parties' respective 'final opinions'.

Evidence

It is the responsibility of a party making an allegation to provide evidentiary support, though if the party is unable to collect evidence, the people's court may choose to collect relevant evidence itself.[82] Should the court want, it may also choose to investigate and collect evidence that it believes to be necessary for the trial. At all times, however, the court must be impartial and comprehensive in its consideration of evidence. Evidence is not anything the party can show to support his or her allegations; Article 63 limits evidence to 'statements of the parties; documentary evidence; material evidence; audio-visual materials; electronic data; witness' testimony; expert opinions; and written records for inspection'. Evidence may only be used to prove or disprove an allegation after it has been verified and authenticated.

Judgment and appeal

At the conclusion of the trial, the judicial officers and court clerk will issue and sign a judgment.[83] The judgment itself must contain specific information, such as the cause of action, the laws applied in the case, the 'facts and causes affirmed by the judgment', the final judgment of the court, the costs and the parties responsible for them and the procedure for filing a timely appeal.[84] If a party wishes his or her case to be heard on 'second instance' or on appeal, he or she must file an appeal with the court listed on the judgment within 15 days of the date of the written judgment or within ten days of a written order.[85]

The appellate court will then hold a public trial with a new collegial panel.[86] The court of second instance also reviews the facts, laws and judgment of the trial court.[87] If the court believes there is no new evidence, and after reading through the file finds no need for a public trial, one may not be held.[88]

Article 170 describes four conclusions the appellate court can come to:

> (1) If, in the original judgment or written order, the facts are clearly ascertained and the law and regulations are correctly applied, the people's court of second instance shall reject the appeal and make a judgment or order to affirm the original judgment or order; (2) If, in the original judgment or written order, the facts are incorrectly ascertained or the law and regulations are incorrectly applied, the people's court of second instance shall make a judgment or order to amend, cancel or change the judgment or order in accordance with the law; (3) If, in the original judgment, the facts are not clearly ascertained, the people's court of second instance may make an order to cancel the original judgment, remand the case to the people's court of original instance for retrial, or the people's court of second instance may amend the judgment after investigating and ascertaining the facts; and (4) If there is serious violation of legal procedures in making the original judgment, for instance, the judgment is made without presence of the parties concerned or a default judgment is made in violation of the law, the people's court of second instance shall rule to cancel the original judgment and remand the case to the people's court of original instance for retrial.

One of the final aspects of a civil lawsuit is enforcement or, as it is labeled in official translations, 'procedure of execution'. The trial court or a court at the same level as the trial court will enforce any 'legally effective judgments or written orders in civil cases, as well as the parts of judgment or written orders that relate to property in criminal cases'.[89] The court responsible for enforcement must be located where the property described in the judgment is located. Other judgments and legal orders that need enforcement will be executed by the court where 'the person subjected to execution has his domicile or where the property subjected to execution is located'.[90]

If the losing party does not comply with the enforcement, he or she must file a truthful report of his or her 'property situation' at the time of enforcement and one year prior to enforcement.[91] If he or she does not, or if the report is not truthful, the losing party, his or her lawyer, or the principal leading person responsible for the omission may be jailed or fined.

As mentioned above, the Civil Procedure Law applies equally to Chinese citizens and legal persons and foreign citizens and legal persons. There are a few special provisions, however, that may change when a 'foreign element' is involved.[92] When international treaties or conventions to which China has acceded conflict with part of the Civil Procedure Law, the international body will override the law, so long as China has not made any relevant reservations to the international convention.[93] Domestic and international provisions regarding diplomatic immunity will govern how civil lawsuits are brought against foreign nationals and those organizations that enjoy diplomatic privilege.[94] For foreign nationals or legal persons to bring lawsuits against Chinese citizens, they must use lawyers admitted to practice in the PRC.[95] Finally, should a party need interpretation or translation of court proceedings, they may be provided, but at the party's expense.[96]

Representative cases

As in all civil law traditions, Chinese judges do not rely on case law to help determine what law to apply or how to apply it. In 2010, however, the SPC issued Provisions of the Supreme People's Court Concerning Work on Guiding Cases,[97] which created quasi-case law. Article 1 of the provisions states that the government created the guiding cases 'to summarize adjudication experiences, unify application of law, enhance adjudication quality, and safeguard judicial justice'. To qualify as a guiding case (and thus create legal precedent), cases must be 'widely concerned by society; [the] legal provisions are of relatively general nature; [they] are of a typical nature; are difficult, complicated or are cases of new types; [or] Other cases having a guiding effect'.[98] The exact language of the provisions states that the courts at all levels 'should refer to' the guiding cases, but the nation's highest judges have said there will be negative consequences for failing to follow these cases.[99]

The guiding cases need not have been decided by the SPC, but were selected because they serve as models for courts across the country to follow. The decisions typically have applied good legal reasoning to replicable fact patterns, and the topics covered are not too narrowly defined so as not to be useful. Ultimately, these cases are meant to help guide courts come to more uniform decisions.

The following six civil law cases were some of those selected by the SPC as either representative cases[100] or guiding cases.[101]

Buluke (Chengdu) Engineering Company Limited v. Sichuan Wanhao Real Estate Management Company Limited & Anor[102]

This is a case of copyright infringement, but also a matter of whether a Chinese company has the standing to bring a lawsuit on behalf of another company. The Higher People's Court of Sichuan Province heard the case on second instance, dismissing the appeal and confirming the judgment of the Intermediate People's Court of Chengdu City, which had held that a Chinese company that is a foreign investment by an overseas company and has permission to use copyrighted materials has standing to bring a case for copyright infringement. Moreover, according to the Berne Convention for the Protection of Arts and Literature, when a photograph is copyrighted in one member state (even if it is not published), it is considered copyrighted under other member states' copyright laws.

In the case, a Chinese company that was a foreign investment of a Swiss company filed a lawsuit against a second Chinese company for copyright infringement. The Swiss parent company had copyrighted under Swiss law 14 pictures that depicted various construction processes, but only published a few. The parent company had given its Chinese subsidiary the right to use the pictures, but the second company used the 14 pictures in its own promotional materials. The intermediate court held that because the parent company had given the plaintiff written authorization to use the pictures, and did not object to the plaintiff's use of the pictures, the plaintiff had the sole right to use the copyrighted material. As such, it had standing to file a lawsuit for copyright infringement under Chinese law.

The court also decided that under the language of the Berne Convention, of which both Switzerland and China are members, the fact that the pictures were copyrighted in Switzerland meant they were similarly protected under Chinese copyright law. The defendant's use of the pictures without the permission of either the subsidiary or the parent company constituted a violation of the law and required compensation.

Shanghai Centaline Property Consultants Limited v. Tao Dehua[103]

In this case, the court had to decide whether contract language prohibited a homebuyer from 'bypassing' an intermediary company that provided the buyer with information, and working with a second intermediary company or acting himself or herself to negotiate a lower price. The No. 2 Intermediate People's Court of Shanghai Municipality ruled on remand that such language is valid, but if the information that a buyer relies on is readily accessible to the public, he or she may use any intermediary to purchase the property without bypassing the original intermediary.

The court held that the previous owner of the home had worked with several housing intermediary companies to sell his home, giving none of them the exclusive right to sell the property. The homebuyer at the heart of the lawsuit and his wife had been shown the home by intermediary buyers prior to contacting the intermediary company that filed the lawsuit. On the day that the homebuyer was shown the property by the plaintiff, the defendant and plaintiff signed a 'confirmation of request to buy real estate' which contained language saying that if the defendant purchased the home without the assistance of the plaintiff within six months of the plaintiff showing the defendant the home, then the defendant would owe the plaintiff liquidated damages.

Though the court found this contractual language to be valid, it reasoned that if the buyer had used 'information, opportunities, or other such conditions provided by the intermediary company' that were otherwise obtainable to the public, there could not have been a breach of the 'bypass' clause. Because the defendant had gathered the same information provided by the plaintiff from several intermediary companies and no company had the exclusive right to sell the property, the court found that the homebuyer did not breach the otherwise valid 'bypass' clause of the contract with the plaintiff.

Wu Mei v. Meishan Xicheng Paper Co., Ltd of Sichuan Province[104]

This case, heard by the Intermediate People's Court of Meishan Municipality, determined whether a judgment on first instance became legally enforceable after an appeal for a hearing on second instance had been withdrawn by one of the parties. The intermediate court held that by withdrawing an appeal, a judgment on first instance 'immediately bec[omes] a legally effective judgment'. Moreover, the court that heard the matter on first instance gained 'compulsory enforcement authority'.

The case arose after an individual attempted to collect on two agreements for payment. When the company that owed the individual refused to pay, the individual brought a lawsuit for the full amount owed plus interest. The Dongpo District People's Court of Meishan Municipality held that the company had to pay what the plaintiff had asked for within ten days of the judgment going into effect, but the company appealed to the intermediate court. Before the actual hearing on second instance, the defendant and the plaintiff agreed to a repayment schedule and the defendant withdrew the appeal.

When the defendant failed to make its payments, the plaintiff asked the court to enforce the original court of first instance's judgment. The intermediate court held that the company's withdrawal of its appeal made the original judgment legally binding, and ordered the company to pay the individual.

Mudanjiang Municipality Hongge Construction and Installation Co., Ltd v. Mudanjiang Municipality Hualong Real Estate Development Co., Ltd and Zhang Jizeng[105]

At issue was whether a court should hear a retrial proceeding if the parties have come to a settlement and completed the terms of the agreement. The SPC held that unless a case was a matter of state, public or social interest, or if a third party's interests would be infringed upon, a court should dismiss a retrial if the parties had worked out and performed a settlement or had withdrawn a petition for retrial. Citing Article 34 of the Interpretation of the Supreme People's Court on Several Issues Concerning the Application of the Adjudication Supervision Procedures of the Civil Procedure Law of the People's Republic of China, as well as social harmony, the court wrote that resolved cases should not be reheard.

In the original case, one company had been unhappy with a second company's performance on a construction project, and filed a lawsuit. After the Higher People's Court of Heilongjiang Province found for one party, the other party sought an appeal. During the retrial period the companies came to a settlement, and both parties had fully performed the terms of the settlement prior to the retrial, prompting the original petitioner to file a petition for withdrawal of the retrial.

For the same reason that the petitioner had filed for a retrial, it also submitted an application for a protest to the Supreme People's Procuratorate. The procuratorate eventually accepted the protest, even though the SPC recommended that it should be withdrawn. The SPC, however, made a final ruling that the case should not be examined because it had been resolved and there were no national, public or social interests involved.

Lin Fangqing v. Changshu Kailai Industry Co., Ltd and Dai Xiaoming[106]

In this case, the Higher People's Court of Jiangsu Province had to determine whether a company had 'serious difficulty in the operation or management of a company' under Article 183 of the Company Law, and thus would need to be dissolved by the people's court. The court determined that a company having two shareholders, both with 50 percent of the company, could constitute difficulty in operation or management. Further, it held that the statute did not refer to a literal difficulty in the functioning of the business, like a difficulty in making a profit.

The parties to the case were the two equal shareholders and the company in which they held stock. One of the shareholders had been unable to agree with the other for some time, and sent a letter to the shareholder and to the company, insisting on dissolving. The other shareholder refused, however, saying that the plaintiff lacked the legal basis to make and pass a shareholder resolution. The parties brought the matter to the Jiangsu

Changshu Garments Town Management Committee, which told the shareholders to undergo mediation. The mediation failed and the case was brought to the Intermediate People's Court of Suzhu Municipality, which held that the shareholder asking for the dissolution of the company lacked the legal authority to do so under the Company Law.

The Higher People's Court of Jiangsu Province, however, held that the structure of this company, as well as its shareholder requirements, made the company extremely difficult to manage and operate. As shareholder meeting resolutions could only be passed by more than 50 percent of the shareholders, nothing would pass without the agreement of both shareholders. Because the company was extremely difficult to operate and manage, and because the shareholder deadlock had not been resolved by outside mediators, it was up to the court to determine whether the company should be dissolved, which the higher court ordered it should.

Li Jianjun v. Shanghai Jiapower Environment Protection Science and Technology Co., Ltd[107]

The issue at hand was whether it was within the scope of a people's court's judicial review to revoke a corporation's decision to terminate its general manager. The No. 2 Intermediate People's Court of Shanghai Municipality held on appeal that the Company Law dictates three reasons why a corporation's board of directors' resolution can be revoked: '(1) The procedure for convening violates laws, administrative regulations, or the articles of association; (2) the voting method violates laws, administrative regulations, or the articles of association; (3) the content of resolutions violates the articles of association.'

In the case at hand, the general manager of a corporation (and owner of 46 percent of the company's stock) was terminated by a resolution passed by the board of directors. The board consisted of the general manager and the owners of the other 54 percent of the stock. Citing the general manager's use of company funds in the stock market without the consent of the board of directors, the two directors with 54 percent of the shares issued the resolution during a board meeting with all three directors present.

The articles of association governing the corporation said that the board of directors had the authority to appoint and dismiss the general manager. They also stipulated that board meetings must have at least two-thirds of the members present and at least two-thirds of the board must agree for a resolution to pass.

As neither the convening of the board members, nor the voting method, nor the content of the resolution itself violated the articles of association, the law or administrative regulations, the intermediate court did not have the authority to revoke the board of directors' resolution.

Notes

1. General Principles of the Civil Law of the People's Republic of China (1986).
2. Ibid., Article 3.
3. Ibid., Article 11.
4. Ibid., Article 84.
5. Ibid.
6. Ibid., Article 85.
7. Ibid., Article 100.
8. Ibid., Article 101.
9. Ibid., Article 134.
10. C. Stephen Hsu (2007) 'Contract law of the People's Republic of China', *Minnesota Journal of International Law*, 16: 115.
11. Ibid., p. 117.
12. Contract Law of the People's Republic of China, Article 1.
13. Daniel C.K. Chow (2009) *The Legal System of the People's Republic of China*, 2nd edn. St Paul, MN: Thomson West, p. 341.
14. Mark Magnier (2007) 'China grants some property rights', *Los Angeles Times*, 16 March; available at: *http://articles.latimes.com/2007/mar/16/world/fg-property16* (accessed: 12 August 2013).
15. Property Law of the People's Republic of China (1 October 2007), Article 1.
16. Ibid.
17. Ibid., Part 2, Ownership.
18. Ibid., Article 43.
19. Ibid.
20. Ibid., Articles 61 and 62.
21. Jeremy Page and Brian Spegele (2011) 'Land dispute in China town sparks revolt', *Wall Street Journal*, 15 December; available at: *http://online.wsj.com/article/SB10001424052970203518404577097532246936046.html* (accessed: 12 August 2013).
22. *Los Angeles Times* (2011) 'China's mass incidents have increased, the government must listen to the people', *Los Angeles Times*, 9 October; available at: *www.rfa.org/mandarin/yataibaodao/yl-10092011191359.html* (accessed: 12 August 2013).
23. Ibid.
24. Tort Liability Law of the People's Republic of China (1 July 2010), Article 15.

25. Ibid., Articles 16–25.
26. Ibid., Articles 8–14.
27. Ibid., Article 24.
28. Laura Wang and James M. Zimmerman (2010) 'China adopts tort liability law', *Lexology*, 3 February; available at: *www.lexology.com/library/detail. aspx?g=ec4b826d-dc76-4a62-8883-2326b213c62f* (accessed: 12 August 2013).
29. Tort Liability Law of the People's Republic of China, Article 1.
30. Ibid., Article 15.
31. Ibid., Article 43.
32. Ibid., Articles 41 and 42.
33. Ibid., Article 43.
34. Ibid., Article 57.
35. Ibid., Article 55.
36. Ibid., Article 66.
37. Ibid., Article 67.
38. See generally Stephen Hsu and Shi Hong (trans) (2006) *A Concise Restatement of Torts*, American Law Institute. Beijing: Law Press; Xiao Yongping, Gong Lefang and Wang Xuefei (trans) (2006) *Restatement of the Law, Third, Torts: Product Liability*, American Law Institute. Beijing: Law Press.
39. Mo Zhang (2011) 'Tort liabilities and torts law: the new frontier of Chinese legal horizon', *Richmond Journal of Global Law and Business*, 10: 415.
40. See generally Xue Hong and Zheng Chengsi (2002) *Chinese Intellectual Property Law: In the 21st Century*. Hong Kong: Sweet & Maxwell Asia.
41. Albert H.Y. Chen (2004) *An Introduction to the Legal System of the People's Republic of China*, 3rd edn. London: LexisNexis Butterworths, p. 240.
42. Chow, note 13 above, p. 331.
43. Company Law of the People's Republic of China (1994), Article 1.
44. Ibid., Article 23.
45. Ibid.
46. Ibid., Article 37.
47. Ibid., Article 77.
48. Ibid., Article 109.
49. Ibid., Articles 126 and 138.
50. Ibid., Article 173.
51. Dan Harris (2009) 'China corporate law: the basics of China's company law', China Law Blog, 14 December; available at: *www.chinalawblog. com/2009/12/china_corporate_law_the_basics.html* (accessed: 12 August 2013).
52. Ibid.
53. Ibid.
54. Ibid.
55. Civil Procedure Law of the People's Republic of China (1991), Article 1.
56. Ibid., Article 2.
57. Ibid., Article 4.

58.   Ibid., Article 10.
59.   Ibid., Article 9.
60.   Ibid., Articles 17 and 18.
61.   Ibid., Article 19.
62.   Ibid., Article 20.
63.   Ibid., Article 21.
64.   Ibid., Article 23.
65.   Ibid., Article 26.
66.   Ibid., Article 39.
67.   Ibid., Articles 39 (courts of first instance) and 40 (courts of second instance).
68.   Ibid., Article 40.
69.   Ibid., Article 39.
70.   Ibid., Article 49.
71.   Ibid., Article 58.
72.   Ibid., Article 119.
73.   Ibid., Article 120.
74.   Ibid.
75.   Ibid., Article 125.
76.   Ibid.
77.   Ibid.
78.   Ibid., Article 127.
79.   Ibid., Article 134.
80.   Ibid., Article 138.
81.   Ibid., Article 141.
82.   Ibid., Article 64.
83.   Ibid., Article 152.
84.   Ibid.
85.   Ibid., Article 164.
86.   Ibid., Article 169.
87.   Ibid., Article 168.
88.   Ibid., Article 169.
89.   Ibid., Article 224.
90.   Ibid.
91.   Ibid., Article 241.
92.   Ibid., Article 259
93.   Ibid., Article 260.
94.   Ibid., Article 261.
95.   Ibid., Article 263.
96.   Ibid., Article 262.
97.   Supreme People's Court (2010) 'Provisions of the Supreme People's Court concerning work on guiding cases', Supreme People's Court of China, Beijing.
98.   Ibid., Article 1.
99.   Garret Anderson, Brian Timm-Brock and Ralph Wang (trans) (2010) 'Provisions of the Supreme People's Court concerning work on guiding cases', China Guiding Cases Project, 27 November; available at: *https:// cgc.law.stanford.edu/supreme-peoples-court-concerning-work-on-guiding-cases/* (accessed: 12 August 2013).

100. Representative cases are published regularly in the *Supreme Court Bulletin*.
101. Partial translations of the guiding cases are available at: *http://cgc.law. stanford.edu/guiding-cases/* (accessed: 12 August 2013).
102. National Judges College and Renmin University Law School (2003) *Overview of Chinese Cases – 2002 Commercial and Administrative Cases*. Beijing: Renmin University Press, p. 270.
103. Partial translation of the case and comments are available at: *https://cgc. law.stanford.edu/guiding-cases/guiding-case-1/* (accessed: 12 August 2013).
104. Partial translation of the case and comments are available at: *https://cgc. law.stanford.edu/guiding-cases/guiding-case-2/* (accessed: 12 August 2013).
105. Partial translation of the case and comments are available at: *https://cgc. law.stanford.edu/guiding-cases/guiding-case-7/* (accessed: 12 August 2013).
106. Partial translation of the case and comments are available at: *https://cgc. law.stanford.edu/guiding-cases/guiding-case-8/* (accessed: 12 August 2013).
107. Partial translation of the case and comments are available at: *https://cgc. law.stanford.edu/guiding-cases/guiding-case-10/* (accessed: 12 August 2013).

7

Criminal laws and criminal cases

Abstract: This chapter looks at criminal law within the People's Republic of China. It starts with an overview of the 1979 Criminal Law and the major differences between this and the 1997 Criminal Law, which is the most recent version. The chapter also looks at the various stages of a criminal investigation, trial and appeal through the Criminal Procedure Law. These legal topics are then illustrated in the case of Liu Xiaobo and other representative cases.

Key words: Liu Xiaobo, criminal law, criminal procedure.

Since its imperial days, criminal law has dominated the Chinese legal system. Previous chapters have explained the concept of 'rule by law', which can be summarized as using the law as an instrument to govern, as opposed to the concept of the 'rule of law', or 'law should govern'.[1] Criminal law is the area in which the Chinese government's use of rule by law is most readily apparent.

The first criminal statute of the PRC was the Regulations of the People's Republic of China on Punishment of Counterrevolutionaries of 1951, which set out various 'counterrevolutionary' crimes, including 'collaborating with imperialism', 'bribing government officials', 'participating in armed rebellion', 'participating in spying or espionage' and 'looting and sabotage'. Under the law, convicted offenders could expect the death penalty or life imprisonment, depending on the seriousness of the crime.[2] These regulations served as the primary 'legal' tool for the CPC to punish class enemies, political dissidents and criminal perpetrators from the beginning of the 1950s to the late 1970s.

Since then, criminal law in China has had two main iterations: the 1979 Criminal Law and the 1997 Criminal Law. These two codes are quite different from each other, and only the 1997 law is currently in effect. The evolution of criminal law has encompassed not just the law itself but also criminal procedure.

Professor Jerome Cohen once wrote: 'As a major instrument of the Communists, the criminal process has faithfully reflected the twists and turns that have occurred in the Party's "general line".'[3] The party views criminal law and criminal procedure as important instruments of political, social and, most recently, economic control. Observers have expressed concern regarding the continued policy of strict social control espoused by the CPC, though there have been limited improvements in procedural due process. As Stanley Lubman commented in his book *Bird in a Cage: Legal Reform in China after Mao*:

> The Chinese criminal process remains dominated not only by the police, but by a blatant instrumentalism that puts it at the service of the CCP and political leaders when they wish to use it. Reforms in both substantive criminal law and the criminal procedure have edged the system toward greater tolerance for the rights of criminal defendants, but have not yet adequately institutionalized protection for those rights.[4]

Criminal law

1979 Criminal Law

Though it is called the 1979 Criminal Law[5] (the year of its publication), the law did not go into effect until 1980. It had several components, including the ideology behind criminal law, the enumerated crimes, the punishments available to the courts and the methods by which to apply the punishments. In addition, the law listed specific crimes, many of which focused on preventing the undermining of the state goal of a socialist society.

While many of the civil laws list their purpose in the first articles, Articles 1 and 2 of the Criminal Law 1979 put forth the ideologies and goals that helped to shape the law. Article 1, for example, says:

> The Criminal Law of the People's Republic of China, which takes Marxism-Leninism-Mao Zedong Thought as its guide and the Constitution as its basis, is formulated in accordance with the policy of combining punishment with leniency and in the light of

the actual circumstances and concrete experiences of the people of all China's nationalities in carrying out the people's democratic dictatorship, led by the proletariat and based on the worker-peasant alliance, that is, the dictatorship of the proletariat, and in conducting the socialist revolution and socialist construction.

Article 2 explains further:

> The tasks of the Criminal Law of the People's Republic of China are to use criminal punishments to fight against all counterrevolutionary and other criminal acts in order to defend the system of the dictatorship of the proletariat; to protect socialist property owned by the whole people and socialist property collectively owned by the working people; to protect the citizens' privately owned lawful property; to protect the citizens' rights of the person and their democratic and other rights; to maintain public order and order in production, education, scientific research and other work and in the life of the masses; and to safeguard the smooth progress of the cause of the socialist revolution and socialist construction.

One of the important crimes listed in the 1979 law is that of counterrevolution. Article 90 defines the crime as 'any act that is committed with the aim of overthrowing the political power of the dictatorship of the proletariat and the socialist system and endangers the People's Republic of China'. The remainder of the section lists various crimes of counterrevolution and the punishment that accompanies such behavior, including working with a foreign state to threaten the 'sovereignty, territorial integrity and security of China';[6] planning to 'subvert the government or dismember the state';[7] bribing or convincing a member of the law enforcement, militia or military to defect or start a rebellion;[8] defecting to the enemy;[9] leading an 'armed mass rebellion' or committing a serious crime;[10] leading a group of people in a prison break;[11] aiding or spying for the enemy;[12] and organizing or leading a 'counterrevolutionary group'.[13] Moreover, crimes of counterrevolution encompassed using 'feudal superstition, superstitious sects or secret societies' to organize a counterrevolution;[14] committing acts of sabotage to further a counterrevolution;[15] poisoning or using germ warfare for counterrevolutionary purposes;[16] and 'inciting the masses to resist or sabotage the implementation of the state's laws or decrees; or propagandizing for and inciting the overthrow of the political power of the dictatorship of the proletariat and the socialist system, through counterrevolutionary slogans, leaflets or by other means'.[17]

Nearly all the crimes of counterrevolution carried sentences of ten years to life in prison, with only a few of the more minor crimes having shorter terms. Article 103 also allowed the courts to sentence to death an individual whose crimes caused 'serious harm to the state and the people and the circumstances [of which were] especially flagrant'. Only defendants convicted of the crimes in Articles 98, 99 and 102 could not be sentenced to death.

Major differences between the 1979 Criminal Law and the 1997 Criminal Law

Though the Criminal Law of the People's Republic of China was reissued in 1997 as a completely new law, it has been amended eight times since then. It is still referred to as the 1997 Criminal Law, as the changes made were less drastic than those between the 1979 and the 1997 laws. The most recent amendments and update were in 2011.

With the exception of the specific provisions listed in Chapter 5, the overall structure of the 1997 Criminal Law mirrors that of the 1979 law. While the structure is the same, the contents are not. In terms of specific provisions, the new law has a section on 'crimes of disrupting the order of the socialist market economy', as opposed to the previous 'crimes of undermining the socialist economic order'. Though this may not seem like a major change, it does reflect the reform and opening of the economic system following Deng Xiaoping's rise to power and the adoption of a socialist market economy instead of a strict socialist or planned economy. In addition, the 1997 law does away with crimes of counterrevolution, instead referring to them as 'crimes of endangering national security'.

Beyond the overall structure, many of the individual articles were changed to create a new criminal justice system. Starting at the very beginning of the law, the mission statement was changed: 'In order to punish crimes and protect the people, this Law is enacted on the basis of the Constitution and in the light of the concrete experiences and actual circumstances in China's fight against crimes.'[18] Moreover, Article 2 reflects a new aim for the law:

> The aim of the Criminal Law of the People's Republic of China is to use criminal punishments to fight against all criminal acts in order to safeguard security of the State, to defend the State power

of the people's democratic dictatorship and the socialist system, to protect property owned by the State, and property collectively owned by the working people and property privately owned by citizens, to protect citizens' rights of the person and their democratic and other rights, to maintain public and economic order, and to ensure the smooth progress of socialist construction.

In a dramatic departure from the previous law, the 1997 law included definitions of crimes, as well as the concepts of equality before the law and proportionality of punishment. Article 3 requires that before someone can be convicted of and punished for a crime, the crime must be concretely defined; if the crime has not been adequately defined, an individual cannot be convicted of it. Article 4 also provides for the law to be 'equally applied to anyone who commits a crime'. It assures citizens that no one is above the law. Finally, the new law also requires that the punishment accurately reflects the crime that was committed, meaning no one should face harsh punishments for relatively minor infractions.[19] These changes were attempts to address fundamental problems in the Chinese system: guilt by analogy, privilege and immunity of political elites, and disproportionality in punishment. The actual effects of these changes, however, are difficult to evaluate.

One of the more noticeable changes, as mentioned, is that the 1997 law eliminated 'crimes of counterrevolution' and replaced them with 'crimes of endangering national security'. There are some crimes that are very similar to the counterrevolutionary crimes listed in the 1979 law (Articles 102, 104, 108), though Article 103 sets forth a new crime: 'organiz[ing], plot[ting] or carry[ing] out the scheme of splitting the State or undermining unity of the country'. Another newer crime that endangers national security is 'subverting the State power or overthrowing the socialist system'.[20] Article 105's subversion of state power has been used in many criminal cases in China, which may indicate its status as a catch-all criminal provision.

The crime of endangering national security also comes with greater ranges of punishment, dictated in part by the convicted individual's role in the commission of the crime. For smaller roles, offenders will be granted lesser sentences; more severe offenses, or those individuals whose crimes involved foreign organizations, will receive a stricter punishment. Article 113 does allow for the death penalty in most crimes of endangering national security if the harm caused was 'particularly grave'.

The 1997 Criminal Law also provided greater clarity on punishments, including principal and supplementary punishments.[21] The principal punishments range from the relatively minor to death: 'public surveillance; criminal detention; fixed-term imprisonment; life imprisonment; and the death penalty'.[22] Article 34 lists the supplemental punishments: 'fine; deprivation of political rights; and confiscation of property'. As the number of foreigners in China has increased exponentially since the 1979 Criminal Law was promulgated, a clause that allows for deportation to be used 'independently or supplementarily to a foreigner who commits a crime'[23] was added.

Of course, China retained the death penalty between the two versions of the Criminal Law, but the 1997 law is somewhat different from the initial 1979 death penalty provisions. Article 48 explains that the penalty is only to be used in cases of 'extremely serious crimes', and allows for an offender to be sentenced simultaneously to a two-year suspension of execution if he or she is not to be executed immediately. The Supreme People's Court must verify and approve all death sentences, but suspensions of executions can be verified and approved by higher people's courts.

The death penalty may apply to anyone convicted of serious crimes, except for those who were not yet 18 years old at the time they committed the crime or women who are pregnant at the time of trial.[24] One of the newer amendments to the 1997 law also restricts the execution of offenders who are 75 years old or older at the time of trial, unless they killed someone by 'especially cruel means'.[25] For those individuals who are granted a suspension of execution, their sentences can be commuted to either life imprisonment or 25 years in prison at the end of the two-year suspension.[26] To be eligible, the offender must not commit an intentional crime during the suspension, and to receive the fixed-term sentence of 25 years he or she must have 'performed major meritorious service'. If the offender does commit an intentional crime, his or her death sentence must be verified and approved by the SPC before it can be carried out.

There is also a new crime of 'defection':

> Any State functionary who, while discharging his official duties at home or abroad, leaves his post without permission and defects to another country, which endangers the security of the People's Republic of China, shall be sentenced to fixed-term imprisonment of not more than five years, criminal detention, public surveillance or deprivation of political rights; if the circumstances are serious, he shall be sentenced to fixed-term imprisonment of not less than five years but not more than 10 years.[27]

If the individual has state secrets, he or she could receive 'heavier punishment'. In 2012 former Chongqing police chief Wang Lijun, after a failed attempt to seek political asylum at the US consulate general in Chengdu, was convicted under the 'defection' provision, among others, and sentenced to 15 years in prison.[28]

Moreover, the 1997 law contains several articles that criminalize espionage and aiding the enemy. Article 110 prohibits an individual from 'joining an espionage organization' or 'directing the enemy to any bombing or shelling target'. Article 111 continues to legislate against spying by outlawing the provision of intelligence to organizations outside China. Finally, anyone convicted of aiding the enemy during wartime by 'providing him with weapons and equipment or military materials' under Article 112 could be sentenced to between ten years and life in prison.

One of the unique features of the 1979 Criminal Law was that the elements of a crime were not defined. With the issue of the 1997 Criminal Law, the four elements of a crime were finally explained, and all four must be present for a suspect to be convicted: 'a criminal subject capable of bearing criminal liability; the requisite mental element or condition; an interest recognized and protected by the state that is infringed; and substantial harm caused by the act or omission of the criminal subject to the interest protected by the state'.[29]

In addition to defining the essential elements of crimes, the 1997 Criminal Law distinguishes between intentional and negligent crimes. An intentional crime, as defined by Article 14, is a crime that is 'committed by a person who clearly knows that his act will entail harmful consequences to society but who wishes or allows such consequences to occur'. In contrast, a negligent crime is 'an act committed by a person who should have foreseen that his act would possibly entail harmful consequences to society but who fails to do so through his negligence or, having foreseen the consequences, readily believes that they can be avoided, so that the consequences do occur'.[30]

The 1997 code was much less political than the 1979 code, both in rhetoric – as illustrated in the earlier comparison of the first two articles – and in substance: 'the 1997 revision also abolished two of the 1979 Law's basic approaches to criminal liability: lack of equal treatment and adjusting punishment in accordance with political needs'.[31] The newer code could be seen as a moderate attempt to make criminal law a legal concept, rather than merely a tool for the CPC to suppress class enemies and counterrevolutionaries, or a supplement to party policies.

Certain concepts advocated by Chinese legal reformists found places in the newer code: 'the authority of the law should be upheld, and there should now be more emphasis on the criminal law's function in protecting citizens' rights, their persons and property, and in safeguarding social productivity, the developing socialist market economy and socialist democracy'[32] and the 'need to affirm in the criminal law principles of justice or fairness, and of socialist humanism'.[33]

The newer code was designed with the intention of removing vague legal language and concepts so as to avoid arbitrary and capricious administration of justice (concrete definitions of crimes, laws that are equally applied to everyone regardless of social or political status, appropriate and proportionate punishment standards, etc.). Ian Dobinson explains that 'There are doubts, however, over the degree to which the revisions are substantial or symbolic.'[34] Viewing these language changes as substantial and positive, 'it can be argued that by making the criminal justice system more rational and predictable, China is moving much closer to the "rule of law" as that term is understood in the West'.[35] On the other hand, it 'can be argued that the changes are mainly illusory and that, underneath the veneer of rhetoric, China's criminal justice system remains a crude and arbitrary tool of state control over enemies both real and imagined'.[36] Both arguments can be supported by empirical studies and evidentiary documentation, as can many hotly debated topics regarding China. Nevertheless, 15 years have passed since 1997, and it appears the second argument is closer to reality.

Criminal procedure

The Criminal Procedure Law of the People's Republic of China[37] first took effect in 1979 and has been amended twice. The first amendment came nearly 20 years later in 1996; the second amendment was made in 2012 and went into effect in 2013. Unlike the Criminal Law, however, a new Criminal Procedure Law has not been issued since it was first promulgated.

The Criminal Procedure Law covers many of the basic topics of legal procedure, including jurisdiction, defense and representation, evidence, etc. Note, however, that there are no separate evidence rules in Chinese criminal process. The second part of the law focuses specifically on filing and investigating criminal cases, as well as how to file a public prosecution. Within the section on investigation there are specific provisions regarding interrogation, witnesses, inquests, search and seizure, and expert evaluations. The law also has sections on trials, including trials of first instance and second instance, and the procedure for reviewing death sentences. The final section lists special situations that have unique procedures, such as trials for minors or involuntary medical treatment for those who are mentally unfit to be found criminally guilty.

According to Article 1, the purposes of the Criminal Procedure Law are to 'ensure[e] correct enforcement of the Criminal Law, punish crimes, protect the people, safeguard State and public security and maintain socialist public order'. In addition, Article 2 lists the following as purposes of the law:

> to ensure that the facts of crimes are ascertained in an accurate and timely manner, that the law is correctly applied, that criminals are punished and innocent people are protected from criminal prosecution, and that citizens are educated to abide by the law and vigorously fight against criminal acts, so as to maintain the socialist legal system, respect and protect human rights, safeguard citizens' personal rights, property rights, democratic rights and other rights, and ensure the smooth progress of the socialist cause.

One unique feature of the Criminal Procedure Law is that it has a section on definitions, and has had this since 1979. Normally, Chinese statutes do not provide a definition section, which often means that the judiciary has complete discretion to define terms how it wishes. In the most recent amendment of the Criminal Procedure Law, Article 106 gives definitions for investigation, parties, legal representatives, participants in the proceedings, agents *ad litem* and close relatives.

Investigation

Generally, criminal investigations are conducted by the public security organs, but in certain situations they will be handled by the people's procuratorates.[38] Typically, the people's procuratorate will take over the investigation when a member of the government has allegedly committed a serious crime, such as dereliction of duty, bribery or embezzlement.[39] It will also investigate claims of a member of the government violating individual citizens' democratic rights. Article 113 clarifies that the purpose of the investigation is to gather evidence 'to prove the criminal suspect guilty or innocent or to prove the crime to be minor or grave'.

Interrogation

Though Article 116 stipulates that interrogation of a criminal suspect must be in the presence of at least two interrogators and in a detention house, there are exceptions to these rules. Article 117 says that if a criminal suspect 'does not need to be arrested or held in custody', he or she can be interrogated outside a detention house. Specifically, the interrogation must take place at his or her domicile, at the scene of a crime or at any other location within the city or county in which the suspect lives. If the individual is ordered to appear in court, he or she will be held for no longer than 12 hours, unless the case is one of 'grave circumstances', when he or she can be held for up to 24 hours.

The investigators who participate in an interrogation will be members of the people's procuratorate or a public security organ.[40] They will begin the interrogation by asking the suspect 'whether or not he has committed any criminal act, and let him state the circumstances of his guilt or explain his innocence; then they may ask him questions'.[41] The interrogators will also tell the criminal suspect that he or she may receive leniency if he or she confesses. While it is expected that the suspect will be honest in his or her responses, he or she does have the 'right to refuse to answer any questions that are irrelevant to the case'.[42] Note that the language does not allow a suspect to refuse to answer a question on the grounds of self-incrimination.

Search and seizure

Usually, investigators must provide a search warrant when conducting a search, but 'if an emergency occurs when an arrest or detention is being made, a search may be conducted without a search warrant'.[43] Investigators are allowed to search a suspect's 'person, belongings and residence', and may also search any other relevant places and people who may be hiding a suspect or criminal evidence.[44]

If property or documents are found during a search that 'may prove a criminal suspect's guilt or innocence', they will be seized by investigators.[45] According to Article 139, only those things that are relevant to the investigation can be taken, and when taken they will be 'preserved or sealed for safekeeping'. The law does not provide any definition or explanation of relevancy in this regard.

Right to counsel

During criminal proceedings, suspects may choose to defend themselves or have someone else defend them, but there are only a few individuals who may be hired as a 'defender':

> lawyers; persons recommended by a public organization or the unit to which the criminal suspect or the defendant belongs; and guardians or relatives and friends of the criminal suspect or the defendant. Persons who are under criminal punishment or whose personal freedom is deprived of or restricted according to law shall not serve as defenders.[46]

Defendants may have no more than two defenders.

Suspects are only able to access a defender following their first interrogations, during which they are informed of their rights to 'entrust a defender'.[47] On occasion, after compulsive measures are taken, a suspect may entrust a defender before his or her first interrogation, provided that the only defender is a lawyer. If the individual has already been named a defendant in the criminal proceedings, however, he or she may have access to a defender at any point.

People's courts and procuratorates have three days from receiving materials on a case transferred to them to inform a suspect of his or her right to work with a defender.[48] If, during detention, a 'criminal suspect or defendant requests for the entrustment of a defender... the people's court, the people's procuratorate and the public security organ concerned shall communicate the request in a timely manner'.[49] Once a defender takes on a case, he or she must inform the body who is prosecuting the case 'in a timely manner'. Finally, a close relative or guardian may entrust a defender on behalf of a detained criminal suspect or defendant.

Compulsory measures

In the Criminal Procedure Law, the section entitled 'compulsory measures' deals with the powers of the people's courts, people's procuratorates and public security organs to compel action. For example, Article 64 allows all three bodies to issue warrants to 'compel the appearance of a criminal suspect or defendant, order him to be released on bail pending trial or subject him to residential surveillance'. In addition, Article 73 allows for residential surveillance of a criminal suspect or defendant at his or her domicile or the place where he or she is staying.

Arrest

For a criminal suspect or defendant to be arrested, a people's procuratorate or people's court must approve the arrest, and it must be made by a public security organ.[50] If there is evidence that the suspect or defendant has committed a crime that would merit a fixed-term imprisonment or more severe punishment, he or she may be arrested without bail prior to trial.[51] The concerns listed as to why a suspect should be denied bail include:

> The criminal suspect or defendant may commit a new crime; [t]here is a real risk that the criminal suspect or defendant may endanger State security, public security or public order; [t]he criminal suspect or defendant may destroy or falsify evidence, interfere with the witnesses who give testimony or collude with others to make confessions tally; [t]he criminal suspect or defendant may retaliate against the victims, informants or accusers; or [t]he criminal suspect or defendant tries to commit suicide or escape.[52]

Someone released on bail or put on residential surveillance can be arrested if he or she 'commits grave violations of the provisions with respect to release on bail pending trial or residential surveillance'.[53]

An arrested person will be taken immediately to a detention house.[54] In addition, his or her family members should be notified within 24 hours after the arrest, but if 'notification cannot be processed' there are exemptions to the 24-hour rule. Finally, in order for a public security officer to make an arrest, he or she must have an arrest warrant.

Though an arrest may only be used as a means of detaining criminals or suspected criminals, Article 80 allows public security organs to:

> initially detain an active criminal or a major suspect under any of the following conditions: if he is preparing to commit a crime, is in the process of committing a crime or is discovered immediately after committing a crime; if he is identified as having committed a crime by a victim or an eyewitness; if criminal evidence is found on his body or at his residence; if he attempts to commit suicide or escape after committing a crime, or he is a fugitive; if there is likelihood of his

destroying or falsifying evidence or tallying confessions; if he does not tell his true name and address and his identity is unknown; and if he is strongly suspected of committing crimes from one place to another, repeatedly, or in a gang.

Time limits

The Criminal Procedure Law provides specific time limits that regulate how long a suspect can be held in custody[55] and how long an investigation can last.[56] A criminal suspect can be held for a maximum of two months in custody, unless the case is complex and the investigation will not be completed within the time frame, in which case the people's procuratorate at the next higher level may extend custody for one month.[57] In some situations a people's procuratorate will find that it is not appropriate to bring a case to trial, even after a long period of time.[58] If this happens, the Supreme People's Procuratorate must file a report with the Standing Committee of the National People's Congress requesting approval for the delayed trial. Finally, if the investigation still cannot be finished within the three months allowed in Article 154, Article 156 allows for an extension of two months; this must be approved by the people's procuratorate of a province, autonomous region or municipality directly under the central government.

Public versus private prosecution

Before the start of a public prosecution, the people's procuratorate must first examine the case,[59] attempting to ascertain:

> whether the facts and circumstances of the crime are clear, whether the evidence is reliable and sufficient and whether the charge and the nature of the crime has been correctly determined; whether there are any crimes that have been omitted or other persons whose criminal responsibility should be investigated; whether it is a case in which criminal responsibility should not be investigated; whether the case has an incidental civil action; and whether the investigation of the case is being lawfully conducted.[60]

There are, however, situations in which private prosecution is more appropriate, including:

cases to be handled only upon complaint; cases for which the victims have evidence to prove that those are minor criminal cases; and cases for which the victims have evidence to prove that the defendants should be investigated for criminal responsibility according to law because their acts have infringed upon the victims' personal or property rights, whereas, the public security organs or the People's Procuratorates do not investigate the criminal responsibility of the accused.[61]

Trial

Following an examination to determine if public prosecution is appropriate, a people's court will decide whether it will try a case, based on if there are sufficiently clear facts in the indictment.[62] If the court chooses to try a case, it will assemble its collegial panel and give the defendant and defender a copy of the indictment filed by the people's procuratorate at least ten days before the start of the trial.[63] Judges may also choose to hold a meeting with the public prosecutor, the defendant and his or her defender and agent *ad litem*. The purpose of the meeting is to 'deliberate and consult their opinions on withdrawal, the list of witnesses, exclusion of illegal evidence and other trial-relevant issues'.[64]

The court will set the trial date, informing the people's procuratorate, the defendant, the defender, the agent *ad litem* and any witnesses, experts and court interpreters participating in the trial. The court will also serve summons and notices three days before the trial date, and publicly announce the 'name of the defendant, the causes of action and the time and location of the court session' if it is a public trial.[65] With the exception of cases that involve 'State secrets or personal privacy', all trials of first instance will be made public.[66] If a concerned party applies for a private trial in cases of trade secrets, a trial of first instance may not be public, either.[67] If there is a reason for a trial to be private, this reason will be announced in court.

At the end of the trial the defendant will make a final statement, after which the collegial panel will deliberate.[68] Article 195 allows the panel to make three possible judgments, after reviewing the facts and evidence established during the trial:

> If the facts of a case are clear, the evidence is reliable and sufficient, and the defendant is found guilty in accordance with law, he shall be pronounced guilty accordingly; [i]f the defendant is found

innocent in accordance with law, he shall be pronounced innocent accordingly; [i]f the evidence is insufficient and thus the defendant cannot be found guilty, he shall be pronounced innocent accordingly on account of the fact that the evidence is insufficient and the accusation unfounded.

Regardless of whether the trial was public or private, however, the judgment will be made public.[69]

Appeal

Should either the defendant or the private prosecutors wish to appeal, they can do so in writing or orally to the next higher level of people's court.[70] In addition, the defenders or a defendant's close relatives may file an appeal with his or her consent.[71] The people's procuratorate can also file a protest with the people's court at the next higher level if it believes there was 'some definite error in a judgment or order of first instance'.[72] Finally, Article 218 allows a victim or his or her legal representative to request the people's procuratorate to file a protest if the victim 'refuses to accept a judgment of first instance'. The people's procuratorate must decide if it will file the protest within five days.

There are three different approaches a people's court of second instance can take following an appeal or protest:

> if the original judgment was correct in the determination of facts and the application of law and appropriate in the meting out of punishment, the People's Court shall order rejection of the appeal or protest and affirm the original judgment. [I]f the original judgment contained no error in the determination of facts but the application of law was incorrect or the punishment was inappropriately meted out, the People's Court shall revise the judgment. [I]f the facts in the original judgment were unclear or the evidence insufficient, the People's Court may revise the judgment after ascertaining the facts, or it may rescind the original judgment and remand the case to the People's Court which originally tried it for retrial.[73]

Should the case be remanded to the court of first instance and the defendant or people's procuratorate wish to file a second appeal or protest, the people's court of second instance will either uphold or reverse the lower court's ruling, but it will not remand for a second time.[74] Finally, Article 233 explains that all judgments from a court of second instance or the Supreme People's Court are final.

Procedure for review of death sentences

When a death sentence has been ordered it must always be approved, either by a higher people's court[75] or the SPC.[76] In addition, if an intermediate people's court has sentenced a defendant to death but has also imposed a two-year suspension of execution, a higher people's court must approve the suspension.[77] Ultimately, collegial panels of three judges at the higher people's court or the SPC will review death sentences or suspensions.[78]

After its review, the SPC will issue a ruling either approving or rejecting the death sentence.[79] If it rejects the sentence, the court may remand the case or revise the sentence itself. Article 240 requires the SPC to speak with the defendant during its review of his or her death sentence. The defense lawyer may also speak with the court, if he or she so requests. The Supreme People's Procuratorate can also choose to submit an opinion on the sentence.

Execution of the death penalty

The official title of the section pertaining to the use of the death penalty is 'execution of the death penalty'. Article 252, the primary article in this section, mandates that all executions will be carried out by shooting or injection. An officer of the people's procuratorate will be present at the execution, which will take place either on the 'execution ground or in a designated place of custody'.[80] Immediately before the execution, a judicial officer will confirm that the person to be executed is the correct offender, and also ask the offender if he or she has any last words before delivering him or her to the executioner.

While executions are publicly announced, they are not open to the public, nor shall they take place in public. The people's court that sentenced the defendant to death is also responsible for notifying the family and submitting a report to the Supreme People's Court following the offender's death.

Since 2007 all courts sentencing criminals to death have required SPC approval,[81] as the court wants to 'ensure capital punishment is reserved only for offenders of extremely serious crimes'.[82] The SPC has been encouraging judges to give 'suspended' death sentences rather than 'immediate execution' for some homicide cases. Lower-court judges are encouraged to use their discretion to recognize mitigating circumstances that would allow them to sentence offenders to a suspended death sentence. As a result, Chinese courts hand down 'death sentence with two years' probation'[83] as frequently as, or more often than, they do actual death sentences.[84] Also, in 2011 the NPC Standing Committee adopted an amendment to reduce the number of capital crimes from 68 to 55.[85] Nevertheless, the latest statistics show that China executes thousands annually, according to an Amnesty International report[86] on the death penalty worldwide, far more than all other nations combined.[87] Amnesty does not provide a precise figure for executions in China, as Beijing keeps such numbers secret.[88]

Criminal Procedure Law amendments

On 30 August 2011 the NPC Standing Committee published a draft and explanatory notes of proposed amendments to China's Criminal Procedure Law on the NPC website, to invite suggestions from the public.[89] This was the first time the public had an opportunity to comment on major criminal procedure legislation before its promulgation, although people had only one month to submit comments by mail or online.[90]

As noted earlier, the current Criminal Procedure Law was promulgated in 1979 and revised in 1996 – with eight amendments since 1999. In 2004 the NPC Standing Committee's Legal Work Committee proposed another major revision, but work on this was delayed due to lack of consensus. Finally, in June 2011, the CPC Central Political-Judicial Committee set up the agenda to revise the law.[91] The proposed amendments were discussed and passed in March 2012 during an NPC meeting, and went into effect on 1 January 2013.[92]

There are 99 amendments to the Criminal Procedure Law in this revision, expanding the number of articles from 225 to 285. The articles cover seven areas: evidentiary system, compulsory measures, defense system, investigation measures, trial procedures, enforcement provisions and special procedures.[93]

Evidence rules

The revision contains new rules against coercing anyone to incriminate himself or herself, as well as rules to exclude illegal evidence: 'the use of torture or extortion to obtain a confession and the use of other illegal means to collect evidence shall be strictly prohibited; no person may be forced to prove his or her own guilt'.[94] The evidence amendments[95] incorporate some essential elements of the SPC'c 2010 judicial interpretation on exclusion of illegal evidence in criminal cases,[96] which was a set of comprehensive rules governing use of such evidence.

Also in the evidence category, there are improvements in types[97] and standards of proof[98] and protection of witnesses.[99]

Criminal defense

While Professor Jerome Cohen believed that, overall, the draft revision 'reflects more of a victory for the police and their allies among prosecutors and judges than for law professors and defense lawyers', he nonetheless said, 'The draft's attempt to reconcile the CPL with more substantial rights conferred on defense counsel and their clients by the revised Lawyers Law demonstrates the limited success of the criminal bar's strenuous lobbying.'[100] In the criminal defense area, the revision confirms lawyers' rights to discuss cases with detained clients before trial, free of jailers' electronic or personal monitoring, and restricts their ability to 'verify' evidence with clients until investigators recommend indictment.[101]

The amendments also encourage and expand the availability of legal aid in criminal proceedings. In the case of a life sentence or higher, 'the people's court, people's prosecutor's office and public security authority shall also provide legal assistance'.[102]

The revision authorizes more benevolent procedures for alleged juvenile offenders.[103] It also makes provisions on compulsory medical treatment for mentally ill persons committing violent acts, allowing courts, not police or prosecutors, to order compulsory treatment.[104]

The amendments explicitly authorize secret arrest and detention tactics, which were previously illegal but commonly used by police and investigators.[105] These 'forced disappearances',[106] as well as other revisions to the Criminal Procedure Law, may be at odds with provisions in current Chinese law that give such legal protections as family notification of detainees' whereabouts and access to counsel,[107] and with international law.[108] The systematic use of arbitrary detention and forced disappearance and the amendments legalizing these tactics have received considerable attention from both academia and media.[109]

- *Non-residential residential surveillance:*[110] in cases of a crime suspected to threaten national security, crimes of terrorist activities and major crimes of bribery, when residential surveillance at the domicile may impede the investigation, surveillance can be carried out in a location other than the residence.[111]

- *Secret residential surveillance:* where a notice cannot be furnished, or where crimes threatening national security or crimes of terrorist activities are suspected and a notice may impede the investigation, family members of the person under surveillance will not be informed of either the reason for the surveillance or the designated non-residential surveillance site.[112] The six months' rule (residential surveillance *may* not exceed six months) remains unchanged.[113]

- *Secret detention:* where notice cannot be furnished, or when *suspected* crimes involve threats to national security, terrorist activities *or other serious offenses* and notice may impede the investigation, family members of the person detained will *not* be informed of the reason for detention and place of custody.[114] This provision has been called the 'Ai Weiwei clause' by some observers.[115]

- *Secret arrest:* where a notice cannot be furnished or crimes threatening national security, terrorist activities *or other serious crimes* are *suspected* and a notice may impede the investigation, family members of the person arrested will *not* be informed of the reason for arrest and place of custody.[116]

'National security' and 'crimes of terrorist activities' are not defined in the revision and are not subject to independent review. Both secret detention and secret arrest provisions include a 'catch-all' clause ('or other serious crimes') which was considered by some legal scholars to be in direct conflict with the International Covenant on Civil and Political Rights.[117]

The case of Liu Xiaobo

The criminal case of Liu Xiaobo exemplifies the contrasting nature and irreconcilability of two provisions of Chinese law: Article 35 of the Constitution and Article 105 of the Criminal Law.

Article 35 of the Constitution of the People's Republic of China guarantees Chinese citizens the 'freedom of speech [and] of the press'.[118] In addition, Article 41 grants citizens the 'right to criticize and make suggestions regarding any state organ or functionary'. These rights seem fairly clear cut, yet there is some dispute about the extent of those rights when compared with Article 105(2) of the Criminal Law of the People's Republic of China:

> Whoever incites others by spreading rumors or slanders or any other means to subvert the State power or overthrow the socialist system shall be sentenced to fixed-term imprisonment of not more than five years, criminal detention, public surveillance or deprivation of political rights; and the ringleaders and the others who commit major crimes shall be sentenced to fixed-term imprisonment of not less than five years.[119]

Indictment

Liu Xiaobo was a key participant in writing and signing Charter '08, a manifesto released on 10 December 2008 to coincide with the sixtieth anniversary of the adoption of the Universal Declaration of Human Rights. It was written in the style of the Czechoslovak Charter 77, calling for more freedom of expression, human rights, more democratic elections, privatization of state enterprises and land, and economic liberalism. A full translation of Charter '08, by Professor Perry Link, is provided in Appendix 3.

Liu Xiaobo was arrested before Charter '08 was released. Almost one year after his arrest, on 10 December 2009, the Beijing Municipal People's Procuratorate Branch No. 1 submitted an indictment to the Beijing Municipal No. 1 Intermediate People's Court, charging Liu with violating Article 105(2) of the Criminal Law.[120] Under Article 141 of the Criminal Procedure Law, the procuratorate asked 'for a judgment and punishment according to law'.

The indictment outlined Liu's criminal history, including a conviction in 1991 for creating 'counterrevolutionary propaganda and incitement' and being sentenced to three years of re-education through labor in 1996 for allegedly disturbing social order. The indictment focuses, however, on the 2009 charge of inciting subversion of state power.

Before filing the indictment, the procuratorate conducted an investigation 'according to law'. The indictment cites a variety of articles in which Liu had apparently written about 'his dissatisfaction with the state power and socialist system of [the] country's people's democratic dictatorship'. It also claims Liu sent his articles to overseas websites for publication, and lists quotes taken from his writing that the procuratorate believed supported its charge of inciting subversion of state power.

Moreover, the indictment cites Liu's authorship of Charter '08 and the 'false... and slander[ous]' language therein. It claims that Liu distributed the document and collected 300 signatures from supporters. He then emailed Charter '08 with the signatures to two overseas websites for publication.

Defense statement

With the exception of the number of people Liu solicited to sign Charter '08, Liu's defense statement agreed with the facts set forth by the indictment.[121] It admitted to Liu writing articles and Charter '08, to publishing documents on overseas websites and to collecting signatures on Charter '08; his defense team argued, however, about the applicable law. The statement reasoned that Liu's writings were protected by his right to freedom of speech and expression and were not in violation of Article 105(2) of the Criminal Law. In addition, the defense statement noted that 'serious procedural flaws exist in the course of investigation, indictment hearings, and the trial'.

The first argument of the defense statement is that there is no evidence to prove Liu intended to incite subversion of state power. Citing the statute under which Liu was indicted, the defense opines that 'intent must be the subjective requisite for a crime of inciting subversion of state power'. It goes on to define this as a defendant knowing that his or her actions will encourage others to overthrow the socialist government and subvert state power. Moreover, the defendant must hope that the individuals he or she incites will succeed in the subversion of state power.

The defense team breaks these two requirements down even further:

> First is the awareness of the fact that one is committing a crime. To be specific, (i) one knows that his/her own action is harmful...; (ii) one should be aware of the causal relationship between the action and the consequence; (iii) one should be aware of the object or target of the action, that is, the victim of the actor must be the object or target that the actor is already aware of... Second is the determination to act, under two types of circumstances: (i) one is aware that his/her action can result in harmful consequences, hopes

that such consequences will occur, and is determined to carry out the act; (ii) one is aware that his/her action can result in harmful consequences but lets things take their course and is still determined to carry out the act.

After explaining that incitement to subvert state power requires intent, and defining intent, the defense team opines that Liu had no reason to know that the articles he sent to overseas websites would be harmful to the socialist system. Without that knowledge there would be no intent to commit the crime.

The defense statement argues that the charges in the indictment are too broad and do not provide the correct context for Liu's statements. Moreover, they muddy the distinction between Liu's constitutional rights (to freedom of speech and expression) and criminal law. The defense team claims that Liu's written work is not criminal, but rather is free speech. Further, even if not constituting free speech, the articles did not pose a threat to national security, nor were they slanderous. Another argument cites the concepts that 'no crime can be committed, and no punishment can be imposed, without an existing penal law' and 'proof beyond a reasonable doubt'. Based on these principles, the defense claimed that Liu cannot be convicted of the crime of inciting subversion of state power.

The second overarching argument of the defense team was that 'there were significant flaws in the investigation, procuracy review and indictment, and trial processes'. Prior to trial, the investigators failed to maintain residential surveillance solely at Liu's home, nor did they allow him free access to his lawyers or his wife, as required under the Criminal Procedure Law and the Provisions on Procedures for Handling Criminal Cases by the Public Security Organs. These errors, claimed Liu's defense, amounted to detention in disguise. If it was indeed detention, the amount of time he was in residential surveillance should be considered time served and deducted from any sentence.

Verdict

Ultimately, however, on 25 December 2009 the Beijing Municipal No. 1 Intermediate People's Court found Liu Xiaobo guilty of incitement to subvert state power.[122] The court held that Liu 'used the Internet's features of rapid transmission of information, broad reach, great social influence, and high degree of public attention, as well as the method of writing and publishing articles on the Internet, to slander and incite others to overthrow our country's state power and the socialist system'. Addressing the issue of malice, the court cited Liu's long history of writing and publishing articles critical of the government. It also appeared to use evidence that the articles were widely read to prove Liu's malice.

The court rejected the defense statement, writing that 'Liu Xiaobo's actions have obviously exceeded the freedom of speech category and constitute criminal offense.' It did not elaborate further on what language made the articles criminal as opposed to protected free speech. The court chose to sentence him to 11 years of fixed-term imprisonment and two years' deprivation of political rights. In addition, anything that Liu used to 'commit the crime' was to be confiscated.

Appeal

Just over one month later, the defense team appealed the intermediate court's verdict.[123] The first claim was that the court erred in not accepting the defense's argument that Liu's *de facto* detention while he was under residential surveillance should be considered time served and subtracted from his sentence. The defense statement for the second instance reiterated that it was entering a plea of not guilty, and that arguing Liu's sentence should be shortened should not be seen as agreement with the court of first instance's verdict. The statement also repeated the problems it found with the investigative organ's surveillance of Liu (see above).

In terms of the application of law, the defense statement made note that government, state power and the ruling party are generally considered distinct in political science. It also points out that freedom of speech is normally defined as 'the right to freely discuss with and to hear the opinion of others as one wishes. Freedom of speech generally is regarded as an indispensable value and idea in modern democracies.' Liu's team argued that 'public power' cannot strip individuals of this right, and the government's attempt to do this had been an abuse of power.

Finally, the defense team argued that there was a lack of procedural justice with regard to the trial, and the court 'turned a blind eye to serious procedural violations'. It noted again that the procedural errors, including refusing to hear the defense counsel's argument during the procuratorate examination and limiting the defendant and defense counsels' speaking times, were a lack of procedural fairness and justice.

Verdict affirmed

The Beijing Municipal High Court ultimately rejected Liu Xiaobo's appeal and affirmed his guilty verdict on 9 February 2010.[124] The court held that there was sufficient evidence to support a conviction of inciting subversion of state power, citing Liu's 'use of Internet features… publishing slanderous essays and extensively collecting signatures online'. Addressing Liu's argument that his actions merely consisted of free (and protected) speech, the court stated that his actions went beyond free speech and thus became criminal:

> His actions constitute the crime of inciting subversion of state power. Furthermore, the crime was committed over a long period of time, and the subjective malice was immense. His articles were widely linked, reproduced, and viewed, spreading vile influence. His criminal acts were grave, and he should be punished according to the law. Liu Xiaobo's grounds for appeal have not been established; his appeal should be overruled.

Moreover, the court found there was 'insufficient reasoning in the defense appeal statement' regarding the issues of trial and criminal procedure and Liu's residential surveillance. Dismissing his arguments, the court determined the conviction and penalty were appropriate, upholding his original sentence. As Chinese criminal procedure only allows one appeal, Liu's conviction and sentence are final.

The Nobel Peace Prize

On 8 October 2010 it was announced: 'The Norwegian Nobel Committee has decided to award the Nobel Peace Prize for 2010 to Liu Xiaobo for his long and non-violent struggle for fundamental human rights in China.'[125] In a press release, the committee stated:

> China's new status must entail increased responsibility. China is in breach of several international agreements to which it is a signatory, as well as of its own provisions concerning political rights. Article 35 of China's constitution lays down that 'Citizens of the People's Republic of China enjoy freedom of speech, of the press, of assembly, of association, of procession and of demonstration.' In practice, these freedoms have proved to be distinctly curtailed for China's citizens.[126]

President Vaclav Havel pointed out the real crime Liu Xiaobo committed – challenging the party:

> In spearheading the creation of Charter 08, Liu Xiaobo crossed the starkest line of all: Do not challenge the Communist Party's monopoly on political power, and do not suggest that China's problems – including widespread corruption, labor unrest, and rampant environmental degradation – might be connected to the lack of progress on political reform.[127]

Representative cases in criminal law

The following pages review several 'guiding cases'[128] selected by the Supreme People's Court of China.

Pan Yumei and Chen Ning

This case[129] determines whether returning bribes negates the crime of accepting them in the first place. The Higher People's Court of Jiangsu Province held that Article 385 of the Criminal Law says that any state employee using his or her office to obtain benefits and profits for an individual and a company which the state employee and the individual jointly organize will be found guilty of accepting bribes even if he or she did not contribute any capital to the company. Moreover, the crime of accepting bribes includes purchasing property or goods at prices far below their market value. When such a situation happens, the amount of the bribe will be calculated as the difference between the purchase price and the fair market value. Finally, attempting to conceal the crime by returning a bribe does not remove the state employee's culpability.

In this case, two state officials were accused of using their offices within Jiangsu province to collect bribes. In total, one defendant was accused of taking RMB11.902 million and the other RMB5.59 million. After their initial conviction by the Intermediate People's Court of Nanjing Municipality, Jiangsu Province, the pair appealed to the higher people's court. The defendants argued that their role in jointly organizing a company with another individual should not be considered as accepting bribes. The court disagreed, however, holding that because the two state employees had not contributed any money to the company but still collected approximately RMB4.8 million each, it was just another form of accepting bribes.

In addition, when one of the defendants argued that her purchase of real estate from a second individual should not be considered as accepting a bribe, the court similarly dismissed her argument. The court found that because she purchased the land for less than half of what it was worth, the difference between the actual market value of the property and the purchase price was a bribe. By later trying to hide her involvement in bribery, the state official's attempt at trying to return bribe money did not negate her culpability for taking the bribe.

Ultimately, the higher people's court upheld the court of first instance's ruling, as well as the punishments it had ordered – the death penalty with a two-year suspension of execution and life imprisonment.

Wang Zhicai

At issue in this case[130] is whether the facts surrounding an intentional homicide can lessen an offender's sentence from the death penalty. The Higher People's Court of Shandong Province determined that even though an offender's actions would normally be punished by death, his or her sentence could potentially be changed to the death penalty with a two-year suspension of execution and the deprivation of political rights for life if there are sufficient mitigating factors.

Though this was a case of intentional homicide, the higher people's court, after having the case remanded following a review by the SPC, determined that certain facts mitigated the defendant's crime. The defendant confessed to killing a young woman with whom he had been romantically involved and who had rejected his marriage proposal. Following her death, he told police what he had done and worked with his parents to provide compensation to the victim's family. The emotional nature of the crime, in addition to the defendant's cooperative behavior, merited a two-year suspension of the death penalty and a restriction on the ability of his sentence to be commuted under Article 50 of the Criminal Law.

Li Fei

Much like the previous case, this is about which factors merit a more lenient sentence under Article 50 for someone convicted of intentional homicide.[131] The court held that when a relative of a suspect actively works with the public security authorities to bring the suspect into custody, the suspect cooperates with police and the victim's family members receive compensation for their loss, the court may award a lighter sentence.

This was a case of intentional homicide in which a young man was sentenced to death by the Intermediate People's Court of Harbin Municipality, Heilongjiang Province. The defendant appealed, but the Higher People's Court of Heilongjiang Province rejected the appeal, sending his case to the Supreme People's Court for review of the penalty. The SPC determined the death penalty was inappropriate and sent the case back to the higher people's court for retrial.

During the retrial, the court held that in most cases of intentional homicide the death penalty should be imposed. Because the defendant's mother not only informed police of her son's whereabouts but also helped bring him into custody, the court elected to impose a two-year suspension on his death sentence and 'restrict the commutation of [the] sentence in accordance with law'. Other factors influencing the decision are that once he was arrested the defendant confessed to his crimes, and the mother paid the victim's family members for their economic loss. Moreover, while the defendant had previously been convicted of a crime, it was only minor larceny.

Yang Yanhu et al.

This case[132] examines which actions constitute the crime of graft under Article 382 of the Criminal Law. In rejecting the defendants' appeal, the Higher People's Court of Zhejiang Province determined that the crime of graft involves 'taking advantage of the conveniences of one's office' to manage or have some kind of influence over public property. The crime also includes taking advantage of acquaintances' roles to handle public property.

The defendant in this case was a deputy director of the Standing Committee of the People's Congress of Yiwu Municipality. In this role, he was accused of conspiring with family members to purchase a home in order to take advantage of demolition and relocation that was scheduled to take place in the village. The defendant used his position to insist that other members of the Construction Directorate of the International Trade City allow him and his family members greater land and construction rights than they deserved. The court ultimately held that the defendant's actions included not only using his own position to exert control over public land, but others' positions as well, both of which constitute the crime of graft. He was sentenced to 15 years of fixed-term imprisonment and fined RMB200,000.

The CPC and criminal law

Ian Dobinson has said that 'From a comparative perspective, especially that of common law, Chinese criminal law would appear to be very different';[133] nevertheless, 'a closer analysis shows that many of the general principles of criminal liability and the way in which they are applied are very similar to common law traditions'.[134] He explained that Chinese criminal law is based on one criminal code – promulgated by the National People's Congress, the highest legislative authority under the Chinese constitution – which forms the basis of legal principles and concepts. The code is supplemented by ancillary legislation from the NPC Standing Committee, the second highest legislative authority. The Criminal Law and supplemental legislations are 'further interpreted and detailed by the directions, interpretations and decisions of the Supreme People's Court'.[135] From these characteristics one can naturally draw the conclusion that Chinese criminal law appears a logical and consistent endeavor to continue to develop and improve the legal system.

This understanding, however, ignores the 'elephant in the room' – the CPC. The CPC's policies carry equal weight to the laws and statutes, if not more. For example, before the NPC promulgated Regulations of the People's Republic of China on Punishment of Counterrevolutionaries (1951), police and military already enforced the CPC Central Committee's Directive on Elimination of Bandits and Establishment of Revolutionary New Order (1950) and Mao Zedong's Directive on Suppression of Counterrevolutionary Activities (1950), also known as the 'Double-ten Directive', both involving large-scale suppression of counterrevolutionaries.[136] The directives stressed the 'educational' effects of the campaign, and cases of execution were publicized to inform the masses.[137] These directives and even speeches by members of the CPC leadership are not defined as legal documents, but they can be implemented and enforced. Moreover, they trump the law if there is a conflict between party policy and the law, as Chen Guangcheng observed: 'The laws are always guided by party policies. That's the fundamental reality of how the law system actually works in China today and the biggest barrier to the law system from improving.'[138]

Perhaps a perfect example to illustrate the institutionalization of this kind of abnormality is the *shuanggui* (双规) system in China, which describes the internal investigation procedure conducted by CPC disciplinary officers for party members under suspicion of violating party policies or the law. This system operates completely outside the legal system. For example, should party members 'be accused of bribery, fraud or any other criminal conduct, they are investigated by the Party first and only turned over to the civilian justice system on its say-so. Even then, any punishment meted out by the courts is at the behest and direction of party organs.'[139] *Shuanggui* is not an exception to the traditional legal process, but constitutes one of two formalized parallel systems. An individual accused of doing something wrong will enter either the *shuanggui* system or the criminal system, depending on whether he or she is a member of the CPC.

While party investigations and disciplines are similar to the codified criminal law, they minimize the severity of criminal offenses, calling them 'minor infractions' or 'mistakes' instead of crimes (also referred to as 'double designations').[140] These infractions do not come with criminal responsibility.

When a party member is accused of a crime, he or she is first investigated by the CPC Central Commission for Discipline Inspection. Throughout questioning and investigation the member is referred to as 'comrade' and is presumed innocent until proven guilty. The internal system does not allow corporal punishment and the secretary-general of the commission insists that the party member's dignity will be respected at all times.[141] If CPC investigators decide that the member will need to be tried by the courts, the case comes with a written opinion from the party. The opinion will dictate what can and cannot be uncovered during the criminal investigation, and nearly all such cases will end up with minor sentences.

As described by Flora Sapio, a legal scholar at the Chinese University of Hong Kong, the *shuanggui* system removes the power of 'independent adjudication' from the courts.[142] Historically, there have been very few cases that the party will turn over to police or the procuracies. The CPC is likely afraid that widespread prosecution of party officials would go against the goal of social harmony. Though the number of cases of corruption by party members topped 1.3 million in 2009, only 100,000 were actually punished within the party system. An even smaller, unknown fraction of those 100,000 were handed over to the police and procuracies for criminal prosecution:[143]

In China the coexistence of arbitrary detention and a transition towards a rule of law is either seen as an oxymoron, or as an aberration... [The] derogations from the rule of law constitute an organic component of the legal order. Hidden behind the law, there lays sovereign power, a power premised on the choice to handle certain issues through procedures that derogate from rights. This theoretically sophisticated study overcomes the current impasses in analyses of China's criminal justice.[144]

While individual party members can be held accountable through the *shuanggui* system, the party itself cannot be held legally accountable for its actions. Since 1949 the CPC's policies have caused death, famine, economic collapse and environmental disaster, but no citizen can sue the CPC in court for damages or anything else. As Professor He Weifang explained: 'It is dangerous and pointless to try to sue the Party. As an organization, the Party sits outside, and above the law. It should have a legal identity, in other words, a person to sue, but it is not even registered as an organization. The Party exists outside the legal system altogether.'[145]

Notes

1. Aristotle (1981) *The Politics*, ed. Trevor J. Saunders, trans. T.A. Sinclair, revised edn. London: Penguin Classics, p. 227, 3.16.
2. Yang Kuisong (2008) 'Reconsidering the campaign to suppress counterrevolutionaries', *China Quarterly*, 193: 102–21.
3. Jerome A. Cohen (1966) 'The criminal process in the People's Republic of China: an introduction', *Harvard Law Review*, 79: 469–532.
4. Stanley B. Lubman (1999) *Bird in a Cage: Legal Reform in China after Mao*. Stanford, CA: Stanford University Press, p. 171.
5. Criminal Law of the People's Republic of China, Zhonghua Renmin Gongheguo Xingfa (1979).
6. Ibid., Article 91.
7. Ibid., Article 92.
8. Ibid., Article 93.
9. Ibid., Article 94.
10. Ibid., Article 95.
11. Ibid., Article 96.
12. Ibid., Article 97.
13. Ibid., Article 98.
14. Ibid., Article 99.
15. Ibid., Article 100.
16. Ibid., Article 101.
17. Ibid., Article 102.

18. Criminal Law of the People's Republic of China, Zhonghua Renmin Gongheguo Xingfa (1997), Article 1.
19. Ibid., Article 5.
20. Ibid., Article 105.
21. Ibid., Article 32.
22. Ibid., Article 33.
23. Ibid., Article 35.
24. Ibid., Article 49.
25. Ibid.
26. Ibid., Article 50.
27. Ibid., Article 109.
28. Austin Ramzy (2012) 'Wang Lijun, police boss who triggered Bo Xilai scandal, sentenced to 15 years', Time World, 24 September; available at: *http://world.time.com/2012/09/24/wang-lijun-police-boss-who-triggered-bo-xilai-scandal-sentenced-to-15-years/* (accessed: 14 August 2013).
29. Daniel C.K. Chow (2009) *The Legal System of the People's Republic of China*, 2nd edn. St Paul, MN: Thomson West, p. 326; see generally Criminal Law of the People's Republic of China (1997), Articles 13–16.
30. Criminal Law of the People's Republic of China (1997), Article 15.
31. Chow, note 29 above, p. 318.
32. Albert H.Y. Chen (2004) *An Introduction to the Legal System of the People's Republic of China*, 3rd edn. Hong Kong: LexisNexis Butterworths, p. 235.
33. Ibid.
34. Ian Dobinson (2002) 'The Criminal Law of the People's Republic of China (1997): real change or rhetoric?'; available at: *http://digital.law.washington.edu/dspace-law/bitstream/handle/1773.1/747/11PacRimLPolyJ001.pdf?sequence=1* (accessed: 14 August 2013).
35. Ibid.
36. Ibid.
37. Criminal Procedure Law of the People's Republic of China (1979).
38. Ibid., Article 18.
39. Ibid.
40. Ibid., Article 116.
41. Ibid., Article 118.
42. Ibid.
43. Ibid., Article 136.
44. Ibid., Article 134.
45. Ibid., Article 139.
46. Ibid., Article 32.
47. Ibid., Article 33.
48. Ibid.
49. Ibid.
50. Ibid., Article 78.
51. Ibid., Article 79.
52. Ibid.
53. Ibid.
54. Ibid., Article 91.
55. Ibid., Article 154.

56. Ibid., Articles 155 and 156.
57. Ibid., Article 154.
58. Ibid., Article 155.
59. Ibid., Article 167.
60. Ibid., Article 168.
61. Ibid., Article 204.
62. Ibid., Article 181.
63. Ibid., Article 182.
64. Ibid.
65. Ibid.
66. Ibid., Article 183.
67. Ibid.
68. Ibid., Article 195.
69. Ibid., Article 196.
70. Ibid., Article 216.
71. Ibid., Article 217.
72. Ibid.
73. Ibid., Article 225.
74. Ibid.
75. Ibid., Article 236.
76. Ibid., Articles 235 and 236.
77. Ibid., Article 237.
78. Ibid., Article 238.
79. Ibid., Article 239.
80. Ibid., Article 252.
81. Criminal Law of the People's Republic of China (1997), Article 48.
82. Wang Shenjun (2013) 'Supreme People's Court work report 2013', 11 March; summary in English available at: *www.globaltimes.cn/ content/767150.shtml* (accessed: 14 August 2013).
83. Criminal Law of the People's Republic of China (1997), Articles 50 and 51.
84. Susan Trevaskes (2008) 'The death penalty in China today: kill fewer, kill cautiously', *Asian Survey*, 48(3): 393–413.
85. *Xinhua News* (2011) 'China exempts 13 crimes from death penalty', *Xinhua News*, 25 February; available at: *http://news.xinhuanet.com/english2010/ china/2011-02/25/c_13750127.htm* (accessed: 14 August 2013).
86. Amnesty International (2012) 'Death penalty in 2011', Amnesty International, 27 March; available at: *www.amnesty.org/en/news/death-penalty-2011-alarming-levels-executions-few-countries-kill-2012-03-27* (accessed: 14 August 2013).
87. Dui Hua Foundation (2010) 'Reducing death penalty crimes in China more symbol than substance'; available at: *http://duihua.org/wp/?p=2343* (accessed: 14 August 2013).
88. Amnesty International, note 86 above.
89. National People's Congress (2011) 'Xingshi Susong fa Xiuzhengan (caoan) tiaowen ji caoan shuoming (刑事诉讼法修正案（草案）条文及草案说明) (Amendments to the Criminal Procedure Law of the People's Republic of China (draft) and Explanatory Notes)', 30 August; available at: *www.npc. gov.cn/npc/xinwen/lfgz/2011-08/30/content_1668503.htm* (accessed: 14 August 2013).

90. Ibid.
91. See Wang Heyan (王和岩) (2011) 'Xingsu fa xiuding zhengqiu yijian: bufen tiaokuan daotui yinfa danyou (刑诉法修订征求意见：部分条款倒退引发担忧) (Amendments to the Criminal Procedure Law invites comments: some provisions go backwards and cause concerns)'; available at: *http://china.caixin.cn/2011-08-30/100296591.html* (accessed: 14 August 2013).
92. Chen Guangzhong (陈光中) (2011) 'Xinsu fa xiugai zhong de jige zhongdian wenti (刑诉法修改中的几个重点问题) (A few important issues in revising the Criminal Procedure Law)'; available at: *www.npc.gov.cn/huiyi/lfzt/xsssfxg/2011-08/24/content_1666933.htm* (accessed: 14 August 2013).
93. National People's Congress, note 89 above, Explanatory Notes.
94. Ibid., (14).
95. Ibid., (14), (17), (21).
96. Supreme People's Court, Supreme People's Procuratorate, Ministry of Public Security, Ministry of State Security and Ministry of Justice (2010) 'Guanyu banli xingshi anjian paichu feifa zhengju ruogan wenti de guiding (关于办理刑事案件排除非法证据若干问题的规定) (Rules concerning questions about exclusion of illegal evidence in handling criminal cases)', 25 June; available at: *http://rmfyb.chinacourt.org/paper/html/2010-06/25/content_11353.htm* (accessed: 14 August 2013).
97. National People's Congress, note 89 above, (12).
98. Ibid., (16).
99. Ibid., (15).
100. Jerome A. Cohen and Yu Han (2011) 'China's struggle for criminal justice', *South China Morning Post*, 28 September; available at: *http://usali.org/media-entities/chinas-struggle-for-criminal-justice* (accessed: 14 August 2013).
101. National People's Congress, note 89 above, (3), (6), (7).
102. Ibid., (4), (95).
103. Ibid., (95).
104. Ibid., (98).
105. In the first half of 2011 authorities reportedly 'disappeared' numerous lawyers and rights activists known for criticizing the CPC and advocating on behalf of politically sensitive causes and groups. See generally Congressional-Executive Commission on China (2011) 'Annual report 2011', 10 October; available at: *http://chrissmith.house.gov/uploadedfiles/china_report_2011.pdf* (accessed: 14 August 2013).
106. Ibid.
107. US Department of State (2011) 'China: Criminal Procedure Law', press release, 31 August; available at: *www.state.gov/r/pa/prs/ps/2011/08/171320.htm* (accessed: 14 August 2013).
108. UN Working Group on Enforced or Involuntary Disappearance (2011) 'China: UN expert body concerned about recent wave of enforced disappearances', press release, 8 April; available at: *www.ohchr.org/en/NewsEvents/Pages/DisplayNews.aspx?NewsID=10928&LangID=E* (accessed: 14 August 2013).

109. See He Weifang (贺卫方) (2011) 'Zheyang de lifa weibei le zhengfu de chengnuo (这样的立法违背了政府的承诺) (This kind of legislation broke the government's promise)', 2 September; available at: *www.caijing.com.cn/2011-09-02/110839364.html* (accessed: 14 August 2013); Donald Clark (2011) 'More on proposed revisions to China's Criminal Procedure Law'; available at: *http://lawprofessors.typepad.com/china_law_prof_blog/2011/10/more-on-proposed-revisions-to-chinas-criminal-procedure-law.html* (accessed: 14 August 2013); Reuters News (2011) 'China announces plans to boost secret detention powers', Reuters, 30 August; available at: *www.reuters.com/article/2011/08/30/us-china-law-detention-idUSTRE77T2HJ20110830* (accessed: 14 August 2013); Wang, note 91 above. Online public comments on the amendments were disproportionally focused on the provisions legalizing secret detention and secret arrest.

110. 'Non-residential residential surveillance' refers to a common practice by Chinese police of locking people up in places other than their residence, but calling it 'residential surveillance'. See Clark, ibid.

111. National People's Congress, note 89 above, (30).

112. Ibid.

113. Criminal Procedure Law of the People's Republic of China (1979), Article 58.

114. National People's Congress, note 89 above, (36).

115. From 3 April to 22 June 2011 artist Ai Weiwei was held by Chinese police at a secret location unknown to his family and the public. The proposed amendment (36) would legalize this kind of secret detention, thus it was called the 'Ai Weiwei clause' by some observers. See Guo Zhiyuan (2011) 'Chance and challenge for Chinese Criminal Procedure Law reform'; available at: *www.usasialaw.org/wp-content/uploads/2011/09/20110926-Chance-and-Challege-for-Chinese-Criminal-Procedure-Law-Reform.pdf* (accessed: 1 April 2013).

116. National People's Congress, note 89 above, (39).

117. See He, note 109 above. China signed the International Covenant on Civil and Political Rights on 5 October 1998, but has not yet ratified the convention. United Nations (1966) 'International Covenant on Civil and Political Rights (ICCPR)', GA Res. 2200A (XXI), 21 UN GAOR Supp. (No. 16), p. 52, UN Doc. A/6316 (1966), 999 UNTS 171, entered into force 23 March 1976.

118. National People's Congress (2007) 'Database of laws and regulations: constitution and the related laws, Constitution of the People's Republic of China', Article 35; available at: *www.npc.gov.cn/englishnpc/Law/2007-12/05/content_1381903.htm* (accessed: 14 August 2013).

119. National People's Congress (2007) 'Database of laws and regulations: criminal law: Criminal Law of the People's Republic of China'; available at: *www.npc.gov.cn/englishnpc/Law/2007-12/13/content_1384075.htm* (accessed: 14 August 2013).

120. Beijing Municipal People's Procuratorate Branch No. 1 (2009) 'Criminal indictment No. 247', 10 December; full translation available at: *www.hrichina.org/crf/article/32065* (accessed: 5 April 2013).

121. Beijing Mo Shaoping Law Firm (2009) 'Concerning Liu Xiaobo's appeal against the charge of inciting subversion of state power, defense statement for the first instance', 23 December; full translation available at: *www. hrichina.org/crf/article/3206* (accessed: 14 August 2013).

122. Beijing Municipal No. 1 Intermediate People's Court (2009) 'Criminal verdict No. 3901'; full translation available at: *www.hrichina.org/crf/ article/3209* (accessed: 14 August 2013).

123. Beijing Mo Shaoping Law Firm (2010) 'Concerning Liu Xiaobo's appeal against the charge of inciting subversion of state power, defense statement of the second instance', 28 January; full translation available at: *www. hrichina.org/crf/article/3210* (accessed: 14 August 2013).

124. Beijing Municipal High People's Court Criminal Division (2010) 'Final verdict No. 64'; full translation available at: *www.hrichina.org/crf/ article/3211* (accessed: 14 August 2013).

125. Nobelprize.org (2010) 'The Nobel Peace Prize 2010', press release, Nobelprize.org, 8 October; available at: *www.nobelprize.org/nobel_ prizes/peace/laureates/2010/press.html* (accessed: 14 August 2013).

126. Ibid.

127. Vaclav Havel, Dana Nemcova and Vaclav Maly (2010) 'A Nobel prize for a Chinese dissident', *New York Times*, 20 September; available at: *www. nytimes.com/2010/09/21/opinion/21iht-edhavel.html?_r=0* (accessed: 14 August 2013).

128. See Chapter 6 for explanations of the 'guiding cases'.

129. Partial translation and comments available at: *https://cgc.law.stanford. edu/guiding-cases/guiding-case-3/* (accessed: 14 August 2013).

130. Partial translation and comments available at: *http://cgc.law.stanford. edu/guiding-cases/guiding-case-4* (accessed: 14 August 2013).

131. Partial translation and comments available at: *http://cgc.law.stanford. edu/guiding-cases/guiding-case-12* (accessed: 14 August 2013).

132. Partial translation and comments available at: *http://cgc.law.stanford. edu/guiding-cases/guiding-case-11* (accessed: 14 August 2013).

133. Ian Dobinson (1997) 'Criminal law', in Wang Chenguang and Zhang Xianchu (eds) *Introduction to Chinese Law*. Hong Kong: Sweet & Maxwell Asia, p. 107.

134. Ibid.

135. Ibid., pp. 107–8.

136. Yang, note 2 above.

137. Ibid.

138. Quoted in Pan Tianyi (2013) 'Communist Party above law, Chinese dissident says', *Yale Daily News*, 25 February; available at: *http:// yaledailynews.com/blog/2013/02/25/communist-party-above-law- chinese-dissident-says/* (accessed: 14 August 2013).

139. Richard McGregor (2010) *The Party: The Secret World of China's Communist Rulers*. London: HarperCollins, p. 15.

140. *Xinhua News* (2006) 'CPC official explains "double designations"', *Xinhua News*, 26 September; available at: *http://english.cri.cn/2946/2006 /09/26/189@143960.htm* (accessed: 14 August 2013).

141. Ibid.

142. Flora Sapio (2010) *Sovereign Power and the Law in China. Zones of Exception in the Criminal Justice System*. Boston, MA, and Leiden: Brill.
143. Stanley Lubman (2012) 'Double jeopardy: crime and China's Communist Party', *Wall Street Journal*, 30 May; available at: *http://blogs.wsj.com/chinarealtime/2012/05/30/double-jeopardy-crime-and-chinas-communist-party/* (accessed: 14 August 2013).
144. Sapio, note 142 above.
145. Ibid., p. 22.

8

The curious case of Ai Weiwei and administrative law

Abstract: This chapter uses the case of Ai Weiwei to explore topics in administrative law. The timeline of the case is presented, along with an analysis of the procedure investigators used during Ai's case and the subsequent tax charges levied against his studio. The legal arguments made by Ai's lawyers and the reasoning of the court in his case are presented and discussed. Finally, broader topics, trends and concerns within Chinese administrative law are covered.

Key words: Ai Weiwei, petition, administrative law, tax law.

On 3 April 2011 the world-renowned Chinese artist Ai Weiwei was taken into custody at Beijing Capital international airport as he was about to fly to Hong Kong. For the next 81 days he was held in secret detention while his friends, family and the international art community demanded information about his condition and asked for his release. Ai's detention is interesting in that its legal basis fell under administrative law, yet the tactics utilized by Chinese authorities often fell outside typical administrative procedures.[1] The timeline of his case also lends credence to the argument that the government used a retroactive application of tax law following Ai's detention to 'legitimize' its actions.[2]

Timeline

Prior to Ai's arrest at 8:30 pm on 3 April, police officers went to his Beijing studio, Fake Cultural Development Company, to question staff members and search the studio.[3] Shortly after his arrest, four new officers arrived to search the studio and did not leave until after midnight. During the searches over 100 pieces of property were taken, all of which were documented on a list that was then given to Ai's wife, Lu Qing. The following day Lu and Ai's assistants were released from custody after being detained. Upon their release, only Ai and his friend Wen Tao were still missing, but within one day of Ai's arrest representatives from Germany, France and the United Kingdom had all voiced their opposition to his arrest and the way China has handled its dissidents.

By 5 April 2011 Ai's mother and sister, Gao Ying and Gao Ge, had still not heard anything about Ai. Lu issued a public request for legal help, and Gao Ying and Gao Ge circulated a missing person's notice.[4] Wen's family also filed a report with the Beijing Nangao police, but the request for information was summarily rejected. A day after the governments of Germany, France and the United Kingdom issued statements regarding Ai's disappearance, the European Union and the US government both requested the artist's release.[5] Adding his voice to the mix was Zhao Lianhai, a human rights activist who was jailed for his role in the 2008 melamine-tainted milk scandal in China.

It was not until the next day that the first state-controlled media organization, the *Global Times*, even acknowledged Ai's detention. On 7 April, however, the government news source, Xinhua, published a report claiming Ai was being held under suspicion of 'economic crimes'; the report was deleted shortly after its publication. At approximately the same time that Xinhua was breaking this news, a Foreign Ministry spokesman confirmed at a press meeting that Ai was indeed being detained for economic crimes. He also warned other countries not to interfere in the investigation. When the official transcript of the meeting was released several hours later, however, all mention of Ai had been removed.[6]

Over the next few days Lu made public a letter asking police for information on her husband, while the accountant for Ai's studio, Hu Minfen, and Ai's driver, Zhang Jingsong, both went missing.[7] By 11 April Liu Zhenggang, Ai's partner at Fake, was also missing. In their first trip to the accounting office, the Beijing Public Security Bureau spent three hours searching the office and seized bookkeeping records, the office computer and more than RMB20,000 in cash.

The Hong Kong radio station RTHK reported that Lu Qing had been asked to bring tax documents to the Beijing Taxation Bureau as part of the investigation.[8] The documents had previously been confiscated by authorities, however, and it was unclear if she was able to provide the paperwork the taxation bureau was after. This request was shortly followed by a story in the pro-Beijing Hong Kong newspaper *Wei Wen Po* claiming Ai was being investigated for bigamy and disseminating pornography, in addition to the charge of tax evasion. Lu and other family members denied the charges.[9]

Twelve days after his initial disappearance, Ai's family and Fake staff and volunteers published an open letter requesting police look into the disappearance of Ai, his colleagues and friends, including the lawyer Liu Xiaoyuan, who had disappeared the day before.[10] The letter, which was originally posted on the website Sina Weibo, the Chinese equivalent of Twitter, asked authorities to follow the normal legal procedures throughout the investigation. Without releasing any information about his or anyone else's disappearance, Liu Xiaoyuan reappeared on 19 April.

By 9 May 2011, 37 days had passed since Ai was escorted from the Beijing airport. This marked an important milestone, as the Criminal Procedure Law allows authorities to hold an individual for 37 days at most before they must release the detainee or file an official charge.[11] According to Jerome Cohen, the law allows police to detain someone for three days without releasing him or her or filing for an arrest warrant with the prosecutors.[12] In certain cases, however, authorities can take up to seven or 30 days to file for a warrant. Because prosecutors can take up to seven days more to approve an arrest warrant, the maximum amount of time someone can be held under current Chinese law is 37 days.

Despite being in custody for 37 days, authorities did not release Ai, nor did they provide any information about his detention or on what charges he was being held. It was another six days before Lu was finally able to visit her husband on 15 May.

On 21 May the first reports emerged indicating that Fake studio was responsible for not paying taxes and destroying evidence of its tax evasion.[13] Though the reports spoke of an investigation of Ai's studio, neither he nor his other disappeared friends and associates were released. By 11 June Lu and the other families had not received any news on their relatives' disappearances, so they filed a joint letter with the public security departments in Beijing.[14] The letter specifically requested that officials properly investigate the kidnappings.

In mid- to late June several artists cancelled their openings at Chinese museums and studios in solidarity with Ai.[15] At the same time, many renowned art museums throughout the world – the Museum of Modern Art, Tate Modern, the Guggenheim Museum and others – pushed for

Ai's release. They created a campaign on Change.org, which collected more than 143,400 signatures demanding Ai's release.[16]

On 22 June 2011, after 81 days of imprisonment, Ai was finally released. Within the next few days his driver, Zhang Jinsong, the manager, Liu Zhenggang, the accountant, Hu Mingfen, and Ai's friend Wen Tao were also released from custody. Upon his release, Ai was instructed to have limited or no contact with several of his colleagues, including his personal videographer Zhao Zhao.[17] Ai was also unable to get in touch with his manager, Liu, who had suffered a heart attack during interrogation.[18]

On 27 June officers from the taxation bureau came to Ai's studio and asked him to sign a document agreeing to pay an alleged RMB12 million in penalties and unpaid taxes.[19] Ai attempted to get in contact with Liu Zhenggang and Hu, but was unable to reach them and so refused to sign.[20] The next day lawyers Pu Zhiqiang and Xia Lin announced they were officially representing Fake in the tax evasion case.

The first thing the lawyers did was submit an appeal to the taxation bureau seeking an accounting of what evidence there was for the case against Fake. The hearing was on 14 July 2011, but it was not open and public as it should have been under law. The government insisted on a closed hearing.[21]

Fake's first appeal was unsuccessful and, on 7 November 2011, the government ordered the studio to pay RMB15 million within 15 days.[22] Though it was Fake which was being ordered to pay the tax bill and accused of evading taxes, Pu said that Ai could be sent back to prison if the RMB15 million was not paid.[23] Remarkably, Fake was able to raise the money through donations. Several thousand people donated to pay the fine, at times throwing the money over the wall of Ai's compound.

On 29 March 2012 the Beijing Local Taxation Bureau turned down a request for a review. On 13 April 2012 Fake sued the Beijing Local Taxation Bureau Second Tax Inspection Bureau at the Chaoyang District People's Court as a matter of administrative litigation; the district court actually heard the tax case on 20 June 2012. On 20 July it ruled against Fake and Ai Weiwei.

On 3 August 2012 Fake lodged an appeal at Beijing No. 2 Intermediate People's Court, and on 27 September 2012 the court upheld the tax evasion conviction and fine against Fake.[24] Ai's second appeal focused primarily on the fine, alleging that the tax bureau had improperly gathered evidence, erred in its examination of company accounts and mishandled witnesses. He also argued that the government had not complied with China's basic criminal and administrative procedures. The appellate court, however, again rejected Ai's arguments.

Finally, on 1 October 2012, the government stripped Fake of its business license, stating that it had failed to meet its registration requirements.[25] It is true that the company was unable to comply with these requirements, but it was because police officers had taken nearly all the studio's materials and its stamp when they first arrested Ai. Ai's lawyer, Liu Xiaoyuan, filed a request for a hearing to resolve the matter.[26]

Procedure

International human rights organizations, such as Human Rights Watch, have publicly questioned the tax case against Ai Weiwei, calling it 'an 11th hour pretext pulled out of a hat by the government to justify Ai's unlawful arrest and secret detention for 81 days'.[27] The belief is that the CPC is creating small bureaucratic and administrative hurdles for Ai that will make clear who is in charge. If these assumptions are true, the Chinese government has blurred the line between criminal and administrative law.[28]

In 1996 the Chinese Criminal Procedure Law was revised to give more rights to suspected criminals and defendants.[29] Though this law was revised again in 2012, the changes did not go into effect until 2013, meaning Ai's arrest and detention fell under the 1996 revisions. According to Andrea J. Worden, the 1996 changes, such as ensuring that suspects had earlier access to a defense attorney, would put China more in line with internationally recognized human rights standards, but the courts, police and procuracy were resistant to implementation.[30] It took until 2000 before the National People's Congress looked at whether the changes had been successfully implemented. The committee investigating the revised Criminal Procedure Law found three 'chronic diseases' still prevalent in the criminal justice system: 'confessions coerced through torture (*xingxun bigong*)… unlawful extended detention (*chaoqi jiya*), and… obstacles facing criminal defense lawyers in providing representation to their clients (*lüshi bianhu nan*)'.[31] Lawyers went on to list the 'three difficulties' that hindered them from representing their clients: 'meeting criminal suspects… obtaining access to case files, and… collecting evidence and cross-examining witnesses at trial'.[32]

Criminal defense lawyers have also been restricted by the perjury statute, which they refer to as 'Big Stick 306'.[33] Article 306 of the Criminal Law of the People's Republic of China reads:

> A defender or an agent ad litem who, in the course of criminal procedures, destroys or forges evidence, assists the party concerned in destroying or forging evidence, or threatens or lures a witness to, contrary to the facts, change testimony or provide false evidence, shall be sentenced to fixed-term imprisonment of not more than three years or criminal detention; and if the circumstance is serious, to fixed-term imprisonment of not less than three years and not more than seven years.

Worden describes this statute as giving the procuracy 'unlimited power' to jail lawyers for presenting evidence that contradicts government evidence.[34] Many lawyers and academics have asked for the repeal of Article 306, as it is what many scholars believe stands in the way of lawyers taking on criminal defense cases. The case of Li Zhuang, a Beijing lawyer who was convicted under this statute, was discussed in Chapter 5.

In addition to regulations and procedures that should give criminal defense attorneys better access to their clients, the Criminal Procedure Law's 1996 revisions contained provisions on notice of and limits to detention. Article 64 states that police are required to notify an individual's family or work unit within 24 hours of the individual's arrest, the reason for detention and where he or she is being held. The article does list some exceptions, one such being where notification would impede the investigation.

There is some debate, however, as to whether written notice of detention must actually be provided. Some scholars believe that local police refrain from providing a written notice to deter defense attorneys from representing a client.[35] Police and prosecutors often insist on a written notice of detention before allowing an attorney to meet with a client, despite no provision in the Criminal Procedure Law requiring such. For Ai, it was clear that the Chinese government failed to provide any notice, written or otherwise, about his detention, his whereabouts or on what charges he was being held. Gradually information was revealed, but it did not happen within the 24-hour time period required by the Criminal Procedure Law.

Another aspect of Ai's case that raised questions within the international legal community was his length of detention. According to the Criminal Procedure Law, there are strict time limits on how long the criminal justice process can take. As Cohen commented: 'Although the Criminal Procedure Law in most cases gives the police only three days to hold someone before deciding whether to release him or apply to the prosecutors for an arrest warrant, exceptions allow them up to seven days and in very limited circumstances up to thirty days.'[36]

Many of these limits can be extended and there is often no way to question an extension, but there is a clear, maximum time limit for how long a suspect can be detained. As described above, Ai was held well past the limit during the pre-arrest and investigation stages of his case, even with extensions.

Several months after Ai's arrest, the NPC Standing Committee made public its draft revisions to the Criminal Procedure Law.[37] One of the changes focused on pre-arraignment and pre-conviction deprivations of liberty, mainly through residential surveillance and detention. Residential surveillance, or *jiasnshi juzhu* (监视居住), is not necessarily surveillance at a suspect's residence, and the draft revision permits police to keep someone under surveillance without notifying the individual's family.[38] Detention, or *juliu* (拘留), and residential surveillance are acceptable in cases of suspected terrorism, bribery or endangerment of state security.

After the initial draft provisions were published, there was an outcry about this deprivation of liberty clause. There were concerns about the lack of notice, so the authorities changed the notice provision to read 'except where notification cannot be processed that there should be notification to the family'.[39] Though the change provided for notification, there are still critics inside and outside of China who believe authorities will not provide sufficient information, such as the location of the detained suspect.[40] The other major concern was that suspected bribery could qualify someone for this deprivation of liberty, and thus the law was changed to make residential surveillance or detention acceptable only for cases of extremely serious bribery.

While there is still a provision requiring family members to be notified within 24 hours of a suspect being taken into custody, Amendment 36, which has unofficially been dubbed the 'Ai Weiwei clause', precludes notification when the detainee is believed to have been involved in crimes of terrorism, threats to national security or any other serious offense and the notice could hinder the investigation.[41] Some scholars see this amendment as a way to legalize retroactively the detention of Ai Weiwei and hundreds of others who were arrested in the so-called Jasmine Revolution of 2011.[42]

Not only was the 81-day secret detention of Ai Weiwei in violation of the notice requirement of Article 91 of the Criminal Procedure Law, but it also violated Article 37 of the Constitution stating 'unlawful detention or deprivation or restriction of a citizen's freedom of the person by other means is prohibited'.[43] Furthermore, the secret detention conflicts with Article 9 of the International Covenant on Civil and Political Rights, which China has signed but not ratified, requiring citizens to be arrested only 'in accordance with such procedures as are established by law'.[44] Ai's arrest and detention were not proper under China's own criminal procedure, and thus not legal under Article 9 of the ICCPR. In addition, the ICCPR requires anyone 'arrested or detained on a criminal charge' to be 'brought promptly before a judge or other officer... [and] entitled to a trial within a reasonable time or to release'.[45] Ai Weiwei's 81-day detention was clearly not in line with this requirement.

On 8 April 2011 the UN Working Group on Enforced or Involuntary Disappearances, after receiving multiple reports of persons being subject to enforced disappearance, including Ai Weiwei and a number of civil rights lawyers, issued a warning to the Chinese government: 'Enforced disappearance is a crime under international law. Even short-term secret detentions can qualify as enforced disappearances, there can never be an excuse to disappear people, especially when those persons are peacefully expressing their dissent with the Government of their country.'[46] The working group stressed: 'China has an obligation to abide by the strictest standards in the field of human rights. It also should fully cooperate with the UN special procedures and in particular with the Working Group.'[47]

The 'tax' case

On 18 November 2011 the lawyer for Fake, Pu Zhiqiang, wrote a legal opinion letter in which he attempted to lay out the legal points of Ai and Fake's case.[48] He suggested that Fake should not pay the back taxes the government alleged it owed, as it disputed the legal decision of the tax authority.[49] He further recommended that Fake request an administrative hearing to raise the procedural concerns within its tax case.

In his letter, Pu questioned the tactics used by authorities in the investigation of the tax evasion. In addition to the numerous disappearances of those close to Ai and in management positions at Fake (see the timeline above), Pu noted that 12 people had been taken into custody by police, including Ai himself, before officers from the Beijing Local Taxation Bureau and Beijing Public Security Bureau first went to the accounting office that was responsible for Fake.[50] Between 3 April (the date of Ai's arrest) and 6 April (the first official notice that Ai was being investigated for 'economic crimes'), police treated this more as a criminal investigation against Ai than an administrative procedure against Fake Company.

When officers went to Beijing Huxin Financial and Accounting Services Limited, they took 'original vouchers, accounting vouchers, accounting documents, tax vouchers, balance sheets, and profit/loss statements and other accounting documents of Fake Company dating from 2000 until February 2011'.[51] The next day the Beijing Public Security Bureau Economic Crime Investigation Unit first questioned Fake's accountant, Hu Mingfen. As described above, she was then put in secret detention until 13 June 2011, and released upon the condition that she no longer contact anyone associated with Fake. It was not until 8 April, however, that agents with the Beijing Local Taxation Bureau first issued Fake Company a tax inspection notice and inquiry notice.[52]

It should also be noted that tax officials failed to provide Fake with a list of the documents seized, as required by Article 25 of the Tax Inspection Work Procedures: whenever officials retrieve account books, accounting vouchers, statements and other relevant information, a notice for retrieving account books and documents should be issued to the target of the inspection and an inventory of retrieved account books and documents completed for the target's signature after being checked and confirmed. Furthermore, the accounting materials that were taken were not returned within the statutory timeframe dictated by Article 25 of the Tax Inspection Work Procedures, which mandate they be returned within three months or 30 days, depending on whether they were more or less than a year old.

Authorities continued to arrest, detain and question people involved with Fake and close to Ai, but on 22 June 2011, the day Ai was released, Xinhua announced that Fake, which it claimed was controlled by Ai Weiwei, had committed the crime of tax evasion and intentionally destroyed some of its financial documents.[53] In addition, Xinhua reported, 'In light of Ai Weiwei's good attitude in admitting his crimes and the fact that he suffers from chronic illness, combined with his multiple expressions of willingness to pay the taxes owed, Ai Weiwei has been released on guarantee pending further investigation in accordance with the law.'[54]

Five days later, however, the Beijing Local Taxation Bureau made it clear that it was Fake Company and not Ai that was being punished for tax evasion. The bureau issued a notice of administrative penalty for taxation ordering Fake to pay RMB12.21 million as a penalty for tax evasion.[55] Given the government had stated this was not an investigation into Ai Weiwei's actions, but rather the alleged economic crimes committed by Fake Company, it is surprising, Pu notes, that Ai said much of the questioning he endured while in detention was in regard to being suspected of inciting subversion of state power.[56]

Pu also described the relationship between Ai Weiwei and Fake, naming Ai as 'merely a designer'.[57] He was not one of the original founders of the company, he did not donate the capital to start it and nor was he the legal representative or the individual in charge of the finances. Beyond Liu Zhenggang, the individual Pu names as in charge of financial and taxation matters, Fake had been using Beijing Huxin Financial and Accounting Services since 2000 to file taxes and handle other accounting issues.

Pu goes into further detail about Ai's role with the company in an attempt to show that he is not a 'person of primary responsibility or other directly responsible person' under Article 31 of the Criminal Law. According to the lawyer, 'The Tax Management Law does not provide for holding anyone other than the taxpayer (which in this case is Fake Company) responsible, so there is clearly no factual or legal basis for the Ministry of Foreign Affairs or the Xinhua News Agency to say that "Ai Weiwei is suspected of economic crimes."'[58]

Pu concludes his first argument – 'The detention of Ai Weiwei et al. appears to have "exceeded authority" and been in violation of the law' – by stating that, because this was an administrative matter, the police had no authority to intervene.[59] The only situation that would give the public security organ the legal authority to handle these taxation issues would be if Fake Company refused to comply with an administrative penalty and administrative authorities relinquished their authority to the police.[60] According to Pu, 'there was no legal basis for the public security organ to step in before taxation authorities had begun investigating the "Fake tax case"... [By doing so,] they exceeded their authority and violated the law in their handling of the case.'[61]

Pu's legal opinion letter also argues that the 'Beijing taxation authorities' handling of the "Fake tax case" involves multiple procedural violations and unclear factual determinations, and its administrative act lacks legality and should be revoked in accordance with the law'.[62] One of his largest grievances was the seizure of Fake Company's accounts and papers by police. Since public security is not authorized to deal with tax cases, Fake's financial records should never have been stored at the Shibalidian police station in Chaoyang district.

Because the public security organ had the financial records, the taxation bureau's evidence of tax evasion was based on photocopies of the originals. Pu and Fake reiterated that they were unable to determine whether the evidence was authentic or accurate from a photocopy, but the taxation bureau did not or could not retrieve the original records from the police. When Fake asked for its records to be 'returned in full', the bureau merely confirmed that the records were with police.

Pu also noted that Fake protested the taxation bureau's refusal to hold a public hearing.[63] According to Pu's letter, the lack of a public hearing is a violation of the law, but the bureau insisted it could only hold a private hearing because the case involved the 'commercial secrets' of a third party.[64] When the No. 2 Audit Office held its private hearing, only appointed counsel and Fake's legal representative were allowed to attend. Not only did the taxation bureau rely on reproductions of the financial records, but it was also unable to show any evidence that a third party had requested that its financial situation be kept secret.[65]

Though the Audit Office ordered Fake to pay over RMB15.22 million in taxes and penalties (approximately RMB8.45 million in missed taxes and RMB6.77 million in fines) on 1 November 2011, Pu 'maintain[s] that the aforementioned decisions were based on factual findings that are not clear and serious procedural violations and that the [tax] authorities were clearly cleaning up for the public security organ's "Ai Weiwei case"'.[66]

The letter ends with the procedures Pu took to protect Fake's legal interests and the seemingly arbitrary and extralegal roadblocks the local administrative organs erected. Pu first recommended Fake only pay a tax guarantee, which would give it the 'right to pursue review and litigation without resulting in outside misunderstanding and misinterpretation'.[67] In an effort to raise the money to pay the guarantee, Ai's mother and brother mortgaged Ai's father's home, yet the government rejected the mortgage, claiming Fake was 'unable in fact to mortgage Ai Qing's [Ai's father] former residence as a taxation guarantee'.[68] So, after over RMB8.69 million were donated to Ai and Fake, Fake pledged its 'bank book' as a guarantee, but the taxation bureau claimed 'bank regulations prohibit an administrative organ like the local taxation bureau from acting as the lawful recipient of a pledge, so it would be impossible to put up the bank book as a pledge'.[69] The only way Fake was able to get an administrative review was by putting money into a tax guarantee funds account, as requested by the local taxation bureau.

Lu Qing, Ai's wife, filed an application for administrative reconsideration on 29 December after Fake was issued a written decision on administrative punishment on 21 November.[70] In it, she argues that the Beijing Local Taxation Bureau erred in using the Notice of the State Administration of Taxation on Some Issues Concerning the Punishments for Acts in Violation of the Regulations on Stamp Tax (Guo Shui Fa), thus Fake wanted a review of the decision and the written decision to be cancelled.

Relying on a close reading of the law, Fake's first application for administrative reconsideration dissected the written decision for errors of law. It highlights part 2(1) of the decision, noting that because the company did 'not affix tax stamps according to relevant provisions' of the Law on the Administration of Tax Collection and the Guo Shui Fa, it was to be fined three times the amount of stamp tax owed.[71] The problem, it argues, is that the ambiguous language of the Tax Law has 'produc[ed] three abnormal situations (i.e. a lower level law contravenes a higher level law, administrative regulations are inconsistent, provisions are inappropriate), because of issuance of the new law and regulation'.[72]

The first situation, a lower-level law contravening a higher-level law, arose because of contradictions between the Law of the People's Republic of China on the Administration of Tax Collection and the Provisional Regulations on Stamp Duty, and between the Detailed Rules for the Implementation of the Law of People's Republic of China to Administer the Levying and Collection of Taxes and the Detailed Rules for Implementation of Provisional Regulations on Stamp Tax. According to Fake, when there is such dissonance, Articles 87 and 88 of the Legislation Law of the People's Republic of China provide that 'laws, administrative regulations, local regulations, autonomous regulations and separate regulations and rules' may be revoked by the NPC Standing Committee:

> The Standing Committee of the National People's Congress has the right to revoke administrative regulations which conflict with the Constitution and the law, has the right to revoke local regulations which conflict with the Constitution, laws and administrative regulations, and has the right to revoke autonomous regulations and separate regulations which are approved by the standing committee of the people's congress in provinces, autonomous regions and municipalities but conflict with the Constitution and provisions of Article 66(2) in this Law.[73]

In addition, 'the State Council has the right to change or revoke inappropriate regulations in departments and local governments'.[74]

Fake insists these regulations specify that the NPC Standing Committee can change the Provisional Regulations on Stamp Duty and the State Council can change the Detailed Rules for Implementation of Provisional Regulations on Stamp Tax. Neither of these rules and regulations, however, can be changed by the State Administration of Taxation that promulgated Guo Shui Fa [2004] 15.

The second situation, in which rules and regulations are inconsistent, focuses on the Detailed Rules for the Implementation of Law to Administer the Levying and Collection of Taxes and the Provisional Regulations on Stamp Duty. As 'both of them are on the same level as administrative regulations', it is up to the State Council to choose whether the newer or older provision is applicable, as decreed by Article 85(2) of the Legislation Law.[75] This provision would also preclude the State Administration of Taxation that issued Guo Shui Fa [2004] 15 from making the same decision.

Finally, when a rule or regulation is inappropriate, the Legislation Law already provides that the State Council can 'change or revoke inappropriate regulations in departments and local governments'.[76] According to Articles 87 and 88, it is up to the State Council to make these changes, not the State Administration of Taxation.

Moreover, the application notes that the taxation bureau cited and applied the wrong law in the written decision. The decision uses the Tax Administration Law that came into effect on 1 May 2001, but section 1(2) of the decision lists alleged tax evasion from 29 November 2000 to 31 December 2010. This means the taxation bureau's decision and punishment were based on a law that was not in effect from 29 November 2000 to 30 April 2001. In addition, Fake states that Article 84 of the Legislation Law does not make laws retroactive unless the law has 'special provisions for a purpose of better protecting the right and interest of the citizens, legal persons and other organizations', which would not apply in a case of tax evasion.[77] Finally, the same law was cited in section 2(2) on punishment.

The next issue raised by Fake is whether the punishment exceeded the statute of limitations. After first determining that the Law of the People's Republic of China on Administrative Punishments has a statute of limitations of two years, meaning any activity that is not 'discovered' within two years of its commission cannot be punished under this law, Fake noted that the Tax Administration Law has a statute of limitations of five years.[78] Again, relying on a close reading of the law, Fake determined that the this tax case would fall under the two-year statute of limitations, and thus being punished for ten years of tax evasion would be inappropriate.

One of the most critical issues Fake addressed in its application for administrative reconsideration is whether the correct degree of punishment was applied. The law requires that similar actions of similar magnitude should be punished to approximately the same degree. The criteria a court can look at when determining punishment can include 'illegal facts, nature, circumstances and extent of social harm excluding the interference of irrelevant factors; the same kind of administrative violations, that is, illegal facts, nature, circumstances and extent of social harm'.[79]

Fake cited a recent case in which a local taxation bureau fined a real estate company an amount that was roughly half of the taxes it owed. In June 2007 the Beijing Taiyue Real Estate Development Co. Ltd was found to have submitted false tax declarations about its income, meaning it had underpaid its sales tax, education surtax and urban maintenance and construction tax. Fake insisted the case was highly sensitive and also named a 'major tax case' by the State Administration of Taxation, yet the construction company was punished at only half the rate of the unpaid taxes. Fake, in contrast, was punished at a rate between one-and-a-half times to three times the rate of unpaid taxes, which Fake argues calls into question the appropriateness of the punishment.

Fake admits there are some situations in which heavier punishment is appropriate, but quotes and dismisses Article 7 of the Several Provisions for Regulating the Free Judging Right of Administrative Penalties in Beijing:

> 'When there is a heavier administrative punishment, the consideration shall be into the following circumstances: (1) acts to cover and destroy illegal evidence or impede law enforcement and etc.; (2) ignore the advice and continue implementation of violations; (3) Offenses resulting in serious consequences; (4) Force [sic], trick, and abet others to commit illegal acts; (5) a major role in joint implementation of the offense; (6) incorrigible, and repeated violations; (7) implementation of the violations in the event of public emergencies; (8) other circumstances which are subject to a heavier punishment.' How can the applicant be subject to the heavier administrative punishment in event of above situations in Article 7 being ruled out?[80]

In its application, Fake's third argument is that the taxation bureau's claim that Fake presented 'illegal facts' – facts that contradict evidence presented by the bureau – is based on unclear facts.[81] The taxation bureau announced that much of the accounting information it had on Fake came from the public security department, but the only instance in which this department can be involved in a tax evasion case is when there are fears that a suspect is 'hiding and intentionally destroying accounting vouchers, account books and financial and accounting reports', according to Article 3 of the Criminal Law Amendment. With many of the accounting materials coming from the police, Fake argues the materials were incomplete and unclear.

In addition, Article 3 of Measures for Verification Collection of Enterprise Income Tax says 'If a taxpayer is under one of the following circumstances, tax authorities shall have the power to verify the enterprise income tax: where account books are established, but the accounts are not in order or information on costs, receipt vouchers and expense vouchers are incomplete, making it difficult to check the books.' Fake noted this, saying the taxation bureau should have used 'verification collection' instead of 'audit collection' in light of the fact that it was 'difficult to check' the studio's accounting books.[82]

Within verification collection, the tax authorities should not have punished Fake because, as the name implies, it is a way first to confirm how much money is owed and then collect it. It is used when 'the taxpayer's account books are not perfect, incomplete information is difficult to audit, or for other reasons is difficult to accurately determine the tax liability. That is, "verification collection" is a collection mode that has to be used by the tax authorities if accurate tax payment information cannot be obtained.'[83] As Fake insists that it is extremely difficult to determine exactly how much money it owes in unpaid taxes, it would be more appropriate to use verification collection.

Fake cites Articles 4 and 30 of the Administrative Punishments Law, which say that administrative punishments, including any punishments for tax evasion, are determined based on facts. When there are unclear facts about a violation of an administrative order, however, Article 30 specifically forbids punishment. Fake summarized its argument that the taxation bureau had incorrectly punished the studio: 'verification collection' is defined as the appropriate form of tax collection when the facts are not entirely clear, there is incomplete information or the taxation bureau is unable to determine tax liability; and as this is a 'case of unclear illegal facts', it was thus important to use verification collection.[84]

Article 63 of the Tax Administration Law defines tax evasion:

> A taxpayer forges, alters, conceals or, without authorization, destroys account books or vouchers for the accounts, or overstates expenses or omits or understates incomes in the account books, or, after being notified by the tax authorities to make tax declaration, refuses to do so or makes false tax declaration, or fails to pay or underpays the amount of tax payable. Where a taxpayer evades tax, the tax authorities shall pursue the payment of the amount of tax he fails to pay or underpays and the surcharge thereon, and he shall also be fined not less than 50 percent but not more than five times the amount of tax he fails to pay or underpays.

Fake alleges the taxation bureau failed to show what actions Fake took that would qualify as tax evasion. Since it also argues that the evidence is unclear, it would be impossible to determine whether Fake violated Article 63 and how much money in taxes went unpaid.[85] Without sufficient evidence, Fake says there is no legal basis for its punishment.

Fake Studio's final argument was that the taxation bureau used the wrong procedures to collect evidence and start an investigation into allegations of tax evasion by the studio. Because of these violations, Fake posits that the punishment against it should be revoked: 'In terms of the respondent in the present case, its law enforcement has committed serious violation of legal procedures and excess of authority or abuse of powers, and thus its penalty decision should of course be revoked according to law.'[86] Relying on the Administrative Reconsideration Law, the Regulation on the Implementation of the Administrative Reconsideration Law and the Rules for Taxation Administrative Reconsideration (No. 21 Decree of the State Administration of Taxation), the taxation bureau's suspected violations preclude it from penalizing Fake.[87]

Fake says the taxation bureau and public security officers violated Article 22(1) of the Tax Audit Regulations when they took Fake's accounting materials from its accounting firm without explaining legal procedure.[88] Article 22 expressly provides for warning before an inspection, 'unless prior notice impedes the inspection'.[89] In addition, Fake argues that no tax inspection notice or tax inspection certificate was issued, as required by Article 59 of the Tax Administration Law and Article 22(2) of the Tax Audit Regulations. Moreover, when police collected the accounting books from Huxin, they never issued a notice for retrieving account book materials or the list of retrieved account book materials, in violation of Article 25 of the Tax Audit Regulations.

One of the final two procedural violations Fake lists in its application is that the taxation bureau failed to return the studio's accounting materials within the three-month and 30-day statutory periods. Article 86 of the Rules for the Implementation of the Law of the People's Republic of China on the Administration of Tax Collection mandates that accounting materials for previous years must be returned within three months of their seizure, and materials for the current year may only be held for 30 days; at the time of Fake's first application for review, the police had not returned any of its account books.[90]

The more serious violation, however, is what Fake terms an illegal penalty hearing.[91] Fake says the taxation bureau failed to provide a public hearing, and by doing so it denied the studio the ability to defend itself properly. Fake cites numerous rules, regulations and laws that mandate a public hearing for tax cases and only allow a private hearing when a third party requests a confidential hearing.[92] Though Fake's hearing was private, the taxation bureau did not provide evidence that a third party requested or needed a confidential hearing to protect its financial interests. In its final appeal for administrative review, Fake noted the lack of original accounting materials, making it impossible to confirm the authenticity of the taxation bureau's evidence:

> However, the respondent, only at the beginning, provided the applicant with copies of relevant evidence materials, and such copies did not bear a signature of the applicant for confirmation. Because the respondent did not produce the originals to be checked with the applicant, the applicant is unable to confirm the evidence for authenticity, legitimacy and effectiveness, and moreover, the applicant was substantially deprived of its rights to statement and defence.[93]

Ultimately, this first application for administrative reconsideration was unsuccessful. Though Pu Zhiqiang presented strong legal arguments with considerable legal citations, the taxation bureau failed to address many of the legal issues addressed in the first (and subsequent) application. This not only highlights the sharp contrast in training and legal knowledge of lawyers and administrative officials, but also reveals the irrelevance of law within administrative decisions. Fake filed its second application for administrative reconsideration on 18 January 2012, which was similarly rejected.[94]

In its second application, Fake first argues that the taxation bureau committed several procedural errors, including the 'early intervention by the public security department, joint action between the public security and taxation departments, [and] making arrests before auditing', all of which contravened administrative rules and regulations.[95] Fake lists sections of the procedural timeline (see above), documenting the involvement of the police and the arrests that took place prior to the beginning of the tax evasion investigation.

The first set of rules and regulations Fake argues the taxation bureau violated all determined that a taxpayer who evaded taxes would not be criminally punished if he or she paid the back taxes and any late fines issued, and he or she had been administratively punished.[96] Article 201 of the Criminal Law of the People's Republic of China makes an exception and allows for criminal liability if the taxpayer 'has been criminally punished in five years for evading tax payment or has been, twice or more, administratively punished by the tax authorities'. Since this did not apply to the studio, Fake argues that police involvement was premature. In addition, Article 57 of the Notice of the Supreme People's Procuratorate and the Ministry of Public Security on Issuing the Provisions (II) of the Supreme People's Procuratorate and the Ministry of Public Security on the Standards for Filing Criminal Cases under the Jurisdiction of the Public Security Organs for Investigation and Prosecution lists an inclusive number of tax evasion scenarios that could lead to criminal prosecution, but none of them describes Fake's alleged actions.[97] The application argues that any evidence gained from this police investigation would be considered 'illegitimate' and should force the taxation bureau to withdraw its punishment.[98]

In analyzing Article 11 of the Provisions on the Transfer of Suspectable Criminal Cases by Administrative Organs for Law Enforcement, Fake concluded that:

> if the public security organs have already been involved in the case, then the tax authorities shall withdraw from it; if the tax authorities are handling the case, it implies that the case has not been transferred to the public security department or the conditions for transfer are not met, then the public security department should not be involved in the case. It is not only a procedural mistake for the respondent and the public security organs to join forces in handling a case, it is also a serious confusion of administrative and judicial boundaries.[99]

Fake reiterated many of the procedural violations it listed in the first application for administrative reconsideration, including that the accounting materials were improperly obtained and not returned within the statutory period, and there was insufficient notice, all of which prevented Fake from adequately defending against charges of tax evasion.

The second application also contested the legal basis used in the written decision for settlement, saying the Beijing Taxation Bureau incorrectly cited the Notification of Beijing Local Taxation Bureau on Definition of Several Policy Business Issues on Enterprise Income Tax in determining that Fake owed over RMB4.7 million in enterprise income tax.[100] The problem, says Fake, is that the Beijing Local Taxation Bureau attempted to define 'tax inspection' in this case without the proper authority.[101]

Fake notes that Article 93 of the Tax Administration Law grants the State Council the power to interpret the phrase 'tax inspection'. Fake admits that interpretation power may also lie with the State Administration of Taxation according to Article 85 of the Rules for the Implementation of the Law of the People's Republic of China on the Administration of Tax Collection, but Fake argues that the Beijing Local Taxation Bureau overstepped its authority by doing so.

Moreover, Fake argues that the power to interpret the 'method for calculating enterprise income tax' lies with either the Ministry of Finance or the State Administration of Taxation, according to Articles 19 and 59 of the Provisional Regulations of the People's Republic of China on Enterprise Income Tax. Again, Fake alleges that the taxation bureau's interpretation of the phrase went beyond its authority.

The studio's final complaint about the legal basis of the settlement decision is that the Notification of Beijing Local Taxation Bureau on Definition of Several Policy Business Issues on Enterprise Income Tax (Jing Di Shui Qi [2002] No. 526) was the incorrect method of determining how much Fake owed in taxes. Not only does Fake argue that the document is in conflict with a higher-level law, but it also notes that 'According to the Legislation Law of the People's Republic of China, Jing Di Shui Qi [2002] No. 526 Document is neither a law, a statute, nor a rule but a regulation of a working department of the local people's government.'[102] What this means is that, according to Article 7 of the Administrative Reconsideration Law, Fake has the right to an administrative reconsideration in light of the confusing regulation.

As in its first application, the studio claims the taxation bureau erred in using the 'audit collection' method because there was insufficient information, and thus the 'verification collection' method was more appropriate. Citing the bureau's reliance on incomplete accounting records, Fake says it should have used verification collection.[103] It also notes that the taxation bureau failed to use the audit collection method correctly by not verifying the studio's 'objective costs, expenses, losses and other reasonable expenditures'.[104] Though the bureau says it discovered more than RMB15.8 million in design fees and engineering income that Fake did not file between 29 November 2000 and 31 December 2010, Fake says 'it is obvious that the respondent has not checked the costs and expenses of the items used to identify income'.[105] Instead, Fake claims the taxation bureau used the audit collection method to come up with a 'ridiculous and peremptory' estimated total enterprise income tax and actual tax paid.

Another contention Fake raises is that the taxation bureau ascribed 'decoration income' to the studio, despite the fact that the studio does not have the construction enterprise qualification certificate necessary to earn decoration income.[106] Because it cannot obtain such income, the money the taxation bureau is calling decoration income cannot be taxed. If the studio were to claim the income, it would need to do so as 'illegal income', for which there is little clarification on how it would be taxed.[107] Though Fake cites Articles 4 and 37 of the Tax Administration Law for guidance, it admits that neither section correctly fits Fake's situation of illegal income. Even if there was a provision that determined how illegal income was to be taxed, Fake notes that Article 65 of the Construction Law vests authority to punish 'an organization which is hired for projects without a certificate of qualification' with the State Council, not with the taxation bureau.

As with the first application for administration review, Pu Zhiqiang and Fake were unsuccessful with the second application. The second and final appeal was rejected on 27 September 2012.

Perhaps inspired by the Al Capone tax evasion case in the United States in 1932,[108] and how the United States handled a infamous gangster and shrewd businessman, in dealing with Ai Weiwei Chinese authorities 'decided to crush him by resorting to economic measures whose illegality would presumably be less apparent both to its own citizens and to the outside world'.[109]

The Ai Weiwei case exemplifies the difficulties of analyzing Chinese law in Western terms, such as the clear distinction between different

has been a jump in the number of people using the petitioning
since 1993. This has caused continued stress on the system,
y with an estimated 10 million petitions between 2003 and 2007
could be low, as this is an official statistic).[118] At any given time,
umbers of people wait in Beijing or provincial capitals as their
ces are heard or received by the authorities.
ely, however, the petitioning system is not an effective way of
ng complaints. This is due, in part, to the non-legal nature of the
g complaints. This is due, in part, to the non-legal nature of the
The State Bureau for Letters and Calls often lacks the authority
ect local or state departments to resolve a petitioner's issue,
ng the central bureau usually sends a petitioner back to his or her
ffice and chastises the local petitioners' bureau.
has led to reports of provincial and local officials hiring individuals
p petitioners reaching the State Bureau for Letters and Calls.[119]
epting petitioners before they can lodge complaints at the national
s a method of protecting local officials, as lower-level officials are
punished for creating situations that lead to national appeals.
ational human rights observers also claim Chinese officials will jail
ners in underground or secret detention centers;[120] in these 'black
petitioners may allegedly face torture and other human rights
es.
ke the labor education system, intercepting and jailing petitioners
common practices in the notorious 'stability maintenance' system,
h has expanded massively in the past two decades.

Designed to weed out any threats to Communist Party rule, funding
for 'stability maintenance' has exceeded the national defense
budget for the past two years, reaching 702 billion yuan, or $110
billion, last year. Payouts fund not just the regular criminal justice
system but also ordinary citizens to watch potential trouble-
makers, bounty hunters hired by local governments to catch
petitioners heading to Beijing and black jails to hold them.[121]

e petitioning system, like many aspects of the administrative law, ha
n largely distorted from its main purpose – to provide a channel f
dinary citizens to voice their grievances. Instead of building trust ir
vernment and a set of resources that lie outside the judicial s'
cal petitioners' bureaus stand to identify individuals who ma'
buble for local officials. The risk of having a complaint file'
em has led many local and provincial authorities to spend cc

categories of law (criminal, administrative, etc.); jurisdiction; and
administrative, civil and criminal procedures. The entire contemporary
legal system started after the Cultural Revolution, less than four decades
ago. China's legal system is still nascent, full of ambiguity, contradictions
and inconsistencies. Ai's case started as a criminal case – on suspicion of
Article 105 of the Criminal Law's 'inciting to subvert the state power' –
but ended up in an administrative law proceeding. During the entire
process, particularly after the legal process started, the authorities tried,
most of the time awkwardly, to use the law to punish an unapologetic
'maverick',[110] but because of their own incompetence and unfamiliarity
with the law, they struggled to cover procedural errors. Ai Weiwei and
his lawyers argued his case is full of abuses and utterly lacked fairness:
'at both the administrative and the judicial levels the proceedings against
him have been a farce'.[111]

Administrative law in China

The primary purpose for administrative law in the People's Republic of
China is to provide oversight to the various departments and committees
within the government. The administrative legal framework first arose in
the 1980s during the period of reform and opening. Though there was a
need for considerable government control during this economic reform,
there was very little administrative law until the mid-1980s. From the
promulgation of the 1982 Constitution to 1988, over 130 administrative
laws, rules and regulations were promulgated that allowed for
administrative litigation. In 1988 the administrative division of the
Supreme People's Court also came into being, along with 1,400 other
administrative panels attached to local courts.

A large part of administrative law was formed by the Administrative
Procedure Law. Though drafted in 1987, it was not until 1989 that it
passed and 1990 before it went into effect. It clarified administrative law
by providing detailed procedures for bringing an administrative lawsuit
against the government. In addition to the Administrative Procedure
Law, the Administrative Supervision Regulations and the Administrative
Reconsideration Regulations were both passed in 1990 and have since
become laws. Legislation in the early to mid-1990s solidified the
administrative system in China. Important laws and regulations
promulgated include the Administrative Procedure Law (1990), or the
Law of Administrative Litigation; the Regulations on Administrative

Supervision (1990); the State Compensation Law (1994); the Law of Administrative Punishment (1996); and the Law of Administrative Review (1999).

Traditionally, China emphasizes political and party control rather than law in the area of state administration. Though China has seen a robust growth of administrative laws, rules and regulations since the 1980s, critics argue administrative law does not have the same strength as other branches of law.[112] There are concerns that this area of law does not properly regulate or control the government, which should be its primary purpose. This is due, at least in part, to a weak judicial branch, corruption and other institutional problems. The Ai Weiwei case is a perfect illustration that the protections the Administrative Procedure Law or Administrative Litigation Law are intended to provide, such as protecting 'legitimate rights and interests'[113] from actions taken by administrative organs, do not always lend themselves to effective litigation.

One area in which there is no doubt that administrative law is not applicable is in regard to the Communist Party of China, as the CPC is not an administrative organ. This was reiterated in a 1991 lawsuit against the CPC by a former professor at Nanjing University, Guo Ruoji.[114] The professor lost his job and was prevented from traveling overseas by the CPC. In his lawsuit against the party, both the Nanjing Intermediate Court and the Higher People's Court of Jiangsu Province held that an administrative lawsuit was inappropriate because the party did not constitute an administrative body.[115]

In Ai's case, however, Pu Zhiqiang and Fake did not pursue litigation. Instead, they relied on administrative reconsideration, which differs from a lawsuit in three ways. The first is that reconsideration provides for a review of an administrative decision, including whether it was proper and legal. Second, an applicant can request consideration of both an act and its basis. Finally, applications for administrative reconsideration are free.

Administrative officials are regulated by the Ministry of Supervision and lower-level supervisory organs. The supervisory organs are allowed to investigate administrative decisions and departments, determine whether decisions are appropriate and impose injunctions on administrative bodies, among other things. The ministry was reformed in 1986 and joined with the CPC's Discipline Committee in 1993. The Administrative Supervision Regulations were passed in 1990, but it was seven years before they became law. These supervisory organs provide

---

the last bit of oversight in a now fully deve government.

Legal scholars, however, have pointed ou the administrative branch that undermines ti the local level, a supervisory organ reports to at the level directly above it and the local g supervisory organ from exercising any overs body at its same level. It cannot be independe body it is meant to supervise. This pattern government.

Albert Chen elucidates another problem of c 'many existing laws only confer powers on adm not contain clear provisions on the limits t sanctions for abuse of the powers'.[117]

The boundaries between administrative law such as civil and criminal law, should be aforementioned structural defects and tradition rather than law, however, the very purpose of a protect citizens from abuse of power by the gove undermined.

Petition

One important aspect of administrative law in (Petitioning describes the system of administrativ individuals to voice their complaints. The system da China, when petitioners would go to an official's cc grievances; if a local official was unable to provide i would travel to the imperial capital to express his Today, petitioners still travel to Beijing if they are un justice they believe they deserve from the courts or lo

The system is officially set up for either a local or receive petitions and pass along problems to the government department. The petitioners' bureaus (or for Letters and Calls at the national level) then contin the respective departments and keep petitioners developments. As with many procedures of the Chinese local official is unable to resolve a complaint, a petitior the provincial- and national-level bureaus.

sums on intercepting petitioners and jailing them when the money could instead be spent on solutions to the problems petitioners are identifying.

Ironically, one extremely encouraging development in administrative law came from Beijing Chaoyang District Court, the very court that ruled against Ai Weiwei in his tax case. On 5 February 2013 the court sentenced ten bounty hunters who had formerly been employed by local authorities to prison for illegally detaining citizens trying to take their local grievances to the central government.[122]

This unprecedented case sparked speculation that the new administration is trying to rein in abuses of some fundamental human rights.[123] As analyzed throughout this book, party control makes China's legal system 'rule by law' rather than 'rule of law'. In the foreseeable future we have no reason to believe this new administration will initiate any political or judicial reform, yet as a 'decentralized predatory state', as Professor Pei Minxin terms it,[124] China is increasingly facing a potentially unanticipated mass revolt that mobilizes a wide range of social groups nationwide.[125] These groups are despondent over the corruption, police brutality, lack of food safety and environmental disasters present in their daily lives. Perhaps, at the very least, the party can address some specific areas where basic due process is ignored, basic human dignity is deprived and basic human rights are violated, such as intercepting and jailing petitioners and the re-education through labor program. By doing so, the CPC can begin to rein in abuses of power, which are currently out of control at local levels and in the administrative systems, without risking its supremacy. If so, the party and the administration may be able to survive for many more years to come.

Notes

1. FakeCase.com (undated) 'The Fake case'; available at: *http://fakecase.com/case* (accessed: 9 August 2013).
2. Ibid.
3. Ibid.
4. Evan Osnos (2011) 'Ai Weiwei and the law', *New Yorker*, 7 April; available at: *www.newyorker.com/online/blogs/evanosnos/2011/04/ai-weiwei-and-the-law.html* (accessed: 9 August 2013).
5. Ibid.
6. FakeCase.com, note 1 above.
7. Ibid.
8. Radio Television Hong Kong (2011) 'Ai Weiwei to fight tax bill', RTHK, 11 November; available at: *http://rthk.hk/rthk/news/englishnews/20111111/news_20111111_56_797318.htm* (accessed: 9 August 2013).

9. Liu Yiheng (2011) 'The real Ai Weiwei: five play artist – full of five poisons', *Wei Wen Po*, 15 April; available at: *http://paper.wenweipo.com/2011/04/15/PL1104150001.htm* (accessed: 25 August 2013).

10. Beijing Fake Cultural Development (2011) 'Public letter from Ai Weiwei's family', 15 April; available at: *www.scribd.com/doc/53066441/Public-Letter-from-Ai-Weiwei-Studio* (accessed: 15 August 2013).

11. Ai Weiwei's lawyers (2012) 'The Ai Weiwei papers', *New Statesman*, 18 October; available at: *www.newstatesman.com/politics/politics/2012/10/ai-weiwei-papers* (accessed: 9 August 2013).

12. Jerome Cohen (2012) 'An introduction to the Ai Weiwei papers', *New Statesman*, 18 October; available at: *www.newstatesman.com/politics/politics/2012/10/ai-weiwei-papers* (accessed: 9 August 2013).

13. Ai Weiwei's lawyers, note 11 above.

14. Lu Qing et al. (2011) 'Joint letter', trans. Jennifer Ng, 10 June; available at: *www.scribd.com/doc/58150935/June-11-Joint-Letter* (accessed: 9 August 2013).

15. Ai Weiwei's lawyers, note 11 above.

16. Solomon R. Guggenheim Foundation (2011) 'Call for the release of Ai Weiwei', June; available at: *www.change.org/petitions/call-for-the-release-of-ai-weiwei* (accessed: 15 August 2013).

17. Ai Weiwei's lawyers, note 11 above.

18. Liu Yanping (@duyanpili) (2011) 'Tweet', 26 July.

19. Ai Weiwei's lawyers, note 11 above.

20. Liu, note 18 above.

21. Ai Weiwei's lawyers, note 11 above.

22. Ibid.

23. *Washington Post* (2011) 'In China, putting a price on democracy', *Washington Post*, 7 November; available at: *www.washingtonpost.com/opinions/in-china-putting-a-price-on-democracy/2011/11/07/gIQA6xUHxM_story.html* (accessed: 7 November 2011).

24. Ai Weiwei's lawyers, note 11 above.

25. *Huffington Post* (2012) 'Ai Weiwei's design license revoked by Chinese officials', *Huffington Post*, 2 October; available at: *www.huffingtonpost.com/2012/10/02/ai-weiweis-design-license_n_1931840.html* (accessed: 15 August 2013).

26. Tania Branigan (2012) 'Ai Weiwei studio to be closed down by Chinese authorities', *The Guardian*, 1 October; available at: *www.guardian.co.uk/world/2012/oct/01/ai-weiwei-firm-closed-china* (accessed: 15 August 2013).

27. Ibid.

28. Ibid.

29. Andrea J. Worden (2009) '"A fair game"? Of law and politics and politics in China, and the "sensitive" case of democracy activist Yang Jianli', *Georgetown Journal of International Law*, 40: 447.

30. Ibid.

31. Ibid.

32. Ibid.

33. *New York Times* (2011) 'Editorial: the Big Stick 306 and China's contempt for the law', *New York Times*, 6 May; available at: *www.nytimes.com/2011/05/06/opinion/06fri3.html?_r=0* (accessed: 15 August 2013).
34. Worden, note 29 above.
35. Ibid.
36. Jerome Cohen (2011) 'Jerome Cohen on the detention of Ai Weiwei'; available at: *www.usasialaw.org/2011/04/jerome-cohen-on-the-detention-of-ai-weiwei/* (accessed: 15 August 2013).
37. Elizabeth M. Lynch (2012) 'Who will be watched: Margaret K. Lewis on China's new CPL & residential surveillance', *China Law & Policy*, 25 September; available at: *http://chinalawandpolicy.com/2012/09/25/who-will-be-watched-margaret-k-lewis-on-chinas-new-cpl-residential-surveillance/* (accessed: 15 August 2013).
38. Ibid.
39. Ibid.
40. Ibid.
41. Ibid.
42. Guo Zhiyuan (2011) 'Presentation chance and challenge for Chinese Criminal Procedure Law reform', 19 September; available at: *www.usasialaw.org/wp-content/uploads/2011/09/20110926-Chance-and-Challege-for-Chinese-Criminal-Procedure-Law-Reform.pdf* (accessed: 15 August 2013).
43. Constitution of the People's Republic of China, Article 37.
44. International Covenant on Civil and Political Rights, Article 9.
45. Ibid.
46. Office of the UN High Commissioner for Human Rights (2011) 'China: UN expert body concerned about recent wave of enforced disappearances', 8 April; available at: *www.ohchr.org/en/NewsEvents/Pages/DisplayNews.aspx?NewsID=10928&LangID=E* (accessed: 15 August 2013).
47. Ibid.
48. Pu Zhiqiang (2011) 'Initial opinions regarding the "Fake tax case" (translation)', Siweiluozi's Blog, 18 November; available at: *www.siweiluozi.net/2011/11/pu-zhiqiang-initial-opinions-regarding.html* (accessed: 7 August 2013).
49. Ibid.
50. Ibid.
51. Ibid.
52. Article 59 of the Law of the People's Republic of China Concerning the Administration of Tax Collection states that 'When making tax inspection, the officials of the tax authorities shall produce… tax inspectional notices', yet officials searched both Ai and Beijing Huxin Ltd prior to the first time notices were presented.
53. Quoted in Pu, note 48 above.
54. Quoted in ibid.
55. Ibid.
56. Ibid.
57. Ibid.

58. Ibid.
59. Ibid.
60. Criminal Law of the People's Republic of China (1997), Article 201(4).
61. Pu, note 48 above.
62. Ibid.
63. Ibid.
64. Ibid.
65. Ibid.
66. Ibid.
67. Ibid.
68. Ibid.
69. Ibid.
70. Fake Design Culture Development (2011) 'Application for administrative reconsideration, Fake Design Culture Development Ltd', 29 November; available at: *http://fakecase.com/documents* (accessed: 25 August 2013).
71. Ibid.
72. Ibid.
73. Ibid.
74. Ibid.
75. Ibid.
76. Ibid.
77. Ibid.
78. Ibid.
79. Ibid.
80. Ibid.
81. Ibid.
82. Ibid.
83. Ibid.
84. Ibid.
85. Ibid.
86. Ibid.
87. Ibid.
88. Ibid.
89. Ibid.
90. Ibid.
91. Ibid.
92. Ibid.
93. Ibid.
94. Fake Design Culture Development (2012) 'Application for administrative reconsideration, Fake Design Culture Development Ltd', 18 January; available at: *http://fakecase.com/documents* (accessed: 25 August 2013).
95. Ibid.
96. Ibid.
97. Ibid.
98. Ibid.
99. Ibid.

100. Ibid.
101. Ibid.
102. Ibid.
103. Ibid.
104. Ibid.
105. Ibid.
106. Ibid.
107. Ibid.
108. *Capone v. United States*, 56 F.2d. 927 (1932).
109. Cohen, note 12 above.
110. See *Global Times* (2011) 'The law will not bend for a maverick', *Global Times*, 6 April; original Chinese version available at: *http://opinion. huanqiu.com/roll/2011-04/1609672.html* (accessed: 15 August 2013); English translation available at: *http://notesonchina.tumblr.com/ post/4387913705/translation-of-the-op-ed-on-ai-wei-wei-in-chinese* (accessed: 15 August 2013).
111. Cohen, note 12 above.
112. Daniel C.K. Chow (2009) *The Legal System of the People's Republic of China*, 2nd edn. St Paul, MN: Thomson West, p. 369.
113. Administrative Procedure Law of the People's Republic of China, Article 1.
114. Guo Luoji (1993) 'How can I sue the Chinese communist territory party punch ball?', 2 March; available at: *http://blog.boxun.com/hero/guolj/80_ 1.shtml* (accessed: 15 August 2013).
115. Ibid.
116. Chow, note 112 above, pp. 370–1.
117. Albert H.Y. Chen (2004) *An Introduction to the Legal System of the People's Republic of China*, 3rd edn. Hong Kong: LexisNexis Butterworths, p. 256.
118. Li Huizi and Zhou Erjie (2007) 'China's public complaint department busiest office in Beijing', Xinhua News Agency, 2 September; available at: *www.chinadaily.com.cn/china/2007-09/02/content_6142475.htm* (accessed: 15 August 2013).
119. Tania Branigan (2009) 'Chinese petitioners held in illicit "black jails", report claims', *The Guardian*, 12 November.
120. Ibid.
121. Ibid.
122. Associated Press (2013) 'China sentences 10 for detaining petitioners', 5 February; available at: *http://bigstory.ap.org/article/china-sentences-10- detaining-petitioners* (accessed: 15 August 2013).
123. Ibid.
124. See generally Pei Minxin (2006) *China's Trapped Transition: The Limits of Developmental Autocracy*. Boston, MA: Harvard University Press.
125. Pei Minxin (2013) 'Five ways China can become a democracy', *The Diplomat*, 13 February; available at: *http://thediplomat.com/2013/02/13/5- ways-china-could-become-a-democracy/* (accessed: 15 August 2013).

Part IV
Conclusion

Afterword

As Chinese historian Ray Huang researched for his book *1587: A Year of No Significance: The Ming Dynasty in Decline*,[1] he found a fatal problem in Chinese politics: the political structure was premature and the administrative methods never grew to support the structure properly, nor were they based on sensible mathematics. Though the population and economy continued to develop, the administrative system was unable to sustain the whole economy. Bureaucrats were working to cope with existing problems while new ones continued to spring forward. Despite the fact that the emperor had been very ambitious and the Chinese people very diligent, these individual efforts never really worked out to save the dynasty from decline.

At first glance 2013, just like any year in the past two decades or so, is a year of no particular significance to China. The CPC, despite political and economic issues, remains firmly in power. Liu Xiaobo, one of two Chinese Nobel Peace laureates, languishes in prison, serving an 11-year sentence. The Tiananmen Square incident of 1989 is still a taboo that cannot be mentioned anywhere in China. Tibet is still burning and the number of monks and civilians who are self-immolating keeps rising, yet Beijing has not changed and shows no sign it plans to change any of its policy in the foreseeable future.[2] There continues to be unrest between the Uyghur and Han populations of Xinjiang. Property prices in Beijing and Shanghai are still sky-high. And blue sky is still a luxury for most Chinese people living in big cities.

Observers like Professor Pei Minxin have argued that China is trapped in a transition from a socialist planned economy to a market economy: 'The market oriented economic policies, pursued in a context of exclusionary politics and predatory practices make the CCP increasingly resemble a self-serving ruling elite.'[3] Pei has also opined that the 'lack of progress in political reform would be the most important factor in constraining China's development – even more important than economic reform'.[4]

Paul Krugman is even more pessimistic:

> China is in big trouble. We're not talking about some minor
> setback along the way, but something more fundamental. The
> country's whole way of doing business, the economic system that
> has driven three decades of incredible growth, has reached its
> limits. You could say that the Chinese model is about to hit its
> Great Wall, and the only question now is just how bad the crash
> will be.[5]

Krugman goes on to pose a poignant question: 'China's political regime
is remarkable, even given the annals of history, for the hypocrisy of its
position: officially it's building the socialist future, in practice it's
presiding over a crony capitalist Gilded Age. Where, then, does the
regime's legitimacy come from?'[6] We believe there are many different
answers.

New president Xi Jinping has used media and propaganda, much like
his predecessors, to speak of the 'China dream'. His propaganda storm
began in earnest after he became president in 2013, and he referenced the
'China dream' numerous times in his first address to the nation as head
of state on 17 March 2013:

> We must make persistent efforts, press ahead with indomitable
> will, continue to push forward the great cause of socialism with
> Chinese characteristics, and strive to achieve the Chinese dream of
> great rejuvenation of the Chinese nation... To realise the Chinese
> road, we must spread the Chinese spirit, which combines the spirit
> of the nation with patriotism as the core and the spirit of the time
> with reform and innovation as the core.[7]

Despite President Xi's call for steadfast support of the China dream, he
has not specified how to put the dream into practice. One thing is clear,
however: this dream is much closer to Mao and farther from the
constitutionalism for which intellectuals and foreign governments had
hoped. In public speeches Xi tends to elevate the CPC above the nation,
and even above the Chinese people. He has tried to clamp down on
criticism of Mao: 'To completely negate Mao Tse-tung would lead to the
demise of the Chinese Communist Party and to great chaos in China.'[8]

At the same time that the state media have extolled the virtues of the
'China dream', they have also launched a campaign against

constitutionalism. Several major party media outlets have written editorials supporting CPC rule by saying that 'Western political concepts like separation of powers are alien and unsuited to China.'[9] Many of the country's intellectuals, however, have been openly advocating for constitutionalism and political reform.[10]

Constitutionalism, which can be defined as the concept of a system of laws and regulations that protect citizens' rights by restraining the government or a political party, has been increasingly ridiculed by the *People's Daily*, the official newspaper of the CPC. One article opines that the drive for constitutionalism is not inherently Chinese, but rather a sign that Western countries have pushed their values on China and injected them into Chinese society. The editorial went so far as to claim that 'the spread of "constitutional-rule" ideas in China has been fostered by foundations affiliated with US intelligence agencies that aim to overturn socialism'.[11]

Is constitutionalism incommensurable with Chinese socialism?

The concept of incommensurability of paradigms is borrowed from the philosophy of science and the philosopher Thomas Kuhn in his book *The Structure of Scientific Revolutions*.[12] He argued that two groups with vastly different paradigms cannot truly understand each other's point of view because they are on two radically different planes. Kuhn suggested that different ideas, vocabularies and experiences all contribute to the inability to see the other group's perspective.

This, of course, raises the question of whether constitutionalism and Chinese communism are incommensurable paradigms. If so, can they ever be reconciled and coexist? If China does adopt constitutionalism, will that mean the end of the CPC as we know it?

If we look at a recent press conference given by US Acting Assistant Secretary of State Uzra Zeya following a conversation on human rights between US and Chinese representatives, we see a split in how the two countries view individual rights. In Zeya's opinion, 'China will be stronger and more stable and more innovative if it represents and respects international human rights norms.'[13] She noted that there continue to be many different incidents the US government has classified as human rights abuses, nearly all of which violated both Chinese law and its international obligations. Yet increasing numbers of individual Chinese citizens are starting publicly to question the CPC.

Though Zeya provided concrete examples of human rights abuses, the Chinese government has noted that the human rights situation is at an all-time high in China.[14] It rejects any claim that things are deteriorating in China, or that it has started to target activists by harassing their relatives. Spokespeople for the government assert that the United States is biased in its criticisms and intentionally distorts the Chinese human rights record.

So, does this mean that constitutionalism and a healthy respect for human rights and Chinese communism are incommensurable? That remains to be seen, at least according to Professor Wang Dong of Peking University School of International Studies, who has said that bilateral talks are an important step toward mutual understanding.[15]

Important updates

Since the main text of the book was first written there have been several important developments within the cases we have presented and Chinese law in general.

The case involving Bo Xilai (Chapter 4) saw an unprecedented five-day trial (22–26 August 2013), and Bo was eventually sentenced to life imprisonment. Professor Pei Minxin believes that 'the Bo Xilai affair has exploded several important myths about one-party rule in China'.[16] One of the most striking lessons from Bo's case is that the idea that 'the post-Mao leadership has perfected a system of managing internal conflict and maintaining elite unity' is false.[17] Instead of a rule of law society, the party has chosen to operate by the rule of the jungle: whoever is the most powerful makes the rules. In *A Death in the Lucky Holiday Hotel: Murder, Money, and an Epic Power Struggle in China*, authors Ho Pin and Huang Wenguang not only discussed the killing of Neil Heywood by Bo's wife, a murder that shocked the international community in 2012, but also the 'stunning and unsettling portrait of the different intertwined interest groups and political factions within the Chinese Communist Party's top decision-making body'.[18] As Bo's case and the cases of those closest to him have shown, the top echelon of the CPC is rife with self-interest, corruption and debauchery.

Contrary to the Chinese government and its supporters' claim that Bo's trial is 'a victory for the rule of law in China',[19] Professor Pei

Minxin and Donald Clarke are less optimistic. In anticipating the most important trial in three decades, the latter first pointed out that:

> China has no separation of powers and so lawmaking is an internal function of government; in other words, the government can pretty much enact any law it wants. It can change any law it finds inconvenient, or pass any law it needs to justify some action, thus enabling it to say (truthfully!) that it is always following the law – should it wish to do so.[20]

Clarke has also argued that the real problem in China today is 'the government ignoring its own law'.[21] For one thing, 'Bo Xilai was being held for months in a form of Party-based investigative detention called *shuanggui*.'[22] As discussed in Chapter 7, in *shuanggui*, or 'double designation', party officials and members are forcibly detained, *extralegally*, for months by party disciplinary officials. They are not held by police, yet they are subject to interrogation. The criminal procedure rules do not apply within the *shuanggui* system at all. Probably few observers would be sympathetic to Bo Xilai and other former high-profile party officials who are in *shuanggui*, which is no different to ordinary citizens being forced to *hecha* ('drink tea') by state security officers (Chapter 4); nevertheless 'the fact that the Party *could* change the law to legalize *shuanggui* but has never done so suggests a defiant declaration of its intent never to subject itself to legal constraints'.[23] This clearly indicates that the party's political agenda carries a much heavier weight than its respect for the law, even its own law.

Probably the most ironic and revealing part of this whole scandal is that Bo Guagua, Bo Xilai's only son, who is in 'exile' in the United States, has enrolled in Columbia Law School to pursue a legal education.[24] Bo Guagua is joining the lawyer Chen Guangcheng, who sought refuge at the US embassy in Beijing,[25] and Wang Lijun, former police chief and Bo Xilai's trusted aide, who attempted to seek political asylum at the US consulate general in Chengdu (Chapter 4), by showing more confidence in the US legal system than in his own.

There have also been two recent news stories about judges and lawyers that shed light on the current state of the Chinese legal system. In the first, two judges and an official were caught participating in some unscrupulous activities. In the second, a noted lawyer who has been critical of the government was arrested because of his previous work.

The CPC recently expelled two judges and an official from the Shanghai high court after a businessman collected video evidence of the three allegedly visiting prostitutes.[26] The men lost their jobs and are facing discipline after the evidence was turned over to the CPC's internal disciplinary body. The businessman used security camera footage and video he collected after following the judges for a year to compile the incriminating evidence; he believed one of the judges had unfairly ruled against him in a lawsuit, and sought evidence to trap the judge in illegal behavior. The footage was embarrassing and public enough that Han Zheng, the CPC secretary of Shanghai, was forced to denounce the judges publicly and warn other court officials against repeating the behavior:

> Although this case involved only a few corrupt and dissolute officials, it has shamed the entire judicial and legal system of Shanghai, and, indeed, the entire city itself... Certain judges have spurned law and discipline, forsaken ethics and morality, and behaved with reckless abandon.[27]

The other story involves Xu Zhiyong, a lawyer who has publicly fought corruption and human rights abuses. Xu was arrested on charges of 'assembling a crowd to disrupt order in a public place'.[28] In early August 2013 Xu, wearing a prison uniform, created a video statement in which he said:

> I encouraged everyone to be a citizen, to proudly and forthrightly be a citizen, to practice their rights as citizens set forth in the constitution and to undertake their responsibilities as citizens; I promoted equal rights in education and allowing children to take the university examination where they have followed their parents to live; I called for officials to disclose their assets. In these absurd times, those are my three crimes.[29]

Though Xu's arrest may seem to be contrary to China's claims that it is moving closer to a more open and reformed society, Ira Belkin of the US-Asia Law Institute at New York University believes the situation to be 'bizarrely consistent'.[30] Especially after the Supreme People's Court recently demonstrated its intention to reduce wrongful convictions[31] and Premier Li Keqiang's pledge to reform the re-education through labor system (Chapter 4),[32] there is hope that the CPC is sincere in building a legitimate legal system. Though the government claims to be embracing the rule of law, it is ultimately focused on social stability, yet the CPC has interpreted 'social stability' to mean both a lack of social unrest and also no questioning of the party's authority. When the government determines someone is a 'troublemaker', it will do everything in its power to silence or stop him or her.

Though the CPC would argue that both these instances are unique and do not represent Chinese society today, they are, to borrow a phrase from Belkin, 'bizarrely consistent'. To remain in control, the party believes it must deter everyone and anyone who questions its actions. At the same time it will turn a blind eye to abuse by its members; but when that abuse becomes public knowledge, the party will distance itself from its members. What this means is that the CPC continues to remain outside of and above the law. Rather than be held accountable under rule of law and constitutionalism, the party uses the law to maintain its power, reinforcing a rule by law system.

Yet 2013 may be a year of significance for China, as all the signs point to either 'the coming collapse of China'[33] or 'when China rules the world'.[34]

Conclusion

While we strove to provide a comprehensive introduction to the Chinese legal system in this book, there are certain issues we did not discuss. In part because each topic could fill volumes, and because of their sensitive nature, we did not cover Tibet, Xinjiang or Inner Mongolia, three 'hotspots' of ethnic conflict; the Falun Gong, an underground religious group that is banned in mainland China; or lesbian, gay, bisexual and transgender issues. While these topics are certainly important, they involve international law, religious freedom, linguistics and legal studies that lie far outside the scope of this introductory volume.

We also wish to emphasize that we, the authors, hold no negative feelings or attitudes toward China. Though this book attempts to provide a neutral, yet critical, analysis of Chinese law, both the authors love China. We travel to and stay in China frequently, which has helped us to understand both Chinese and American culture. We are most fortunate to be able to appreciate the beauty of the language, literature and traditions of China. At the same time, we are able to function freely in an American system of justice and fundamental fairness. We feel obligated to serve as a bridge to both countries. We hope to provide a better understanding of the Chinese legal system while remaining zealous advocates for democratic values, business ethics, due process and rule of law.

Moreover, we are certainly aware of the concept of legal orientalism,[35] namely 'a set of globally circulating narratives about what law is and who has it... and how a European tradition of philosophical prejudices about Chinese law developed into a distinctively American ideology of empire'.[36] Though we try to shy away from legal orientalism and present an unbiased look at Chinese law, we recognize that it is not always possible to escape our own paradigms and preconceived notions. To the best of our ability, however, we have questioned our presumptions and others, examined authors' prejudice and, most importantly, taken nothing at face value.

It is amazing to watch China, this enormous and extremely complicated country, managing to maintain its power and balance. It is amazing to see a legal system in the making, and we believe the creation of the rule of law and transformation of 1.5 billion human beings' lives will be one of the greatest dramas in our lifetime. We feel privileged to witness this long and rather painful process.

As we end our analysis of the Chinese legal system, we would like to quote a paragraph from the preface to the autobiography of Yung Wing, the first Chinese student to graduate from an American university:

> Would it not be strange, if an Occidental education, continually exemplified by an Occidental civilization, had not wrought upon an Oriental such a metamorphosis in his inward nature as to make him feel and act as though he were a being coming from a different world, when he confronted one so diametrically different? This was precisely my case, and yet neither patriotism nor the love of my fellow countrymen had been weakened. On the contrary, they had increased in strength from sympathy.[37]

Notes

1. Ray Huang (1982) *1587: A Year of No Significance: The Ming Dynasty in Decline*. New Haven, CT: Yale University Press.
2. Steve Wilson (2013) 'Tibetan monk dies after self-immolation in China', *Daily Telegraph*, 21 July; available at: *www.telegraph.co.uk/news/ worldnews/asia/tibet/10193139/Tibetan-monk-dies-after-self-immolation-in-China.html* (accessed: 8 August 2013).

3. Pei Minxin (2006) *China's Trapped Transition: The Limits of Developmental Autocracy*. Cambridge, MA: Harvard University Press, p. 8.
4. Ibid., p. 11.
5. Paul Krugman (2013) 'Hitting China's wall', *New York Times*, 18 July; available at: *www.nytimes.com/2013/07/19/opinion/krugman-hitting-chinas-wall.html* (accessed: 8 August 2013).
6. Paul Krugman (2013) 'How much should we worry about a China shock?', *New York Times*, 20 July; available at: *http://krugman.blogs.nytimes.com/2013/07/20/how-much-should-we-worry-about-a-china-shock/* (accessed: 15 August 2013).
7. BBC (2013) 'What does Xi Jinping's China dream mean?', BBC News, 5 June; available at: *www.bbc.co.uk/news/world-asia-china-22726375* (accessed: 8 August 2013).
8. Barbara Demick (2013) 'China's Xi more Maoist than reformer thus far', *Los Angeles Times*, 8 June; available at: *http://articles.latimes.com/2013/jun/08/world/la-fg-china-xi-20130608* (accessed: 8 August 2013).
9. Oiwan Lam (2013) 'China: constitutionalism is for capitalists', *Global Voices*, 27 May; available at: *http://globalvoicesonline.org/2013/05/27/clinging-to-chinese-constitution-is-to-deny-china/* (accessed: 10 August 2013).
10. Rogier Creeemers (2013) 'The constitutionalism debate in China', 17 July; available at: *www.iconnectblog.com/2013/07/the-constitutionalism-debate-in-china/* (accessed: 10 August 2013).
11. *Want China Times* (2013) '*People's Daily* slams "constitutionalism" as Beidaihe retreat begins', *Want China Times*, 6 August; available at: *www.wantchinatimes.com/news-subclass-cnt.aspx?id=20130806000072&cid=1101&MainCatID=0* (accessed: 8 August 2013).
12. Thomas S. Kuhn (1996) *The Structure of Scientific Revolutions*, 3rd edn. Chicago, IL: University of Chicago Press.
13. Uzra Zeya (2013) 'Press conference following US-China human rights dialogue', US Department of State, 2 August; available at: *www.state.gov/j/drl/rls/rm/2013/212667.htm* (accessed: 7 August 2013).
14. *Washington Post* (2013) 'China says human rights situation is at a historic best, rejects US criticism', *Washington Post*, 2 August; available at: *http://articles.washingtonpost.com/2013-08-02/world/41015432_1_activists-liu-xiaobo-xu-zhiyong* (accessed: 8 August 2013).
15. Quoted in ibid.
16. Pei Minxin (2013) 'Bo Xilai's trial exposes truth about China', *Bloomberg News*, 6 August; available at: *www.bloomberg.com/news/2013-08-06/bo-xilai-s-trial-exposes-truth-about-china.html* (accessed: 8 August 2013).
17. Ibid.
18. Ho Pin and Huang Wenguang (2013) *A Death in the Lucky Holiday Hotel: Murder, Money, and an Epic Power Struggle in China*. New York: Public Affairs, p. viii.
19. Rebecca Liao (2013) 'Why Bo Xilai's trial is a victory for the rule of law in China', *The Atlantic*, 7 August; available at: *www.theatlantic.com/china/archive/2013/08/why-bo-xilais-trial-is-a-victory-for-the-rule-of-law-in-china/278448/* (accessed: 26 August 2013).

20. Donald Clarke (2013) 'The Bo Xilai trial and China's "rule of law": same old, same old', *The Atlantic*, 21 August; available at: *www.theatlantic.com/china/archive/2013/08/the-bo-xilai-trial-and-chinas-rule-of-law-same-old-same-old/278868/* (accessed: 26 August 2013). Content in parentheses in the original.
21. Ibid.
22. Ibid.
23. Ibid.
24. Tom Phillips and Jon Swaine (2013) 'Bo Xilai's son Bo Guagua "enrolls at Columbia Law School"', *Daily Telegraph*, 29 July; available at *www.telegraph.co.uk/news/worldnews/asia/china/10208303/Bo-Xilais-son-Bo-Guagua-enrolls-at-Columbia-Law-School.html* (accessed: 26 August 2013).
25. BBC (2012) 'China dissident Chen Guangcheng "in US embassy"', BBC News, 27 April; available at: *www.bbc.co.uk/news/world-asia-china-17877005* (accessed: 26 August 2013).
26. Jane Perlez (2013) 'Chinese judges disciplined in prostitution scandal after videos circulate online', *New York Times*, 7 August; available at: *www.nytimes.com/2013/08/08/world/asia/chinese-judges-disciplined-for-cavorting-with-prostitutes.html?_r=0* (accessed: 8 August 2013).
27. Ibid.
28. BBC (2013) 'China detains activist Xu Zhiyong', BBC News, 17 July; available at: *www.bbc.co.uk/news/world-asia-china-23339401* (accessed: 8 August 2013).
29. China Law Prof Blog (2013) 'Jailhouse statement of Xu Zhiyong', trans. Donald Clarke; available at: *http://lawprofessors.typepad.com/china_law_prof_blog/* (accessed: 8 August 2013).
30. *The Economist* (2013) 'The rule of law: bizarrely consistent', *The Economist*, 27 July, p. 38.
31. Stanley Lubman (2013) 'What China's wrongful convictions mean for legal reform', *Wall Street Journal*, 17 July; available at: *http://blogs.wsj.com/chinarealtime/2013/07/17/wrongful-convictions-and-chinas-legal-reform-push/* (accessed: 26 August 2013).
32. *Xinhua News* (2013) 'Li Keqiang: Chinese re-education through labor reform plan expected to be unveiled by the end of the year', *Xinhua News*, 17 March; available at: *http://news.xinhuanet.com/2013lh/2013-03/17/c_115054123.htm* (accessed: 26 August 2013).
33. Gordon G. Chang (2001) *The Coming Collapse of China*. New York: Random House.
34. Martin Jacques (2009) *When China Rules the World*. New York: Penguin.
35. Teemu Ruskola (2013) *Legal Orientalism: China, the United States, and Modern Law*. Cambridge, MA: Harvard University Press.
36. Ibid.
37. Yung Wing (1909) *My Life in China and America*. New York: Henry Holt and Company, p. iii.

Appendix 1
Constitution of the People's Republic of China

Full text after amendment on 14 March 2004. Amended in accordance with the Amendments to the Constitution of the People's Republic of China adopted respectively at the First Session of the Seventh National People's Congress on 12 April 1988, the First Session of the Eighth National People's Congress on 29 March 1993, the Second Session of the Ninth National People's Congress on 15 March 1999 and the Second Session of the Tenth National People's Congress on 14 March 2004. Adopted at the Fifth Session of the Fifth National People's Congress and promulgated for implementation by the Announcement of the National People's Congress on 4 December 1982.

Preamble

China is a country with one of the longest histories in the world. The people of all of China's nationalities have jointly created a culture of grandeur and have a glorious revolutionary tradition.

After 1840, feudal China was gradually turned into a semi-colonial and semi-feudal country. The Chinese people waged many successive heroic struggles for national independence and liberation and for democracy and freedom.

Great and earthshaking historical changes have taken place in China in the 20th century.

The Revolution of 1911, led by Dr. Sun Yat-sen, abolished the feudal monarchy and gave birth to the Republic of China. But the historic mission of the Chinese people to overthrow imperialism and feudalism remained unaccomplished.

After waging protracted and arduous struggles, armed and otherwise, along a zigzag course, the Chinese people of all nationalities led by the Communist Party of China with Chairman Mao Zedong as its leader ultimately, in 1949, overthrew the rule of imperialism, feudalism and bureaucrat-capitalism, won a great victory in the New-Democratic Revolution and founded the People's Republic of China. Since then the Chinese people have taken control of state power and become masters of the country.

After the founding of the People's Republic, China gradually achieved its transition from a New-Democratic to a socialist society. The socialist transformation of the private ownership of the means of production has been completed, the system of exploitation of man by man abolished and the socialist system established. The people's democratic dictatorship led by the working class and based on the alliance of workers and peasants, which is in essence the dictatorship of the proletariat, has been consolidated and developed. The Chinese people and the Chinese People's Liberation Army have defeated imperialist and hegemonist aggression, sabotage and armed provocations and have thereby safeguarded China's national independence and security and strengthened its national defence. Major successes have been achieved in economic development. An independent and relatively comprehensive socialist system of industry has basically been established. There has been a marked increase in agricultural production. Significant advances have been made in educational, scientific and cultural undertakings, while education in socialist ideology has produced noteworthy results. The life of the people has improved considerably.

The victory in China's New-Democratic Revolution and the successes in its socialist cause have been achieved by the Chinese people of all nationalities, under the leadership of the Communist Party of China and the guidance of Marxism-Leninism and Mao Zedong Thought, by upholding truth, correcting errors and surmounting numerous difficulties and hardships. China will be in the primary stage of socialism for a long time to come. The basic task of the nation is to concentrate its effort on socialist modernization along the road of Chinese-style socialism. Under the leadership of the Communist Party of China and the guidance of Marxism-Leninism, Mao Zedong Thought, Deng Xiaoping Theory and the important thought of Three Represents, the Chinese people of all nationalities will continue to adhere to the people's democratic dictatorship and the socialist road, persevere in reform and opening to the outside world, steadily improve socialist institutions, develop the socialist market economy, develop socialist democracy, improve the socialist legal system and work hard and self-reliantly to modernize the country's industry, agriculture, national defence and science and technology step by step and promote the coordinated development of the material, political and spiritual civilizations, to turn China into a socialist country that is prosperous, powerful, democratic and culturally advanced.

The exploiting classes as such have been abolished in our country. However, class struggle will continue to exist within certain bounds for a long time to come. The Chinese people must fight against those forces and elements, both at home and abroad, that are hostile to China's socialist system and try to undermine it.

Taiwan is part of the sacred territory of the People's Republic of China. It is the inviolable duty of all Chinese people, including our compatriots in Taiwan, to accomplish the great task of reunifying the motherland.

In building socialism it is essential to rely on workers, peasants and intellectuals and to unite all forces that can be united. In the long years of revolution and construction, there has been formed under the leadership of the Communist Party of China a broad patriotic united front which is composed of the democratic parties and people's organizations and which embraces all socialist working people, all builders of socialism, all patriots who support socialism, and all patriots who stand for the reunification of the motherland. This united front will continue to be consolidated and developed. The Chinese People's Political Consultative Conference, a broadly based representative organization of the united front which has played a significant historical role, will play a still more important role in the country's political and social life, in promoting friendship with other countries and in the struggle for socialist modernization and for the reunification and unity of the country. The system of the multi-party cooperation and political consultation led by the Communist Party of China will exist and develop for a long time to come.

The People's Republic of China is a unitary multi-national State created jointly by the people of all its nationalities. Socialist relations of equality, unity and mutual assistance have been established among the nationalities and will continue to be strengthened. In the struggle to safeguard the unity of the nationalities, it is necessary to combat big-nation chauvinism, mainly Han chauvinism, and to combat local national chauvinism. The State will do its utmost to promote the common prosperity of all the nationalities.

China's achievements in revolution and construction are inseparable from the support of the people of the world. The future of China is closely linked to the future of the world. China consistently carries out an independent foreign policy and adheres to the five principles of mutual respect for sovereignty and territorial integrity, mutual non-aggression, non-interference in each other's internal affairs, equality and mutual benefit, and peaceful coexistence in developing diplomatic relations and economic and cultural exchanges with other countries. China consistently opposes imperialism, hegemonism and colonialism, works to strengthen unity with the people of other countries, supports the oppressed nations and the developing countries in their just struggle to win and preserve national independence and develop their national economies, and strives to safeguard world peace and promote the cause of human progress.

This Constitution, in legal form, affirms the achievements of the struggles of the Chinese people of all nationalities and defines the basic system and basic tasks of the State; it is the fundamental law of the State and has supreme legal authority. The people of all nationalities, all State organs, the armed forces, all political parties and public organizations and all enterprises and institutions in the country must take the Constitution as the basic standard of conduct, and they have the duty to uphold the dignity of the Constitution and ensure its implementation.

Chapter I: General Principles

Article 1 The People's Republic of China is a socialist state under the people's democratic dictatorship led by the working class and based on the alliance of workers and peasants.

The socialist system is the basic system of the People's Republic of China. Disruption of the socialist system by any organization or individual is prohibited.

Article 2 All power in the People's Republic of China belongs to the people.

The National People's Congress and the local people's congresses at various levels are the organs through which the people exercise state power.

The people administer State affairs and manage economic and cultural undertakings and social affairs through various channels and in various ways in accordance with the provisions of law.

Article 3 The State organs of the People's Republic of China apply the principle of democratic centralism.

The National People's Congress and the local people's congresses at various levels are constituted through democratic elections. They are responsible to the people and subject to their supervision.

All administrative, judicial and procuratorial organs of the State are created by the people's congresses to which they are responsible and by which they are supervised.

The division of functions and powers between the central and local State organs is guided by the principle of giving full scope to the initiative and enthusiasm of the local authorities under the unified leadership of the central authorities.

Article 4 All nationalities in the People's Republic of China are equal. The State protects the lawful rights and interests of the minority nationalities and upholds and develops a relationship of equality, unity and mutual assistance among all of China's nationalities. Discrimination against and oppression of any nationality are prohibited; any act which undermines the unity of the nationalities or instigates division is prohibited.

The State assists areas inhabited by minority nationalities in accelerating their economic and cultural development according to the characteristics and needs of the various minority nationalities.

Regional autonomy is practised in areas where people of minority nationalities live in concentrated communities; in these areas organs of self-government are established to exercise the power of autonomy. All national autonomous areas are integral parts of the People's Republic of China.

All nationalities have the freedom to use and develop their own spoken and written languages and to preserve or reform their own folkways and customs.

Article 5 The People's Republic of China governs the country according to law and makes it a socialist country under rule of law.

The State upholds the uniformity and dignity of the socialist legal system.

No laws or administrative or local regulations may contravene the Constitution.

All State organs, the armed forces, all political parties and public organizations and all enterprises and institutions must abide by the Constitution and other laws. All acts in violation of the Constitution or other laws must be investigated.

No organization or individual is privileged to be beyond the Constitution or other laws.

Article 6 The basis of the socialist economic system of the People's Republic of China is socialist public ownership of the means of production, namely, ownership by the whole people and collective ownership by the working people. The system of socialist public ownership supersedes the system of exploitation of man by man; it applies the principle of 'from each according to his ability, to each according to his work'.

In the primary stage of socialism, the State upholds the basic economic system in which the public ownership is dominant and diverse forms of ownership develop side by side and keeps to the distribution system in which distribution according to work is dominant and diverse modes of distribution coexist.

Article 7 The State-owned economy, namely, the socialist economy under ownership by the whole people, is the leading force in the national economy. The State ensures the consolidation and growth of the State-owned economy.

Article 8 The rural collective economic organizations apply the dual operation system characterized by the combination of centralized operation with decentralized operation on the basis of operation by households under a contract. In rural areas, all forms of cooperative economy, such as producers', supply and marketing, credit and consumers' cooperatives, belong to the sector of socialist economy under collective ownership by the working people. Working people who are members of rural economic collectives have the right, within the limits prescribed by law, to farm plots of cropland and hilly land allotted for their private use, engage in household sideline production and raise privately owned livestock.

The various forms of cooperative economy in cities and towns, such as those in the handicraft, industrial, building, transport, commercial and service trades, all belong to the sector of socialist economy under collective ownership by the working people.

The State protects the lawful rights and interests of the urban and rural economic collectives and encourages, guides and helps the growth of the collective economy.

Article 9 All mineral resources, waters, forests, mountains, grasslands, unreclaimed land, beaches and other natural resources are owned by the State, that is, by the whole people, with the exception of the forests, mountains, grasslands, unreclaimed land and beaches that are owned by collectives as prescribed by law.

The State ensures the rational use of natural resources and protects rare animals and plants. Appropriation or damaging of natural resources by any organization or individual by whatever means is prohibited.

Article 10 Land in the cities is owned by the State.

Land in the rural and suburban areas is owned by collectives except for those portions which belong to the State as prescribed by law; house sites and privately farmed plots of cropland and hilly land are also owned by collectives.

The State may, in the public interest and in accordance with law, expropriate or requisition land for its use and make compensation for the land expropriated or requisitioned.

No organization or individual may appropriate, buy, sell or otherwise engage in the transfer of land by unlawful means. The right to the use of land may be transferred according to law.

All organizations and individuals using land must ensure its rational use.

Article 11 The non-public sectors of the economy such as the individual and private sectors of the economy, operating within the limits prescribed by law, constitute an important component of the socialist market economy.

The State protects the lawful rights and interests of the non-public sectors of the economy such as the individual and private sectors of the economy. The State encourages, supports and guides the development of the non-public sectors of the economy and, in accordance with law, exercises supervision and control over the non-public sectors of the economy.

Article 12 Socialist public property is inviolable.

The State protects socialist public property. Appropriation or damaging of State or collective property by any organization or individual by whatever means is prohibited.

Article 13 Citizens' lawful private property is inviolable.

The State, in accordance with law, protects the rights of citizens to private property and to its inheritance.

The State may, in the public interest and in accordance with law, expropriate or requisition private property for its use and make compensation for the private property expropriated or requisitioned.

Article 14 The State continuously raises labour productivity, improves economic results and develops the productive forces by enhancing the enthusiasm of the working people, raising the level of their technical skill, disseminating advanced science and technology, improving the systems of economic administration and enterprise operation and management, instituting the socialist system of responsibility in various forms and improving the organization of work.

The State practises strict economy and combats waste.

The State properly apportions accumulation and consumption, concerns itself with the interests of the collective and the individual as well as of the State and, on the basis of expanded production, gradually improves the material and cultural life of the people.

The State establishes a sound social security system compatible with the level of economic development.

Article 15 The State practises socialist market economy.

The State strengthens economic legislation, improves macro-regulation and control.

The State prohibits in accordance with law any organization or individual from disturbing the socio-economic order.

Article 16 State-owned enterprises have decision-making power with regard to their operation within the limits prescribed by law.

State-owned enterprises practise democratic management through congresses of workers and staff and in other ways in accordance with law.

Article 17 Collective economic organizations have decision-making power in conducting independent economic activities, on condition that they abide by the relevant laws.

Collective economic organizations practise democratic management and, in accordance with law, elect or remove their managerial personnel and decide on major issues concerning operation and management.

Article 18 The People's Republic of China permits foreign enterprises, other foreign economic organizations and individual foreigners to invest in China and to enter into various forms of economic cooperation with Chinese enterprises and other Chinese economic organizations in accordance with the provisions of the laws of the People's Republic of China.

All foreign enterprises, other foreign economic organizations as well as Chinese-foreign joint ventures within Chinese territory shall abide by the laws of the People's Republic of China. Their lawful rights and interests are protected by the laws of the People's Republic of China.

Article 19 The State undertakes the development of socialist education and works to raise the scientific and cultural level of the whole nation.

The State establishes and administers schools of various types, universalizes compulsory primary education and promotes secondary, vocational and higher education as well as pre-school education.

The State develops educational facilities in order to eliminate illiteracy and provide political, scientific, technical and professional education for workers, peasants, State functionaries and other working people. It encourages people to become educated through independent study.

The State encourages the collective economic organizations, State enterprises and institutions and other sectors of society to establish educational institutions of various types in accordance with law.

The State promotes the nationwide use of Putonghua [common speech based on Beijing pronunciation – Tr.].

Article 20 The State promotes the development of the natural and social sciences, disseminates knowledge of science and technology, and commends and rewards achievements in scientific research as well as technological innovations and inventions.

Article 21 The State develops medical and health services, promotes modern medicine and traditional Chinese medicine, encourages and supports the setting up of various medical and health facilities by the rural economic collectives, State enterprises and institutions and neighbourhood organizations, and promotes health and sanitation activities of a mass character, all for the protection of the people's health.

The State develops physical culture and promotes mass sports activities to improve the people's physical fitness.

Article 22 The State promotes the development of art and literature, the press, radio and television broadcasting, publishing and distribution services, libraries, museums, cultural centres and other cultural undertakings that serve the people and socialism, and it sponsors mass cultural activities.

The State protects sites of scenic and historical interest, valuable cultural monuments and relics and other significant items of China's historical and cultural heritage.

Article 23 The State trains specialized personnel in all fields who serve socialism, expands the ranks of intellectuals and creates conditions to give full scope to their role in socialist modernization.

Article 24 The State strengthens the building of a socialist society with an advanced culture and ideology by promoting education in high ideals, ethics, general knowledge, discipline and the legal system, and by promoting the formulation and observance of rules of conduct and common pledges by various sections of the people in urban and rural areas.

The State advocates the civic virtues of love of the motherland, of the people, of labour, of science and of socialism. It conducts education among the people in patriotism and collectivism, in internationalism and communism and in dialectical and historical materialism, to combat capitalist, feudal and other decadent ideas.

Article 25 The State promotes family planning so that population growth may fit the plans for economic and social development.

Article 26 The State protects and improves the environment in which people live and the ecological environment. It prevents and controls pollution and other public hazards.

The State organizes and encourages afforestation and the protection of forests.

Article 27 All State organs carry out the principle of simple and efficient administration, the system of responsibility for work and the system of training functionaries and appraising their performance in order constantly to improve the quality of work and efficiency and combat bureaucratism.

All State organs and functionaries must rely on the support of the people, keep in close touch with them, heed their opinions and suggestions, accept their supervision and do their best to serve them.

Article 28 The State maintains public order and suppresses treasonable and other criminal activities that endanger State security; it penalizes criminal activities that endanger public security and disrupt the socialist economy as well as other criminal activities; and it punishes and reforms criminals.

Article 29 The armed forces of the People's Republic of China belong to the people. Their tasks are to strengthen national defence, resist aggression, defend the motherland, safeguard the people's peaceful labour, participate in national reconstruction and do their best to serve the people.

The State strengthens the revolutionization, modernization and regularization of the armed forces in order to increase national defence capability.

Article 30 The administrative division of the People's Republic of China is as follows:

1. The country is divided into provinces, autonomous regions, and municipalities directly under the Central Government;

2. Provinces and autonomous regions are divided into autonomous prefectures, counties, autonomous counties, and cities; and

3. Counties and autonomous counties are divided into townships, nationality townships, and towns.

Municipalities directly under the Central Government and other large cities are divided into districts and counties. Autonomous prefectures are divided into counties, autonomous counties, and cities.

All autonomous regions, autonomous prefectures and autonomous counties are national autonomous areas.

Article 31 The State may establish special administrative regions when necessary. The systems to be instituted in special administrative regions shall be prescribed by law enacted by the National People's Congress in the light of specific conditions.

Article 32 The People's Republic of China protects the lawful rights and interests of foreigners within Chinese territory; foreigners on Chinese territory must abide by the laws of the People's Republic of China.

The People's Republic of China may grant asylum to foreigners who request it for political reasons.

Chapter II: The Fundamental Rights and Duties of Citizens

Article 33 All persons holding the nationality of the People's Republic of China are citizens of the People's Republic of China.

All citizens of the People's Republic of China are equal before the law.

The State respects and preserves human rights.

Every citizen is entitled to the rights and at the same time must perform the duties prescribed by the Constitution and other laws.

Article 34 All citizens of the People's Republic of China who have reached the age of 18 have the right to vote and stand for election, regardless of ethnic status, race, sex, occupation, family background, religious belief, education, property status or length of residence, except persons deprived of political rights according to law.

Article 35 Citizens of the People's Republic of China enjoy freedom of speech, of the press, of assembly, of association, of procession and of demonstration.

Article 36 Citizens of the People's Republic of China enjoy freedom of religious belief.

No State organ, public organization or individual may compel citizens to believe in, or not to believe in, any religion; nor may they discriminate against citizens who believe in, or do not believe in, any religion.

The State protects normal religious activities. No one may make use of religion to engage in activities that disrupt public order, impair the health of citizens or interfere with the educational system of the State.

Religious bodies and religious affairs are not subject to any foreign domination.

Article 37 Freedom of the person of citizens of the People's Republic of China is inviolable.

No citizen may be arrested except with the approval or by decision of a people's procuratorate or by decision of a people's court, and arrests must be made by a public security organ.

Unlawful detention or deprivation or restriction of citizens' freedom of the person by other means is prohibited, and unlawful search of the person of citizens is prohibited.

Article 38 The personal dignity of citizens of the People's Republic of China is inviolable. Insult, libel, false accusation or false incrimination directed against citizens by any means is prohibited.

Article 39 The residences of citizens of the People's Republic of China are inviolable. Unlawful search of, or intrusion into, a citizen's residence is prohibited.

Article 40 Freedom and privacy of correspondence of citizens of the People's Republic of China are protected by law. No organization or individual may, on any ground, infringe upon citizens' freedom and privacy of correspondence, except in cases where, to meet the needs of State security or of criminal investigation, public security or procuratorial organs are permitted to censor correspondence in accordance with the procedures prescribed by law.

Article 41 Citizens of the People's Republic of China have the right to criticize and make suggestions regarding any State organ or functionary. Citizens have the right to make to relevant State organs complaints or charges against, or exposures of, any State organ or functionary for violation of law or dereliction of duty; but fabrication or distortion of facts for purposes of libel or false incrimination is prohibited.

The State organ concerned must, in a responsible manner and by ascertaining the facts, deal with the complaints, charges or exposures made by citizens. No one may suppress such complaints, charges and exposures or retaliate against the citizens making them.

Citizens who have suffered losses as a result of infringement of their civic rights by any State organ or functionary have the right to compensation in accordance with the provisions of law.

Article 42 Citizens of the People's Republic of China have the right as well as the duty to work.

Through various channels, the State creates conditions for employment, enhances occupational safety and health, improves working conditions and, on the basis of expanded production, increases remuneration for work and welfare benefits.

Work is a matter of honour for every citizen who is able to work. All working people in State-owned enterprises and in urban and rural economic collectives should approach their work as the masters of the country that they are. The State promotes socialist labour emulation, and commends and rewards model and advanced workers. The State encourages citizens to take part in voluntary labour.

The State provides necessary vocational training for citizens before they are employed.

Article 43 Working people in the People's Republic of China have the right to rest.

The State expands facilities for the rest and recuperation of the working people and prescribes working hours and vacations for workers and staff.

Article 44 The State applies the system of retirement for workers and staff members of enterprises and institutions and for functionaries of organs of State according to law. The livelihood of retired persons is ensured by the State and society.

Article 45 Citizens of the People's Republic of China have the right to material assistance from the State and society when they are old, ill or disabled. The State develops social insurance, social relief and medical and health services that are required for citizens to enjoy this right.

The State and society ensure the livelihood of disabled members of the armed forces, provide pensions to the families of martyrs and give preferential treatment to the families of military personnel.

The State and society help make arrangements for the work, livelihood and education of the blind, deaf-mutes and other handicapped citizens.

Article 46 Citizens of the People's Republic of China have the duty as well as the right to receive education.

The State promotes the all-round development of children and young people, morally, intellectually and physically.

Article 47 Citizens of the People's Republic of China have the freedom to engage in scientific research, literary and artistic creation and other cultural pursuits. The State encourages and assists creative endeavours conducive to the interests of the people that are made by citizens engaged in education, science, technology, literature, art and other cultural work.

Article 48 Women in the People's Republic of China enjoy equal rights with men in all spheres of life, in political, economic, cultural, social and family life.

The State protects the rights and interests of women, applies the principle of equal pay for equal work to men and women alike and trains and selects cadres from among women.

Article 49 Marriage, the family and mother and child are protected by the State.

Both husband and wife have the duty to practise family planning.

Parents have the duty to rear and educate their children who are minors, and children who have come of age have the duty to support and assist their parents.

Violation of the freedom of marriage is prohibited. Maltreatment of old people, women and children is prohibited.

Article 50 The People's Republic of China protects the legitimate rights and interests of Chinese nationals residing abroad and protects the lawful rights and interests of returned overseas Chinese and of the family members of Chinese nationals residing abroad.

Article 51 Citizens of the People's Republic of China, in exercising their freedoms and rights, may not infringe upon the interests of the State, of society or of the collective, or upon the lawful freedoms and rights of other citizens.

Article 52 It is the duty of citizens of the People's Republic of China to safeguard the unification of the country and the unity of all its nationalities.

Article 53 Citizens of the People's Republic of China must abide by the Constitution and other laws, keep State secrets, protect public property, observe labour discipline and public order and respect social ethics.

Article 54 It is the duty of citizens of the People's Republic of China to safeguard the security, honour and interests of the motherland; they must not commit acts detrimental to the security, honour and interests of the motherland.

Article 55 It is the sacred duty of every citizen of the People's Republic of China to defend the motherland and resist aggression.

It is the honourable duty of citizens of the People's Republic of China to perform military service and join the militia in accordance with law.

Article 56 It is the duty of citizens of the People's Republic of China to pay taxes in accordance with law.

Chapter III: The Structure of the State

Section 1: The National People's Congress

Article 57 The National People's Congress of the People's Republic of China is the highest organ of state power. Its permanent body is the Standing Committee of the National People's Congress.

Article 58 The National People's Congress and its Standing Committee exercise the legislative power of the State.

Article 59 The National People's Congress is composed of deputies elected from the provinces, autonomous regions, municipalities directly under the Central Government, and special administrative regions, and of deputies elected from the armed forces. All the minority nationalities are entitled to appropriate representation.

Election of deputies to the National People's Congress is conducted by the Standing Committee of the National People's Congress.

The number of deputies to the National People's Congress and the procedure of their election are prescribed by law.

Article 60 The National People's Congress is elected for a term of five years.

The Standing Committee of the National People's Congress must ensure the completion of election of deputies to the succeeding National People's Congress two months prior to the expiration of the term of office of the current National People's Congress. Should extraordinary circumstances prevent such an election, it may be postponed and the term of office of the current National People's Congress extended by the decision of a vote of more than two-thirds of all those on the Standing Committee of the current National People's Congress. The election of deputies to the succeeding National People's Congress must be completed within one year after the termination of such extraordinary circumstances.

Article 61 The National People's Congress meets in session once a year and is convened by its Standing Committee. A session of the National People's Congress may be convened at any time the Standing Committee deems it necessary or when more than one-fifth of the deputies to the National People's Congress so propose.

When the National People's Congress meets, it elects a Presidium to conduct its session.

Article 62 The National People's Congress exercises the following functions and powers:

1.   to amend the Constitution;

2.   to supervise the enforcement of the Constitution;

3.   to enact and amend basic laws governing criminal offences, civil affairs, the State organs and other matters;

4.   to elect the President and the Vice-President of the People's Republic of China;

5.   to decide on the choice of the Premier of the State Council upon nomination by the President of the People's Republic of China, and on the choice of the Vice-Premiers, State Councillors, Ministers in charge of ministries or commissions, the Auditor-General and the Secretary-General of the State Council upon nomination by the Premier;

6. to elect the Chairman of the Central Military Commission and, upon nomination by the Chairman, to decide on the choice of all other members of the Central Military Commission;

7. to elect the President of the Supreme People's Court;

8. to elect the Procurator-General of the Supreme People's Procuratorate;

9. to examine and approve the plan for national economic and social development and the report on its implementation;

10. to examine and approve the State budget and the report on its implementation;

11. to alter or annul inappropriate decisions of the Standing Committee of the National People's Congress;

12. to approve the establishment of provinces, autonomous regions, and municipalities directly under the Central Government;

13. to decide on the establishment of special administrative regions and the systems to be instituted there;

14. to decide on questions of war and peace; and

15. to exercise such other functions and powers as the highest organ of state power should exercise.

Article 63 The National People's Congress has the power to remove from office the following persons:

1. the President and the Vice-President of the People's Republic of China;

2. the Premier, Vice-Premiers, State Councillors, Ministers in charge of ministries or commissions, the Auditor-General and the Secretary-General of the State Council;

3. the Chairman of the Central Military Commission and other members of the Commission;

4. the President of the Supreme People's Court; and

5. the Procurator-General of the Supreme People's Procuratorate.

Article 64 Amendments to the Constitution are to be proposed by the Standing Committee of the National People's Congress or by more than one-fifth of the deputies to the National People's Congress and adopted by a vote of more than two-thirds of all the deputies to the Congress.

Laws and resolutions are to be adopted by a majority vote of all the deputies to the National People's Congress.

Article 65 The Standing Committee of the National People's Congress is composed of the following:

- the Chairman;
- the Vice-Chairmen;
- the Secretary-General; and
- the members.

Minority nationalities are entitled to appropriate representation on the Standing Committee of the National People's Congress.

The National People's Congress elects, and has the power to recall, members of its Standing Committee.

No one on the Standing Committee of the National People's Congress shall hold office in any of the administrative, judicial or procuratorial organs of the State.

Article 66 The Standing Committee of the National People's Congress is elected for the same term as the National People's Congress; it shall exercise its functions and powers until a new Standing Committee is elected by the succeeding National People's Congress.

The Chairman and Vice-Chairmen of the Standing Committee shall serve no more than two consecutive terms.

Article 67 The Standing Committee of the National People's Congress exercises the following functions and powers:

1. to interpret the Constitution and supervise its enforcement;
2. to enact and amend laws, with the exception of those which should be enacted by the National People's Congress;
3. to partially supplement and amend, when the National People's Congress is not in session, laws enacted by the National People's Congress, provided that the basic principles of these laws are not contravened;
4. to interpret laws;
5. to review and approve, when the National People's Congress is not in session, partial adjustments to the plan for national economic and social development or to the State budget that prove necessary in the course of their implementation;

6. to supervise the work of the State Council, the Central Military Commission, the Supreme People's Court and the Supreme People's Procuratorate;

7. to annul those administrative regulations, decisions or orders of the State Council that contravene the Constitution or other laws;

8. to annul those local regulations or decisions of the organs of state power of provinces, autonomous regions, and municipalities directly under the Central Government that contravene the Constitution, other laws or administrative regulations;

9. to decide, when the National People's Congress is not in session, on the choice of Ministers in charge of ministries or commissions, the Auditor-General or the Secretary-General of the State Council upon nomination by the Premier of the State Council;

10. to decide, when the National People's Congress is not in session, on the choice of other members of the Central Military Commission upon nomination by the Chairman of the Commission;

11. to appoint or remove, at the recommendation of the President of the Supreme People's Court, the Vice-Presidents and Judges of the Supreme People's Court, members of its Judicial Committee and the President of the Military Court;

12. to appoint or remove, at the recommendation of the Procurator-General of the Supreme People's Procuratorate, the Deputy Procurators-General and procurators of the Supreme People's Procuratorate, members of its Procuratorial Committee and the Chief Procurator of the Military Procuratorate, and to approve the appointment or removal of the chief procurators of the people's procuratorates of provinces, autonomous regions, and municipalities directly under the Central Government;

13. to decide on the appointment or recall of plenipotentiary representatives abroad;

14. to decide on the ratification or abrogation of treaties and important agreements concluded with foreign states;

15. to institute systems of titles and ranks for military and diplomatic personnel and of other specific titles and ranks;

16. to institute State medals and titles of honour and decide on their conferment;

17. to decide on the granting of special pardons;

18. to decide, when the National People's Congress is not in session, on the proclamation of a state of war in the event of an armed attack on the country or in fulfilment of international treaty obligations concerning common defence against aggression;

19. to decide on general or partial mobilization;

20. to decide on entering the state of emergency throughout the country or in particular provinces, autonomous regions, or municipalities directly under the Central Government; and

21. to exercise such other functions and powers as the National People's Congress may assign to it.

Article 68 The Chairman of the Standing Committee of the National People's Congress directs the work of the Standing Committee and convenes its meetings. The Vice-Chairmen and the Secretary-General assist the Chairman in his work.

The Chairman, the Vice-Chairmen and the Secretary-General constitute the Council of Chairmen which handles the important day-to-day work of the Standing Committee of the National People's Congress.

Article 69 The Standing Committee of the National People's Congress is responsible to the National People's Congress and reports on its work to the Congress.

Article 70 The National People's Congress establishes a Nationalities Committee, a Law Committee, a Finance and Economic Committee, an Education, Science, Culture and Public Health Committee, a Foreign Affairs Committee, an Overseas Chinese Committee and such other special committees as are necessary. These special committees work under the direction of the Standing Committee of the National People's Congress when the Congress is not in session.

The special committees examine, discuss and draw up relevant bills and draft resolutions under the direction of the National People's Congress and its Standing Committee.

Article 71 The National People's Congress and its Standing Committee may, when they deem it necessary, appoint committees of inquiry into specific questions and adopt relevant resolutions in the light of their reports.

All organs of State, public organizations and citizens concerned are obliged to furnish the necessary information to the committees of inquiry when they conduct investigations.

Article 72 Deputies to the National People's Congress and members of its Standing Committee have the right, in accordance with procedures prescribed by law, to submit bills and proposals within the scope of the respective functions and powers of the National People's Congress and its Standing Committee.

Article 73 Deputies to the National People's Congress and members of the Standing Committee have the right, during the sessions of the Congress and the meetings of the Committee, to address questions, in accordance with procedures prescribed by law, to the State Council or the ministries and commissions under the State Council, which must answer the questions in a responsible manner.

Article 74 No deputy to the National People's Congress may be arrested or placed on criminal trial without the consent of the Presidium of the current session of the National People's Congress or, when the National People's Congress is not in session, without the consent of its Standing Committee.

Article 75 Deputies to the National People's Congress may not be held legally liable for their speeches or votes at its meetings.

Article 76 Deputies to the National People's Congress must play an exemplary role in abiding by the Constitution and other laws and keeping State secrets and, in public activities, production and other work, assist in the enforcement of the Constitution and other laws.

Deputies to the National People's Congress should maintain close contact with the units which elected them and with the people, heed and convey the opinions and demands of the people and work hard to serve them.

Article 77 Deputies to the National People's Congress are subject to supervision by the units which elected them. The electoral units have the power, through procedures prescribed by law, to recall deputies they elected.

Article 78 The organization and working procedures of the National People's Congress and its Standing Committee are prescribed by law.

Section 2: The President of the People's Republic of China

Article 79 The President and Vice-President of the People's Republic of China are elected by the National People's Congress.

Citizens of the People's Republic of China who have the right to vote and to stand for election and who have reached the age of 45 are eligible for election as President or Vice-President of the People's Republic of China.

The term of office of the President and Vice-President of the People's Republic of China is the same as that of the National People's Congress, and they shall serve no more than two consecutive terms.

Article 80 The President of the People's Republic of China, in pursuance of the decisions of the National People's Congress and its Standing Committee, promulgates statutes, appoints or removes the Premier, Vice-Premiers, State Councillors, Ministers in charge of ministries or commissions, the Auditor-General and the Secretary-General of the State Council; confers State medals and titles of honour; issues orders of special pardons; proclaims entering of the state of emergency; proclaims a state of war; and issues mobilization orders.

Article 81 The President of the People's Republic of China, on behalf of the People's Republic of China, engages in activities involving State affairs and receives foreign diplomatic representatives and, in pursuance of the decisions of the Standing Committee of the National People's Congress, appoints or recalls plenipotentiary representatives abroad, and ratifies or abrogates treaties and important agreements concluded with foreign states.

Article 82 The Vice-President of the People's Republic of China assists the President in his work.

The Vice-President of the People's Republic of China may exercise such functions and powers of the President as the President may entrust to him.

Article 83 The President and Vice-President of the People's Republic of China exercise their functions and powers until the new President and Vice-President elected by the succeeding National People's Congress assume office.

Article 84 In the event that the office of the President of the People's Republic of China falls vacant, the Vice-President succeeds to the office of the President.

In the event that the office of the Vice-President of the People's Republic of China falls vacant, the National People's Congress shall elect a new Vice-President to fill the vacancy.

In the event that the offices of both the President and the Vice-President of the People's Republic of China fall vacant, the National People's

Congress shall elect a new President and a new Vice-President. Prior to such election, the Chairman of the Standing Committee of the National People's Congress shall temporarily act as the President of the People's Republic of China.

Section 3: The State Council

Article 85 The State Council, that is, the Central People's Government, of the People's Republic of China is the executive body of the highest organ of state power; it is the highest organ of State administration.

Article 86 The State Council is composed of the following:

- the Premier;
- the Vice-Premiers;
- the State Councillors;
- the Ministers in charge of ministries;
- the Ministers in charge of commissions;
- the Auditor-General; and
- the Secretary-General.

The Premier assumes overall responsibility for the work of the State Council. The ministers assume overall responsibility for the work of the ministries and commissions. The organization of the State Council is prescribed by law.

Article 87 The term of office of the State Council is the same as that of the National People's Congress.

The Premier, Vice-Premiers and State Councillors shall serve no more than two consecutive terms.

Article 88 The Premier directs the work of the State Council. The Vice-Premiers and State Councillors assist the Premier in his work.

Executive meetings of the State Council are to be attended by the Premier, the Vice-Premiers, the State Councillors and the Secretary-General of the State Council.

The Premier convenes and presides over the executive meetings and plenary meetings of the State Council.

Article 89 The State Council exercises the following functions and powers:

1. to adopt administrative measures, enact administrative regulations and issue decisions and orders in accordance with the Constitution and other laws;

2. to submit proposals to the National People's Congress or its Standing Committee;

3. to formulate the tasks and responsibilities of the ministries and commissions of the State Council, to exercise unified leadership over the work of the ministries and commissions and to direct all other administrative work of a national character that does not fall within the jurisdiction of the ministries and commissions;

4. to exercise unified leadership over the work of local organs of State administration at various levels throughout the country, and to formulate the detailed division of functions and powers between the Central Government and the organs of State administration of provinces, autonomous regions, and municipalities directly under the Central Government;

5. to draw up and implement the plan for national economic and social development and the State budget;

6. to direct and administer economic affairs and urban and rural development;

7. to direct and administer the affairs of education, science, culture, public health, physical culture and family planning;

8. to direct and administer civil affairs, public security, judicial administration, supervision and other related matters;

9. to conduct foreign affairs and conclude treaties and agreements with foreign States;

10. to direct and administer the building of national defence;

11. to direct and administer affairs concerning the nationalities and to safeguard the equal rights of minority nationalities and the right to autonomy of the national autonomous areas;

12. to protect the legitimate rights and interests of Chinese nationals residing abroad and protect the lawful rights and interests of returned overseas Chinese and of the family members of Chinese nationals residing abroad;

13. to alter or annul inappropriate orders, directives and regulations issued by the ministries or commissions;

14. to alter or annul inappropriate decisions and orders issued by local organs of State administration at various levels;

15. to approve the geographic division of provinces, autonomous regions, and municipalities directly under the Central Government, and to approve the establishment and geographic division of autonomous prefectures, counties, autonomous counties, and cities;

16. in accordance with the provisions of law, to decide on entering into the state of emergency in parts of provinces, autonomous regions, and municipalities directly under the Central Government;

17. to examine and decide on the size of administrative organs and, in accordance with the provisions of law, to appoint or remove administrative officials, train them, appraise their performance and reward or punish them; and

18. to exercise such other functions and powers as the National People's Congress or its Standing Committee may assign to it.

Article 90 Ministers in charge of the ministries or commissions of the State Council are responsible for the work of their respective departments and they convene and preside over ministerial meetings or general and executive meetings of the commissions to discuss and decide on major issues in the work of their respective departments.

The ministries and commissions issue orders, directives and regulations within the jurisdiction of their respective departments and in accordance with law and the administrative regulations, decisions and orders issued by the State Council.

Article 91 The State Council establishes an auditing body to supervise through auditing the revenue and expenditure of all departments under the State Council and of the local governments at various levels, and the revenue and expenditure of all financial and monetary organizations, enterprises and institutions of the State.

Under the direction of the Premier of the State Council and in accordance with the provisions of law, the auditing body independently exercises its power of supervision through auditing, subject to no interference by any other administrative organ or any public organization or individual.

Article 92 The State Council is responsible and reports on its work to the National People's Congress or, when the National People's Congress is not in session, to its Standing Committee.

Section 4: The Central Military Commission

Article 93 The Central Military Commission of the People's Republic of China directs the armed forces of the country.

The Central Military Commission is composed of the following:

- the Chairman;
- the Vice-Chairmen; and
- the members.

The Chairman assumes overall responsibility for the work of the Central Military Commission.

The term of office of the Central Military Commission is the same as that of the National People's Congress.

Article 94 The Chairman of the Central Military Commission is responsible to the National People's Congress and its Standing Committee.

Section 5: The Local People's Congresses and Local People's Government at Various Levels

Article 95 People's congresses and people's governments are established in provinces, municipalities directly under the Central Government, counties, cities, municipal districts, townships, nationality townships, and towns.

The organization of local people's congresses and local people's governments at various levels is prescribed by law.

Organs of self-government are established in autonomous regions, autonomous prefectures and autonomous counties. The organization and working procedures of organs of self-government are prescribed by law in accordance with the basic principles laid down in Sections 5 and 6 of Chapter III of the Constitution.

Article 96 Local people's congresses at various levels are local organs of state power.

Local people's congresses at or above the county level establish standing committees.

Article 97 Deputies to the people's congresses of provinces, municipalities directly under the Central Government and cities divided into districts are elected by the people's congresses at the next lower level; deputies to the people's congresses of counties, cities not divided into districts, municipal districts, townships, nationality townships, and towns are elected directly by their constituencies.

The number of deputies to local people's congresses at various levels and the manner of their election are prescribed by law.

Article 98 The term of office of the local people's congresses at various levels is five years.

Article 99 Local people's congresses at various levels ensure the observance and implementation of the Constitution and other laws and the administrative regulations in their respective administrative areas. Within the limits of their authority as prescribed by law, they adopt and issue resolutions and examine and decide on plans for local economic and cultural development and for the development of public services.

Local people's congresses at or above the county level shall examine and approve the plans for economic and social development and the budgets of their respective administrative areas and examine and approve the reports on their implementation. They have the power to alter or annul inappropriate decisions of their own standing committees.

The people's congresses of nationality townships may, within the limits of their authority as prescribed by law, take specific measures suited to the characteristics of the nationalities concerned.

Article 100 The people's congresses of provinces, and municipalities directly under the Central Government, and their standing committees may adopt local regulations, which must not contravene the Constitution and other laws and administrative regulations, and they shall report such local regulations to the Standing Committee of the National People's Congress for the record.

Article 101 Local people's congresses at their respective levels elect and have the power to recall governors and deputy governors, or mayors and deputy mayors, or heads and deputy heads of counties, districts, townships and towns.

Local people's congresses at or above the county level elect, and have the power to recall, presidents of people's courts and chief procurators of people's procuratorates at the corresponding level. The election or recall of chief procurators of people's procuratorates shall be reported to the chief procurators of the people's procuratorates at the next higher level for submission to the standing committees of the people's congresses at the corresponding level for approval.

Article 102 Deputies to the people's congresses of provinces, municipalities directly under the Central Government and cities divided into districts are subject to supervision by the units which elected them; deputies to the people's congresses of counties, cities not divided into districts, municipal districts, townships, nationality townships, and towns are subject to supervision by their constituencies.

The units and constituencies which elect deputies to local people's congresses at various levels have the power to recall the deputies according to procedures prescribed by law.

Article 103 The standing committee of a local people's congress at or above the county level is composed of a chairman, vice-chairmen and members, and is responsible and reports on its work to the people's congress at the corresponding level.

A local people's congress at or above the county level elects, and has the power to recall, members of its standing committee.

No one on the standing committee of a local people's congress at or above the county level shall hold office in State administrative, judicial and procuratorial organs.

Article 104 The standing committee of a local people's congress at or above the county level discusses and decides on major issues in all fields of work in its administrative area; supervises the work of the people's government, people's court and people's procuratorate at the corresponding level; annuls inappropriate decisions and orders of the people's government at the corresponding level; annuls inappropriate resolutions of the people's congress at the next lower level; decides on the appointment or removal of functionaries of State organs within the limits of its authority as prescribed by law; and, when the people's congress at the corresponding level is not in session, recalls individual deputies to the people's congress at the next higher level and elects individual deputies to fill vacancies in that people's congress.

Article 105 Local people's governments at various levels are the executive bodies of local organs of state power as well as the local organs of State administration at the corresponding levels.

Governors, mayors and heads of counties, districts, townships and towns assume overall responsibility for local people's governments at various levels.

Article 106 The term of office of local people's governments at various levels is the same as that of the people's congresses at the corresponding levels.

Article 107 Local people's governments at or above the county level, within the limits of their authority as prescribed by law, conduct administrative work concerning the economy, education, science, culture, public health, physical culture, urban and rural development, finance, civil affairs, public security, nationalities affairs, judicial administration, supervision and family planning in their respective administrative areas; issue decisions and orders; appoint or remove administrative functionaries, train them, appraise their performance and reward or punish them.

People's governments of townships, nationality townships, and towns execute the resolutions of the people's congresses at the corresponding levels as well as the decisions and orders of the State administrative organs at the next higher level and conduct administrative work in their respective administrative areas.

People's governments of provinces, and of municipalities directly under the Central Government decide on the establishment and geographic division of townships, nationality townships, and towns.

Article 108 Local people's governments at or above the county level direct the work of their subordinate departments and of people's governments at lower levels, and have the power to alter or annul inappropriate decisions of their subordinate departments and of the people's governments at lower levels.

Article 109 Auditing bodies are established by local people's governments at or above the county level. Local auditing bodies at various levels, independently and in accordance with the provisions of law, exercise their power of supervision through auditing and are responsible to the people's government at the corresponding level and to the auditing body at the next higher level.

Article 110 Local people's governments at various levels are responsible and report on their work to people's congresses at the corresponding levels. Local people's governments at or above the county level are responsible and report on their work to the standing committees of the people's congresses at the corresponding levels when the congresses are not in session.

Local people's governments at various levels are responsible and report on their work to the State administrative organs at the next higher level. Local people's governments at various levels throughout the country are State administrative organs under the unified leadership of the State Council and are subordinate to it.

Article 111 The residents committees and villagers committees established among urban and rural residents on the basis of their place of residence are mass organizations of self-management at the grass-roots level. The chairman, vice-chairmen and members of each residents or villagers committee are elected by the residents. The relationship between the residents and villagers committees and the grass-roots organs of state power is prescribed by law.

The residents and villagers committees establish sub-committees for people's mediation, public security, public health and other matters in order to manage public affairs and social services in their areas, mediate civil disputes, help maintain public order and convey residents' opinions and demands and make suggestions to the people's government.

Section 6: The Organs of Self-Government of National Autonomous Areas

Article 112 The organs of self-government of national autonomous areas are the people's congresses and people's governments of autonomous regions, autonomous prefectures and autonomous counties.

Article 113 In the people's congress of an autonomous region, autonomous prefecture or autonomous county, in addition to the deputies of the nationality exercising regional autonomy in the administrative area, the other nationalities inhabiting the area are also entitled to appropriate representation.

Among the chairman and vice-chairmen of the standing committee of the people's congress of an autonomous region, autonomous prefecture or autonomous county there shall be one or more citizens of the nationality or nationalities exercising regional autonomy in the area concerned.

Article 114 The chairman of an autonomous region, the prefect of an autonomous prefecture or the head of an autonomous county shall be a citizen of the nationality exercising regional autonomy in the area concerned.

Article 115 The organs of self-government of autonomous regions, autonomous prefectures and autonomous counties exercise the functions and powers of local organs of State as specified in Section 5 of Chapter III of the Constitution. At the same time, they exercise the power of autonomy within the limits of their authority as prescribed by the Constitution, the Law of the People's Republic of China on Regional

National Autonomy and other laws and implement the laws and policies of the State in the light of the existing local situation.

Article 116 The people's congresses of national autonomous areas have the power to enact regulations on the exercise of autonomy and other separate regulations in the light of the political, economic and cultural characteristics of the nationality or nationalities in the areas concerned. The regulations on the exercise of autonomy and other separate regulations of autonomous regions shall be submitted to the Standing Committee of the National People's Congress for approval before they go into effect. Those of autonomous prefectures and counties shall be submitted to the standing committees of the people's congresses of provinces or autonomous regions for approval before they go into effect, and they shall be reported to the Standing Committee of the National People's Congress for the record.

Article 117 The organs of self-government of the national autonomous areas have the power of autonomy in administering the finances of their areas. All revenues accruing to the national autonomous areas under the financial system of the State shall be managed and used by the organs of self-government of those areas on their own.

Article 118 The organs of self-government of the national autonomous areas independently arrange for and administer local economic development under the guidance of State plans.

In exploiting natural resources and building enterprises in the national autonomous areas, the State shall give due consideration to the interests of those areas.

Article 119 The organs of self-government of the national autonomous areas independently administer educational, scientific, cultural, public health and physical culture affairs in their respective areas, protect and sift through the cultural heritage of the nationalities and work for a vigorous development of their cultures.

Article 120 The organs of self-government of the national autonomous areas may, according to the military system of the State and practical local needs and with the approval of the State Council, organize local public security forces for the maintenance of public order.

Article 121 In performing their functions, the organs of self-government of the national autonomous areas, in accordance with the provisions of the regulations on the exercise of autonomy in those areas, employ the spoken and written language or languages in common use in the locality.

Article 122 The State provides financial, material and technical assistance to the minority nationalities to help accelerate their economic and cultural development.

The State helps the national autonomous areas train large numbers of cadres at various levels and specialized personnel and skilled workers of various professions and trades from among the nationality or nationalities in those areas.

Section 7: The People's Courts and the People's Procuratorates

Article 123 The people's courts of the People's Republic of China are the judicial organs of the State.

Article 124 The People's Republic of China establishes the Supreme People's Court and the people's courts at various local levels, military courts and other special people's courts.

The term of office of the President of the Supreme People's Court is the same as that of the National People's Congress. The President shall serve no more than two consecutive terms.

The organization of the people's courts is prescribed by law.

Article 125 Except in special circumstances as specified by law, all cases in the people's courts are heard in public. The accused has the right to defence.

Article 126 The people's courts exercise judicial power independently, in accordance with the provisions of law, and not subject to interference by any administrative organ, public organization or individual.

Article 127 The Supreme People's Court is the highest judicial organ.

The Supreme People's Court supervises the administration of justice by the people's courts at various local levels and by the special people's courts. People's courts at higher levels supervise the administration of justice by those at lower levels.

Article 128 The Supreme People's Court is responsible to the National People's Congress and its Standing Committee. Local people's courts at various levels are responsible to the organs of state power which created them.

Article 129 The people's procuratorates of the People's Republic of China are State organs for legal supervision.

Article 130 The People's Republic of China establishes the Supreme People's Procuratorate and the people's procuratorates at various local levels, military procuratorates and other special people's procuratorates.

The term of office of the Procurator-General of the Supreme People's Procuratorate is the same as that of the National People's Congress; the Procurator-General shall serve no more than two consecutive terms.

The organization of the people's procuratorates is prescribed by law.

Article 131 The people's procuratorates exercise procuratorial power independently, in accordance with the provisions of law, and not subject to interference by any administrative organ, public organization or individual.

Article 132 The Supreme People's Procuratorate is the highest procuratorial organ.

The Supreme People's Procuratorate directs the work of the people's procuratorates at various local levels and of the special people's procuratorates. People's procuratorates at higher levels direct the work of those at lower levels.

Article 133 The Supreme People's Procuratorate is responsible to the National People's Congress and its Standing Committee. People's procuratorates at various local levels are responsible to the organs of state power which created them and to the people's procuratorates at higher levels.

Article 134 Citizens of all China's nationalities have the right to use their native spoken and written languages in court proceedings. The people's courts and people's procuratorates should provide translation for any party to the court proceedings who is not familiar with the spoken or written languages commonly used in the locality.

In an area where people of a minority nationality live in a concentrated community or where a number of nationalities live together, court hearings should be conducted in the language or languages commonly used in the locality; indictments, judgments, notices and other documents should be written, according to actual needs, in the language or languages commonly used in the locality.

Article 135 The people's courts, the people's procuratorates and the public security organs shall, in handling criminal cases, divide their functions, each taking responsibility for its own work, and they shall coordinate their efforts and check each other to ensure the correct and effective enforcement of law.

Chapter IV: The National Flag, the National Anthem, the National Emblem and the Capital

Article 136 The national flag of the People's Republic of China is a red flag with five stars.

The national anthem of the People's Republic of China is the March of the Volunteers.

Article 137 The national emblem of the People's Republic of China consists of an image of Tian'anmen in its centre illuminated by five stars and encircled by ears of grain and a cogwheel.

Article 138 The capital of the People's Republic of China is Beijing.

Appendix 2
The socialist legal system with Chinese characteristics

Information Office of the State Council of the People's Republic of China, 27 October 2011

Foreword

Governing the country by law and building a socialist country under the rule of law is a fundamental principle for the Communist Party of China (CPC) to lead the people and effectively govern the country. We need to bring into being a socialist system of laws with Chinese characteristics so as to ensure there are laws to abide by for the carrying on of state affairs and social life; this is a precondition and foundation for us to implement the fundamental principle of the rule of law in all respects, and an institutional guarantee for China's development and progress.

In 1949 the People's Republic of China was founded, marking the great transition from the centuries-old dictatorial system of feudalism to the system of people's democracy, putting an end to the period of semi-colonialism and semi-feudalism in China, and enabling the people to become masters of the country, society and their own life. For over 62 years, particularly since the policy of reform and opening up was adopted in 1978, the CPC has led the Chinese people in making the Constitution and laws. With concerted and unremitting efforts, by the end of 2010 we had put in place a socialist system of laws with Chinese characteristics, which is based on the conditions and reality of China, meets the needs of reform, opening up and the socialist modernization drive, and reflects the will of the CPC and the Chinese people. This legal system, headed by the Constitution, with laws related to the Constitution, civil and commercial laws and several other branches as the mainstay, and consisting of laws, administrative regulations, local regulations and other tiers of legal provisions, ensures that there are laws to abide by in economic, political, cultural and social development, as well as in ecological civilization building.

The socialist system of laws with Chinese characteristics is a legal foundation for socialism with Chinese characteristics to retain its nature, a legal reflection of the innovative practice of socialism with Chinese characteristics, and a legal guarantee for the prosperity of socialism with Chinese characteristics. Its establishment is an important milestone in China's development of socialist democracy and the legal system, and showcases the great achievements of reform, opening up and the socialist modernization drive. It is of great realistic and far-reaching historic significance.

I. Establishment of the socialist system of laws with Chinese characteristics

The socialist system of laws with Chinese characteristics was formed gradually under the leadership of the CPC in the course of adapting itself to the cause of building socialism with Chinese characteristics.

When the People's Republic of China was founded, it was confronted with the difficult tasks of organizing and consolidating the new political power, restoring and developing the national economy, and realizing and guaranteeing the people's right to be masters of the country. To meet the needs of construction of the political power, from 1949 to 1954, before the convening of the First National People's Congress (NPC), China promulgated and implemented the Common Program of the Chinese People's Political Consultative Conference, which acted as a temporary constitution, and enacted the Organic Law of the Central People's Government, Trade Union Law, Marriage Law, Land Reform Law, Interim Regulations on the Organization of the People's Courts, Interim Regulations on the Organization of the Supreme People's Procuratorate, Regulations on Punishment of Counter-revolutionaries, Interim Regulations on Punishment for Impairment of the State Currency, Regulations on Punishment for Embezzlement, Electoral Law of the National People's Congress and Local People's Congresses, and laws and regulations on the organization of local people's governments and local judicial organs, on regional ethnic autonomy, on the management of public and private enterprises, and on labor protection. With these laws and regulations, New China embarked on its course of development of democracy and the legal system.

In 1954 the First Session of the First NPC was held. The session adopted the first Constitution of New China, which established the principles for people's democracy and socialism, established the people's congress system as a fundamental political system, and provided for the basic rights and obligations of Chinese citizens. The session also adopted organic laws of the NPC, the State Council, local people's congresses and local people's committees, people's courts, and people's procuratorates, thus establishing the basic principles for state affairs. In 1956 the Eighth National Congress of the CPC proposed that 'the state must make a complete legal system gradually and systematically according to its needs.' Before the 'cultural revolution' broke out in 1966, China's legislature had enacted over 130 laws and decrees. The building of democracy and the legal system in this period provided valuable experiences for building a socialist system of laws with Chinese characteristics. During the 'cultural revolution,' China suffered grave setbacks in its work to improve democracy and the legal system, and its legislation almost came to a standstill.

In 1978 the Third Plenary Session of the 11th Central Committee of the CPC summarized the experience and lessons since the founding of New China, made a historic decision to shift the focus of the work of the Party and the state to economic development and to adopt the policy of reform and opening up, and stated, 'To ensure people's democracy, we must strengthen our socialist legal system, which will enable democracy to be institutionalized and codified, and ensure that such system and laws are stable, continuous and authoritative. All this will ensure that there are laws to go by, that they are observed and strictly enforced, and that violators are brought to book.' This session ushered in a new chapter in China's history of reform and opening up, and the building of the socialist democracy and legal system. Legislation in this period focused on restoring and re-establishing state order, and carrying out and advancing reform and opening up. In 1979 the Second Session of the Fifth NPC passed a resolution concerning the amendment to several provisions of the Constitution, which provided that local people's congresses at and above the county level established standing committees, and deputies to the people's congresses of counties were to be elected directly by their constituencies. The meeting also enacted the Electoral

Law of the National People's Congress and Local People's Congresses, Organic Law of the Local People's Congresses and Local People's Governments, Organic Law of the People's Courts, Organic Law of the People's Procuratorates, Criminal Law, Criminal Procedure Law, and Law on Chinese-Foreign Equity Joint Ventures, marking the beginning of large-scale legislation work in the new period.

In 1982, to adapt to the great changes in the economic, political, cultural and social life of China, the Fifth Session of the Fifth NPC adopted the present Constitution, establishing the fundamental system of the country and fundamental principles for state affairs, and setting basic tasks for the country, providing basic guarantees for reform and opening up, and the socialist modernization drive in the new period and symbolizing that China's efforts to improve democracy and the legal system had entered a new era. As reform and opening up deepened, and profound changes took place in China's economy and society, China made amendments to the Constitution in 1988, 1993, 1999 and 2004, respectively. These amendments affirmed the important status of the non-public sector of the economy, and wrote into the Constitution that the state 'practices a socialist market economy,' 'exercises the rule of law, building a socialist country governed according to law,' and 'respects and protects human rights,' that 'citizens' lawful private property is inviolable,' and that 'the system of multi-party cooperation and political consultation led by the Communist Party of China will exist and develop in China for a long time to come.' These amendments contributed to China's economic, political, cultural and social development and progress. During this period, to meet the needs for centering on economic development and promoting reform and opening up, the legislature enacted the General Principles of the Civil Law, Law on Industrial Enterprises Owned by the Whole People, Law on Chinese-Foreign Cooperative Joint Ventures, Law on Foreign-funded Enterprises, Patent Law, Trademark Law, Copyright Law, Economic Contract Law, Law on Enterprise Bankruptcy, and some other laws. To carry out the policy of 'one country, two systems,' the legislature enacted the Basic Law of the Hong Kong Special Administrative Region and the Basic Law of the Macao Special Administrative Region. To strengthen ethnic unity, develop socialist democracy and safeguard citizens' legitimate rights and interests, the legislature enacted the Law on Regional Ethnic Autonomy, Organic Law of the Villagers' Committees, Criminal Procedure Law, Civil Procedure Law, Administrative Procedure Law, and some other laws. To protect and improve the living and ecological environment, the legislature enacted the Environmental Protection Law, Law on the Prevention and Control of Water Pollution, Law on the Prevention and Control of Atmospheric Pollution, and some other laws. To promote education and culture, the legislature enacted the Compulsory Education Law, Law on the Protection of Cultural Relics, and some other laws. These great achievements in legislation laid an important foundation for the establishment of the socialist system of laws with Chinese characteristics.

In 1992 the 14th National Congress of the CPC made an important strategic decision to establish a socialist market economy. It expressly stated that the establishment and improvement of this socialist market economy must be regulated and guaranteed by a complete legal regime. To meet the requirements for establishing a socialist market economy, the Chinese legislature accelerated the pace of enacting economic laws; to regulate market players, maintain market order, strengthen macro-control and promote opening to the outside world, the legislature enacted the Company Law, Partnership Enterprise Law, Law on Commercial Banks, Law on Township Enterprises, Anti-Unfair Competition Law, Law on the Protection of Consumers' Rights and Interests, Product Quality Law, Auction Law, Guaranty Law, Maritime Code, Insurance Law, Negotiable Instruments Law, Law on Urban Real Estate Administration, Advertising Law, Law on Certified Public Accountants, Arbitration Law, Audit Law, Budget Law, Law on the People's Bank of China, Foreign Trade Law, Labor Law, and some other laws. To improve criminal laws, the legislature revised the Criminal Law, making it unified and complete, and revised the Criminal Procedure Law, improving criminal procedure. To regulate and supervise the use of power, the legislature enacted the Law on Administrative Penalty, Law on State Compensation, Judges Law, Public Procurators Law, Law on Lawyers, and some other laws. To strengthen the protection of the environment and resources, the legislature enacted the Law on the Prevention and Control of Environmental Pollution by Solid Waste, and some other laws while revising the Mineral Resources Law and some other laws.

In 1997 as the socialist market economy was gradually put in place, the level of opening up was constantly enhanced, the efforts to improve democracy and the legal system were advanced, and all undertakings were developing, to advance the cause of building socialism with Chinese characteristics in all aspects in the 21st century, the CPC, at its 15th National Congress, set the first ten-year target for the national economic and social development for the new century, established a basic strategy of 'governing the country according to law and building a socialist country ruled by law' and set the goal of completing the socialist system of laws with Chinese characteristics by the year 2010. To achieve this goal, to guarantee and promote the socialist market economy, and to meet the requirements of joining the World Trade Organization (WTO), the Chinese legislature kept on making new economic laws. It enacted the Securities Law, Contract Law, Law on Bid Invitation and Bidding, Trust Law, Law on Individual Proprietorship Enterprises, Law on the Contracting of Rural Land, Government Procurement Law, and some other laws, while revising the Foreign Trade Law, Law on Chinese-Foreign Equity Joint Ventures, Law on Chinese-Foreign Cooperative Joint Ventures, Law on Foreign-funded Enterprises, Patent Law, Trademark Law, Copyright Law, and some other laws. To regulate legislative activities and improve the legislation system, the NPC enacted the Law on Legislation, systematizing and codifying the principles, mechanism, extent of power and procedure of legislation, and the systems of legal interpretation, application of law, and registration and other systems. To develop socialist democracy, foster socialist culture, protect the ecological environment, and develop social undertakings, the legislature enacted the Administrative Reconsideration Law, Higher Education Law, Law on Prevention and Control of Occupational Diseases, and some other laws; revised the Trade Union Law, Law on the Protection of Cultural Relics, Marine Environmental Protection Law, Pharmaceuticals Administration Law, and some other laws. And to ensure that the laws are effectively carried out, the NPC Standing Committee made legal interpretations of articles in the Criminal Law, Basic Law of the Hong Kong Special Administrative Region and some other laws. These efforts enabled a socialist system of laws with Chinese characteristics to take shape.

Entering the new century, the CPC set the goal of building a moderately prosperous society of a higher level in all aspects for the benefit of over one billion people by 2020 at its 16th and 17th national congresses. To meet this goal, and to improve socialist democracy and the socialist legal system, fully carry out the basic strategy of governing the country by law, better safeguard the people's rights and interests, social fairness and justice, and promote social harmony, the Chinese legislature strengthened legislation work and constantly improved the quality of legislation. To safeguard China's sovereignty and territorial integrity, and promote the peaceful reunification of the country, the legislature enacted the Anti-Secession Law. To develop socialist democracy, it enacted the Law on the Supervision of

Standing Committees of People's Congresses at All Levels, Administrative Licensing Law, Administrative Coercion Law, and some other laws. To protect the lawful rights and interests of the citizens, legal persons and other organizations, and guarantee and promote the healthy development of the socialist market economy, the legislature enacted the Property Law, Tort Law, Law on Enterprise Bankruptcy, Anti-monopoly Law, Law on Anti-money Laundering, Enterprise Income Tax Law, Law on Vehicle and Vessel Taxation, Law on the State-owned Assets of Enterprises, Banking Supervision Law, and some other laws. To improve the social security system, and ensure and improve the people's livelihood, the legislature enacted the Social Insurance Law, Labor Contract Law, Employment Promotion Law, People's Mediation Law, Law on Labor Dispute Mediation and Arbitration, Food Safety Law, and some other laws. To conserve resources, protect the environment and build a resource-conserving and environmentally-friendly society, the legislature enacted the Law on Renewable Energy, Circular Economy Promotion Law, Law on Environmental Impact Assessment, and some other laws. In addition, the Chinese legislature also promulgated and revised a group of laws to strengthen social management and safeguard social order.

As the NPC and its Standing Committee enact laws, the State Council and local people's congresses and their standing committees, based on their scope of legislative power as prescribed in the Constitution and related laws, have adopted many administrative regulations and local regulations, which play an important role in improving China's socialist democracy and legal system, and promoting the establishment of the socialist system of laws with Chinese characteristics.

To ensure a unified legal system and make it more scientific and consistent, legislative bodies at different levels sorted out laws and regulations on several occasions. From 2009, the NPC Standing Committee, the State Council, and local people's congresses and their standing committees started to sort out laws and regulations in an all-round way. The NPC Standing Committee annulled eight laws and decisions about legal issues, and revised 59 laws. The State Council annulled seven administrative regulations and revised 107 administrative regulations. Local people's congresses and their standing committees annulled 455 local regulations, and revised 1,417 local regulations. Such work has helped to solve the problem of incompatibility among laws and regulations.

Since New China was founded, and particularly since the policy of reform and opening up was introduced in 1978, China has made remarkable achievements in its legislation work. By the end of August 2011, the Chinese legislature had enacted 240 effective laws including the current Constitution, 706 administrative regulations, and over 8,600 local regulations. As a result, all legal branches have been set up, covering all aspects of social relations; basic and major laws of each branch have been made; related administrative regulations and local regulations are fairly complete; and the whole legal system is scientific and consistent. A socialist system of laws with Chinese characteristics has been solidly put into place.

II. Composition of the socialist system of laws with Chinese characteristics

The socialist system of laws with Chinese characteristics is an organic integration of the related laws of the Constitution, civil and commercial laws, administrative laws, economic laws, social laws, criminal laws, litigation and non-litigation procedural laws, and other legal branches, with the Constitution in the supreme place, the laws as the main body, and administrative and local regulations as the major components.

1. Tiers of the socialist system of laws with Chinese characteristics

The Constitution is the paramount law of the socialist system of laws with Chinese characteristics. As China's fundamental law, the Constitution assumes the commanding position in the socialist system of laws with Chinese characteristics and is the fundamental guarantee of lasting stability and security, unity of ethnic groups, economic development and social progress. In China, people of all ethnic groups, all state organs, the armed forces, all political parties and public organizations, and all enterprises and institutions in the country must take the Constitution as the basic standard of conduct, and they have the duty to uphold the dignity of the Constitution and ensure its implementation.

China's present Constitution is one with Chinese characteristics and geared to the needs of socialist modernization, and is the general charter for governance of the country and good order of the nation. It was passed by the NPC in 1982 after nationwide discussion. Later, in accordance with the national economic and social development, the NPC passed four

Amendments to the Constitution. China's Constitution defines the basic system and basic tasks of the state, affirms the leadership of the CPC, establishes the guiding role of Marxism-Leninism, Mao Zedong Thought, Deng Xiaoping Theory and the important thought of the Three Represents, determines the state system as a people's democratic dictatorship led by the working class and based on the alliance of workers and peasants, and takes the system of people's congresses as the form of administration. It rules that all state power belongs to the people and that the citizens enjoy extensive rights and freedom in accordance with the law, establishes the system of multi-party cooperation and political consultation led by the CPC, the system of regional ethnic autonomy and the system of primary-level self-governance, and specifies the basic economic system in which public ownership is dominant and diverse forms of ownership develop side by side and the distribution system in which distribution according to work is dominant and diverse modes of distribution coexist. While maintaining its stability, China's Constitution is constantly improving and advancing with the times, along with the reform and opening up and the progress of the cause of socialist modernization. Promptly written into the Constitution are important experience, principles and systems that have been proven mature by practice, which fully reflects the outstanding achievements of China's reform and opening up, the great achievements of the cause of socialist construction with Chinese characteristics and the self-improvement and constant development of the socialist system, providing a fundamental guarantee for the progress of the reform and opening up, and socialist modernization.

The Constitution has supreme legal authority in the socialist system of laws with Chinese characteristics. All laws, administrative and local regulations must be made in accordance with the Constitution and follow its basic principles, and must not contravene the Constitution.

The laws are the main body of the socialist system of laws with Chinese characteristics. The Constitution stipulates that the NPC and its Standing Committee exercise the legislative power of the state. The laws formulated by the NPC and its Standing Committee are the main body of the socialist system of laws with Chinese characteristics, and deal with matters of fundamental and overall importance to national development and those which affect the country's stability and long-term development. The laws are the basis of the nation's legal system, and must not be contravened by administrative or local regulations.

The Law on Legislation ensures exclusive legislative power to the NPC and its Standing Committee. The NPC enacts and amends basic laws governing criminal offences, civil affairs, state organs and other matters;

the Standing Committee of the NPC enacts and amends laws other than the ones to be enacted by the NPC. When the NPC is not in session, it may supplement and amend laws enacted by the NPC, but must not contradict the basic principles of such laws. The Law on Legislation also stipulates that the following must be governed by law: affairs concerning state sovereignty; formation, organization, and functions and powers of state organs; the system of regional ethnic autonomy; the system of special administrative regions; the system of primary-level self-governance; criminal offences and their punishment; mandatory measures and penalties involving deprivation of citizens' political rights or restriction of the freedom of the person; requisition of non-state-owned property; basic civil system; basic economic system; basic systems of fiscal administration, taxation, customs, finance and foreign trade; systems of litigation and arbitration; and other affairs.

The laws enacted by the NPC and its Standing Committee establish the important and basic legal systems in the nation's economic, political, cultural, social and ecological civilization construction, are the main body of the socialist system of laws with Chinese characteristics and provide an important basis for the formulation of administrative and local regulations.

Administrative regulations are an important component of the socialist system of laws with Chinese characteristics. The State Council formulates administrative regulations in accordance with the Constitution and laws, which is an important form of the State Council's implementation of its responsibility endowed by the Constitution and laws. The administrative regulations may regulate matters concerning the implementation of the provisions of the laws and performance of the administrative functions and powers of the State Council. For matters that shall be governed by laws to be formulated by the NPC and its Standing Committee, the State Council may enact administrative regulations first in its place with authorization from the NPC and its Standing Committee. The administrative regulations occupy an important position in the socialist system of laws with Chinese characteristics by detailing the related systems stipulated by laws, elaborating and supplementing the laws.

The State Council, in accordance with the actual needs of socioeconomic development and administrative work, has enacted – within its statutory power limits and conforming to legal procedures – a large number of administrative regulations which cover all areas of administration, concerning the nation's economic, political, cultural and social matters. They play an important role in the implementation of the Constitution and laws, the guaranteeing of the reform and opening up and socialist modernization, the promotion of comprehensive, balanced and sustainable economic and social development and the advancement of administration in accordance with law of the people's governments at all levels.

Local regulations are another important component of the socialist system of laws with Chinese characteristics. The people's congresses and their standing committees of the provinces, autonomous regions, municipalities directly under the central government, and the larger cities may, in accordance with the Constitution and laws, formulate local regulations, which is an important channel and form of the people's participation in the administration of state affairs and promotion of local economic and social development by law. The people's congresses and their standing committees of the provinces, autonomous regions and municipalities directly under the central government may, in the light of the specific local conditions and actual needs, formulate local regulations, provided that they do not contradict the Constitution, the laws and the administrative regulations. The people's congresses and their standing committees of the larger cities may, in the light of the specific local conditions and actual needs, formulate local regulations, provided that they do not contradict the Constitution, laws, administrative regulations and local regulations of their respective provinces or autonomous regions. Moreover, they shall submit such regulations to the standing committees of the people's congresses of the provinces or autonomous regions for approval before implementation. The people's congresses of the ethnic autonomous areas have the power to formulate autonomous regulations and separate regulations on the basis of the political, economic and cultural characteristics of the local ethnic group(s). Where certain provisions of the laws and administrative regulations are concerned, adaptation may be made in autonomous regulations and separate regulations, but such adaptation may not contradict the basic principles of the laws and administrative regulations. However, no adaptation may be made to the provisions of the Constitution and the Law on Regional Ethnic Autonomy, or the provisions in other laws and administrative regulations that are specially formulated to govern the ethnic autonomous areas. The autonomous regulations and separate regulations of the autonomous regions shall be submitted to the Standing Committee of the NPC for approval before they go into effect. The autonomous regulations and separate regulations of the autonomous prefectures or counties shall be submitted to the standing committees of the people's congresses of the relevant provinces, autonomous regions or municipalities directly under the central government for approval before they go into effect. The people's congresses and their standing committees of the provinces and cities where special economic zones are located may, upon authorization by the NPC and its Standing Committee and in the light of specific local conditions and actual needs, formulate regulations in accordance with provisions of the Constitution and basic principles of the laws and administrative regulations, and enforce them within the limits of the special economic zones. Local regulations may be formulated to govern matters requiring the formulation of rules to implement the provisions of laws and administrative regulations, and matters pertaining to local affairs. Except for matters governed by laws exclusively formulated by the NPC and its Standing Committee, local regulations can also be made on other matters which are not yet covered by existing laws and administrative regulations. The local regulations also occupy an important position in the socialist system of laws with Chinese characteristics. They elaborate and supplement the laws and administrative regulations, extend and improve national legislation and accumulate useful experience for national legislation.

Local people's congresses and their standing committees, which actively exercise local legislative functions and powers, have enacted a large number of local regulations in the light of the actual conditions of local economic and social development, playing an important role in guaranteeing the effective implementation of the Constitution, laws and administrative regulations within their respective administrative regions, and promoting the reform and opening up and socialist modernization drive.

2. Branches of the socialist system of laws with Chinese characteristics

Laws related to the Constitution

The laws related to the Constitution are the collection of legal norms supporting the Constitution and directly guaranteeing its enforcement and the operation of state power. They regulate the political relationships of the state and mainly consist of laws in relation to the establishment, organization, functions, powers and basic working principles of state organs; laws on the system of regional ethnic autonomy, the system of special administrative regions and the primary-level self-governance;

laws in relation to maintaining state sovereignty, territorial integrity, national security and national symbols; and laws in relation to guaranteeing the basic political rights of citizens. By the end of August 2011 China had enacted 38 laws related to the Constitution, as well as a number of administrative and local regulations.

China has formulated electoral laws related to the NPC and local people's congresses at all levels, organic laws of local people's congresses and people's governments at all levels, and developed mechanisms for the election of deputies of the people's congresses and the leadership of state organs, providing an institutional guarantee for the people's exercise of state power and a legal basis for the formation of state organs. It has enacted organic laws of the NPC, the State Council, the People's Courts and the People's Procuratorates, and established systems concerning the organization, function and power and limits of related state organs. To implement the 'one country, two systems' policy and realize national reunification, it has promulgated the basic laws of the Hong Kong and Macao special administrative regions and established the system of special administrative region which has ensured the long-term prosperity and stability of Hong Kong and Macao. It has formulated organic laws governing urban residents' committees and villagers' committees for the establishment of urban and rural primary-level self-governance. In this way, citizens directly exercise the rights of democratic election, decision, administration and supervision by law, and implement democratic self-government of public and welfare affairs at the grassroots level, which have become the most direct and extensive democratic practices in the country. China has promulgated the Law on the Procedure for the Conclusion of Treaties, Law on Territorial Waters and the Contiguous Zones, Law on Exclusive Economic Zones and the Continental Shelf, Anti-Secession Law, Law on the National Flag, Law on the National Emblem, and other laws, and established a legal system which maintains state sovereignty and territorial integrity while safeguarding the fundamental interests of the country. It has enacted the Law on Assemblies, Processions and Demonstrations, Law on State Compensation, and other laws, as well as administrative regulations concerning ethnic group, religion, petition, and publication and registration of mass organizations, which guarantee the basic political rights of the citizens.

China fully protects its citizens' right to vote and stand for election. Elections follow the principles of universal suffrage and equality, and are carried out in the forms of direct, indirect and competitive elections. The Constitution stipulates that all citizens of the People's Republic of China who have reached the age of 18, except persons who have been deprived of their political rights in accordance with the law, shall have the right to vote and stand for election, regardless of ethnic status, race, sex, occupation, family background, religious belief, education, property status or length of residence. To guarantee its citizens' right to vote and stand for election, China is constantly modifying and improving the electoral system in accordance with the country's actual conditions, and has gradually realized the election of deputies to the people's congresses consonant with the proportion of the populations in urban and rural areas, and ensured that an appropriate number of representatives can appear at the NPC from all regions, ethnic groups and walks of life, realizing complete equality of the voting right of urban and rural residents.

China has enacted the Law on Regional Ethnic Autonomy, which ensures the implementation of the system of regional ethnic autonomy, fully respects and guarantees the right of ethnic minorities to administer their own affairs, and protects the legitimate rights and interests of the ethnic minorities by law. According to the Constitution and laws, China has currently 155 ethnic autonomous areas, i.e. five autonomous regions, 30 autonomous prefectures and 120 autonomous counties (banners). In addition, there are over 1,100 villages where ethnic minorities live in concentrated communities. According to the Constitution and the Law on Regional Ethnic Autonomy, ethnic autonomous areas have extensive autonomous power. First, they have the exclusive right to govern the local affairs of their ethnic groups and other affairs within their respective administrative regions. The chairman or vice-chairmen of the standing committee of the people's congress of an ethnic autonomous area must be a member of the ethnic group exercising regional autonomy in the area, and the head of an autonomous region, autonomous prefecture or autonomous county must be a citizen of the ethnic group exercising regional autonomy in the area concerned. Secondly, the people's congresses of ethnic autonomous areas have the power to enact regulations on the exercise of autonomy and separate regulations in the light of the political, economic and cultural characteristics of the ethnic group or groups in the areas concerned, and by law may also make adaptations to the provisions of laws and administrative regulations in the light of the characteristics of the ethnic group(s) in the areas concerned. By the end of August 2011, the ethnic autonomous areas had enacted more than 780 regulations on the exercise of autonomy, as well as separate regulations, which are currently in force. Thirdly, ethnic autonomous areas use and develop their own spoken and written languages. Fifty-three of the 55 minority groups have their own languages, and there are altogether 72 languages; 29 minority groups have their own scripts. The system of regional ethnic autonomy established by the Constitution and the Law on Regional Ethnic Autonomy is consistent with the common interests and development needs of all China's ethnic groups. It guarantees the minority groups' self-government of their own affairs by law, their democratic participation in the administration of state and social affairs, and their equal entitlement to economic, political, social and cultural rights, and maintains relations of equality, solidarity, mutual assistance and harmony among ethnic groups.

China respects and upholds human rights. The Constitution has comprehensive stipulations on the fundamental rights and freedoms of the citizens. The state has promulgated a series of laws and regulations and has developed a comparatively complete legal system to protect human rights, and ensures the citizens' right to subsistence and development, personal rights and property rights, freedom of religious belief, of speech, of the press, of the assembly, of association, of procession and of demonstration, the right to social security and education, as well as other economic, political, social and cultural rights. The Constitution stipulates that citizens of the People's Republic of China enjoy the freedom of religious belief. No state organ, public organization or individual may compel citizens to believe in, or not to believe in, any religion; nor may they discriminate against citizens who believe in, or do not believe in, any religion. The State Council has also promulgated the Regulations on Religious Affairs. Currently China has a total of more than 100 million believers in various religions, and the state fully protects its citizens' freedom of religious belief. The Constitution also provides that citizens who have suffered losses as a result of infringement of their civic rights by any state organ or functionary have the right to compensation in accordance with the provisions of the law. The state has enacted the Law on State Compensation and established the system of state compensation to effectively guarantee the right to state compensation of all citizens, legal persons and other organizations in accordance with the law.

Civil and commercial laws

Civil laws adjust property and personal relationships between civil subjects with equal status, that is, between citizens, between legal persons and between citizens and legal persons, and follow the principles of equal status between civil subjects, autonomy of will, fairness, honesty and credibility, and other basic principles. Commercial laws adjust commercial relationships between business subjects, and follow the basic principles of Civil Law and the principles of the freedom of commercial transaction, compensation of equal value and convenience and safety, among other principles. By the end of August 2011 China had promulgated 33 civil and commercial laws, as well as a large number of administrative and local regulations concerning commercial activities.

The state enacted the General Principles of the Civil Law, which establishes the basic principles that shall be followed in civil and commercial activities, and defines the target of regulation and basic principles of civil laws, as well as the systems concerning civil subjects, civil activities, civil rights and civil liability. With the development of the market economy, China gradually formulated the Contract Law, Property Law, Law on the Contracting of Rural Land and other laws, and established and improved the system of creditors' rights and the system of property rights including the proprietary rights, usufructuary rights and collateral rights; enacted the Tort Law and improved the tort responsibility system; promulgated the Marriage Law, Adoption Law, Succession Law and other laws and established and improved the marriage and family system; formulated the Law of the Application of Law in Foreign-related Civil Relations and improved the legal system of civil relations with foreigners; made the Company Law, Partnership Enterprise Law, Law on Individual Proprietorship Enterprises, Law on Commercial Banks, Law on Securities Investment Fund, Law on Specialized Farmers' Cooperatives, and other laws, and established and improved the system of business subjects. It also promulgated the Securities Law, Maritime Code, Negotiable Instruments Law, Insurance Law and other laws, and established and improved the system of commercial activities. The systems of maritime trade, negotiable instruments, insurance, securities and other market economic activities gradually took form and quickly developed.

China attaches great importance to the protection of intellectual property rights, and has promulgated a large number of laws and regulations, including the Patent Law, Trademark Law, Copyright Law, Regulations on the Protection of Computer Software, Regulations on the Protection of Integrated Circuit Layout Design, Regulations on the Collective Administration of Copyright, Regulations on the Protection of the Right to Network Dissemination of Information, Regulations on the

Protection of New Varieties of Plants, Regulations on the Customs Protection of Intellectual Property Rights, Regulations on the Administration of Special Signs, Regulations on the Protection of Olympic Symbols, and other laws and regulations, centered on the protection of intellectual property rights. The promulgation of the Trademark Law in 1982 marked the beginning of China's systematic development of a modern legal system covering intellectual property rights. To further enhance the protection of intellectual property rights in China and meet the requirements for joining the WTO, China has been constantly improving the legal system of intellectual property rights, and has made a number of amendments to the Patent Law, Trademark Law, Copyright Law and other laws to highlight legal protection of the promotion of scientific and technological advancement and innovation from the perspectives of the principles of legislation, the contents of rights, the standard of protection and the means of legal remedy, among others. By the end of 2010, the state had approved over 3,890,000 patents of various types, and effectively registered over 4,600,000 trademarks, including 670,000 trademarks from 177 countries and regions. According to incomplete statistics, during the period 2001–2010 copyright administration organs at various levels confiscated 707 million pirated copies, delivered 93,000 administrative penalties and transferred 2,500 cases to judicial organs.

To promote the reform and opening up, and expand international economic cooperation and technical exchanges, China enacted the Law on Chinese-Foreign Equity Joint Ventures, Law on Foreign-funded Enterprises and Law on Chinese-Foreign Cooperative Joint Ventures, with provisions on the investment conditions, procedures, operation, supervision, administration, and the protection of legitimate rights and interests of foreign investors in China. The state has established the principle that foreign investors should respect China's sovereignty when investing in China and other principles, including the protection of investors' legitimate rights and interests, equality and mutual benefit, extending of preferential policies and conforming to international prevailing norms, creating a favorable environment for foreign investors in China. To better implement the principles of equality and mutual benefit and conforming to international prevailing norms, China has made several amendments to the above three laws, and fully guarantees the legitimate rights and interests of foreign investors in their investment and commercial activities in China. By the end of 2010 China had approved the establishment of 710,747 foreign-funded enterprises with an actual investment of US$1.107858 trillion, which fully demonstrates the constant improvement of China's legal system regarding the protection of foreign investors.

Administrative laws

Administrative laws are the collection of legal norms on the granting, execution and supervision of administrative power. They regulate the relationships between administrative authorities and subjects of administration because of administrative activities, follow the principles of statutory remit, statutory procedure, fairness and openness, and effective supervision, and guarantee the discharge of the functions and powers of administrative organs, as well as the rights of citizens, legal persons and other organizations. By the end of August 2011 China had enacted 79 administrative laws and a large number of administrative and local regulations regulating administrative power.

China attaches great importance to the regulation of the administrative organs' execution of their power, strengthens the supervision of the execution of administrative power in accordance with the law, and ensures the correct execution of administrative power by administrative organs. China has formulated the Law on Administrative Penalties, established the basic principles of penalty by law, fairness and openness, corresponding penalty for offence and combination of penalty and education, standardized the enactment rights of administrative penalties, developed fairly complete procedures of the decision and execution of administrative penalties, and established the hearing system of administrative penalties, by which an administrative organ, before making a decision on administrative penalty that may have a significant influence on the production and life of the party concerned, shall notify the party the right to request a hearing. The state has promulgated the Administrative Reconsideration Law, established the self-correction mechanism within administrative organs, and provided remedies to citizens, legal persons and other organizations for the protection of their legitimate rights and interests. Under this law, about 80,000 cases of administrative dispute are handled each year. The state has enacted the Administrative Licensing Law, which regulates the institution, executive organs and procedures of administrative licensing, standardizes the system of administrative licensing, and, in order to reduce the number of administrative licensing, defines the matters involved in the application for administrative licensing. It also stipulates that administrative licensing will not be used for matters in which citizens, legal persons and other organizations can make decisions themselves, matters which can be effectively regulated by the competitive mechanism of the market, matters which the organizations of trades or intermediary bodies can manage through self-discipline, and matters which administrative departments can solve by other administrative means such as subsequent supervision. In order to thoroughly implement the Administrative Licensing Law, the 11th meeting of the Standing Committee of the 10th NPC passed nine amendments, removing 11 types of administrative licensing. The State Council canceled 1,749 matters of administrative licensing at the central level, changed the administrative method for 121 matters and transferred 46 matters to lower administrative levels. The state has promulgated the Administrative Coercion Law, which clearly defines the principles of the institution and execution of administrative enforcement, standardizes the types, statutory limits, executive bodies and procedures of administrative enforcement, providing a legal basis for the guarantee and supervision of the administrative organs' performance of administrative functions and powers in accordance with the law, and the protection of the legitimate rights and interests of citizens, legal persons and other organizations.

China attaches great importance to the protection of the ecological environment for mankind's survival and sustainable development. The state has promulgated the Environmental Protection Law, which lays down the basic principle of coordinated development of economic construction, social development and environmental protection, and dictates that governments at all levels, all organizations and individuals have the right and duty to protect the environment. To prevent negative impact on the environment in the course of project construction, the state has enacted the Law on Environmental Impact Assessment. The state has enacted laws for specific targets in environmental protection, such as those on prevention and control of water pollution, marine environment, atmospheric pollution, environmental noise pollution, environmental pollution by solid waste, radioactive pollution, and other laws. The State Council has formulated the Regulations on the Administration of Environmental Protection of Project Construction, Regulations on the Safe Management of Hazardous Chemicals, Regulations on the Collection and Use of Pollutant Discharge Fees, Measures on the Administration of Permits for Operations Involving Hazardous Waste, and other administrative regulations. The local people's congresses, in the light of the specific local conditions in their respective areas, have drawn up a large number of local regulations on environmental protection. China has established a system of national environmental protection standards, and had implemented over 1,300 national environmental protection standards by the end of 2010. China is also constantly strengthening the administrative enforcement of environmental protection laws. Over the past five years the state has investigated over 80,000 cases of violation of environmental protection laws, and has closed down 7,293 offending operations in accordance with the law.

China has also enacted the Education Law, Compulsory Education Law, Higher Education Law, Vocational Education Law, Teachers Law, Regulations on the Administration of Kindergartens, Regulations on the Qualifications of Teachers, and Regulations on Chinese-Foreign Cooperation in Running Schools to establish and improve its national education system. It has enacted the Drug Administration Law, Law on Maternal and Infant Health Care, Blood Donation Law, Law on the Prevention and Treatment of Infectious Diseases, Law on Physical Culture and Sport, Frontier Health and Quarantine Law, Food Safety Law, Regulations on the Supervision and Administration of Medical Devices, Regulations on Traditional Chinese Medicine and Anti-Doping Regulations to establish and improve the medical health system to ensure the people's health and safety. It has enacted the Law on Residents' Identity Cards, Law on the Control of Frontier Exit and Entry of Citizens, Law on the Control of Guns, Fire Prevention Law, Law on the Control of Narcotics, Law on Public Security Penalties, Emergency Response Law, Regulations on Detention Centers, Regulations on Safety Management of Large-Scale Mass Activities, and Regulations on the Safety Administration of Fireworks and Firecrackers to establish and improve systems aimed at maintaining social order and stability, promoting social harmony and ensuring public security. China has enacted the Civil Servants Law, People's Police Law, Law on Diplomatic Personnel, and Punishment Ordinance for Civil Servants Working in Administrative Organs to set up and improve the system of public service. China has enacted the National Defense Mobilization Law, Law on the Protection of Military Installations, Civil Air Defense Law, Military Service Law, Law on National Defense Education, Regulations on the Recruitment of Soldiers, and Militia Work Regulations to establish and improve the system of national defense and armed forces building. It has formulated the Law on Science and Technology Progress, Law on Popularization of Science and Technology, Law on the Protection of

Cultural Relics, Law on the Intangible Cultural Heritage, Regulations on the Protection of Fossils, Regulations on the Protection of the Great Wall, and Regulations on the Administration of Films to establish and improve the system to promote scientific and technological progress, and protect and nourish culture.

Economic laws

Economic laws are a collection of laws and regulations which adjust social and economic relations arising from the state's intervening in, managing and regulating economic activities for the society's overall interests. They provide legal devices and an institutional framework for the state to conduct appropriate intervention in and macro-control of the market economy, thereby preventing malpractices resulting from spontaneous and blind operation of the market economy. By the end of August 2011 China had formulated 60 economic laws and a large number of related administrative and local regulations.

China has enacted the Budget Law, Price Law, and Law on the People's Bank of China to exercise macro-control and management over economic activities. It has formulated the Law on Corporate Income Tax, Individual Income Tax Law, Law on Vehicle and Vessel Taxation, Law on the Administration of Tax Collection, Provisional Regulations on Value-Added Tax, Provisional Regulations on Business Tax, and Provisional Regulations on City Maintenance and Construction Tax to improve the taxation system. It has enacted the Law on Regulation and Supervision of the Banking Industry, and Law on Anti-Money Laundering to supervise and regulate the banking industry to ensure its safe operation. It has enacted the Agriculture Law, Seed Law, and Law on Agricultural Product Quality and Safety to guarantee agricultural development and food safety of the country. It has formulated the Railway Law, Highway Law, Civil Aviation Law, and Electric Power Law to supervise and administer key industries and promote their development. It has formulated the Land Administration Law, Forest Law, Water Law, and Mineral Resources Law to regulate the rational exploitation and utilization of important natural resources. It has enacted the Energy Conservation Law, Renewable Energy Law, Circular Economy Promotion Law, and Law on the Promotion of Clean Production to promote the effective utilization of energy and development of renewable energy.

China stresses the use of laws to safeguard fair and orderly competition among market players. The Anti-Unfair Competition Law is an important law formulated by China during its transition from the planned economy to the market economy. By drawing lessons from other countries, it makes provisions to forbid counterfeiting, commercial bribery, false publicity, infringement on trade secrets, unfair lottery-attached sales and vilifying competitors to safeguard the rights and interests of commercial operators and enable them to compete fairly and justly. The Price Law stipulates that the state institutes and gradually improves a mechanism under which prices are formed mainly by the market under the state's macro-economic control. The prices of most commodities and services shall be regulated by the market while the prices of a very small number of commodities and services shall be guided or fixed by the government. The Anti-Monopoly Law has prohibitive provisions on monopolistic agreements, abuse of dominant market positions, and concentration of business operators that eliminates or restricts competition. China has carried out reforms to its fiscal, taxation, banking, foreign exchange and investment systems, establishing a macro-management system suited to the market economy. Remarkable achievements have been made in the deregulation of markets within the Chinese economy.

China actively discharges its obligations within the framework of the WTO, constantly improves its legal system regarding foreign trade, and has established a foreign trade system suited to the socialist market economy. It has clearly defined the rights and obligations of those engaged in foreign trade, and has improved the system of managing import and export of goods, technologies and the international service trade. It has established a foreign trade survey and promotion system with Chinese characteristics. In the light of WTO rules, China has improved its trade remedy system, customs supervision, and import and export commodity inspection and quarantine system, and established a unified and transparent foreign trade system. China's foreign trade has been expanding rapidly, and the ratio of its total export-import volume to the international trade volumes keeps rising. In 2010 the ratio of China's exports in the world's total was 10.4 percent.

Social laws

China's social laws are the collection of laws and regulations with respect to the adjustment of labor relations, social security, social welfare and protection of the rights and interests of special groups. It follows the principle of justice, harmony and appropriate state intervention. By performing their duties, the state and society provide necessary protection for the rights and interests of laborers, the unemployed, the incapacitated for work, as well as other special groups in need of help so as to safeguard social equity and promote social harmony. By the end of August 2011, China had enacted 18 laws in this particular field and a large number of administrative and local regulations to regulate labor relations and social security.

China's Labor Law deals with labor relations and other relationships closely related to them, such as labor protection, labor safety and hygiene, occupational training, labor disputes and labor supervision, thus establishing China's basic labor system. China has enacted the Law on Mine Safety, Law on Prevention and Control of Occupational Diseases, and Production Safety Law and some other laws, making provisions for safe production and prevention of occupational diseases, and strengthening the protection of the rights and interests of laborers. It has enacted the Labor Contract Law, Employment Promotion Law, and Law on Labor Dispute Mediation and Arbitration, thus establishing and improving the system, which is suited to the socialist market economy, of labor contract, employment promotion and labor dispute settlement. It has enacted the Red Cross Society Law, Law on Donation for Public Welfare Undertakings and Regulations on Foundation Administration, thereby establishing and improving the system that promotes the development and administration of public welfare undertakings. It has formulated the Trade Union Law and revised it twice, defining the status of trade unions in the country's political, economic and social life, clarifying the rights and obligations of trade unions, and playing an active role in safeguarding laborers' legitimate rights and interests in accordance with the law.

China attaches importance to the building of its social security system. It has enacted the Social Insurance Law, established a social insurance system which covers both rural and urban residents, basic endowment insurance, basic health insurance, work-related injury insurance, unemployment insurance and maternity insurance, guaranteeing that all citizens can get necessary material aid and living allowances when they get old, sick, injured or unemployed, or give birth. It stipulates that the basic endowment funds should be managed at the national level, and other social insurance funds managed at the provincial level. It has set up a system for the inter-regional transfer of laborers' social security. The State Council has enacted the Regulations on Unemployment Insurance, Regulations on Work-related Injury Insurance, Provisional Regulations on Collection and Payment of Social Insurance Premiums, and Regulations on the Work Regarding the Rural Five Guarantees. It has decided to establish a new rural endowment insurance and new rural cooperative health care system. They all play an important role in promoting the building of a social security system. The gradual establishment of the social security system provides legal guarantee for the Chinese government to accelerate the building of the social security network in accordance with the law, safeguard social equality and build a harmonious society. At present, the coverage of China's social security is expanding from state-owned enterprises to various social and economic organizations, from workers and staff members of organizations to self-employed people and other residents, and from the urban areas to the rural areas. By the end of 2010 the endowment insurance system of urban workers covered 257 million people, an increase of 1.7 times compared with 2002, and the new rural endowment insurance system covered 103 million people. The basic health insurance for rural and urban residents covered 1.26 billion people, 13 times the number in 2002. Work-related injury insurance covered 161 million people. The coverage of unemployment insurance and maternity insurance is also expanding rapidly. The State Council has also formulated the Measures for Assisting Vagrants and Beggars with No Means of Support in Cities, Regulations on Legal Aid, Regulations on Natural Disaster Relief, and Regulations on Minimum Subsistence Allowance for Urban Residents, and has decided to set up a minimum subsistence allowance program for rural residents, thus basically establishing a social relief system covering both urban and rural areas. By the end of 2010 some 77 million residents with financial difficulties in China received minimum subsistence allowance. The level of China's social security is constantly improving, and people are sharing the fruits of development.

China pays great attention to the protection of the rights and interests of special groups. It has enacted the Law on the Protection of Disabled Persons, Law on the Protection of Minors, Law on the Protection of Rights and Interests of Women, Law on the Protection of the Rights and Interests of the Elderly, and Law on the Prevention of Juvenile Delinquency. It has developed a comparatively complete legal system to protect the rights and interests of special groups, which plays an important role in protecting the legitimate rights and interests of special groups, and in safeguarding social equity and justice.

Criminal law

This is the law that defines crimes and penalties. It aims to punish crime and protect the people, maintain social order and public security, and safeguard national security through regulating the state's power of punishment. By the end of August 2011 China had enacted the Criminal Law and eight amendments to it, as well as decisions on punishing fraudulent purchase of foreign exchange, evading foreign exchange control, and illegal trade in foreign exchange, plus nine legal interpretations on the Criminal Law.

The Criminal Law defines clearly these basic principles: punishment of crimes is defined by law, everyone is equal before the law, and punishment should match the severity of the crime. It expressly stipulates that any act deemed by explicit stipulations of the law as a crime is to be convicted and given punishment by law, and that any act that is not deemed a crime by the explicit stipulations of the law is not to be convicted or given punishment. The law shall be equally applied to anyone who commits a crime. No one shall have the privilege of transcending the law. The degree of punishment shall be commensurate with the crime committed and the criminal responsibility to be borne by the offender. The Criminal Law of China defines various types of crime and types of punishment, including public surveillance, criminal detention, fixed-term imprisonment, life imprisonment and the death penalty. It also includes three accessory penalties – fine, deprivation of political rights and confiscation of property. In addition, it states the concrete application of punishments. It identifies ten criminal acts and corresponding criminal liability, namely the crimes of endangering national security, endangering public security, undermining the order of the socialist market economy, infringing upon the rights of the person and the democratic rights of citizens, encroaching on property, disrupting the order of social administration, endangering the interests of national defense, embezzlement and bribery, dereliction of duty, and servicemen's transgression of duties.

In the light of the actual situation brought about by economic and social development, China promptly revises and interprets its Criminal Law in an effort to improve the criminal legal system. Amendment VIII to the Criminal Law, passed in February 2011, made major revisions of the previous Criminal Law. It eliminates capital punishment for 13 non-violent economic-related offences, thus reducing the number of crimes subject to the death penalty by 19.1 percent; it improves legal provisions that give more lenient punishment and non-custodial penalties to minors and elderly people who have reached the age of 75; it stipulates that refusing to pay wages, seriously infringing upon the legal rights and interests of laborers, and drunk driving are criminal offences; it gives harsher punishment for criminal offences in violation of citizens' personal freedom, life and health. All this has improved China's criminal justice system, strengthened the protection of human rights, reflecting the development of China's social civilization and progress in the spheres of democracy and rule of law.

Litigation and non-litigation procedure laws

These are laws giving standard solutions to various litigation and non-litigation activities arising from social disputes. The litigation system aims to regulate the state's judicial activities in settling social disputes, and the non-litigation system aims to regulate arbitration agencies and people's mediation organizations in settling social disputes. By the end of August 2011 China had enacted ten laws in the fields of litigation and non-litigation procedure.

China's Criminal Procedure Law stipulates the basic system and principles of criminal procedures. For instance, the law applies equally to all citizens; the people's courts and people's procuratorates exercise judicial authority and procuratorial powers independently; the people's courts, people's procuratorates and public security organs divide their responsibilities, coordinate their efforts and check each other; ensure that criminal suspects and defendants obtain defense; and no one shall be convicted without a court decision. It also specifies the procedures such as jurisdiction, withdrawal, defense, evidence, enforcement measures, investigation, prosecution, trial and execution, which effectively guarantee the correct application of the Criminal Law, and protect the personal, property, democratic and other rights of citizens so as to ensure the smooth progress of the cause of socialism.

China's Civil Procedure Law stipulates the following basic principles and system: the parties to civil litigation shall have equal litigation rights; mediation shall be conducted for the parties on a voluntary and lawful basis; the court shall follow the system of public trial and the court of second instance being that of last instance. It makes clear the litigation rights and obligations of the parties concerned, the use of evidence, the civil trial procedures such as ordinary procedure of first instance, procedure of second instance, summary procedure, special procedure, procedure for trial supervision, and procedure of execution and enforcement execution measures.

China's Administrative Procedure Law defines the legal remedy system in administrative lawsuits. It explicitly stipulates that a citizen, a legal person or other organization has the right to initiate an administrative lawsuit at a people's court in accordance with this law if they believe their lawful rights and interests are infringed upon by an administrative organ or staff working in it, and the people's court exercises judicial power independently with respect to administrative cases to protect the legal rights and interests of the citizens. Since the promulgation and implementation of the Administrative Procedure Law, the people's courts have accepted over 100,000 cases annually on average, protecting the lawful rights and interests of the citizens and making the administrative organs exercise their administrative powers according to law.

China's Arbitration Law has provisions for the establishment of domestic arbitration and foreign-related arbitration agencies, stipulates that an arbitration commission shall be independent of any administrative organ, which guarantees its independence. It also specifies that arbitration should be conducted upon a voluntary and independent basis, and that a system of a single and final award shall be practiced for arbitration. It also contains details about arbitration procedures. Since the promulgation of this law over 500,000 cases of economic disputes have been handled, involving a total sum of 700 billion yuan. It has played an important role in settling civil and economic disputes fairly, promptly and effectively, protecting the lawful rights and interests of the parties concerned, maintaining social and economic stability and promoting social harmony.

People's mediation is a Chinese way of resolving contradictions and settling disputes without resorting to legal proceedings. The Constitution and Civil Procedure Law specify the nature and fundamental principles of people's mediation, and the State Council has promulgated the Organic Regulations on the People's Mediation Commissions. In 2009 people's mediation organizations mediated over 7.67 million civil disputes, with a success rate of over 96 percent. In order to further promote people's mediation work and improve the system, China has formulated the People's Mediation Law, making the good experience and practices accumulated in this field into law. At present, there are more than 820,000 people's mediation organizations in China, and 4.67 million people's mediators, forming a mediation network covering both rural and urban areas. They are playing an important role in preventing and reducing civil disputes, resolving social conflicts, and maintaining social harmony and stability.

In addition, China has formulated the Extradition Law, Special Maritime Procedure Law, Law on Labor Dispute Mediation and Arbitration, and Law on the Mediation and Arbitration of Rural Land

Contracting Disputes, thereby establishing and improving the system of litigation and non-litigation procedure laws.

The above-mentioned laws and regulations made by legislative bodies cover all aspects of society, bring all the work of the state and all aspects of social life under the rule of law, laying a solid foundation for the rule of law and construction of a socialist country under the rule of law. Law has become an important means for Chinese citizens, legal persons and other organizations to resolve disputes and conflicts. It also provides an important basis for the people's courts at all levels to safeguard the lawful rights and interests of citizens, legal persons and other organizations.

III. Features of the socialist system of laws with Chinese characteristics

The differences between countries in their historical and cultural traditions, actual situations and paths of development, their social, political and economic systems determine that their systems of laws have different features. The socialist system of laws with Chinese characteristics is the concentrated reflection of the institutionalization and codification of China's practice in its economic and social development since the founding of the People's Republic of China in 1949, and especially in the past 30-odd years since the adoption of the reform and opening up policy. As an important component of the socialist system with Chinese characteristics, it has distinct features.

1. The socialist system of laws with Chinese characteristics embodies the essential requirements of socialism with Chinese characteristics

The nature of a country's legal system depends on the nature of its social system established in law. China is a socialist country under the people's democratic dictatorship, led by the working class and based on the alliance of workers and peasants. In the primary stage of socialism, China practices a basic economic system with public ownership as the mainstay and the joint development of diverse forms of ownership, which determines that China's legal institutions are bound to be socialist ones and that China's legal system is bound to be a socialist one with

Chinese characteristics. All legal norms covered in and all legal institutions established by the socialist legal system contribute to consolidating and developing socialism, reflect the people's common aspirations, safeguard their fundamental interests and make sure that the people are the masters of their own country. China proceeds from the essential requirement of socialism with Chinese characteristics and the will and long-term interests of the people in making its laws and determining the relevant provisions. The aim and outcome of all the work of the state are to realize, safeguard and expand the fundamental interests of the overwhelming majority of the people.

2. Socialist system of laws with Chinese characteristics meets the demand of the reform, opening up and socialist modernization of the current times

The most salient characteristic of this new period in China is reform and opening up. The socialist system of laws with Chinese characteristics comes into existence and develops along with reform and opening up, and they complement each other. The establishment of the socialist system of laws with Chinese characteristics is the inherent requirement for the progress of reform, opening up and socialist modernization. It is carried out on the basis of in-depth analysis of those practices. At the same time, the establishment of the socialist system of laws with Chinese characteristics provides a favorable legal environment for reform, opening up and socialist modernization, and serves as a good regulator, guide, guarantee and impetus for the latter. Meanwhile, by appropriately handling the relationship between the stability of law and the mobility of reform, the socialist system of laws with Chinese characteristics reflects the successful practice of reform, opening up and modernization, and leaves enough space for their future development.

3. The socialist system of laws with Chinese characteristics reflects the requirements of an inherently unified and structurally multilevel legal system

The constitution of a country's legal system is determined by its legal traditions, political and legislative systems, and other factors. China is a united multi-ethnic country as well as a state with a unified governmental system. Due to historical reasons, economic and social development is unbalanced among different regions. To accommodate the requirements of this national condition, the Constitution and laws define the unified and multilevel structure of China's legislative system with Chinese characteristics, which further determines the inherently unified and structurally multilevel feature of the socialist system of laws with Chinese characteristics. It reflects the inner logic of the legal system itself, and conforms to China's national conditions and practices. Therefore, the socialist system of laws with Chinese characteristics is headed by the Constitution, composed of multilevel legal norms, including laws, administrative and local regulations. The legal norms are laid down by various legislative bodies according to their respective legislative competence prescribed by the Constitution and laws. They have different legal effect, but together constitute the scientific, harmonious and unified whole of the socialist system of laws with Chinese characteristics as its organic parts.

4. The socialist system of laws with Chinese characteristics meets the cultural demand of carrying forward the fine traditions of Chinese legal culture and drawing on the achievements of human legal civilizations

All countries base and develop their legal systems on their historical and cultural traditions, and actual social conditions, and their legal systems' communication and exchange with and learning from each other as economic globalization deepens. The constitution of the socialist system of laws with Chinese characteristics is always based on China's national conditions, combining the inheritance of historical traditions, the introduction of the fruits of other civilizations with system innovations. It attaches great importance to the inheritance of fine traditional legal culture, carries out system innovations according to the requirements of reform, opening up and socialist modernization, thus realizing the integration of traditional culture and modern civilization; at the same time, it studies and draws on the good legislative experience of other countries and learns from their legislative achievements, but never slavishly imitates their models, which makes the current legal system conform to China's national conditions and practices as well as the trend of contemporary world legal civilization. China's legal system, featuring both inclusiveness and openness, has fully demonstrated its unique cultural characteristics.

5. The socialist system of laws with Chinese characteristics reflects the development demand of being dynamic and open, and of advancing with the times

A country's legal system is normally the reflection of its conditions at a specific historical stage. With the country's economic and social development, its legal system needs to be enriched and improved, and innovations introduced. Currently China is in the primary stage of socialism, and will remain so for a long time to come. The country is still in the stage of structural reforms and social transformation, and its socialist system calls for constant self-improvement and development, which determines that the socialist system of laws with Chinese characteristics is bound to have the features of both stability and mobility, both periodical variations and continuity, and both actuality and foresightedness. China's legal system is dynamic, open, developing, not static, closed or fixed; it will constantly improve with China's economic and social development and the practice of building a socialist country under the rule of law.

In the course of formulation of the socialist system of laws with Chinese characteristics, China's legislative bodies have integrated the leadership of the CPC, the people's status as masters of their country and the rule of law, actively exercised their legislative power, and carried out legislative work in a planned, focused and step-by-step manner, with attention always fixed on the priorities of the country. We have thereby accumulated some precious experience and successfully blazed a new path of legislation with Chinese characteristics.

Persisting in promoting legislation in a planned and phase-by-phase manner with clear objectives

In the practice of building socialism with Chinese characteristics under the leadership of the CPC over the past 30-odd years since the adoption of the reform and opening up policies, China's legislative bodies have, on the basis of their central tasks at different stages, proceeded from reality, focused on key issues, carried out careful organization work, established priorities, and formulated scientific, rational and practical five-year legislation plans and annual legislation work plans. They have enacted laws and regulations urgently needed for economic and social development, promoted legislation actively and steadily, and gradually formulated methods of building a socialist legal system in a planned, focused and phase-by-phase manner with clear objectives. We should pool legislative resources, focus on key legislation work and promptly meet the requirements of the fast-developing reform and opening up, thereby providing an effective path for building a socialist system of laws with Chinese characteristics.

Persisting in promoting the side-by-side advancement of legislation at various levels

China is a united multi-ethnic country as well as a state with a unified government system, and economic and social development is unbalanced among different regions. In accordance with the national conditions, it is stipulated in the Constitution that under the guidance of the principle of giving full scope to the initiative and enthusiasm of the local authorities under the unified leadership of the central authorities, on the condition of maintenance of a unified legal system, the NPC and its Standing Committee exercise the legislative power of the state, the State Council formulates administrative regulations in accordance with the Constitution and the law, the people's congresses of provinces, autonomous regions, municipalities directly under the central government, comparatively larger cities and their standing committees may adopt local regulations, the people's congresses of ethnic autonomous areas have the power to enact regulations on the exercise of autonomy and other separate regulations, and the people's congresses or their standing committees of the provinces and cities where special economic zones are located may, upon authorization by the NPC, formulate regulations and enforce them within the limits of the special economic zones. A legislation work pattern of side-by-side advancement of legislation at various levels has gradually taken shape, which greatly accelerates the building of our legal system and at the same time takes into consideration the actual needs of economic and social development in various regions. This is a practical working model for the socialist system of laws with Chinese characteristics.

Persisting in the combination of various legislative forms

The building of the socialist system of laws with Chinese characteristics is a scientific and systematic project. Since the reform and opening up started, in accordance with the demands of economic and social development, China's legislative bodies have lost no time in enacting laws and regulations urgently needed for the development of all social undertakings, attached importance to their amendment or abolition, and explained and checked them in a timely manner. They have adopted various legislative forms, such as formulation, amendment, abolition and interpretation, and promoted legislation in an all-round way. In this way, we have improved the quality of legislation and guaranteed the scientific nature and harmony of the legal system while laying a solid foundation for the effective implementation of legal norms.

IV. Improvement of the socialist system of laws with Chinese characteristics

The task remains arduous to improve the socialist system of laws with Chinese characteristics which we have successfully built. To improve that system from a new starting point is an inherent requirement of promotion of the development and improvement of the socialist system with Chinese characteristics. This will also be the primary task for our legislation work in future.

China is now at a critical stage in deepening reform and opening up, and building a moderately prosperous society in an all-round way, as it has established the development goal for the first 20 years of the 21st century. The need for legal system improvement is urgent in order to meet the challenges of new domestic and international situations, and new demands and expectations of the people, as well as new issues and problems facing China's reform, development and stability. To realize scientific development, accelerate transformation of the economic development mode, and further guarantee and improve the people's livelihood, all need a legal system to promote and give guidance. There is a rising demand for more scientific and democratic legislation, as increasingly diversified stakeholders and complicated interest patterns make it harder to regulate social interests through legislation.

China will endeavor to meet the requirements of its basic strategies of promoting scientific development, improving social harmony and ruling the country by law. At present and for some time to come, and in accordance with the requirements of economic and social development, as well as scientific development, China will accelerate the transformation of the economic development mode, guarantee and improve the people's livelihood, improve social harmony, and continuously improve the laws and regulations, so as to build a better socialist system of laws with Chinese characteristics.

China will continuously improve legislation in the economic field. In order to meet the requirements of the development of the socialist market economy, we will improve the legal institutions for civil and commercial affairs. To meet the requirements of deepening the reforms of the fiscal, taxation and financial systems, we will improve legal institutions concerned with budget management, fiscal transfer payment, financial risk control and taxation. We will, in particular, attach importance to taxation legislation, and turn taxation regulations made by the State Council on authorization into laws. We will also improve laws regarding the state's management and control of economic activities in order to safeguard the country's economic security, and promote the healthy development of the socialist market economy.

China will take active measures to strengthen legislation on socialist democracy. In order to meet the requirements of actively yet steadily advancing political reform, we will improve legal institutions concerning election, self-governance among people at the grassroots level and organization of state organs; we will improve legislation regarding administrative procedures to regulate administrative actions, and improve laws concerning audit supervision and administrative reconsideration. In order to meet the requirements of reforming the judicial system, we will revise the Criminal Procedure Law, the Civil Procedure Law and the Administrative Procedure Law, so as to improve the procedure law system. We will also improve the legal system concerning the exercise of power by state organs and the punishment and prevention of corruption, in order to expand socialist democracy, standardize and supervise the exercise of power, and continuously develop socialist democracy.

China will strengthen legislation in the social field. We will always put people first, guarantee and improve the people's livelihood, advance social undertakings, improve the social security system, encourage innovation in social management, gradually improve the legal institutions concerning employment, labor protection, social security, social assistance, social welfare, income distribution, education, medical care, housing and social organizations, constantly explore an innovative social management mechanism, and push forward the development of social undertakings.

China will attach more importance to legislation in the cultural, scientific and technological fields. In order to meet the requirements of promoting reform in the cultural system and advancing science and technology, we will improve the legal institutions which support public cultural undertakings, develop the culture industry, encourage cultural and scientific innovation, and protect intellectual property rights, so as to realize cultural prosperity and build an innovation-oriented country.

China will attach importance to legislation in the field of the environment. In order to meet the requirements of building an energy-saving and environmentally-friendly society, we will strengthen laws on energy saving and eco-environmental protection, and improve our institutions so as to accelerate the transformation of the economic development mode, solve the contradictions between socioeconomic development and environmental protection, and promote harmony between man and nature.

While improving various laws, we will attach importance to their implementation, working mechanism and supporting regulations. We will improve the channels and methods for the interpretation of laws, and make it our regular work. We will give timely legal interpretations when the specific meaning of certain provisions needs further clarification, or the application of laws in certain new circumstances needs further explanation. We need to improve the organization, mechanism and method for reviewing and filing regulations, rules, and legal interpretations. Meanwhile, we will improve the revision mechanism as applied to laws and regulations, and make it work on a regular basis in order to make our legal system more scientific and consistent.

We will work to promote scientific and democratic legislation, and improve legislation quality. We will improve the mechanism whereby NPC deputies are involved in legislation, and bring their role to the full. We will improve the motion deliberation system and establish a scientific and democratic examination and voting mechanism. We will explore channels and forms for the public to participate in legislation activities in an orderly manner, improve panel discussions, feasibility study meetings, hearings on legislation and the gathering of public opinion through the publication of draft laws and regulations, and establish and improve the mechanism through which public opinion can be heard and feedback can be given, so as to let legislation reflect the will of the public.

We will establish and improve a mechanism featuring feasibility studies before making legislation and evaluation after making legislation, constantly endeavor to make legislation more scientific and reasonable, and further improve the practicality of laws and regulations.

Concluding remarks

Social practice is the foundation of laws, and laws encapsulate practical experience. Social practice is endless, and legislative work should also constantly move forward with the times. Building socialism with Chinese characteristics is a long-term historic task. Improving the socialist system of laws with Chinese characteristics is also a long-term and arduous historic task, and it must advance in tandem with the practice of socialism with Chinese characteristics.

The vitality of laws lies in their enforcement. The formation of the socialist system of laws with Chinese characteristics has generally solved the basic problem of having laws for people to follow. Now, the problem of ensuring that laws are observed and strictly enforced and that lawbreakers are prosecuted has become more pronounced and pressing. Therefore, China will take active and effective steps to guarantee the effective enforcement of the Constitution and laws, and accelerate the advance of the rule of law and the building of a socialist country under the rule of law.

Appendix 3 Charter '08

I. Foreword

A hundred years have passed since the writing of China's first constitution. 2008 also marks the sixtieth anniversary of the promulgation of the *Universal Declaration of Human Rights*, the thirtieth anniversary of the appearance of the Democracy Wall in Beijing, and the tenth of China's signing of the International Covenant on Civil and Political Rights. We are approaching the twentieth anniversary of the 1989 Tiananmen massacre of pro-democracy student protesters. The Chinese people, who have endured human rights disasters and uncountable struggles across these same years, now include many who see clearly that freedom, equality, and human rights are universal values of humankind and that democracy and constitutional government are the fundamental framework for protecting these values.

By departing from these values, the Chinese government's approach to 'modernization' has proven disastrous. It has stripped people of their rights, destroyed their dignity, and corrupted normal human intercourse. So we ask: Where is China headed in the twenty-first century? Will it continue with 'modernization' under authoritarian rule, or will it embrace universal human values, join the mainstream of civilized nations, and build a democratic system? There can be no avoiding these questions.

The shock of the Western impact upon China in the nineteenth century laid bare a decadent authoritarian system and marked the beginning of what is often called 'the greatest changes in thousands of years' for China. A 'self-strengthening movement' followed, but this aimed simply at appropriating the technology to build gunboats and other Western material objects. China's humiliating naval defeat at the hands of Japan in 1895 only confirmed the obsolescence of China's system of government. The first attempts at modern political change came with the ill-fated summer of reforms in 1898, but these were cruelly crushed by ultraconservatives at China's imperial court. With the revolution of 1911, which inaugurated Asia's first republic, the authoritarian imperial system that had lasted for centuries was finally supposed to have been laid to rest. But social conflict inside our country and external pressures were to prevent it; China fell into a patchwork of warlord fiefdoms and the new republic became a fleeting dream.

The failure of both 'self-strengthening' and political renovation caused many of our forebears to reflect deeply on whether a 'cultural illness' was afflicting our country. This mood gave rise, during the May Fourth Movement of the late 1910s, to the championing of 'science and democracy.' Yet that effort, too, foundered as warlord chaos persisted and the Japanese invasion [beginning in Manchuria in 1931] brought national crisis.

Victory over Japan in 1945 offered one more chance for China to move toward modern government, but the Communist defeat of the Nationalists in the civil war thrust the nation into the abyss of totalitarianism. The 'new China' that emerged in 1949 proclaimed that 'the people are sovereign' but in fact set up a system in which 'the Party is all-powerful.' The Communist Party of China seized control of all organs of the state and all political, economic, and social resources, and, using these, has produced a long trail of human rights disasters, including, among many others, the Anti-Rightist Campaign (1957), the Great Leap Forward (1958–1960), the Cultural Revolution (1966–1976), the June Fourth [Tiananmen Square] Massacre (1989), and the current repression of all unauthorized religions and the suppression of the *weiquan* rights movement [a movement aiming to defend citizens' rights promulgated in the Chinese constitution and fight for human rights recognized by international conventions that the Chinese government has signed]. During all this, the Chinese people have paid a gargantuan price. Tens of millions have lost their lives, and several generations have seen their freedom, their happiness, and their human dignity cruelly trampled.

During the last two decades of the twentieth century the government policy of 'Reform and Opening' gave the Chinese people relief from the pervasive poverty and totalitarianism of the Mao Zedong era, and brought substantial increases in the wealth and living standards of many Chinese as well as a partial restoration of economic freedom and economic rights. Civil society began to grow, and popular calls for more rights and more political freedom have grown apace. As the ruling elite itself moved toward private ownership and the market economy, it began to shift from an outright rejection of 'rights' to a partial acknowledgment of them.

In 1998 the Chinese government signed two important international human rights conventions; in 2004 it amended its constitution to include the phrase 'respect and protect human rights'; and this year, 2008, it has promised to promote a 'national human rights action plan.' Unfortunately most of this political progress has extended no further than the paper on which it is written. The political reality, which is plain for anyone to see, is that China has many laws but no rule of law; it has a constitution but no constitutional government. The ruling elite continues to cling to its authoritarian power and fights off any move toward political change.

The stultifying results are endemic official corruption, an undermining of the rule of law, weak human rights, decay in public ethics, crony capitalism, growing inequality between the wealthy and the poor, pillage of the natural environment as well as of the human and historical environments, and the exacerbation of a long list of social conflicts, especially, in recent times, a sharpening animosity between officials and ordinary people.

As these conflicts and crises grow ever more intense, and as the ruling elite continues with impunity to crush and to strip away the rights of citizens to freedom, to property, and to the pursuit of happiness, we see the powerless in our society – the vulnerable groups, the people who have been suppressed and monitored, who have suffered cruelty and even torture, and who have had no adequate avenues for their protests, no courts to hear their pleas – becoming more militant and raising the possibility of a violent conflict of disastrous proportions. The decline of the current system has reached the point where change is no longer optional.

II. Our fundamental principles

This is a historic moment for China, and our future hangs in the balance. In reviewing the political modernization process of the past hundred years or more, we reiterate and endorse basic universal values as follows:

- *Freedom.* Freedom is at the core of universal human values. Freedom of speech, freedom of the press, freedom of assembly, freedom of association, freedom in where to live, and the freedoms to strike, to demonstrate, and to protest, among others, are the forms that freedom takes. Without freedom, China will always remain far from civilized ideals.

- *Human rights.* Human rights are not bestowed by a state. Every person is born with inherent rights to dignity and freedom. The government exists for the protection of the human rights of its citizens. The exercise of state power must be authorized by the people. The succession of political disasters in China's recent history is a direct consequence of the ruling regime's disregard for human rights.

- *Equality.* The integrity, dignity, and freedom of every person – regardless of social station, occupation, sex, economic condition, ethnicity, skin color, religion, or political belief – are the same as those of any other. Principles of equality before the law and equality of social, economic, cultural, civil, and political rights must be upheld.

- *Republicanism.* Republicanism, which holds that power should be balanced among different branches of government and competing interests should be served, resembles the traditional Chinese political ideal of 'fairness in all under heaven.' It allows different interest groups and social assemblies, and people with a variety of cultures and beliefs, to exercise democratic self-government and to deliberate in order to reach peaceful resolution of public questions on a basis of equal access to government and free and fair competition.

- *Democracy.* The most fundamental principles of democracy are that the people are sovereign and the people select their government. Democracy has these characteristics: (1) Political power begins with the people and the legitimacy of a regime derives from the people. (2) Political power is exercised through choices that the people make. (3) The holders of major official posts in government at all levels are determined through periodic competitive elections. (4) While honoring the will of the majority, the fundamental dignity, freedom, and human rights of minorities are protected. In short, democracy is a modern means for achieving government truly 'of the people, by the people, and for the people.'

- *Constitutional rule.* Constitutional rule is rule through a legal system and legal regulations to implement principles that are spelled out in a constitution. It means protecting the freedom and the rights of citizens, limiting and defining the scope of legitimate government power, and providing the administrative apparatus necessary to serve these ends.

III. What we advocate

Authoritarianism is in general decline throughout the world; in China, too, the era of emperors and overlords is on the way out. The time is arriving everywhere for citizens to be masters of states. For China the path that leads out of our current predicament is to divest ourselves of the authoritarian notion of reliance on an 'enlightened overlord' or an 'honest official' and to turn instead toward a system of liberties, democracy, and the rule of law, and toward fostering the consciousness of modern citizens who see rights as fundamental and participation as a duty. Accordingly, and in a spirit of this duty as responsible and constructive citizens, we offer the following recommendations on national governance, citizens' rights, and social development:

1. *A new constitution.* We should recast our present constitution, rescinding its provisions that contradict the principle that sovereignty resides with the people and turning it into a document that genuinely guarantees human rights, authorizes the exercise of public power, and serves as the legal underpinning of China's democratization. The constitution must be the highest law in the land, beyond violation by any individual, group, or political party.

2. *Separation of powers.* We should construct a modern government in which the separation of legislative, judicial, and executive power is guaranteed. We need an Administrative Law that defines the scope of government responsibility and prevents abuse of administrative power. Government should be responsible to taxpayers. Division of power between provincial governments and the central government should adhere to the principle that central powers are only those specifically granted by the constitution and all other powers belong to the local governments.

3. *Legislative democracy.* Members of legislative bodies at all levels should be chosen by direct election, and legislative democracy should observe just and impartial principles.

4. *An independent judiciary.* The rule of law must be above the interests of any particular political party and judges must be independent. We need to establish a constitutional supreme court and institute procedures for constitutional review. As soon as possible, we should abolish all of the Committees on Political and Legal Affairs that now allow Communist Party officials at every level to decide politically sensitive cases in advance and out of court. We should strictly forbid the use of public offices for private purposes.

5. *Public control of public servants.* The military should be made answerable to the national government, not to a political party, and should be made more professional. Military personnel should swear

allegiance to the constitution and remain nonpartisan. Political party organizations must be prohibited in the military. All public officials including police should serve as nonpartisans, and the current practice of favoring one political party in the hiring of public servants must end.

6. *Guarantee of human rights.* There must be strict guarantees of human rights and respect for human dignity. There should be a Human Rights Committee, responsible to the highest legislative body, that will prevent the government from abusing public power in violation of human rights. A democratic and constitutional China especially must guarantee the personal freedom of citizens. No one should suffer illegal arrest, detention, arraignment, interrogation, or punishment. The system of 'Reeducation through Labor' must be abolished.

7. *Election of public officials.* There should be a comprehensive system of democratic elections based on 'one person, one vote.' The direct election of administrative heads at the levels of county, city, province, and nation should be systematically implemented. The rights to hold periodic free elections and to participate in them as a citizen are inalienable.

8. *Rural–urban equality.* The two-tier household registry system must be abolished. This system favors urban residents and harms rural residents. We should establish instead a system that gives every citizen the same constitutional rights and the same freedom to choose where to live.

9. *Freedom to form groups.* The right of citizens to form groups must be guaranteed. The current system for registering nongovernment groups, which requires a group to be 'approved,' should be replaced by a system in which a group simply registers itself. The formation of political parties should be governed by the constitution and the laws, which means that we must abolish the special privilege of one party to monopolize power and must guarantee principles of free and fair competition among political parties.

10. *Freedom to assemble.* The constitution provides that peaceful assembly, demonstration, protest, and freedom of expression are fundamental rights of a citizen. The ruling party and the government must not be permitted to subject these to illegal interference or unconstitutional obstruction.

11. *Freedom of expression.* We should make freedom of speech, freedom of the press, and academic freedom universal, thereby guaranteeing that citizens can be informed and can exercise their right of political supervision. These freedoms should be upheld by a Press Law that abolishes political restrictions on the press. The provision in the current Criminal Law that refers to 'the crime of incitement to subvert state power' must be abolished. We should end the practice of viewing words as crimes.

12. *Freedom of religion.* We must guarantee freedom of religion and belief, and institute a separation of religion and state. There must be no governmental interference in peaceful religious activities. We should abolish any laws, regulations, or local rules that limit or suppress the religious freedom of citizens. We should abolish the current system that requires religious groups (and their places of worship) to get official approval in advance and substitute for it a system in which registry is optional and, for those who choose to register, automatic.

13. *Civic education.* In our schools we should abolish political curriculums and examinations that are designed to indoctrinate students in state ideology and to instill support for the rule of one party. We should replace them with civic education that advances universal values and citizens' rights, fosters civic consciousness, and promotes civic virtues that serve society.

14. *Protection of private property.* We should establish and protect the right to private property and promote an economic system of free and fair markets. We should do away with government monopolies in commerce and industry and guarantee the freedom to start new enterprises. We should establish a Committee on State-Owned Property, reporting to the national legislature, that will monitor the transfer of state-owned enterprises to private ownership in a fair, competitive, and orderly manner. We should institute a land reform that promotes private ownership of land, guarantees the right to buy and sell land, and allows the true value of private property to be adequately reflected in the market.

15. *Financial and tax reform.* We should establish a democratically regulated and accountable system of public finance that ensures the protection of taxpayer rights and that operates through legal procedures. We need a system by which public revenues that belong to a certain level of government – central, provincial, county or local –

are controlled at that level. We need major tax reform that will abolish any unfair taxes, simplify the tax system, and spread the tax burden fairly. Government officials should not be able to raise taxes, or institute new ones, without public deliberation and the approval of a democratic assembly. We should reform the ownership system in order to encourage competition among a wider variety of market participants.

16. *Social security.* We should establish a fair and adequate social security system that covers all citizens and ensures basic access to education, health care, retirement security, and employment.

17. *Protection of the environment.* We need to protect the natural environment and to promote development in a way that is sustainable and responsible to our descendants and to the rest of humanity. This means insisting that the state and its officials at all levels not only do what they must do to achieve these goals, but also accept the supervision and participation of nongovernmental organizations.

18. *A federated republic.* A democratic China should seek to act as a responsible major power contributing toward peace and development in the Asian Pacific region by approaching others in a spirit of equality and fairness. In Hong Kong and Macao, we should support the freedoms that already exist. With respect to Taiwan, we should declare our commitment to the principles of freedom and democracy and then, negotiating as equals and ready to compromise, seek a formula for peaceful unification. We should approach disputes in the national-minority areas of China with an open mind, seeking ways to find a workable framework within which all ethnic and religious groups can flourish. We should aim ultimately at a federation of democratic communities of China.

19. *Truth in reconciliation.* We should restore the reputations of all people, including their family members, who suffered political stigma in the political campaigns of the past or who have been labeled as criminals because of their thought, speech, or faith. The state should pay reparations to these people. All political prisoners and prisoners of conscience must be released. There should be a Truth Investigation Commission charged with finding the facts about past injustices and atrocities, determining responsibility for them, upholding justice, and, on these bases, seeking social reconciliation.

China, as a major nation of the world, as one of five permanent members of the United Nations Security Council, and as a member of the UN Council on Human Rights, should be contributing to peace for humankind and progress toward human rights. Unfortunately, we stand today as the only country among the major nations that remains mired in authoritarian politics. Our political system continues to produce human rights disasters and social crises, thereby not only constricting China's own development but also limiting the progress of all of human civilization. This must change, truly it must. The democratization of Chinese politics can be put off no longer.

Accordingly, we dare to put civic spirit into practice by announcing Charter '08. We hope that our fellow citizens who feel a similar sense of crisis, responsibility, and mission, whether they are inside the government or not, and regardless of their social status, will set aside small differences to embrace the broad goals of this citizens' movement. Together we can work for major changes in Chinese society and for the rapid establishment of a free, democratic, and constitutional country. We can bring to reality the goals and ideals that our people have incessantly been seeking for more than a hundred years, and can bring a brilliant new chapter to Chinese civilization.

Source: New York Review of Books.
Translation from Chinese © 2009, Perry Link.

Selected readings and resources for further research in Chinese law and history

Books

Alford, William P. (1997) *To Steal a Book Is an Elegant Offense: Intellectual Property Law in Chinese Civilization*. Stanford, CA: Stanford University Press.

Balme, Stéphanie and Dowdle, Michael W. (eds) (2009) *Building Constitutionalism in China*. New York: Palgrave Macmillan.

Brook, Timothy, Bourgon, Jérôme and Blue, Gregory (2008) *Death by a Thousand Cuts*. Cambridge, MA: Harvard University Press.

Chang, Gordon G. (2001) *The Coming Collapse of China*. New York: Random House.

Chang, Jung and Halliday, Jon (2006) *Mao: The Unknown Story*. New York: Anchor Books.

Chen, Albert H.Y. (2004) *An Introduction to the Legal System of the People's Republic of China*, 3rd edn. Hong Kong: LexisNexis Butterworths.

Cheng, Pei-kai (ed.) (1999) *The Search for Modern China: A Documentary Collection*. New York: W.W. Norton.

Ching, Frank (2008) *China: The Truth about Its Human Rights Record*. London: Rider.

Chow, Daniel C.K. (2009) *The Legal System of the People's Republic of China in a Nutshell*, 2nd edn. St Paul, MN: Thomson West.

Clarke, Donald (ed.) (2008) *China's Legal System: New Developments, New Challenges*. Cambridge: Cambridge University Press.

Cohen, Jerome Allan (1968) *The Criminal Process in the People's Republic of China, 1949–1963: An Introduction*. Cambridge, MA: Harvard University Press.

Cohen, Jerome Allan (1974) *People's China and International Law: A Documentary Study*. Princeton, NJ: Princeton University Press.

Diamant, Neil, Lubman, Stanley and O'Brien, Kevin (eds) (2010) *Engaging the Law in China: State, Society, and Possibilities for Justice*. Stanford, CA: Stanford University Press.

Dautcher, Jay (2009) *Down a Narrow Road: Identity and Masculinity in a Uyghur Community in Xinjiang China*. Cambridge, MA: Harvard University Press.

Fairbank, John King (1976) *The United States and China*. Cambridge, MA: Harvard University Press.

Fairbank, John King (1982) *Chinabound: A Fifty-Year Memoir*. New York: Harper & Row.

Fairbank, John King (1986) *The Great Chinese Revolution: 1800–1985*. New York: Harper & Row.

Fairbank, John King (1992) *China: A New History*. Cambridge, MA: Belknap Press.

Fewsmith, Joseph (2001) *China since Tiananmen: The Politics of Transition*, Modern China Series. New York: Cambridge University Press.

Gilley, Bruce (2004) *China's Democratic Future: How It Will Happen and Where It Will Lead*. New York: Columbia University Press.

Ginsburg, Tom and Moustafa, Tamir (2008) *Rule By Law: The Politics of Courts in Authoritarian Regimes*. Cambridge: Cambridge University Press.

Gladney, Dru C. (2004) *Dislocating China: Muslims, Minorities, and Other Subaltern Subjects*. Chicago, IL: University of Chicago Press.

Gray, John Henry (2002) *China: A History of the Laws, Manners and Customs of the People*. Mineola, NY: Dover Publications.

Halper, Stefan (2010) *The Beijing Consensus*. New York: Basic Books.

He, Weifang (2012) *In the Name of Justice: Striving for the Rule of Law in China*. Washington, DC: Brookings Institution Press.

Head, John W. (2009) *China's Legal Soul: The Modern Chinese Legal Identity in Historic Context*. Durham, NC: Carolina Academic Press.

Head, John W. (2011) *Great Legal Traditions: Civil Law, Common Law and Chinese Law in Historical and Operational Perspective*. Durham, NC: Carolina Academic Press.

Hegel, Robert E. (ed.) (2009) *True Crimes in Eighteenth-Century China: Twenty Case Histories*. Seattle, WA: University of Washington Press.

Hegel, Robert E. and Carlitz, Katherine (eds) (2007) *Writing and Law in Late Imperial China: Crime, Conflict and Judgment*. Seattle, WA: University of Washington Press.

Ho, Pin and Huang, Wenguang (2013) *A Death in the Lucky Holiday Hotel: Murder, Money, and an Epic Power Struggle in China*. New York: Public Affairs.

Hsu, C. Stephen (2003) *Understanding China's Legal System: Essays in Honor of Jerome Cohen*. New York: New York University Press.

Huang, Philip C. (2010) *Chinese Civil Justice, Past and Present*. Lanham, MD: Rowman & Littlefield.

Huang, Ray (1982) *1587: A Year of No Significance: The Ming Dynasty in Decline*. New Haven, CT: Yale University Press.

Huang, Ray (1997) *China: A Macro History*. New York: East Gate.

Huang, Ray (1999) *Broadening the Horizons of Chinese History: Discourses, Syntheses and Comparisons*. Armonk, NY: M.E. Sharpe.

Jacques, Martin (2009) *When China Rules the World*. New York: Penguin.

Jenner, W.J.F. (1992) *The Tyranny of History: The Roots of China's Crisis*. London: Allen Lane.

Keith, Ron (2005) *New Crime in China: Public Order and Human Rights*. London: Routledge.

Kennedy, David and Stiglitz, Joseph E. (2013) *Law and Economics with Chinese Characteristics: Institutions for Promoting Development in the Twenty-First Century*. Oxford: Oxford University Press.

Kissinger, Henry (2011) *On China*. New York: Penguin.

Kolås, Åshlid and Thowsen, Monica P. (2005) *On the Margins of Tibet: Cultural Survival on the Sino-Tibetan Frontier*. Seattle, WA: University of Washington Press.

Leung, Priscilla M.F. (ed.) (2005) *Selected Edition of China Law Reports, 1991–2004*. Hong Kong and Beijing: Isinolaw Holding/People's Court Press/Renmin University Press.

Levenson, Joseph R. (2008) *Confucian China and Its Modern Fate: A Trilogy*. New York: ACLS Humanities.

Liao, Yiwu (2008) *The Corpse Walker: Real Life Stories, China from the Bottom Up*. New York: Pantheon.

Liao, Yiwu (2013) *For a Song and a Hundred Songs: Poet's Journey through a Chinese Prison*. Boston, MA: New Harvest.

Lieberthal, Kenneth (1997) *Governing China*. New York: R.S. Means.

Liu, Xiaobo (2012) *No Enemies, No Hatred: Selected Essays and Poems*. Cambridge, MA: Belknap Press.

Lovell, Julia (2006) *The Politics of Cultural Capital: China's Quest for a Nobel Prize*. Honolulu, HI: University of Hawaii Press.

Lubman, Stanley B. (1996) *China's Legal Reforms*. Oxford: Oxford University Press.

Lubman, Stanley B. (1999) *Bird in a Cage: Legal Reform in China after Mao*. Stanford, CA: Stanford University Press.

Luo, Wei (2006) *Chinese Law and Legal Research*. Littleton, CO: Fred B. Rothman.

Lutze, Thomas D. (2007) *China's Inevitable Revolution: Rethinking America's Loss to the Communists*. New York: Palgrave Macmillan.

MacCormack, Geoffrey (1996) *The Spirit of Traditional Chinese Law*. Atlanta, GA: University of Georgia Press.

MacFarquhar, Roderick (1987) *The Politics of China: The Eras of Mao and Deng*. Cambridge: Cambridge University Press.

MacFarquhar, Roderick (2006) *Mao's Last Revolution*. Cambridge, MA: Belknap Press.

MacFarquhar, Roderick (ed.) (2011) *The Politics of China: Sixty Years of the People's Republic of China*. Cambridge: Cambridge University Press.

Mackerras, Colin (2000) *Sinophiles and Sinophobes: Western Views of China*, Literary Anthologies of Asia Series. New York: Oxford University Press.

Mackerras, Colin (2001) *The New Cambridge Handbook of Contemporary China*. New York: Cambridge University Press.

McGranahan, Carole (2010) *Arrested Histories: Tibet, the CIA, and Memories of a Forgotten War*. Durham, NC: Duke University Press.

McGregor, Richard (2010) *The Party: The Secret World of China's Communist Rulers*. New York: Harper Collins.

Meisner, Maurice (1999) *Mao's China and After: A History of the People's Republic*, 3rd edn. New York: Simon & Schuster.

Mungello, David E. (2009) *The Great Encounter of China and the West, 1500–1800*. Lanham, MD: Rowman & Littlefield.

Nyberg, Albert and Rozelle, Scott (1999) *Accelerating China's Rural Transformation*. Washington, DC: World Bank.

Peerenboom, Randall (2002) *China's Long March toward Rule of Law*. Cambridge: Cambridge University Press.

Peerenboom, Randall (2009) *Judicial Independence in China: Lessons for Global Rule of Law Promotion*. Cambridge: Cambridge University Press.

Pei, Minxin (1998) *From Reform to Revolution: The Demise of Communism in China and the Soviet Union*. Cambridge, MA: Harvard University Press.

Pei, Minxin (2006) *China's Trapped Transition: The Limits of Developmental Autocracy*. Cambridge, MA: Harvard University Press.

Perry, Keller (ed.) (2001) *Chinese Law and Legal Theory*. Aldershot: Ashgate.

Potter, Pitman B. (2001) *The Chinese Legal System: Globalization and Local Legal Culture*. London: Routledge.

Rajah, Jothie (2012) *Authoritarian Rule of Law: Legislation, Discourse and Legitimacy in Singapore*. Cambridge: Cambridge University Press.

Ruskola, Teemu (2013) *Legal Orientalism: China, the United States, and Modern Law*. Cambridge, MA: Harvard University Press.

Schell, Orville and Delury, John (2013) *Wealth and Power: China's Long March to the Twenty-First Century*. New York: Random House.

Schell, Orville and Shambaugh, David (eds) (1999) *The China Reader: The Reform Era*. New York: Vintage Books.

Shih, Chih-yu (1999) *Collective Democracy: Political and Legal Reform in China*. Hong Kong: Chinese University Press.

Shirk, Susan L. (2007) *China: Fragile Superpower*. New York: Oxford University Press.

Sorman, Guy (2008) *The Empire of Lies: The Truth about China in the Twenty-First Century*. New York: Encounter Books.

Spence, Jonathan D. (1979) *The Death of Woman Wang*. New York: Penguin.

Spence, Jonathan D. (1980) *To Change China: Western Advisers in China*. New York: Penguin.

Spence, Jonathan D. (1982) *The Gate of Heavenly Peace: The Chinese and Their Revolution, 1895–1980*. New York: Penguin.

Spence, Jonathan D. (1990) *The Search for Modern China*. New York: W.W. Norton.

Spence, Jonathan D. (1992) *Chinese Roundabout: Essays in History and Culture*. New York: W.W. Norton.

Spence, Jonathan D. (2001) *Treason by the Book*. New York: Viking.

Sutter, Robert (2005) *Historical Dictionary of United States-China Relations*. Lanham, MD: Rowman & Littlefield.

Tanner, Murray Scott (1999) *Politics of Lawmaking in Post-Mao China: Institutions, Processes, and Democratic Prospects*. New York: Oxford University Press.

Tsai, Kellee S. (2007) *Capitalism without Democracy: The Private Sector in Contemporary China*. Ithaca, NY: Cornell University Press.

Zhang, Liang (2001) *The Tiananmen Papers*. New York: Public Affairs.

Zhao, Ziyang (2009) *Prisoner of the State: The Secret Journal of Premier Zhao Ziyang*. New York: Simon & Schuster.

Zimmerman, James M. (2010) *China Law Deskbook: A Legal Guide for Foreign-Invested Enterprises,* 3rd edn. Chicago, IL: American Bar Association.

Online resources

National People's Congress of China
www.npc.gov.cn/englishnpc/news/index.htm
National People's Consultative Conference
www.cppcc.gov.cn/zxww/zxyw/home/
Central People's Government of the People's Republic of China
http://english.gov.cn/ and *www.china.org.cn/index.htm*
Legislative Affairs Office of the State Council of the People's Republic
of China
www.chinalaw.gov.cn/article/english/
Gazette of the State Council of the People's Republic of China
www.china.org.cn/e-gongbao/gazette/index.htm
Supreme People's Court of the People's Republic of China
http://en.chinacourt.org/
Supreme People's Procuratorate of the People's Republic of China
www.spp.gov.cn/
Ministry of Justice of the People's Republic of China
www.legalinfo.gov.cn/english/
Ministry of Public Security of the People's Republic of China
www.mps.gov.cn/English/
Ministry of Foreign Affairs of the People's Republic of China
www.fmprc.gov.cn/eng/
China Information and Sources: China Law and Justice
www.chinatoday.com/law/a.htm
China Law Digest
www.chinalawdigest.com/
China National Knowledge Infrastructure
http://oversea.cnki.net/kns55/default.aspx
Lawinfochina
www.lawinfochina.com/
Westlaw China
www.westlawchina.com/index_en.html
LexisNexis China
www.lexisnexis.com.cn/english/
AsianLII: Laws of the People's Republic of China
www.asianlii.org/cn/legis/cen/laws/
US Congressional-Executive Commission on China
www.cecc.gov/
US-China Economic and Security Review Commission
www.uscc.gov/

New York University US Asian Law Institute
www.usasialaw.org/
Yale Law School: China Law Center
www.law.yale.edu/intellectuallife/ChinaLawCenter.htm
Chinese Law Prof Blog
http://lawprofessors.typepad.com/china_law_prof_blog/
WorldLII: People's Republic of China
www.worldlii.org/catalog/214.html
Xinhua News Agency
www.chinaview.cn/
China Daily
www.chinadaily.com.cn/
China Digital Times
http://chinadigitaltimes.net/
Library of Congress China Law Research Guide
www.loc.gov/law/help/china.php
American Bar Association China Committee Bibliography, Seattle
University Law Library
*www.abanet.org/intlaw/committees/africa_eurasia/china/bibliography.
shtml*
Research Guide to Chinese Law
http://docs.law.gwu.edu/facweb/dclarke/public/Research_Guides.html
Harvard Law School China Legal Research
http://guides.library.harvard.edu/ChineseLegalResearch
NYU China Law Research Links
*www.law.nyu.edu/library/research/foreign_intl/foreigndatabasesby
jurisdiction/china*
Chinese Studies WWW Virtual Library, University of Melbourne
*www.lib.unimelb.edu.au/collections/asian/chi-web/chihp-law.
html#china*
Chinalaw Deskbook Research Guide
*www.chinalawdeskbook.com/pdf/CLD%20Bibliography%20Electro
nic%20Research%20Guide.pdf*
Chinese Legal Research
http://lib.law.washington.edu/eald/clr/cres.html
University of Minnesota Human Rights Library
www1.umn.edu/humanrts/
China Guiding Case Project
https://cgc.law.stanford.edu/

Index